THE CENTURY-MAKERS
The Men Behind the Ashes 1877-1977

KU-503-250

Don Bradman and Charles Bannerman —
century-makers who span the century

THE CENTURY-MAKERS

The Men Behind the Ashes 1877~1977

FRANK TYSON

SIDGWICK & JACKSON

LONDON

By the same author
The Hapless Hookers
Complete Cricket Coaching-Illustrated
Cricket Diversions
Test of Nerves

First published in Great Britain in 1980
by Sidgwick and Jackson Limited

Copyright © Frank Tyson 1980

ISBN 0 283 98676 X

HERTFORDSHIRE
COUNTY LIBRARY

796.358

9936907

12 NOV 1980

Printed in Singapore by Times Printers Sdn Bhd
for Sidgwick and Jackson Limited
1 Tavistock Chambers, Bloomsbury Way,
London WC1A 2SG

Contents

Foreword

Frank Tyson has made the best of two worlds. It seems no time ago that he opened the telegram that told him he had become a B.A. and said, 'Now I can play cricket for as long as I want—and no longer'. He has read as few Test match fast bowlers have done—and bowled faster than most students of cricket history. His idea to assess Test match cricketers in the light of the opinions of their elders and contemporaries is as good as it is original. The fact is that there is no other accurate yardstick of cricketing ability. Statistics, of course, are valuable; but the 'damned dots' cannot afford a *relative* basis for comparison except with others of the same period. For instance, how does one compare an innings of W.G. Grace against fast round-arm slingers on a Lord's pitch so rough that the crowd rose to him for stopping an entire over (four balls at that time) of plumb shooters, on the one hand, with, on the other, a century on an utterly plumb wicket at The Oval, Karachi, or Kanpore?

Only those who have closely watched—preferably played with or against—a cricketer can give a just evaluation of his quality. The films and tele-recordings being made nowadays will give a fair idea of comparative performances. Anyone who has tried to compile an historic film about first-class cricket, though, knows how pathetically little material there is of even relatively recent events. A few jerky feet of W.G. Grace taking a net; Victor Trumper trying vainly to cut wides which were clearly thrown by the non-cricketing photographer; a few demonstration strokes played by Jack Hobbs for a short instructional film, seemed almost all the material on most of the pre-1946, and even pre-1954, period. Recently, by a delightful accident, Frank Woodhead came by and recognized an amateur's film of Test cricket at Trent Bridge in the 1930s. It has some memorable shots of Bradman and McCabe. Even that, though, is pitifully little by comparison with the hunger of the enthusiast to see Woolley, Tate, MacDonald, Jackson, Sutcliffe, Hobbs, and Verity play. Whole generations before them are barely pictured at all.

The nearest substitute is the opinion of those who saw and knew them. As Frank Tyson has discovered, relatively few, until C.B. Fry, contributed precise analysis to their opinions. Anyone who has tried to discover whether some first-class cricketer at the start of this century was right or left-handed can appreciate how loose definition was in sports writing—even that classed as reference—in relatively recent times. Indeed, without going so far back as that, one could wish devoutly for complete film coverage of Frank Tyson's fast bowling which defeated Australia in 1954-5.

JOHN ARLOTT

The Lone Century

During my early days in the Central Lancashire League my batting prowess received general if unflattering recognition. On one occasion, however, at Middleton's Towncroft Avenue ground, I rose to unprecedented heights—I survived for three balls! As I was leaving the ground, the resident Smart Alec who inevitably occupied one of the front seats in the pavilion, tugged down on the peak of his flat cap and tightened his muffler around his neck as he gave me a baleful glance of dissatisfaction. 'I knew that you were no good as a batsman, Frank', he said, 'but this time . . . you were lucky to make a duck!'

An acquaintance of those distant formative days matched my own ineptitude with the bat; but he more than compensated for his shortcomings with a superb sense of gamesmanship. Before each away match, he would walk into the pavilion, look around the ground and announce in loud tones for the benefit of the opposition players: 'No-o-o . . . I don't think I've made a hundred on this ground—yet!'

My friend, like myself, never reached the century mark with the bat in any class of cricket. Apart from several forgettable bowling analyses, this book and its account of the Hundred Years War of Test Cricket is the first triple-figure score I have achieved in the game. Like my innings, this literary knock contains blemishes which emanate from my dependence on oral history and my character. I am no Hutton of literary style and no Bradman of statistics. To adapt Descartes: I write, therefore I am. This book is the expression of my thoughts and the collated opinions of other cricket-lovers expressed to me in personal terms. It is a picaresque stroll down the century-long lane of Test matches, peopled with reminiscences and anecdotes, some apocryphal and some true.

Like all of my previous innings, this, my longest knock is full of flaws. I should have described more fully the savage elegance of Peter May's batting and his reliance on his bottom hand, his guide and master, for the crunching power of his drives. I could have perhaps dwelt whimsically on his habit of enunciating in the squeaky tones which seem characteristic of great batsmen, 'Do you mind!', when his composure was disturbed. Neil Harvey, that nuggety left-hander against whom I hated to bowl because, whilst I could dismiss him, I could never suppress him, is worthy of more attention than he is given in these pages. I have not even discussed George Tribe's three different kinds of wrong 'uns, Bruce Dooland's top-spinner or Cecil George Pepper's flipper. There is no mention of the bulkless timing of Colin Cowdrey's massive driving or the unflinching courage of the other Colin, McDonald, Australia's opener, against the fastest bowling. How can one do justice to the nervous brilliance of Norman O'Neill at the crease or sketch in words the circumambulatory path of his unintended running between the wickets which provoked the downfall of so many of his partners?

'Slasher' Mackay, Australia's Groucho Marx of the middle-order, demands a long descriptive essay in the manner of P.G.Wodehouse to do humorous justice to his cricketing idiosyncrasies. How can I capture in words the assured and affected arrogance of the basically insecure Tony Lock? I am as unqualified to play the psychologist as I am to explain Lock's uncanny control of his spinners in the twilight of his career with Western Australia: a state for whom Lock was the Bismarck of cricket unification.

This catalogue is only a minute cross-section of my sins of literary omission. I can only say of the following lines: here I am, take me—for there is much of my personality in them. The book is not strictured by the temporal limits of a hundred years of Test cricket; its subject is the world around the game for it deals in the personalities, individualities and character inherent in a sport of people. I hope that, unlike the little man described by Browning in *The Grammarian's Funeral*, I have not 'gone on adding one to one' until the hundred's soon hit. I would sooner, like the great man in the poem, aim at a million. Like him I shall probably miss my mark by many human units. If so, I shall throw myself on your understanding of my motives and, seeking your unperplexed enjoyment, I hope that I shall find it.

FRANK TYSON

1. Different Times, Different Customs

Cricket historians dwell with delight upon the romantic origins and antiquity of the game. They linger over the Anglo-Saxon word for a shepherd's crook: 'Cricc'—the implement which gave the game a name. They point out with pride how this humble pastime of driving a ball with a shepherd's stave had spread so far from its native Sussex Weald by the year 1300 that Master John De Leek, Chaplain to Prince Edward the King's son, was claiming the £6 from the Wardrobe Accounts of the Royal Household so that his princely charge might play at cricket at Newenton and Westminster.

The welfare of cricket in the days of its early development was essentially the concern of autocratic and independent bodies such as the Marylebone, the Hambledon, the All Kent, the Melbourne, and the Calcutta Cricket Clubs. Great patrons such as the fourth Duke of Richmond, the Duke of Dorset, the Earl of Winchelsea and Lord Frederick Beauclerk fostered the sport and wagered on the game in a most extravagant manner.

In spite of the venerable age of the informal game, organized international cricket is but a youthful stripling upon the sporting stage. The first shots in the Hundred Years Test War between those two inveterate enemies, England and Australia, were fired as recently as 15 March, 1877. Test cricket as we know it, is such a modern concept that players like Australia's Jack Ryder and England's Frank Woolley and 'Tiger' Smith, who were born less than a score of years after the inaugural Test and who fought out many of the ensuing duels, were still alive to celebrate Test cricket's hundredth birthday and see Melbourne's Centenary Test.

The relative youth of the international game of cricket can be shown by an historical perspective: many of the political problems which faced the British Empire of 1877 still existed within the British Commonwealth of 1977. In those days there were no bombs in the streets of Belfast, but a young Irishman by the name of Charles Stewart Parnell was eloquently pleading the cause of Irish Home Rule in the House of Commons. In South Africa, black faced white, not in the streets of Sharpeville or Soweto, but in the pitched battles of the Zulu wars at

The earliest cricket illustration — from Bede, Life of St Cuthbert

Isandhlwana and Rorkes Drift. The English lion confronted the Russian bear in the cold war in Kabul and Afghanistan and not in Eastern Europe. Massacres were commonplace, not in Africa or Timor, but closer home to England in Bulgaria. Politicians such as Gladstone, like some early-day Barry Goldwater, thumped the jingoistic drum and demanded that the Russians be packed out of the Balkans 'bag and baggage'. Europe was in the grip of an agricultural depression, comparable to the current world recession. The picture is so familiar that the hundred years which have passed since then seem only a drop in the ocean of time.

Insignificant though the past hundred years of cricket development seem against the broader context of history, they contained major achievements in the realms of international cricket progress. The passage of the years has seen the establishment of organized national and international competitions and Boards of Control. In England, the infant Test and County Cricket Board acts as the modern guardian over matches and competitions as diverse as Test rubbers, the County Championship, and the one-day matches sponsored by the Benson and Hedges, John Player, and the Gillette Companies. The respective Cricket Boards of Australia, New Zealand, India, Pakistan, and the West Indies are the watchdogs over first-class competitions which rejoice in the exotic names of the Ranji, the Duleep, the Quaid-e-Azam trophies, the Sheffield, Plunket and Shell Shields, and the Currie Cup. Over all, lies the aegis of the International Cricket Conference, the direct descendant of the Imperial Cricket Conference. Theirs is the authority which governs the Anglo-Australian contests for the Ashes, supervises the England-West Indies clashes for the Wisden Trophy, arranges the Tests between England and New Zealand to determine the winner of the W. J. Jordan Trophy, and sits in administrative judgement over the arrangements of the F. M. Worrell Trophy, contested between Australia and the West Indies. More recently the International Cricket Conference has acted in the capacity of organizer of the inaugural Prudential World Cup Competition, contested on the basis of an international round-robin series of one-day matches in England in 1975.

These activities reveal no more than the tip of the iceberg of an organization which is now so large that it embraces twenty-one full and associate members. From the small beginnings of that first Melbourne Test one hundred years ago, there has developed an administrative body which, in the passage of time has organized, in an official or unofficial capacity, more than 800 Test matches between nineteen pairs of competitors. In fact, the One Hundred Years War of Test Cricket is something of a misnomer. Like the Hundred Years War between England and France in the fourteenth and fifteenth century, the cricket conflict between nations extends some sixteen years beyond the century mark.

It was in 1861 that an English side led by the Surrey professional, H. H. Stephenson, first visited the shores of Australia. His side was an entertaining substitute for a cancelled lecture tour by the famous English author, Charles Dickens. This was a touring party which was

H.H. Stephenson's Eleven 1861, the first English touring side to Australia

followed in quick succession by expeditionary forces captained by W. G. Grace and Lillywhite; but it was not until 1877 that these visitations were placed upon an official footing by the instigation of matches played between Australian and English sides based on an eleven-a-side equality.

The story of international cricket since the mid-nineteenth century is a true but strange tale. Since cricket is a game which gives free rein to the personality of its participants, human strength, weakness, vacillation, and steadfastness have been, and will continue to be, shown throughout the course of its continuing evolution. Carlyle stated that the history of the world is but the biography of great men. If one accepts that greatness does not preclude human foibles, he might easily have said the same thing about the history of Test cricket. For me the humanistic charms of the sport have always rested in the character of the players.

The expression of the players' diverse personalities has sometimes led them even to ignore the bonds of loyalty. Some of them represented both countries. Murdoch, Trott, Woods, Ferris, and Midwinter, all played both for Australia and England. Indeed, Midwinter, having first appeared for Australia in 1876, transferred his allegiance to England for the year 1881, only to turn his coat again as the seasons changed in 1882. Englishmen Hearne and Mitchell represented both England and South Africa whilst Sammy Guillen played both for the West Indies against New Zealand, and for New Zealand against the West Indies. Other cricket transfers were compulsory. Ranjitsinhji, Duleepsinhji and the elder Nawab of Pataudi all played for England before their native India had an entity or a being in the cricket world. Pakistanis, Kardar, Amir Elahi and Gul Mahomad all had perforce to represent India before religious and political differences brought about the partition of the sub-continent into two nations and created Pakistan.

The disputatious and querulous side of man's nature was often reflected in many and diverse fashions on the cricket field. Test cricket has not always been the gentleman's game and the character-builder that many educationalists would lead us to believe. Only too often human quirks were reflected in the behaviour of the cricketing greats. In 1876, the famous Nottinghamshire all-rounder, Alfred Shaw, refused to accompany W. G. Grace's touring side to Australia on the grounds that only second-class accommodation was offered to the professional members of the team. In 1888 and 1890, the South Australian all-rounder Giffen, was unable to come to a financial agreement with the Australian organizers of the tour to England and consequently did not make the trip. Some say that he demanded as a pre-condition to his making the visit that his brother be included in the party. This inference was later vigorously denied.

Whole series have been placed in jeopardy by the actions of spectators, individual players and administrators. The hooliganism of the Sydney crowd in 1879 created a strong anti-Australian bias in English cricketing circles. As a result, when Murdoch's team visited England in 1880 they were awarded the belated consolation prize of a single Test and had to advertise to fill their fixture list with matches of less than first-class standing. The source of their embarrassment was the antipathy towards them aroused in the breast of Lord Harris, the English captain, as a result of a riot directed against him in the previous year on the Sydney Cricket Ground during his side's visit to Australia.

In 1912, Victor Trumper, Clem Hill, Tibby Cotter, Warwick Armstrong and Vernon Ransford were all missing from the Australian team which contested the Triangular Tournament of that year in England. The absence of the rebellious sextet arose from their disgruntlement at not being permitted to choose their own player-manager for the tour.

Jardine's 'bodyline' tactics of the 1932-3 England tour of Australia almost caused the cancellation of the rubber at the half-way mark and in the words of cricket historian, Harry Altham, came near to 'antagonizing a dominion'. The ill-considered Australian Board of Control telegram which denounced the Jardine tactics and used the term 'unsportsmanlike', caused the M.C.C. to react with the reluctant suggestion that the rest of the series be cancelled if the sportsmanship of the English side remained in doubt. Such was the violence of partisan feelings in this injurious year that the whole diplomatic might of the Dominions Office had to be brought into play to prevent an open breach between England and Australia.

These, then, are the heights of feeling and the depths of behaviour to which the noble game of Test cricket has risen and fallen. It seems that the accusations of loutish behaviour, which are not infrequently levelled at present-day Test players, were not without precedent in the good old days. In the words of the French proverb: 'The more everything changes the more it remains the same'.

Many things, however, have altered in the make-up of Test cricket since that significant inaugural day in March 1877. Not the least of these innovations has been the transformation of the grounds which have seen the Test match dramas unfold. The Melbourne Cricket Ground of 1877 was crowded when 12,000 people crammed into its confines to see Bannerman score his 165—the first Test century. The new grandstand which was constructed specifically for the English games could hold no more than 2,000 people. In summer it accommodated the cricket spectators of the central ground itself; in winter the seating was rearranged to face outwards towards Richmond Park and the football scene. In those days the turf of the M.C.G. was hallowed and reserved exclusively for cricket as that of Lords is today. Nowadays the vast concrete amphitheatre of the Melbourne Cricket Ground accommodates more than 120,000 spectators. The sprawling barren splendour of the southern stand alone can accommodate more than the totality of the crowd which witnessed the first clash between England and Australia a hundred years ago.

Grounds have been added to the Test circuit; other venues have been subtracted. Adelaide's picturesque Central Oval saw its first Test in 1884-5. The smutty grimness of Sheffield's Brammall Lane remained uncheered by any Test match entertainment until 1902—its unique year of international fame. For a brief moment, in 1928-9, Brisbane's Exhibition Ground basked in the glory of a Test; its distinction was transient, for it hosted only one more game against South Africa in 1930-1. On the occasion of the next English visit to Brisbane, the 'Ground of the Flowering Gum-Trees', the Woolloongabba, claimed the honour of staging all of Brisbane's first-class and international cricket.

Test grounds have come and gone, but it seems that Lords and The Oval go on forever. They were the scenes of Australia's first Test encounters in England, and they have survived two World Wars and their accompanying vicissitudes. Something of a heathen was the German pilot who, in 1941, disturbed the pigeons and the sacred turf of Thomas Lord's ground by dropping two bombs on it and setting fire to the secretary's house. Something of a Philistine was the civil servant who signed the authorization which turned The Oval into a prisoner-of-war camp in 1944. In spite of these disturbances of their cricketing tradition, Lords and The Oval remain the same centres of cricket culture as they were when the first ball between England and Australia was bowled.

Test wickets, too, have had their ups and downs. There was a time when batting captains had the option of choosing their ground. In the

1880s it was not unusual to see Australia batting on one pitch and England batting on another preferred strip of turf alongside the Australian wicket. Before the progressive evolution of laws in the 1950s governing the covering of Test pitches, the possibility of rain during the match and a resultant 'sticky dog' made the toss of the coin a critical factor in determining the fate of the two sides. Australian captains Monty Noble, Lindsay Hassett and English skipper F. S. Jackson feared neither the wickets nor the toss in one series. They won the toss on all five occasions!

Controversy has raged through the years about the preparation of Test wickets. In 1956 an Old Trafford dust bowl enabled Jim Laker to capture an unprecedented and so far unsurpassed total of 19 wickets in one game. The howls of anguish which arose from the Australian camp on that occasion could be heard from Manchester to Melbourne, as could the tourists' protests in 1972 when a mysterious fungus-affected wicket at Leeds enabled the English spinners to wreak havoc amongst the Australian batting line-up to win the game on a disputed premise. On the other side of the world in Melbourne in 1955 a puzzling subterranean spring reputedly flowed from beneath the ground on the

The social scene at Lords in the nineteenth century

David Gregory's first Australian team in England 1878

rest day of the Third Test to bind the mosaic of a disintegrating wicket once again to the semblance of a pitch. It was fortunate on that occasion that the damp surface favoured Len Hutton's touring Englishmen and enabled them to win the game; otherwise there is no doubt that the wails of protest which would have arisen about the alleged illegal watering of the wicket would have been equally as mournful as those of the unfortunate Australians in 1956 and 1972.

In July 1976, the International Cricket Conference meeting at Lords, ruled that advertising on players clothing and equipment would not be permitted. This ruling has even been extended to the banning of colours, other than those of clubs, on players' dress. Yet it is not to be fondly imagined that cricketers never wore distinctive and identifying colours in the early days of Test cricket. Indeed, in the 1850 to 1880 period, coloured shirts were common uniform in the game. Patterns of vivid spots, stripes or checks upon the white background of the shirt were the insignia of both teams and individual players. The All-England uniform shirt was one of pink spots on a white background. Multi-coloured ribbons around hats, which varied from the top to the bowler styles as the game evolved, were the mark of clubs and sometimes, in celebrity games, of noted individual players. Cricket in the nineteenth century must have been an extremely uncomfortable game. Shirts were starched and chokingly buttoned up to the Adam's apple; bow ties were 'de rigueur'. Footwear was generally heavy and cumbersome; it was not until 1882 that white buckskin boots replaced solid brown brogues.

Nineteenth-century Tests would have been a strange sight indeed for modern spectators. Not only were pitches and players vastly different from those of modern times, the laws of the game were also dissimilar in some respects. It was not until 1884 that the five- or six-ball over

16

gained general recognition. The earliest bowlers had to content themselves with four balls in an over: a custom probably handed down from the times when four individual players each bowled a ball in succession. Tests in the 1870s and 1880s seldom went beyond three days. Did not immortal Dr W. G. Grace pass the opinion that if no decision could be reached within that space of time, the match was abortive and should be recommenced?

Until 1902 the distance of the return crease from the stumps was three and not four feet, and the bowler's target of the wicket in pre-1936 days was one inch narrower than the present set of stumps. Leg-before-wicket decisions were more difficult to come by in the days of Shaw and Lillywhite than they are in the times of Thomson and Lillee. Before 1937 the umpire raised his finger in answer to an appeal only when the ball hit the batsman on the pad and pitched in a straight line between wicket and wicket. Regulations governing tours, pitches, times, experimental laws and fair and unfair tactics have been in a continual state of flux over the past hundred years. It would be hard to choose a single season in which the game has not, at least in one respect, been modified and modernized.

Nowadays we live in an era of ersatz one-day cricket, and the commercial sponsorship of a game which has moved into the realms of public entertainment rather than that of private enjoyment. The upheavals which have sometimes shaken the conservative foundations of the Lords pavilion have not been suffered in silence by their reactionary opponents. It is the differing opinions which people hold about the nature of cricket and its diverse circumstances which give it its varied and often stormy appeal. It is said that cricket has been played in such disparate places as on top of Table Mountain, which is not as flat as it appears from sea level, at Spitzbergen on ice, and even on top of

W.G. Grace's final appearance for England-Nottingham 1899. Standing (L to R) R.G. Barlow (umpire), T. Hayward, G.H. Hirst, W. Gunn, J.T. Hearne, W. Storer, Brockwell, V.A. Titchmarsh (umpire). Seated (L to R) C.B. Fry, K.S. Ranjitsinhji, W.G. Grace, F.S. Jackson. Squatting (L to R) W. Rhodes, J.T. Tyldesley the Eiffel Tower with a French bun as the ball and a wine bottle, empty naturally, as the bat!

Varying reasons have caused the game to be halted inopportunely. Once during a county game, a bull advanced onto the field of play and tossed both sets of stumps high into the air. A troop of weasels on one occasion paraded across the centre of the playing area bringing the players an unlooked-for breather. Once during a first-class game, a spectator left the headlights of his car on, blinding the enemy batsman at the opposite end of the ground, whilst at another time a spectator suffering from an attack of lock-jaw halted the game prematurely. It is perhaps not unusal for midsummer snow to stop play in Manchester; what *was* rare was the midsummer heat which caused the abandonment of play. But by far the most illuminating and silently eloquent commentary on the character of the game of cricket was that made by the match in which both scorers fell asleep and the game had to be restarted!

The truth about Test cricket over the past hundred years is that it has been a sport and recreation whose raw material is people. Because of this it remains today what it was in 1877, a game which

Age can not wither, nor custom stale
Her infinite variety.

2. 'There's nowt so queer as folk'

A small pub in my Lancashire home town rejoiced in the name of 'The Owd Who'd 've Thowt It'. In the Queen's English this title amounts to the expression of surprise contained in the words: 'The Old Who Would Have Thought It'. It would have been a bizarre title for an inn in any part of the world; but in Lancashire, amongst perhaps the most phlegmatic people in the world, the words emblazoned on the front of that hostelry were extraordinarily uncharacteristic of the people who frequented it. Lancastrians have a saying which states 'there's nowt so queer as folk'. They expect people to be characters and individuals in their own right. My native stock has its lovable peculiarities, in sport just as much as in the ordinary walks of life. I well recall the story of the Central Lancashire League professional. He had been rewarded on the previous Saturday by the spectators with a handsome collection for his achievements with the ball, so decided to recompense his supporting fellow players in the following game with the handsome gift of a single cigarette. He passed the packet around the dressing-room but, reaching an individual who had not played on the previous weekend, he withdrew the offer of the unearned reward and passed on to the next man sitting expectantly on the pavilion bench.

As it is in minor cricket, so it is in the major affair of Tests. There is no game so individualistic as cricket, even at the highest levels; there is no sport which gives so much scope to the idiosyncrasies of the people who play. Greed and magnanimity, envy and generosity, fear and courage; these are but a small cross-section of the sentiments and qualities of character which have, at some time or another, found their way on to the Test match scene. Test cricket only reflects the human facets and the interests of the people who play it. Sometimes these attributes are almost as unexpected as the strange sounding name of my home-town pub. For instance Freddy Trueman has a great interest in ornithology. Nicholas Wanostrocht, or Felix, as he was known to his fellow professional players of the early nineteenth century, was as adept with the artist's crayon and brush as he was with the cricket ball. Perhaps it was no coincidence that the imaginative Felix was the inventor of the catapult bowling machine. The great pre-First World

War left-handed English bowler, Colin Blythe, was an accomplished violinist. By profession 'Horseshoe' Collins, the Australian captain of the early 1920s was a bookmaker with a more professional and long-term profitable interest in betting than Baron Tennyson who in 1920 once wagered a friend 1,000 to 1 against his captaining England—and lost. Rubbing shoulders in those days with the noble Lord was Hanson Carter, the Australian wicketkeeper, who followed the lugubrious profession of an undertaker. England fast bowler John Snow swings a mean ball, a dangerous bat, and a low-scoring golf club and can still aspire to be a poet and littérateur. C. B. Fry found his delight in working with the youth of England in naval training ships. Ted Dexter and Gary Sobers often returned low golf scores which, had they been emulated on the cricket field, would have certainly prevented their gaining Test pre-eminence. The leisure inclinations of ex-Australian opener Ian Redpath are peacefully inclined toward the less active sport of fishing.

Over the years cricket has caused the death of the heir to the English throne, the shades of its fields have been lit by the batting brilliance of an Indian Prince, yet such is the democratic charm of the game that Test fame was not denied the three-fingered left hand of Bert Ironmonger, a city council worker. On the one hand, cricket is egalitarian,

John McCarthy Blackham, 'The Prince of Wicketkeepers'

and on the other, it awards its own honours. It allows skilful commoners to rise to the royal ranks of sporting craftsmen. One of the first in this dynasty of ability was John McCarthy Blackham, whose obituary in the Melbourne *Argus* of 1932 described him as 'the Prince of Wicketkeepers'. He was not universally recognized at the outset of his career as being possessed of regal qualities behind the stumps. In Australia's first Test against England in Melbourne in 1877, the budding demon bowler, Spofforth, was absent from the Australian line-up. This was because of his stubborn insistence on the presence of Murdoch, behind the stumps, the only wicketkeeper who, in his opinion, understood his bowling. How misguided was Spofforth's judgment was revealed when, in the subsequent Test, Blackham stumped the English opener Shaw off a chest-high Spofforth 'kicker' when the batsman had scored only a single! Blackham was a stumper rather than a wicketkeeper. His belief was that the wickets should always be within the reach of the man behind the stumps irrespective of the speed of the bowler.

To his great-nephew, with whom in later life he dined each week, the ex-bank clerk confided that even the suave Bert Oldfield, gathering the thunderbolts of McDonald and Gregory in the 1920s, did not meet his high criterion of wicketkeeping. Oldfield was apparently, in Blackham's opinion, a stopper rather than a stumper. Blackham refused to retreat from the wicket to take any fast bowler. It was small wonder that in his old age the fingers of both of his hands, all of which were broken at one stage or another of his career, resembled bunched and knotted mallee roots. All of his front teeth were long departed in the keeping service of his country and in his chest there was a cavity: the hollow broken-ribbed legacy of a fast, rising delivery.

The courage of the man was immense. Not for him the accoutrements of the present-day keeper; he was content with pads and gloves which could have scarcely kept his hands warm on a cold day, let alone protect them from injury. The Blackham gloves are on display in the Baer Museum at the Melbourne Cricket Ground to this very day. Each time I see them I am convinced that Blackham must have bought them as riding gauntlets from a men's outfitters rather than as wicketkeeping gloves from a sports store.

Blackham's wicket-keeping gloves, Baer Museum, Melbourne Cricket Ground

In that inaugural Test match of March 1877, whilst Blackham kept, Midwinter bowled; indeed he bowled with such efficiency that he captured 5/78 in England's first innings. Midwinter's all-round capabilities earned him a professional engagement with W. G. Grace's county of Gloucester in the following English season. He was already in England when Dave Gregory's touring Australian side of 1878 arrived there. The Australian all-rounder attempted to discard his county allegiance to help his fellow-countrymen and suffered the indignity of being 'Player-napped'! He was changing in the dressing-room to take the field for Australia against Middlesex when, post-haste in a hansom cab, W. G. Grace and J. A. Bush arrived from The Oval to haul him away to play for Gloucester against Surrey. Apparently this was an occasion when player considerations outweighed gentlemanly conduct and selection for a county was considered more important than

H.H. Stephenson's
Eleven at the
Melbourne Cricket
Ground 1862

nomination in an Australian side. It is worthwhile remembering that the early games between England and Australia enjoyed only the status of a colonial side playing against an English team of varying strength. The term 'Test match' was only used to describe a match between England and Australia seven years after the first game between the two countries.

In August 1876, W. G. Grace accumulated no fewer than 839 runs in a single week and was only twice dismissed. It was a performance which caused the Yorkshire professional, Emmett, to comment during the course of his side's tribulation that they would have 'Grace before meat, Grace after dinner, and I guess we will have Grace tomorrow'. W.G. scored no less than 318 not out against Yorkshire. In spite of this performance, the Grand Old Man of Cricket did not set any store on accompanying the Lillywhite side to Australasia, and when the first official Test was played some seven months later Grace was not in the England team. Indeed, it is hard to realize that whilst W.G.'s Test career officially spanned nineteen years and twenty-two Tests, all of which were played against Australia, only three of those official games took place on Australian soil. It must be added, however, that W.G. did, in fact, pay an earlier visit to Australia in 1873, before the instigation of official Tests: a visit which was for him and his bride, the former Miss Agnes Day, a silver-lined cricketing honeymoon.

The truth about the early England-Australia Tests is that they did not enjoy a general prestigious recognition. It was quite common for players to be unwilling or unavailable to make tours. Before the foundation of the respective Boards of Control, English and Australian touring sides were organized and invited by private clubs such as the Melbourne and Marylebone Cricket Clubs and individuals like A. C. MacLaren. Australian grounds never saw such leading England players as the Hon. F. S. Jackson or C. B. Fry. These players of the golden age of cricket were never available or willing to make the tour. On the Australian side of .the coin, George Giffen was not infrequently unavailable to make the westward voyage to England. Selection of the early international sides was arbitrary, but at least it allowed scope for the imagination.

The experience of the past makes one wonder whether a knowledge-able dictator such as A. C. MacLaren is not sometimes a better solution to selection problems than the more democratic but not necessarily more discerning committee of selectors. After all, was it not MacLaren who, in 1901, subtracted the great England bowler, Sydney Barnes, from the Lancashire League and brought him to Australia, thereby giving his country a striking force which was to hang like the Sword of Damocles over Australia until the beginning of the First World War.

Archie MacLaren, the Lancashire and England leader beloved of Neville Cardus, was more than a legend in his own lifetime; his cricket-ing career was a legend in itself. He played the first of his Tests against Australia in 1894, captained his country's side in twenty-two games between 1899 and 1909 and still had enough nationalistic pride left in him to emerge from retirement, grey-headed in 1921, and lead the largely amateur team which lowered the colours of Warwick Arm-strong's all-conquering Australians on one of the two occasions on which they were beaten in that season. In the eyes of Neville Cardus, writing his way upwards from the Manchester slum of Moss Side into the aristocracy of the Old Trafford press box, MacLaren was endowed with royal proportions, disdaining anything that was puny or un-worthy. The great writer described MacLaren as not merely hooking the ball but 'dismissing it from his presence'. Once in a Test match in Sydney the English captain was aghast at the Australian captain Joe Darling's audacity in setting three short-legs for fast bowler Jones's first over of a Test match. He exclaimed: 'Joe, what's the meaning of this? What are all these people doing here? How do you expect me to play my celebrated hook shot with all these damn silly people in the way?' But Darling was adamant, insisting that this was his chosen field. Three drives in the first over were sufficient to remove the threatening on-side formation. 'Thank you', exclaimed Archie MacLaren, 'Now we can proceed with the match like gentlemen!' MacLaren's gallantry was of the Sir Walter Raleigh type. He was known to have shed his raincoat on a cold and bleak evening and offered it to a waitress who was cowering and sheltering in the entrance of his hotel waiting for the torrential rain storm outside to abate.

MacLaren's gentlemanly counterpart in the opposition camp and the 'Noblest Australian of them all' was Victor Trumper. His ambition was not to make cricket a personal financial bonanza; so little respect did the impractical Victor have for financial gain, that he would take a new bat from the highly-priced 7s 6d rack in his sports store, use it once in a game, and give it to a child waiting outside the pavilion. His skill with the bat was such that he was described as having no style since he was all style. His contemporaries stated that whilst most batsmen were content to have one answer for each ball, Trumper could produce half a dozen different and effective strokes for the same delivery.

Archie MacLaren. 'He dismissed the ball from his presence'

Arthur Mailey. 'Felt like a boy who had killed a dove'

During the Manchester Test of 1902, on a saturated wicket and after a delayed start, Trumper scored a hundred before lunch. The eventual margin of Australia's victory was only 3 runs, due largely to Trumper's innings and a crucial catch missed by Fred Tate, Maurice's father, off the bat of Joe Darling. When, in later years, the England captain, Archie MacLaren, was taxed with his inabilty to stem the spate of runs which flowed from Trumper's bat, his answer was that his field placement was sensibly dictated by the direction of his bowlers; but since Victor put two balls into the practice ground, he deemed it highly unlikely that he would be permitted to put fieldsmen there. Trumper was in the words of those who were privileged to see him 'the most gallant and handsome batsman of them all'.

The great Australian spin bowler, cartoonist and wag, Arthur Mailey, once described his encounter with his idol Trumper in a Sydney club match. His first delivery was a leg spinner, perfect in length, loop and maximum spin. The batsman hit it to the boundary with a grace and elegance that was all the more astonishing since a similar delivery would have probably only evoked a forward defensive shot from a mortal batsman. A few balls later, Mailey attempted the only other desperate shot which he had in his locker—a bosie or wrong 'un. A temporary aberration on the part of the great man led to the ball passing between bat and pad and to his being stumped by two yards. Trumper walked past Mailey on the way back to the pavilion and with the humility of the great expressed the opinion that the ball was too good for him. It did little for Mailey's mixed feelings of personal delight at his success and chagrin at having been deprived of further batting joys. In Mailey's own words: 'There was no triumph in me as I watched the receding figure. I felt like a boy who had killed the dove'. Trumper's sporting greatness and gentility was too good for this world. As Byron said, 'Whom the Gods love, die young'. Wisden's records of births and deaths show that Mr Trumper V.T. of New South Wales died on 28 June 1915, at the age of thirty-seven of Bright's disease.

Of a different ilk and temperament was G. L. Jessop, 'The Croucher' of Gloucester and England. C. B. Fry wrote of him in his obituary that

> ...it is not an overstatement to characterize Jessop's manner of batsmanship as altogether unique. His stance was such, so was his footwork, so was his swing. He crouched low over his bat as he grounded it, he dipped his head almost to his sloped bat handle as he sighted the flight, then he catapulted himself into a sort of rapid chassé towards the pitch of the ball and flung his bat at it with a long elastic sweep, arms at full length, but with abruptly locked-back wrists which he unloosed into the stroke at the finish.

Each time that I see an illustration of Jessop playing his famous pull drive, I am amazed by his statistical record. It seems incredible that such a visually agricultural player, addicted to what can only be described in modern parlance as 'the slog', could score no fewer than 26,698 runs in first-class cricket.

It would be an over-simplification to dismiss Jessop as a hitter pure and simple. Certainly he smote the ball hard and scored twelve of his fifty-three first-class centuries in under an hour; but he had style. Fry described Jessop's methods as

> . . . belting the ball high and hard all around the clock from over coverpoint's head to over the ropes behind square-leg. Besides his hard driving, he used a positively terrific square cut which he administered to the short-pitched ball which he squeezed out of the bowler who tried to mitigate punishment from the quick-footed drive.
>
> Naturally such methods entailed risks, but it was remarkable how consistent a scorer was this apparent gambler. He said himself that he gambled on a system, a careful system. He certainly made a huge success of taking what looked like the wildest chances.

'The Croucher' Gilbert Jessop

Perhaps in a lesser way he was England's Bradman: a batsman who was in position so quickly that he could indulge in apparently agricultural yet fruitful strokes with a minimum of risk. Jessop was once described as the human catapult 'who wrecks the roofs of distant towns'. His record shows that it was an apt description, for he personally never scored at less than 80 runs an hour; an amazing achievement when one considers that Woolley and Trumper scored at 55 runs per hour and Bradman at 50. Twice Jessop plundered no fewer than 28 runs off a six-ball over, one of which was delivered by that redoubtable England bowler, Len Braund.

Undoubtedly Jessop's greatest moment of glory was in The Oval Test of 1902. England in their second innings were set 263 to win on a wicket which, wet and inhospitable in its early stages, had become distinctly unpleasant on the third day. When Jessop, batting at number seven, joined F. S. Jackson, England were in the dire predicament of having lost 5/48; 215 were needed for victory on a vicious pitch with only 5 wickets in hand. It was at this stage that Jessop and Jackson added 109 for the sixth wicket, Jessop contributing a personal and improbable century in only 75 minutes. In the final analysis it was left to the cool Yorkshire heads of the last men at the wicket, George Hirst and Wilfred Rhodes to steer England home by one wicket, after the ninth wicket fell 15 runs short of their ultimate target. This was the heroic, last ditch crisis which, according to apocryphal cricket legend, was prefaced by the Hirst instruction to Rhodes to 'get 'em in singles'. The irony of the England victory at The Oval in 1902 was that both Hirst and Jessop, the eventual match-winners, were recalled to the England side after having been omitted from the previous Old Trafford Test—another cliff-hanger which England lost by 3 runs.

The astonishing factor about Jessop's volcanic century in the context of the whimsical game of cricket, is that his hundred is not the most rapid ever recorded on the Test field. The distinction of notching a three-figure score in only seventy minutes went to 'Dynamite' Jack Gregory some nineteen years later in Johannesburg, South Africa. What a dynamic cricketer this all-rounder, discovered by the Australian Services Team in England during the war years of 1914-18, must have been. His whirlwind batting brought him a further century against England in Melbourne, whilst his eruptive pace with a new ball made

Frank Woolley state that Gregory was to be more feared than even the tigerish and lithe Ted McDonald. As a close-to-the-wicket fieldsman, Gregory was fearless, and in his halcyon year of 1920-1 accepted a record 15 catches in a single series against England.

The name of Donald George Bradman commands almost half a page just in the index of Wisden, cricket's bible. The amplification of these terse references could be, and indeed have been, transcribed into whole volumes of praise about the greatest scoring-machine ever seen. A cross-section of a statistical survey of Bradman's first-class career reveals that he scored no fewer than 28,067 runs, 6,996 of them in Test matches. The unfortunate English bowlers suffered to the extent of 5,028 runs, whilst, as if to prove that Bradman set the science of run-scoring above nationalistic pride, he took 1,690 runs off his fellow Australian bowlers in one Sheffield Shield season. His batting feats are legion. He averaged over 99 in all of his Test matches, scored 974 in a single rubber against England, and plundered the attack of the old enemy to the tune of 309 runs on one fine Leeds day in 1930. The fact that he scored 6 hundreds in succession, and hit 117 centuries, are but mere cyphers. The interesting and unfathomable mystery which will probably remain submerged forever like the lost city of Atlantis, is: what was Bradman's motivating force? What made him continue hour after hour, batting in search of an unending stream of runs?

The secret of his successful batting technique is more of an open book. In the opinion of such competent judges as ex-Australian captain and his contemporary, Lindsay Hassett, Bradman's reaction to a bowler's delivery was so rapid that he was in a position to employ both orthodox and unexpected attacking strokes to deliveries which for normal mortals would simply have evoked a defensive and respectful response. In a word, Bradman will go down in the annals of cricket history as the Muhammad Ali of the game. He was undoubtedly, in terms of batting success, the greatest.

This history of cricket is studded with the names of great players; but only a select band of cricketers have ever earned general acclaim, like Jack Hobbs, for being both a great player and a thorough gentleman. A monthly occurrence during the latter years of John Berry Hobb's life was a luncheon held in a Fleet Street restaurant by his contemporary player-associates in county cricket. The event itself was an eloquent testimony to the general esteem in which the ex-England opening batsman was held. The name of the luncheon—The Master's Luncheon—was a tribute to his skill as a complete batsman. How often amidst a lively chatter and clatter of utensils have I heard Alf Gover, the ex-England fast bowler, tell the story of how the Master shielded him, a number eleven batsman, from every ball of a Northampton attack for more than an hour while victory drew ever closer to their Surrey side.

Great Hearts have abounded in Anglo-Australian Test cricket history equally as much as they did in Bunyan's *Pilgrim's Progress*. One of the largest ever to beat, lay within the breast of the England fast bowler of the turn of the century, Tom Richardson. He enjoyed the herculean reputation in his native county of Surrey of walking ten miles to home games with his cricket bag on his shoulder, bowling his 20 or

30 overs in a day, and walking wearily home again with his cricket bag under his arm. In the Old Trafford Test of 1896, he sent down 68 overs in Australia's first innings and 42.3 in their second to capture 13 wickets for 244 runs. His side lost the game by 3 wickets and Richardson was led, bemused and exhausted, from a field of play which had seen him deserve the bowler's V.C. for courage and fortitude. Perhaps after such and other harrowing experiences of being bowled to his knees, it is not surprising to learn that Richardson ended his own life on a mountainside at St Jean d'Arvay at the age of forty-one.

Anglo-Australian cricket has also seen a degree of egocentricity. Albert Trott appearing for the M.C.C. against the Australians at Lords in 1899 drove the slow off-spin bowling of Monty Noble so high and so far that the ball hit a chimney pot on top of the pavilion and fell behind it. To this very day it is the only recorded instance of a hit carrying such a distance at Cricket Headquarters; but I do recall a hit by Cecil Pepper of the Australian Services' side reaching the top tier of the stand in 1945. The strange fact about Trott's enormous smite was that before the occurrence, he was an accomplished all-rounder, completing the double of 1,000 runs and 200 wickets in an English season on two occasions. It is reputed that, after his big-hitting achievement at Lords, his batting deteriorated into mere hitting because of his ambition to repeat the feat. Ill health provoked Trott into ending his own life in 1914 with a bullet through the brain.

Albert Trott

The inventive nature of cricketers has also played an important part in the development of the game. B. J. T. Bosanquet was, until the time of his playing for Oxford University in 1898, a fast-medium bowler. A convivial evening at the billiard table, however, saw him playing a game of 'twisty-grab' with his fellow students: an event which was to transform his own bowling style and radically influence the evolution of leg-spin bowling. Noticing the peculiar behaviour of the billiard ball when it spun in the opposite direction to the turn of the wrist because too much spin was imparted, Bosanquet translated this experience into bowling and invented the 'bosie' or 'wrong 'un'. He experimented with it at Lords in 1900 and captured his first wicket with this novel ball, after it had bounced four times. Greater days, however, lay around the corner for him and with more control he mystified the Australians in Sydney in 1904 and captured 6/51 to win the game for his side by 157 runs. He repeated this success one year later at Trent Bridge where he took 8/107 in Australia's second innings.

England-Australian contests have seen batting performances which have bordered on the mystic. To have bowled at Ranjitsinhji, and to have witnessed the Indian prince glance a delivery off the middle stump to fine leg for 4, must have made one contribute to the opinion of Wainwright, the Yorkshire professional, who stated quite simply that 'Ranji never played a Christian stroke in his life'.

Some players like the famous England opening attack of 1911-12 tour of Australia, the left-handed F. R. Foster, and Sydney Barnes, deserved the epithet 'great' on merit. Few who saw it, ever forgot their reducing the Australian batting might of Kelleway, Bardsley, Hill, Armstrong, Trumper and Minnett to the shambles of 6 for 38 on a

Victor Trumper. 'The noblest Australian of them all'

flawless Melbourne wicket. It was perhaps the greatest exhibition of medium-pace swing and cut, that the past hundred years of England-Australia Tests have ever seen and it resulted in an England win by 8 wickets. The bowling records of that rubber reveal that Foster captured 32 wickets and Barnes 34: an incredible dual bowling success.

Other individuals in the past one hundred years of Test cricket have more or less had greatness thrust upon them. Such was the case of George Gunn, the Nottinghamshire professional, who was in Australia in 1907 for the sake of his health, when Jones, the captain of the England side and a martyr to tuberculosis, fell sick and was able to play in only the Fourth and Fifth Tests. Gunn, press-ganged into the service of his country, proved a remarkable success, topping the England Test batting honours with an aggregate of 462 runs and an average of 51.33 and scoring two centuries in the rubber.

I would like to be convinced that the most dominant personality trait which has characterized the players in Anglo-Australian Tests in the last century has been the good humour and friendliness between the two sides both on and off the field. I chuckle at the remark passed by Arthur Wood, the England wicketkeeper, who, coming in to bat at The Oval in 1938 with the home side's total standing at a massive 6/770, commented that he was just the man for a crisis.

The puckish Arthur Mailey, the man who spun his leg-spinners for Australia like a millionaire in the early 1920s and an employee of the Sydney Metropolitan Water Board, was not averse to turning up to a function in a hotel where he had been instrumental in cutting off the water supply for a full day, and listening with equanimity to the tales of woe of his hosts, bemoaning the inadequaces of the reception because of the lack of consideration of the local Water Board. Another Australian 'wag' was the captain visiting England who, whilst attending a mayoral reception, amused the audience in his speech in response to the welcome by asking His Worship whether he would flush if he pulled his chain!

For the future I would hope that the cricket relationships between England and Australia will be based on the same spirit of friendliness which existed between Arthur Morris, the Australian opener, and J.J. Warr, the England medium-pace bowler of the 1950-1 touring side. J.J.'s only success in the two Test matches in which he played was Ian Johnson's wicket, captured at Adelaide for an overall cost of 281 runs. During the M.C.C. game against New South Wales, Arthur Morris, having edged J.J. faintly to the wicketkeeper and seeing the umpire in something of a quandary as to whether to give the decision in J.J.'s favour, nodded his head vigorously in the affirmative and made off in voluntary capitulation towards the pavilion.

3. Bligh's Bounty: The Legend of the Ashes

Nineteenth-century England was a country dedicated to the economic policy of free-trade or 'laissez-faire'. Cricket can be grateful that it was; for it was the spirit of private enterprise and imagination which produced the very beginnings of Test cricket. In 1859, the Nottinghamshire professional George Parr, visualizing that there was a profit to be made out of displaying the home-grown cricket product in the colonies, accepted the invitation of a certain Mr Pickering and the Montreal Cricket Club to export a team of his English colleagues, temporarily, to Canada and as a result reaped a golden harvest both for his players and himself.

Other entrepreneurs were not slow in following Parr's example. The Melbourne Cricket Club's catering firm of Messrs Spiers and Ponds, disappointed by the inability of the famous author, Charles Dickens, to make a lecture tour, despatched a representative in the person of Mr Mallam to England in the summer of 1861 to negotiate for a cricket tour of Australasia. Their sponsored proposition was quickly accepted by Surrey's H. H. Stephenson, and the monetary success of that particular visit can be easily gauged by the fact that 25,000 people each paid half a crown to witness the tourists' game in Melbourne and the players and sponsors alike made a handsome profit. On the cricket field they did not have matters all their own way. In the former Victorian boom gold mining town of Castlemaine, on a now deserted paddock called Wattle Flats, stands a slender plinth surmounted by a bronze plaque; inscribed in the metal are the indelible facts of the first defeat sustained by an English side in Australia against the Twenty-Two of Victoria on that ground.

The El Dorado of Australia attracted other Sir Walter Raleighs of English cricket. In 1863-4 George Parr led the next expeditionary force which included such illustrious names as Julius Caesar, Billy Caffyn, E. M. Grace and Tom Hayward. The famous Dr W. G. Grace followed his brother to the colonies on a lucrative honeymoon trip in 1873-4; the tour yielded the amateur captain a fee which was the equivalent of $30,000 in modern currency. It was an eventful visit prefaced by the unwillingness of the great Nottinghamshire all-rounder Alfred

Shaw to accompany Grace because of the stingy provision of second-class accommodation and travel arrangements for the professionals in the party.

A less publicized Australian tour of England took place in the year 1868. It was in this year that an Englishman by the name of Charles Lawrence, a player who remained in Australia to coach after the Stephenson tour, assembled an Aboriginal team of cricketers on the shores of Lake Wallace at Edenhope in the Western District of Victoria to train them for a tour of England. To this day, a cairn in the grounds of the local school by the side of the lake marks the practice area on which the Aboriginals perfected their rude skills. From the outset, Lawrence was hampered by red tape and regulations. The emigration of Aborigines was frowned upon by the colonial government and the Central Board for the Protection of the Race; it was only by the subterfuge of pretending that his group was embarking upon a fishing trip that Lawrence managed to smuggle his team of true Australians out of the Port Phillip township of Queenscliff in the barque, *The Rangatara*. They were a colourful bunch. They embroidered their cricketing performances in England by giving displays of their native skills of throwing boomerangs and wielding nula-nulas during the tea and luncheon intervals. Their names were equally as bizarre as their reportedly unorthodox methods of play and they included in their ranks such unheard of cricketing celebrities as Dick-a-Dick, Peter, Mullagh, Cuzens, Sundown, King Cole, Jim Crow, Tiger, Red Cap, Bullocky, Twopenny, Mosquito, Charlie Dumas and Tarpot.

Tarpot was an interesting character who, according to Ballarat legend, obtained his nickname in a strange fashion. In the early days of touring sides in the Victorian goldfields and against a background which included the profit-making necessity of charging admission fees in the complete absence of anything but low, picket fences, the policing

The Aboriginal side in Sydney 1867. Standing rear row (L to R) Tarpot, T.W. Wills, Mullagh.
Front row (L to R) King Cole (leg on chair), Dick-a-Dick, Jellico, Peter, Red Cap, Harry Rose, Bullocky, Cuzens

The Melbourne Cricket
Ground at the time of
the First Test 1877

of the gate was almost impossible. More spectators gained access to the ground over the low fences than through the primitive turnstiles. It was Tarpot who, in his occasional capacity as a gatekeeper, devised the ingenious scheme of smearing the top of the surrounding picket fence with liquid tar. Unpaying intruders into the ground were then identified by the black, tell-tale marks on their breeches and expelled. The inventor of this novel admission check was dubbed thereafter Tarpot; not surprisingly the name stuck and he was identified on every subsequent score sheet by his nickname. Amongst Tarpot's other accomplishments was the ability to run 100 yards backwards in fourteen seconds! Sadly for him he fell sick before the departure of the 1868 touring team and had to be removed from the ship.

The first so-called official Test match between England and Australia took place on the Melbourne Cricket Ground on 15-17 March 1877. The ambition of the colonists to play their cricket mentors on an equal footing was stimulated by the early successes of Australian fifteens, eighteens and twenty-twos against the touring sides of W. G. Grace in 1873-4 and James Lillywhite's professionals in 1876-7. Lillywhite's XI were beaten by the fifteens of Victoria and New South Wales and even held to a level-teams draw by the latter side whilst en route to New Zealand. Such victories stimulated the opinion within the breasts of the former Australian underdog that their ability on the field was the equal of that of the previously dominant Englishmen. So ardent was this belief that even the cut-throat rivalry between Melbourne and Sydney sportsmen was forgotten and a combined side chosen to meet Lillywhite's team in even contest in the first official 'Test' upon their return from New Zealand.

In spite of the common Australian desire to meet England on an equal footing it must not be supposed that all was sweetness and light for the first match. The sides were far from fully representative of their countries. The famous Sydney bowler Evans—the equal of any English county bowler in the opinion of the tourists—was not available because of pressure of business. Spofforth, at this stage just an unruly spirit rather than the 'Demon' that he was later to become, refused to play when the Victorian wicketkeeper, John McCarthy Blackham, was chosen in preference to the New South Welshman, Murdoch. To make matters worse for Australia, the Victorian 'bowler of the century', Frank Allan, declined to appear since he was working in Warrnambool and the local fair, which coincided with the First Test, afforded a rare and not-to-be-neglected opportunity of meeting all his old friends.

Lillywhite's England side was weakened by the absence of Pooley, their regular star wicketkeeper. In a local game against the Twenty-two of Canterbury in Christchurch, New Zealand, Pooley wagered that he could nominate the scores of all the opposing batsmen. When his bet was accepted, on the basis that Pooley would lose a shilling when he was wrong and gain a pound when he was right, the astute wicketkeeper worked the pea-and-thimble trick of nominating a duck as the score of all the opposing batsmen. Since a high proportion of the Canterbury players was less than expert with the bat, the shrewd Surrey man made a handsome profit.

A certain Mr Donkin, however, refused to take his loss graciously and the ensuing brawl resulted in the subsequent arrest of Pooley and the English baggage-man and supporter, Alf Bramall, in Otago on a charge of assault and battery and causing damage in excess of five pounds. Tried before the Supreme Court of Canterbury, the English-men were acquitted and freed with the additional compensation of a purse of sovereigns and a gold ring from their local sympathizers; but the cricket damage was done and Pooley was delayed sufficiently to miss the First Test against Australia.

England's cause was scarcely helped by the fact that the sea journey from New Zealand's Bluff was so rough that most of the team were compelled to sleep on deck throughout the voyage. Their ship was delayed and they arrived in Melbourne a bare day before the match, and were forced to take the field, still reeling on sea legs ill-suited to the demands of the Test field. Indeed, when the staggering and exhausted Armitage, England's lob bowler, bowled his first delivery in the game, it passed so high over the head of Bannerman that the local press was moved to write that the batsman could not have reached it with a clothes prop. Armitage's second delivery was in violent contrast to his first. It rolled along the ground causing much amusement amongst the spectators.

In the final analysis Australia won the game by 45 runs, thanks to the heroic Charles Bannerman, who scored 165 before the Yorkshire fast bowler, 'Happy Jack' Ulyett, so badly split his finger that it caused him to retire hurt. The magnitude of Bannerman's contribution to the Australia first innings score of 245 can be assessed from the fact that not one of Bannerman's fellow-players scored more than 18! The Melbourne public showed their non-partisan gratitude to their N.S.W. hero by subscribing £87 7s 6d to a well-deserved collection.

The best colonial bowlers were Tom Kendall and Billy Midwinter. The slow left-handed Kendall, operating off a two-pace approach, bowled virtually unchanged throughout England's second innings, when the tourists needed only 155 runs to win. His final analysis of 7/55 saw Lillywhite's side all out for 108. Whilst he received the Australasian trophy for the best home-side bowler, Kendall was never to recapture his form again. He played only in the two Tests of 1877.

Midwinter returned the figures of 5/78 in England's first innings of 196 and so impressed the visitors that he was recruited to play for the county of his birth, Gloucestershire, in the following season. This division of loyalties subsequently caused Midwinter to appear for England before he again represented Australia, the country for whom he first appeared. Sadly Midwinter, the 'Bendigo Infant' as he was called, went mad after the premature death of his wife and children. He was confined to the Kew Asylum and died of general paralysis before he was forty.

Australia's initial victory in the embryo competition for the then unknown trophy of the Ashes stimulated two main reactions; the first was the demand for revenge by Lillywhite's side. The return match took place on the Melbourne Cricket Ground between 31 March and 4 April. By this stage, a fortnight on land had restored the Englishmen to their status of landlubbers and consequently improved cricketers. Even the strengthening of the Australian side by the inclusion of the formerly recalcitrant Spofforth and Murdoch could not prevent England from carrying off a handsome victory by 4 wickets. The five Yorkshiremen in Lillywhite's team, Greenwood, Ulyett, Emmett, Hill and Armitage shouldered the main responsibility of the tourists' batting to steer them home to victory.

Lillywhite's English Eleven in Australia 1877

The second consequence of Gregory's victory was that their opponents were suitably impressed by the improved quality of Australian cricket. After the visit of H. H. Stephenson's XI in 1862, Roger Iddison, the Yorkshire professional, remarked of the Australians that 'He didn't think much of their play, but they are a wonderful lot of drinking men'. This English judgment was completely revised after the events in Melbourne in March and April 1877. Australian cricket had obviously arrived and one local Melbourne writer was moved to advise future sponsors of English tours that: 'Whoever may enter into future speculations reporting an English XI, he should bear in mind the great improvement of colonial cricket and not imagine that anything will do for Australia'. This was the message which David Gregory and his team were to underline when, at the invitation of their English guests of the previous year, they toured England in the summer of 1878.

There was no place for weaklings in Gregory's basic party of a dozen tourists. Their visit was prefaced by a long toning-up tour of Australia and New Zealand and matches were played in both America and Canada en route and on the way back from England. In that country itself no fewer than thirty-seven matches were arranged, twenty of them

Fred Spofforth, 'The Demon Bowler'

against odds. Nor was that the end of the long, long cricket trail. Upon their return home, the first Australian tourists were obliged to display their improvement by touring their own country once again. It was small wonder that on this fifteen-month Odyssey Spofforth developed into the 'Demon' later batsmen knew. He captured an incredible 764 wickets at an average of 6.08!

Their busy enthusiasm and the English hospitality ensured Gregory's men of a warm welcome, but the bleak European summer was far from welcoming, and the tourists soon found their thin silk shirts and hard wicket techniques ill-suited to the biting winds and the soft pitches. Their predicament was almost poetic justice since the fate which befell Lillywhite's men in the antipodes only a few months previously was one of almost identical hardship. At one stage of their journey to Australasia the diary of one of the tourists reported a member of the side as suffering such martyrdom from rheumatism that he could not even get out of his bunk without assistance; two others were miserable with the cold whilst another appeared afflicted with the measles. I wonder what a modern-day manager would have made of such a sick list?

Gregory's men began inauspiciously at Nottingham by losing by an innings, but the Australian underdogs had their day when, on 27 May 1878, they defeated the flower of English cricket and the M.C.C. in a single, soggy day on a waterlogged Lords pitch. Illustrious batsmen such as W. G. Grace, Hornby and bowlers of the ability of Shaw and Morley could do little against a colonial combination which won by 9 wickets. Spofforth, in the M.C.C. first innings total of 33, captured 6/4; but even that exceptional performance was not sufficient to win the match with ease since the home side trailed by only 8 runs on the first innings. When the Grand Old Man of English Cricket, W. G. Grace, opened the M.C.C.'s second innings, few people even contemplated the possibility of his failing twice in a single game; yet W.G. was dropped off the very first ball which he received, whilst the second bowled him. Boyle improved on Spofforth's first innings gambit by taking 6/3. The whole of London was agog as the M.C.C., teetering to a paltry second innings total of 19, set the tourists only 12 to win and so lost by 9 wickets before the close of play on the first day.

Mobs of admiring sports fans crowded around the Australians' hotel to catch a glimpse of their heroes. Not the least in demand was F. R. Spofforth; a man who began the tour as an express bowler with a fast yorker, yet matured so much that he returned to Australia as a master in the art of change of pace, and was hailed by W.G. Grace as the greatest bowler in the world. If 'damned statistics' do not lie then Spofforth must indeed have been the doyen of all bowlers of all ages; the almost incredible truth about Spofforth's performance in those few short months of wandering around Australia, England, America and Canada was that he captured in a single year as many wickets as some bowlers take in a whole career.

In 1878 England did not accord to Australia the satisfaction of meeting her on level terms in a single Test. Indeed, in spite of the resounding victory of Gregory's team over the M.C.C., there appears to have been a reluctance on the part of the English cricketing world to award full international status to the colonials. Such at least was the inference drawn from the refusal of most of the leading English players to embark on the next expeditionary force to Australia in 1878-9. Perhaps their reluctance was understandable in view of the touring hardships and privations experienced by their predecessors in the course of the preceding seventeen years.

Originally the party to Australia in 1878-9 was conceived as a completely amateur band led by I. D. Walker, one of the famous cricketing Southgate family. In the final analysis, however, none of the brothers was able to make the trip and the mantle of captaincy fell upon Lord Harris's shoulders. His side was strengthened by the professional bowling talents of Yorkshiremen Ulyett and Emmett. It was scarcely a fully representative England XI. Gregory's side had to wait until the New Year of 1879 before their next and the third international. In the only Test played against Lord Harris's side in Melbourne between 2 and 4 January 1879, Australia were victorious by 10 wickets against an English side of obvious bowling limitations. In the tourists' innings of 113 and 160, the 'Demon' Spofforth once again proved indomitable and bettered his Lords performance of the previous English summer by returning match figures of 13/110.

Far more significant for the immediate future of Australian cricket than the Melbourne Test, however, was the match between Lord Harris's XI and New South Wales in Sydney. In the course of the New South Wales second innings, Billy Murdoch, the darling of the Sydney crowd and the scorer of 82 in the home side's first innings total of 177, was adjudged run out for 10. The perpetrator of this apparently dastardly decision was the English umpire, Coulthard. Those were the days when touring sides contributed not only players to a game but also their own umpire. The fact that Coulthard was a hated Victorian, recruited during an earlier part of the tour, caused an outcry amongst the Sydney spectators which would only have been rivalled eighty years later by a Yorkshire crowd who had seen their own Len Hutton given run out on 99, one run short of victory, by a Lancastrian umpire in the traditional Roses match. The New South Wales captain, David Gregory, advanced on to the field and objected to Coulthard on the grounds of incompetency. This was the signal for a full scale riot amongst the betting fraternity around the Sydney ground and a prolonged invasion of the playing area which almost resulted in Lord Harris claiming the match by default. In the course of the scrimmage, wickets were torn from the pavilion fence, the noble Lord was assaulted and the English batsman, 'Monkey' Hornby, who had apprehended one of the more blatant offenders and was delivering him to the hands of the law, had his shirt torn from his back. Lord Harris received an apology from the New South Wales cricket authorities, but it was no coincidence that in the aftermath of this violent insult to a leading English cricket administrator the Australian touring side in England in 1880 were hard-pressed to fill their fixture list.

Many excuses were offered for the inability of the Australians to find opponents. It was alleged that the main cause of their difficulties was the lateness of their final agreement to make the tour. The brutal truth of the matter was, however, that the Australians were effectively snubbed by the English counties because of the manhandling of Lord Harris and his side in Sydney only a few months previously. At one stage the Australian side were reduced to the indignity of having to advertise for matches. It was only due to the forgiving nature of Lord Harris and the organizing efficiency of a certain Mr C. W. Alcock that the first Test match between England and Australia on English soil was played at The Oval from 6 to 8 September 1880.

In that game Grace scored 152 but Murdoch riposted with an unbeaten 153 in the Australians' second innings. It was said that Murdoch bet his companion-in-arms, Grace, at the conclusion of his memorable innings, that he would outscore him. The guinea which Murdoch won, he wore on his watch chain until his death. Murdoch's not inconsiderable achievement in 'outgracing' Grace was in vain and England, blessed by the absence of the injured Spofforth, struggled home by 5 wickets after half their side were dismissed by Boyle and Palmer in the second innings for a mere 57. This was the one and only time that all the three Grace brothers, E.M., W.G. and G.F., played in the same Test match. It was to be the last important game in Fred Grace's life. A few months later he was dead, the victim of pneumonia contracted after sleeping in a damp bed.

W.G. Grace, 'The Champion shows his style'

In the English winter of 1881-2 the famous triumvirate of Shaw, Lillywhite and Shrewsbury led the first of their all-professional sides to Australia, enduring the rigours of Buffalo Bill's pioneer America en route. For the first time a full series of four Tests was played between the two countries. An innings of 124 from Horan—later to become 'Felix' of Australian journalism—in the First Test, and 149 from Ulyett in the fourth encounter ensured that these games were drawn. Victory went to Australia in the Second and Third Tests by 5 and 6 wickets respectively. The second game saw Murdoch keeping wicket on the third morning; at this stage he yielded up the gloves to Blackham who kept them in his possession until 1895. It was a match distinguished also by the endurance of Australian bowlers Evans and Palmer, who bowled unchanged for over three hours in England's first innings —a joint record which still stands to this present day.

The third match saw Australia advantaged by being permitted to choose an alternative wicket for their first innings, after England had batted on a sub-standard pitch in their first knock. As a result McDonnell scored 147: an amazing feat when one considers that this was his initial century in first-class cricket. Scandal struck the tour when it was rumoured that two members of the England side had contracted to sell the Victorian game to the home state when they required only 94 runs to win in their second innings. Fortunately for the good name of cricket, the rumour was laid bare as pure calumny: Shaw's team proved that there was no selling plate in the game by winning by 18 runs.

The year 1882 witnessed the coming-of-age of Australian cricket. In the unique Test match of that year—if not of all time—Australia won a remarkable first victory in Tests on English soil against the full might of the home country's cricketers. The England side was replete with great names: R. G. Barlow, W. G. Grace, A. N. Hornby, A. G. Steel, G. Uylett, C. T. Studd, A. P. Lucas, the Hon. A. Lyttelton, J. M. Read, W. Barnes and E. Peate were, at that stage, the best talent that England could put on to the cricket field. In spite of this opposition and the fact that Australia, batting first on a ground which Barlow the England player described as unfit, could only score 63, Murdoch's men registered a thrilling victory by 7 runs. England's lead on the first innings was 38 and this appeared to be an advantage of match-winning dimensions, for in their second attempt Australia could manage only 122 and were thus only 84 runs away from outright defeat.

Fred Spofforth, the bowling hero of England's first innings in which he captured 7/46 was in the van of the Australian team as they set foot on The Oval for the last English innings of this celebrated Test; as he strode determinedly on to the field to play he declared with conviction: 'This thing can be done'. He dismissed seven Englishmen for 44 to bring his match tally to 14/90; Spofforth's herculean effort was supported by that of the bearded Boyle and together they tumbled out the mighty England batsmen for 77 and steered Australia home to a palpitating victory by 7 runs.

It was a match of almost unbearable tension. The Australian player Horan later described how in the final phases, the excitement rose to such a fever pitch that one spectator dropped down dead whilst another gnawed through the handle of his umbrella. 'Buns' Thornton—the man who was later to gain fame by striking the ball from the Scarborough Cricket Ground into the adjoining Trafalgar Square, to be subsequently asked by a lady admirer whether he was batting at The Oval or Lords—drew a vivid picture of the predicament of C. T. Studd as The Oval drama drew to its climax. Studd, he said, was 'walking around the pavilion with a blanket around him'. His anticipatory shivering was needless anxiety; as Peate, the last English batsman, flailed at the final ball and was bowled, Studd stood disconsolately at the non-striker's end. He did not face a ball!

Spofforth, the Australian bowling hero, was carried shoulder high to the pavilion. If ever a man made cricket history it was he on that day. In the final crisis he bowled his last 11 overs for 2 runs and 4 wickets! Ironically, however, it was the English captain, W. G. Grace, who reputedly did almost as much as Spofforth to stiffen the Australian determination to win the game. In Australia's second innings, their 21-year-old batsman S. P. Jones had just completed a single and moved off down the wet pitch to pat down a divot raised by the last delivery, when W. G. picked up the ball and unsportingly ran him out. The story goes that Jones went to do his 'gardening' at the invitation of the champion, but one must doubt that even W.G.'s gamesmanship reached such extremes.

The English sporting public took the Australian victory very much to heart. They paid little heed to the press statement of 1877 about the improved quality of Australian cricket. They preferred to believe that The Oval defeat emanated from a deterioration in the standard of the English game. Apparently, even in those days, the press preferred to criticize the English performance rather than praise the Australian achievement. At the end of the week of The Oval Test, the London newspaper, *The Sporting Times,* published the now famous obituary notice which paradoxically gave birth, if not immediate substance, to the legend of the Ashes. The notice read:

In affectionate remembrance
of English Cricket
which died at The Oval
on
29th August, 1882.

Deeply lamented by a large circle of
sorrowing friends and acquaintances R.I.P.

N.B. The body will be cremated and
the Ashes taken to Australia.

The idea that the 'Ashes' should become the perpetual trophy to be contested by England and Australia was self-evident in *The Sporting Times* paragraph. The notion did not become reality, however, until the following winter when the Hon. Ivo Bligh, later to become Lord Darnley, led a team of eight amateurs and four professionals to the antipodes. In a speech in Adelaide Ivo Bligh described his mission in

Australia as: 'A crusade to regain the Ashes, which had been so rudely wrested from England's possession in the previous summer'.

The holy mission of Captain Bligh gained him a character which was in complete contrast to his more famous and maligned namesake of the *Bounty;* he became known as Saint Ivo and after the third match of the series in Sydney, when the rubber based on the scheduled matches had been won, a group of ladies burnt a bail, enclosed the ashes in a small funeral urn and presented it with due solemnity to the English captain. Contrary to public belief, that urn now resides permanently in the Imperial Cricket Memorial Gallery at Lords, and does not, as is commonly supposed, pass into the possession of the winner of the series.

The Bligh tour of Australia was, to say the least, eventful. It began disastrously when the team's ship, the *Peshawar,* was in collision with the barque *Glencoy* 600 miles south of Colombo. In the accident English fast bowler, Fred Morley, fell from his bunk and broke several ribs. It was an injury which was to not only decimate Bligh's attack, since Morley was their only fast bowler, but was also to lead to the premature retirement and death of the unfortunate player. Australia defeated England by 9 wickets in the First Test in Melbourne; a game which saw the giant George Bonnor score 85 and smite the English bowler Bates with blacksmithian might 150 yards over the skittle alley and into the elm trees in Richmond Park. Bates, however, was to have his revenge and it was he who, by capturing 13/102, was largely instrumental in England winning the second game of the rubber by an innings and 27 runs. In the course of the second knock Bates took the first hat-trick for England against Australia by capturing the wickets of McDonnell, Giffen and, ironically, Bonnor. It was a remarkably successful game for Bates for not only did he capture his 14 wickets, but he also scored 55 runs in England's one and only innings; he thus became the first of only three cricketers who have ever taken 10 wickets and scored a half-century in the same game.

The 1882-3 series was in many respects a remarkably casual affair. It was a feature of each match that the teams had the option of choosing a different wicket for each innings. Apparently during the Third Test in Sydney Billy Murdoch made a miscalculation about the appropriate surface to use for his final innings. With his side needing 153 runs to win, they floundered against the fast left-handed medium-pace of Barlow who captured 7/40 and bundled out Australia for 83 for England to win by 69 runs.

With little or no regard for an official itinerary or programme, a fourth supplementary Test was arranged. Australia won by 4 wickets in a game which saw the return of the ubiquitous Billy Midwinter to the Australian camp after having consecutively represented Australia and England in earlier series. Equally strange in this Australian victory was the performance of the home batsmen before play began on the fourth day. Several wickets had been prepared for their second innings; before the wondering eyes of the English players the Australians tested the qualities of each strip before play began with a fast bowler operating from either end! Small wonder the laws now state that trial balls are not allowed after the call of play.

The Countess of Darnley

The Australian Eleven in England 1882. Standing (L to R) G.E. Palmer, H.F. Boyle, W.L. Murdoch (captain), P.S. McDonnell, F.R. Spofforth, T.P. Horan, S.P. Jones. Seated (L to R) C.W. Beal (manager), G. Giffen, A.C. Bannerman, T.W. Garrett, H.H. Massie, G.T. Bonnor

Bligh's England party was the first to visit the northern outpost of Queensland. It is worth recording that their captain took back to England not only the Ashes, but also a wife, in the person of Miss Florence Morphy of Beechworth, Victoria. On the *Peshawar* en route to Australia Bligh, whilst playing deck tennis, slipped and gashed his hand badly. He was bandaged and nursed by the future Lady Darnley. In statistical terms, the Hon. Ivo contributed little to Anglo-Australian Tests. His first innings in Australia yielded nought and he returned from the tour with a meagre Test aggregate of 62 and an average of 10.33. Shortly afterwards a heart ailment caused his retirement and he transferred his sporting allegiances to golf. Yet in spite of statistics it is an incontrovertible fact that Bligh, the practical author of the Ashes tradition and a fine ambassador, established strong cricketing and romantic links between England and Australia. Upon his death in 1927, Lady Darnley donated the 'Ashes' urn to the M.C.C.

4. Australia's Lean Years

Billy Murdoch's Australian tour of England in 1882 was a watershed in his country's cricket history. Paradoxically, Australia's initial moment of glory at The Oval produced a defeatist reaction which spanned more than a decade. Facts speak for themselves. In twelve series in the fourteen years subsequent to 1882, Australia won only one rubber—that of 1891-2—and conceded twenty-three Test losses with only a modicum of compensation in ten victories. Eleven wins in twelve series must have almost convinced the English partisans that the Ashes were never destined to leave their niche at Lords.

Australia contributed as much to its own downfall in these years as did its opponents. These were divisive and turbulent times in the history of Australian cricket. More often than not the source of dispute was the perennial bone of contention—money. It was seldom that Australia managed to field either a fully representative team or its strongest side. The 1884 team in England was perhaps one of its most formidable. It is true that there was no Garrett or Horan and the hard-hitting batting hero of The Oval in 1882, Massie, was also absent. Nonetheless the illustrious names of Bannerman, McDonnell, Murdoch, Scott, Giffen, Bonnor, Midwinter, Blackham, Palmer, Spofforth, and Boyle were enough to daunt all but the staunchest of opposing cricketing hearts. It was bad luck for Murdoch's combination that they were confronted by what George Giffen estimated to be the strongest English side of the nineteenth century.

(L to R) W.L. Murdoch, F.R. Spofforth, H.F. Boyle, A.C. Bannerman

In typical Manchester fashion, the First Test at Old Trafford was curtailed by rain. The pitch itself was a mud heap when the match began. It was only a masterly 43 from Shrewsbury, the inventor of defensive pad-play, which enabled England to score 95 in their first innings against the wiles of Spofforth and Boyle. In the final analysis, the lost first day and a succession of fortunate edges from the surprise-choice batsman, O'Brien, permitted England to draw the game. When stumps were drawn England had lost 6 wickets in their second innings and were still only 27 runs ahead.

It was a different story at Lords where A. G. Steele compiled a commanding 148 to steer England home by an innings and 5 runs. In a

strange interlude of democratic captaincy which would be unknown in present times, Murdoch, the Australian skipper, substituted for W. G. Grace and had the temerity to catch Scott, his own side's highest scorer, for 75 in Australia's first innings! Other times obviously breed other customs, or at least such is the inference to be drawn from the fact that Blackham, the Australian keeper, elected to bat without gloves against fast bowler Ulyett and had to retire hurt as a result of a damaged finger. One would have thought that the risks which he ran in keeping wicket in his flimsy gauntlets would have been sufficient for J. McCarthy Blackham. Apparently they were not. Fast bowler Ulyett clinched the match for England by capturing 7/36 by cutting the ball back viciously from outside the off-stump, off a patch of turf roughed by Spofforth's follow-through.

The Third and Final Test at The Oval was drawn in historic fashion. In the Australian first innings total of 551, three of their batsmen scored a century on the first day! Lord Harris, the English captain, became so exasperated that he invited the wicketkeeper, the Hon. A. Lyttelton, to abandon his pads and gloves and take up the ball. Astonishingly, Lyttelton, 'purveying' what one post-war English cricket writer would have described as 'seemingly guileless deliveries', lobbed his way into Test history by sending down 12 tempting underarm overs to capture 4/19, and emerge from the match as England's most successful bowler. All of the England players bowled whilst Murdoch the Australian captain compiled a crushing 211: a score which was to remain the highest Test total in England until Bradman exceeded it forty-six years later. On the last day England were a precarious 8/181 until a stubborn 90 in five and three-quarter hours from the famous stone-waller Scotton of 'block, block, block at the foot of the wicket, O, Scotton' poetic fame, rescued them from their dilemma. To cap one of the most extraordinary Test matches of all time, Walter Read, furious at being relegated to the number ten position, came to the wicket to lash a cyclonic century in less than two hours.

The Oval in the nine-
teenth century

Shrewsbury's touring side of 1884-5 returned from Australia with a
3-2 victory from the first five-match series played between the two
countries. There is no gainsaying the fact, however, that the English
side was extremely lucky. In the first instance, the Australian camp was
a house divided against itself. In the space of five Tests Australia was
led by no fewer than four captains. On the eve of the Second Test in
Melbourne, Murdoch's 1884 touring side of England demanded half of
the game's gate money as a reward for their impending efforts; the
Melbourne Cricket Club's answer was a completely new Australian side
in which only Horan and Jones retained their places. No fewer than five
Australian players made their first and last Test bow in the one and
same game.

The tour began badly for Australia in Adelaide where England won
by 8 wickets largely to a personally unique century from the all-rounder
Barnes and high wicket-taking performances from both Bates and Peel.
Coincidentally, Bannerman was unable to bat in the second Australian
innings because of an injured hand, damaged as it had been in the very
first Anglo-Australian Test by fast bowler Ulyett.

Australian public opinion attributed their country's initial defeat of
1884 to their men's lack of practice after their return from England. No
amount of work at the nets could save the novice side which the home
country fielded against England for the Second Test; the tourists won
by 10 wickets, with their left-handed spin bowler, Johnny Briggs
scoring 121. The Third Test in Sydney saw the old backbone of the
previously filleted Australian side restored to its former rigidity. The
10-run bonus gained by Australia before the onset of a ferocious hailstorm enabled them to slip home by 6 runs on a wicket rendered
treacherous by an icy mantle which at one stage made the Sydney
Cricket Ground resemble a polar ice-cap.

There is no doubt that if sponsors had awarded today's Player of the
Match trophy in the era of the Fourth Sydney Test of 1884-5, the
winner on that occasion would have been Bonnor. He came to the

43

'Happy Jack' Ulyett. A fast bowling character

wicket with his side 7 wickets down for 134 in pursuit of a first England innings total of 265. In the space of only eighty-five minutes after the tea interval, Bonnor smote the bowling of Ulyett, Peel, Attewell, Bates, Barnes and Flowers to all corners of the Sydney Cricket Ground, to score 113 of his eventual total of 128. The astonishing feature of his innings was that it was compiled on a spiteful wicket on which the ball kicked so much that England at their second attempt could only manage 77 against the bowling of Spofforth and Palmer. Bonnor did not offer a chance in this innings until he was missed at slip off the shot which brought him simultaneously to his century. After being annihilated by 8 wickets, England clinched the series in the Fifth Test by an innings and 98 against an Australian side who were still bickering amongst themselves and with the administrators. Bonnor, the deciding influence in the previous Test, was missing from the Australian line-up, as indeed was McDonnell, the scorer of 174 and 83 in the first match and Blackham who had not only kept wicket in the fourth game in Sydney but had also captained the side. Reports on the Final Test provided illuminating evidence that even in those early days umpires had to contend with derision and abuse from players. Umpire Hodges refused to appear after tea on the third day after Shrewsbury's men complained about his decisions. His substitute proved to be Tom Garrett, who was so far from being a superannuated player that he was to represent Australia in their very next encounter with England at Old Trafford in 1886.

That year's touring party was characterized by its inexperience. It was the first team to leave Australian shores under the sponsorship of the Melbourne Cricket Club and the first not to be backed by private individuals. Sweetness and light were again lacking from the Australian camp of 1886. The established names of McDonnell, Bannerman, Murdoch and Horan were missing from the team when it was announced. Their leader was the untried H. J. H. Scott and, when crisis loomed, the side proved unequal to the challenge. Even the great Spofforth was not his former bowling self. He injured a finger and whilst he was later to return to live in England and play for Derbyshire, this proved to be his last visit as a tourist to that country. The impact of Spofforth on the development of fast bowling can be gauged from the fact that in the course of five visits to England he collected 1,236 wickets. Disastrously for Scott's team, Spofforth's injury coincided with an equally important deprivation; the hard-hitting Bonnor was also injured at the end of July, and the series deteriorated into a 3-0 walk-over for England and a complete fiasco for Australia.

Double misfortune courted Scott's side since their year of injury and callowness coincided with the emergence of a great England bowler, Lohmann. As a result of this combination of factors the home side won the First Test by 4 wickets and annihilated the tourists by an innings and 106 runs at Lords. In the second encounter at Cricket Headquarters rain fell a quarter of an hour after start of play: this climatic quirk produced two performances which were probably amongst the greatest by England players. Lancashire's ill-starred left-hand bowler, Johnny Briggs, returned a match-winning analysis of 11/74; he was supported by a magnificent century from the bat of Arthur Shrewsbury. The Nottinghamshire batsman proved his artistry by scoring 164 on a wicket which was described as being treacherous and sticky in the extreme. It constantly kicked and turned unpredictably, but for nearly seven hours Shrewsbury defied the wiles of Spofforth, Palmer, Evans, Garrett, Trumble and Giffen: one of the finest bowling combinations ever to play for Australia.

The English victory in the Third Test at The Oval by an innings and 217 runs was the heaviest defeat sustained by either England or Australia until 1934. W. G. Grace, by reaching 170 attained the highest pinnacle of scoring achievement scaled by a home batsman until Mead surpassed him in 1921. A wicket freshened by rain added to Australia's misfortunes, and Lohmann captured 12/104 to end a tour which was one of the most unhappy experienced by an Australian side in England.

Even the fact that the years 1886-7 saw the emergence of those two formidable Australian bowlers 'Terror' Turner and Jack Ferris, failed to stem the tide of English supremacy. In the opinion of W. G. Grace, Turner, a fast-medium bowler, came off the pitch quicker than any other person he played against except the Yorkshireman, George Freeman. In spite of Turner's chest-on action and low delivery, he made the ball lift abruptly and brought it back sharply from the off. In addition, he possessed the capacity to move the ball away off the wicket from leg to off and could pitch his yorker at will. During the 1888 tour of England he captured 283 wickets and his career record of 101 Test wickets at intervals of 51 balls and at an average of 16.53 has never been rivalled in numbers or striking rate by any other Australian bowler. In spite of the dual assets of Turner and Ferris, Australia in 1886-7 were no match for the strong professional batting ability of the English side, personified in the joint captains, Shaw and Shrewsbury, and the bowling talents of Barnes, Lohmann and Briggs. In the First Test in Sydney, England achieved the apparently impossible by scoring 45 in their first innings and winning by 13 runs! That total of 45 remains the lowest score by an England side in Australia. The hero of the game was the all-rounder Barnes, who scored 32 in England's meagre second innings total of 184 and captured 8 wickets in the match including 6/28 in Australia's second knock.

In the second match against Australia, which England won by 71 runs, Barnes was unable to play. Australia fielded an extraordinary team since they not only dropped Spofforth but also suffered the disability of having Bannerman and Giffen unavailable and Trott injured. One could also say that England laboured under some selection difficulties. In the previous game Barnes, the burgeoning English star, had a slight disagreement with the Australian captain, McDonnell, whom he attempted to punch in the nose. Unfortunately for Barnes, McDonnell, with the true genius of perfect timing, ducked at precisely the right moment and Barnes, observing the coaching criterion of following-through, hit the brick wall behind the Australian skipper. He so badly bruised his hand that he was unable to play in the subsequent Test.

In the following Australian season the Melbourne Cricket Club continued its role as sponsor of cricket tours, begun with Scott's tour of

George Giffen. An all-rounder without peer

England in 1886, by acting as host to an English side captained by Lord Hawke. The entry of the M.C.C. into the sponsorship field in no way discouraged the enterprise of individuals such as Shaw, Shrewsbury and Lillywhite. They too, brought a professional side to Australia in 1887 in a business venture which proved nothing short of a financial disaster, due to the rival attractions of Lord Hawke's team. Lord Hawke himself was compelled to return to England by a family death and he left Vernon to preside over a composite England side drawn from the two touring parties, and to contest the single Sydney Test of the tour. The comparative strengths of the two teams was completely disparate. Indeed, so strong were both of the English sides that each, in its own right, defeated representative Australian elevens in the weeks before the official Test. Shrewsbury was in devastating form with the bat and in the course of the tour compiled two double centuries whilst Lohmann showed his skill by literally mowing down the wickets with a regularity which made him the second most potent striking force in the history of English bowling.

The Test itself was a farce, with England winning by 126 runs on a pitch which was rendered impossible by torrential rain just before the start of play. The Australian captain McDonnell won the toss and sent England into bat; it was a decision which was apparently well justified, as the left-handed Ferris turned some deliveries so abruptly that they were fielded by first slip without the wicketkeeper interposing a glove! By dint of a masterly 44 from Shrewsbury in the first innings and a gambler's 39 from Maurice Read in the second, England twice exceeded the century mark. Australia for her part could only manage totals of 42 and 82—the first of which remains to this day the second lowest score in England-Australia Tests. It was on this tour that A. E. Stoddart—'dear and gentle Stod'—made his debut for England; he was to go on to earn a reputation for himself in cricket 'as a man to win the heart of every sportsman in Australia'.

The Australian tale of woe and failure continued in 1888 when a side led by McDonnell visited England. The sum total of their batting experience was confined to the names of the McDonnell himself, Bonnor, Bannerman and Jones. Even this moderate strength was further depleted when Jones contracted smallpox and could not make an appearance in any of the three Tests. George Giffen's all-round skills would have greatly enhanced the winning chances of the 1888 tourists; but Giffen remained at home in Adelaide with his brother.

The main bowling responsibilities of McDonnell's side therefore devolved upon the shoulders of Turner and Ferris. The nippy right and left-handed opening bowlers did not let their side down; they captured 534 wickets on the tour—405 more victims than all of the other bowlers combined in a short space of twenty weeks. It was an astonishing but not altogether disproportionate achievement, since the amount of work which Ferris and Turner performed in the absence of Spofforth and Boyle was immense. In the course of three Tests alone the two opening bowlers sent down 287.2 overs and captured 32 wickets; the other Australian bowlers between them contributed 69.1 overs for 5 additional wickets.

C.T.B. Turner, 'The Terror'

The main support for Ferris and Turner came from Sammy Woods, the young Australian and Cambridge undergraduate fast bowler, who in this year made his début for his native land and who, ten years later, would play in three Tests for England against South Africa. In the First Test at Lords, Turner and Ferris captured a joint 18 wickets to dismiss England for 53 and 62 and steer their side home to victory by 61 runs. This was Australia's first win since the Sydney Test of 17 March 1885. The muddy wicket of Lords however was not repeated at The Oval and England ran out victors by an innings and 137 runs. Five Surrey men represented their country on their home ground and bundled Australia out for successive totals of 80 and 100. Quite a feature of this series was the regularity of Australia's batting failures; on four of the six occasions on which they batted they could not surpass the century mark.

Such batting fragility was self-evident at Old Trafford where England won by an innings and 21 runs after only totalling 172 in their first innings. With typical Manchester reliability, rain fell forty-eight hours before the start of play and England thus gained the advantage of batting first on a wicket which was soft but not as yet at its drying, sticky worst. That nadir of its development was reserved for the second day, when a hot sun created such a monster of a pitch that the match was all over before lunch. Thus Manchester gained for itself the dubious honour of being the scene of the shortest Test ever played. At one stage in their second innings of 70 Australia were a horrendous 6/7. Bobby Peel, the Yorkshire left-handed spinner, who was later to fall foul of Lord Hawke and be subsequently banished from Yorkshire cricket for appearing drunk on the field at Chesterfield, returned match figures of 11/68 and was virtually unplayable.

Jack Ferris

In the mid-1880s, the Australian captain Billy Murdoch, then resident in England, temporarily abandoned cricket in favour of shooting; in 1890 he was persuaded to return to lead the Australian touring side. 'Johnny' Moyes, in his book *Australian Cricket,* described Murdoch as being, at this stage of his career, past his best. He was not as effective on wickets which were less than good, since he had lost something of the nimbleness of his youth. The Australian side included K.E. Burn, a Tasmanian and an excellent batsman; Burn was initially chosen as a reserve wicketkeeper as a result of the Melbourne and Sydney selectors being unable to resolve their differences about who should act as substitute to Blackham. When the ship carrying the Australian side was on the high seas, Burn enquired about who was to keep wicket in emergencies and was told that the task was reserved for him. It transpired that he had never kept wicket in his life and that the wrong Burn from Tasmania had been selected!

As it was in 1888, so it was in 1890. Giffen again refused to tour and more than half of Murdoch's side were completely unused to English conditions. The upshot of this unfortunate set of circumstances was that Australia lost more matches than they won. Once again the main burden of the bowling fell on the broad shoulders of Turner and Ferris, who, between them, captured 430 wickets during the tour. This was to be Jack Ferris's swan-song for Australia. In 1891-2 he accompanied an English side to South Africa where he took 235 wickets during the tour at an average of 5.9 runs. Subsequently he journeyed to England to play for W. G. Grace's county of Gloucestershire. Shortly afterwards he returned to his native Adelaide for a holiday, played a single game for South Australia, bowled one over, scored a duck, and then unexpectedly retired from first-class cricket at the ripe old age of thirty-three.

The 1890 Old Trafford Test was washed out without a ball being bowled; a climatic disaster which was repeated in Manchester in 1938 and in Melbourne in 1970-1. Victory went to England at Lords by 7 wickets in a game which saw the Australian, Dr J. E. Barrett, become the first player to carry his bat through a Test innings. Remarkably, on a treacherous pitch neither Blackham nor the English wicketkeeper, MacGregor, permitted a single bye. In The Oval Test, England were deprived of the services of Peel and Ulyett. Not unusually in those far-off days of parochial partisanship, they were claimed by Yorkshire for their county championship game. England bereft of the services of Stoddart, who opted to play for Middlesex, won by 2 wickets. The home hero was undoubtedly the tall left-handed Kentish fast bowler, Martin, who only a week previously was instrumental in enabling his county side to defeat the tourists at Canterbury. Martin captured 6/50 in Australia's first innings and followed this performance with a further 6/52 in the second. The astonishing feature of this fine double was that Martin was not retained in the England side. Indeed the bowler from Kent who, five years later was to take 4 wickets with consecutive balls in an M.C.C. game against Derbyshire, played only one further game for his country against South Africa in 1891. He must certainly be one of the unluckiest players in Test history and his omission a prime example of the whimsical vagaries of selectors. In spite of Martin's outstanding performance, the English victory was far from comfortable. Had Harry Trott caught W. G. Grace off the very first ball which he received in England's second innings, 'The Champion' would not only have 'bagged a pair'; he would have also given the Australians a further 16 runs with which to gamble. As it was, there was great excitement in the Australian camp as, with 2 wickets to fall and 2 runs to score, England's number 10, Sharp of Surrey, played and missed at every ball in one Ferris over. Successive maidens were bowled as the tension steadily mounted. The excitement was further accentuated when Sharp played the ball towards cover and embarked on the most optimistic of singles. Both batsmen were stranded in mid-wicket as Dr Barrett, with a most unmedical lack of precision, threw erratically and the resultant overthrows won England the game.

The year 1891-2 was a notable season for Australian cricket watchers. It saw the return of W. G. Grace as captain of a touring England side after an interval of eighteen years. Grace's party landed in Australia under the generous patronage of Lord Sheffield. England's noble sponsor not only spent more than £10,000 on the tour, but he also became an early major patron of Australian cricket by donating a trophy which became known as the Sheffield Shield for competition between the Australian states. The series itself was happily crowned for the home supporters by an Australian 2-1 victory; the first time that

Australia had won the Ashes since their initial victory in 1882.

It was a new-look Australia which brought Blackham success and earned him the further honour of leading the touring party to England in 1893. George Giffen won back his spurs and his position in the Australian side by a marathon performance for South Australia against Victoria which saw him score 271 and take 16/166 in the match—truly the greatest all-round performance in first-class cricket. Alec Bannerman, the N.S.W. captain, captured the dim limelight in the first two Tests by batting for fifteen and a quarter hours for an aggregate of 189 runs. Joe Lyons, however, more than compensated for Bannerman's sluggardly approach by hitting a brilliant 134 out of the 174 added by Lyons and Australia's go-slow opener in 165 minutes for the second wicket of the Sydney game. In the First Test in Melbourne over the New Year period, England quickly realized how much they missed the services of Shrewsbury and Gunn, both of whom refused terms. The tourists went down by 54 runs in a game which saw George Giffen make the statement that he did not doubt his lbw decision in Australia's first innings against Peel was out, but he certainly questioned the right and judgment of W. G. Grace at point in appealing. When Blackham clustered his fieldsmen around the illustrious Doctor in an effort to upset him when he opened England's second innings, W.G. added further fuel to the fires of contention by asking the home skipper whether he wanted a funeral in his side!

W.G. Grace's stature in cricket (caricature by Beerbohm)

Wherever Grace went it seemed that he stirred up controversy. Before the Second Test match in Sydney, Blackham made the fateful decision to play the dubiously fit Moses, who pulled a leg muscle during the previous game. Grace warned Blackham that he could expect no sympathy if Moses broke down again. Inevitably Moses's leg gave way beneath him, but the pride of the Australian captain would not permit him to ask for a runner. When England batted again, Moses hobbled stoically around the field, much to the anger of the crowd who were openly hostile towards the unbending Doctor. It was in this game that Bobby Abel, to whom was once ascribed the doubly dubious honour of being 'the best mid-off in the land and the father of ten', became the first Englishman to carry his bat through an innings by scoring 132 not out. The left-handed spinner, Johnny Briggs, ended the Australian second innings of 391 with a hat-trick of the wickets of Giffen, Callaway and Blackham. At this stage the pitch was a distinctly lively proposition and Grace made the unwise decision of opening with his normal batsman rather than sending in the tail-enders until the wicket improved. As a result, at the close of play on the fourth day England were 3/11: a situation from which they never recovered in spite of a fine second innings of 69 from Stoddart on a much improved fifth-day pitch.

W.G. climaxed his final tour of Australia by crushing the home side by an innings and 230 runs in the Final Test in Adelaide. Stoddart scored 134 including one enormous hit on to the bicycle track surrounding the grassless, almost polished, surface of the Adelaide Oval. This physical factor was quickly changed when, with the English innings ending at 499, rain cascaded down, transforming the Adelaide surface into a 'sticky-dog' and making Johnny Briggs completely unplayable: a truism witnessed by his match analysis of 12/136.

The Australian 1893 side to England was led by Blackham; a man who, in the opinion of expert observers of the game, lacked the finesse and judgment which had characterized Murdoch's captaincy. It was a considerable source of controversy that Murdoch himself, who was playing for the English county of Sussex at the time, was not included in the Australian party. Neither he nor Ferris, who was playing county cricket for Gloucestershire, was invited to participate in the Australian tour. A dry summer robbed 'Terror' Turner of much of his bite and Australia's greatest wicket-takers proved to be off-spinners Trumble and Giffen. Trumble captured 100 wickets on the tour but lacked support. The batting strength of the Australian side was reflected by the fact that seven men reached the thousand-run mark during the English season and that on one occasion Australia totalled 843 against an Oxford and Cambridge team of past and present players. The tourists' overall performance, however, was far from impressive. They lost ten first-class games and the series resulted in a 1-0 victory in England's favour. The Lords Test saw the introduction of the Hon. F. S. Jackson, the Cambridge University captain, into the international game. He scored 91 on his début in a remarkable match. At one stage in their first innings Australia were 5/75 when novitiate 'Dasher' Harry Graham came to the wicket to notch a rumbustious 107 and, in association with Syd Gregory, added 142 for the sixth wicket.

The century which eluded Jackson at Lords came his way in the Second Test at The Oval where England won by an innings and 43. When England's last man, Lancashire fast bowler, Mold, joined Jackson at the wicket, the future Governor of Bengal was 98 not out. Mold's running between the wickets, which was later to lead to Jackson's dismissal, was so irrational that Jackson was consistently deprived of the strike and only reached his hundred with a desperate and enormous hit over long-on onto the roof of the stand next to The Oval pavilion. A strange feature of this Oval Test was that it was played as a benefit game for the Old England professional, Maurice Read. It is hard to envisage modern Test authorities foregoing such gate receipts for such a generous reason.

Stranger things, however, were to follow in the drawn Final Test at Manchester. Jackson exercised his amateur's prerogative of free and independent choice and, on the heels of his maiden Test century, opted to play for Yorkshire in the county championship rather than his country. Peel, the professional, did not have the freedom of choice and was not released by that county. With fast bowler Lockwood injured, England chose the gypsy-eyed, dark-haired, Surrey bowler, Tom Richardson, to replace him. Richardson responded with a magnificent début of 10/156. He was supported by Lancashire fast bowler Mold, whose suspect action would probably have caused a few raised eyebrows amongst the modern umpiring fraternity. Some English counties even spoke of not playing against Lancashire because of it. In the dying moments of the Third Test England required 198 runs in two and a quarter hours to win. With the Ashes already securely in their possession, they refused to take up the unprofitable challenge.

The gentlemanly Stoddart led the next English expeditionary force to Australia in the winter of the following year. It proved to be a five-game rubber which hung in the balance until the final deciding Test in Melbourne. The flagging fortunes of Australia were revived by the enthusiastic public interest stirred in the major cities of Australia. The Tests were dominated by the physical fast-bowling magnetism of Richardson, who captured 32 wickets, the all-round competency of Giffen, who scored more runs and took more wickets than anyone in either side, and the batting dominance of Englishmen Ward, Brown and Stoddart.

The Tests began in spectacular fashion in Sydney with Richardson capturing 3 wickets in the space of 21 runs. Australia lost the game by 10 runs as a result of a series of cruel misfortunes, which revolved around the almost habitual injury to Blackham's mangled fingers, and the weather, which made Australia's last innings a nightmare on a sticky quagmire against the unplayable left-handers Briggs and Peel. England appeared to be about to dominate the series when they won the Second Test in Melbourne by 94 runs. After being bundled out by Turner, Coningham and Trumble on a saturated wicket, England retaliated through the agency of magnificently sustained pace bowling from Tom Richardson who took 5/57 to limit Australia's first innings lead to a mere 48 runs. The English captain, Stoddart, thereupon rubbed salt into the Australian wounds by plundering the Australian bowlers to the extent of 173 runs: a record score by an English captain in Australia which was to endure until Mike Denness surpassed his feat during the tour of 1974-5.

George Giffen, who took over the Australian captaincy subsequent to Blackham's injury, led his side back along the road to revival in the Third Test in Adelaide by winning by 382 runs before his home crowd. It was a victory achieved in spite of the formidable selection problems which confronted Australia. Their star bowler, Turner, was suffering from a chill and with Lyons and Graham out of form and Moses unfit, England began the game with fond hopes of clinching the series in three straight encounters. On this occasion, however, it was the Englishmen's turn to suffer the slings and arrows of outrageous fortune, hurled in their faces by the intense heat, an under-prepared pitch, and frequently showery conditions. Fast-medium bowler, Albert Trott, in a rewarding debut, captured 8/43 in England's second innings and the tourists could do no better than mediocre totals of 124 and 143. In spite of his initial impact on international cricket, Bert Trott failed to gain selection for England in the following year.

The Fourth Test in Sydney was to prove an infinitely worse batting débâcle on England's part. Bad weather ruined the prepared pitch and an impromptu surface, cut and rolled at the last moment, transformed the Test into a game of pure chance. The match was won and lost on the performance of one Australian player, Harry Graham, 'The Little Dasher'. He was a player whose unpredictable talents must have resembled those of the modern Doug Walters. Graham scored 105 in the sole Australian total of 284 by the crudely effective expedient of

A.E. Stoddart

51

bounding down the wicket to fast bowler Richardson. On one occasion he despatched Richardson's first bounce into the crowd, ducked the next predictable bouncer, and again struck the third ball for 4. His batting partner, Gregory, could only stand, stare and be amazed at such daring techniques. Albert Trott followed his bowling success in Adelaide by scoring an invaluable 85 not out at number nine, though astonishingly he was not afforded the opportunity of bowling a ball. It was certainly a game of big hits. Joe Darling, batting at number eight, lofted Briggs into the tennis courts behind the pavilion where what is now Sydney's number two ground is located. It was an immense blow of some 120 yards carry. The English batsmen could not emulate the spirit of Graham's aggression, and succumbed supinely to the bowling of G. H. S. Trott, Turner and Giffen to be all out for successive totals of 65 and 72. After it had rained throughout the whole of Saturday and on Sunday night, the English captain, Stoddart, forecast his side's eventual fate. As he predicted, England were dismissed twice in the space of a single day.

The Test in Melbourne decided the series and stimulated a spectator interest which could be compared with that evoked by Worrell's West Indian side who found themselves in a similar position in 1960-1. Predictably the Victorian spectators turned out in force, only to be disappointed by seeing their side go down by 6 wickets. Many people believed that the Australian discomfiture was of their own making since fast bowler 'Terror' Turner was omitted from the side in which he had commanded a place since 1886. The strange facet of his non-selection was the fact that he was a selector and it was rumoured that he was voted out of the side by his colleagues, Blackham and Giffen. Richardson bowled like a man inspired for England, taking 9 wickets in the game and dismissing Iredale with a ball which trimmed the bails before it almost broke the pickets. MacLaren was fortunate to reach a first innings total of 120 since Giffen twice dropped caught and bowled chances off him as a result of an injured finger sustained while batting. With rain threatening in the second English innings, Ward, defending stubbornly, contributed 93, whilst Brown compiled an aggressive 140 to knock off the required 297 runs for victory after the tourists had lost their first 2 wickets for 28. The closeness of the series was, however, significant. It proved beyond a doubt that the period of Australia's drifting in the Test doldrums was drawing rapidly to a close.

This judgment was vindicated by the performance of the 1896 Australian side in England. Their achievements were probably the best by a touring side in that country since those of the great eleven of 1882. Their record against the counties was remarkable. It is true that the side led by G. H. S. Trott were bowled out for 18 in their first innings against the M.C.C. by Pougher and Jack Hearne and lost by an innings and 18 runs; but they more than avenged this defeat by vanquishing the strong counties of Nottinghamshire, Yorkshire, Kent, Sussex and Gloucestershire. Gloucestershire suffered the indignity of being bowled out in their second innings for 17 runs: the smallest total ever scored by an English county against Australian bowlers. Trott's team lost only to the M.C.C., Thornton's XI at Scarborough, Lord De La Warr's side at

Bexhill on a pitch which was described as 'curious', the South of England, and England. The tourists easily accounted for a strong Lancashire team, the formidable Players' XI and the might of the North of England. The new emergent batting forces of Joe Darling, Clem Hill and Syd Gregory scored heavily on many occasions and against Derbyshire, on a perfect pitch, the Australians compiled 625 in a single innings.

In spite of the fact that the odd omission of Albert Trott, the hero of the Third and Fourth Tests in Australia in 1894-5, illogically weakened their side, the Australians performed consistently better than their English counterparts and could be counted extremely unlucky to lose the rubber by the margin of 2-1. In the persons of Ernie Jones and McKibbin, Australia possessed two exceptionally fast bowlers who were occasionally stigmatized as possessing actions which, unlike Caesar's wife, were not above suspicion. It was Jones who was reputed to have sent a ball whistling through the now greying beard of the venerable Dr W. G. Grace, and excused himself with the comment: 'Sorry Doc, she slipped'.

An immense crowd of 30,000 poured into Lords to see the first day's play of the First Test. They overflowed on to the playing area, impeding the movement of players, and, in the mood of the modern Sydney crowd, threw any object which came to hand at people who obstructed their view of play. On a good dry wicket, the Australian batsmen in their first innings were hurried to and from the wicket by a devastating piece of fast bowling from Tom Richardson. He captured 6/39 in a paltry first innings total of 53 and it was this initial batting débâcle which cost Australia the game. They recovered admirably in their second innings against an England side which was perhaps one of the strongest of all time, including as it did Grace, Stoddart, Abel, Brown, Gunn, Jackson, Hayward, Lilley, Lohmann, Hearne and Richardson. In the second Australian innings Harry Trott notched 143 and was supported in wonderful fashion by Syd Gregory who reached 103; but the second innings total of 347 was not enough and, in spite of a damp wicket on the third day, England coasted home to victory by 6 wickets.

Vengeance came Australia's way in the Second Test at Old Trafford by three wickets. Prince Ranjitsinhji became the first Indian chosen for England in this game, after having been passed over for the Lords encounter. His selection caused much surprise amongst the Anglophiles and it was said that the Australian camp welcomed his inclusion with glee. Ranji later caused this glee to turn into wormwood and gall. In England's second innings 6 wickets were down with the home side still 2 runs behind Australia's first innings total. Ranji transformed certain defeat into a close call for Australia by scoring 154 not out, following his 62 in the first innings. He thereby occasioned many moments of anxiety for the tourists who lost 7 wickets for 125 before victory finally came their way. The Old Trafford Test also witnessed one of the greatest feats of fast bowling endurance. Tom Richardson, the England and Surrey fast bowler, sent down 110.3 overs in the game to take 13/244. He bowled unchanged for over three hours on the final day, in times when there was no interval for tea. At the conclusion of the match he

K.S. Ranjitsinhji, Jam
Saheb of Nawanaga

was led, bemused and exhausted from the field, still not knowing whether his side had won or lost.

England won the final and deciding encounter at The Oval by 66 runs. It was not a match without incident. Before the game started Gunn, Richardson, Hayward, Abel and Lohmann confronted the ground authority, the Surrey Committee, with a demand that their match fee of £10 be doubled before they would play. When the Surrey administrators refused to even listen to their terms, three of the rebels withdrew their demands, but England had to take the field without Gunn and Lohmann. The professionals' ultimatum was based on the contention that amateurs in the England side received the equivalent in expenses of the paid player's fee: a fact that was later proved to be true in the case of W. G. Grace. The only conclusion that the impartial observer can deduce from the wrangle, was that even in those days the 'shamateur' was not unknown to English cricket. The match itself was ruined by rain and a soft pitch. Hugh Trumble bowled magnificently to capture 12 wickets in the match for 89; but his effort was more than counterbalanced by the joint bowling of Peel and Hearne who captured 18 wickets between them. England won with moderate totals of 145 and 84. The game did, however, contain one unpleasant surprise for Australia's batsman Iredale; he was run out by a Ranji throw from a distance of well over 100 yards as he was embarking on his fifth run!

The closeness, the excitement and the quality of the play throughout this 1896 series was significant. It revealed beyond a shadow of doubt that the fourteen-year imbalance between the two sides was at an end. Moreover, names were emerging into the spotlight of centre stage which were to bring a new dimension into the game. In the mid-1990s English cricket was leavened by a youthful additive. The era of Grace was virtually at an end; the chief role which he occupied in English cricket for over thirty years was now to be played by young understudies such as Jackson, Ranjitsinhji, MacLaren and Hayward. Waiting in the wings ready to step into the left-handed bowling lead, formerly occupied by Peel and Briggs, were Rhodes and Hirst.

Cheek by batting jowl with them were Jessop and Fry. The Australian prodigies Joe Darling, Syd Gregory, the 19-year-old Clem Hill, Hugh Trumble and Ernie Jones were already in centre stage. Monty Noble, Victor Trumper, and Warwick Armstrong were eagerly awaiting their cues. After the 1899 series, the cricketing public could say with sad justification that Dr W. G. Grace, the King of Cricket, had abdicated; that year marked his last Test appearance. In 1896, however, it was quite obvious that there were numerous heir apparents to the crown of Grace. His successors were to usher in an era of cricket which was to become known as 'The Golden Age' of the game.

5. The Golden Dawn

The historical coastline of western civilization has been buffeted by waves of 'golden ages', in the same way that England, according to authors Sellars and Yeats in *1066 and All That,* was subjected to waves of Romans and Celts. Art connoisseurs hold that the Renaissance was the golden age of painting and sculpture; the classical theatre and Shakespeare ushered in the golden age of English literature and poetry. In Melbourne there is even a hotel called The Golden Age which presumably pays tribute to high standards of journalism observed by Melbourne's *Age* newspaper, located around the corner from the pub. Nothing could therefore be more natural than to subscribe to the theory that, as in most other art forms, there was a golden age of cricket.

The generally accepted historical theory of cricket's development is that Dr W. G. Grace steered it from its middle ages, variable wickets and questionable techniques, into the calmer waters of modernity. His tighter scientific batting methods and truer pitches produced a higher degree of scoring reliability. The passing of Grace from the Test scene bequeathed to cricket a legacy of technical maturity. Players, building upon the sound foundations established by W.G., perfected a game of elegance and produced batsmen of great competence and skill. The Trumpers, Rhodes, Hirsts, Hobbs, Nobles, Jacksons and Gregorys were but natural evolutionary products of the 'Peking cricketing man' who played the game only a century before.

The players of the years 1896 to 1914 were, however, more than products of preceding generations of cricketers. It is my firm contention that they were not merely the epitome of ability in a golden age of cricket, they were reflections of the times in which they lived. Therefore to understand them better, it is necessary to comprehend their social background in the years just before and just after the turn of the twentieth century. The late Victorian and Edwardian eras were times of great welfare advancement and brought the emergence of a new aggressive spirit in social awareness. England was the scene of an increasing appreciation of the importance of the individual. The labour and liberal movements were finding new strength and insisting upon the social rights of the people. The English liberal government of the early 1900s,

quick to sense the new spirit abroad, was the first government in the western hemisphere to introduce legislation dealing with health insurance, free and secular education, and unemployment benefits. The power of the House of Lords to veto money bills was abolished. In the streets, women suffragettes were agitating for the rights of women to vote. The philosophy of free-trade and laissez-faire was the generally accepted theory that individuals had the right to make their own way in the world with a minimum of governmental interference. British foreign affairs were characterized by a feeling of belligerent infallibility, for this was the era of gunboat politics, the naval and armament races, and jingoism.

The sombreness of Queen Victoria's reign was dramatically changed when her son, Edward VII, took the throne. He was a man with a passion for uniforms, decorations, possessions and entertainments of all kinds. In 1901 the King opened Parliament in person, reviving a ceremony which had fallen into disuse since 1881. It was as if England was awakening after a long period of Victorian hibernation to the Edwardian glamour and appeal of pomp and spectacle. This was a time of supreme self-confidence and affluence which put jingling coins in the pockets of the man in the street. Cricket in the Edwardian era reflected this extroversion, wealth and belief in oneself. The game went through one of its most assertive stages which, allied to its scientific development, brought cricket to its golden apogee in the early twentieth century. Players and spectators alike were made aware of the natural beauty of the athletic prowess of their age.

In terms of the improvement in players' ability, innovations in the

The Great Australian Eleven in England 1902. Back row (L to R) W.P. Howell, W. Armstrong, E. Jones, H. Trumble, Major R.J. Wardill (manager), A.J. Hopkins, C. Hill. Front row (L to R) V. Trumper, J. Saunders, J. Darling, M.A. Noble, J.J. Kelly, S.E. Gregory. Squatting (L to R) W. Carter, R.A. Duff.

B.J.T. Bosanquet, the
inventor of the 'googly'

game, and administrative initiative, the years between 1896 and 1914 were amongst the most fruitful in the game of cricket. Not only did Australia achieve political federation during this period, but she also established herself as an organized and democratic cricketing entity with the foundation of the first Board of Control at a meeting at Wesley College, Melbourne, in 1905. These, too, were the years that saw Bosanquet invent the googly and Hirst reduce the swinging ball to a reliable and scientifically predictable weapon. Trumper, Ranji, Jackson, Hayward and Hobbs raised the science of batting to previously unknown heights. Bowling reached the zenith of achievement embodied in such names as Barnes, Foster, Trumble and Noble. International organization advanced to such a degree that in 1902 Joe Darling captained an Australian side to South Africa and only eight years later saw that visit reciprocated by a Springbok team under Sherwell. Two years before the outbreak of the First World War, an unfortunate Triangular Test Tournament between South Africa, England and Australia was literally floated during the catastrophically wet English summer of 1912. In terms of the comparative successes of the two sides there was little to choose during these years between England and Australia; of the eight series played between the years 1897 and 1912 Australia won five and England three.

The evidence that the tide had turned against the previous English supremacy was very clear between 1897 to 1902: a period which saw Australia win four successive rubbers. The first in Australia in 1897-8 went Australia's way by the handsome margin of 4-1. The English side was dogged by desperately hard luck; players such as Gunn, Abel, Ward, and Brown were no longer on the selector's short list, whilst ill-health severely hampered Ranji's form, and a family death caused the English captain Stoddart to be unavailable for the first two Test matches. In contrast Australia unearthed a new vein of golden batting ability in the person of Clem Hill. The English bowling strength, outside the persons of Richardson and Hearne was so suspect that wicketkeeper Storer was compelled in four of the five Test matches to remove his pads to bowl his supremely optimistic leg spinners. A magnificent 175 from the ailing Ranjitsinhji enabled England to win the First Test by 9 wickets. It was not a match without incident since the Australian batsman McLeod, having been bowled by a no-ball without hearing the umpire's call, walked out and was thereupon run out in the heat of the moment by wicketkeeper Storer.

McLeod and Australia both had their revenge in Melbourne in the Second Test where the home side won by an innings and 55 runs with McLeod scoring 112 before he was bowled, ironically enough, by his former wicketkeeping persecutor, Storer. Ranji, though far from well and in fact being absent for the whole of the first day in order to have an abscess in his throat lanced, scored a magnificent 71 in England's first innings. The sensation of the match occurred when Jim Phillips, the Australian umpire who was to no-ball C.B. Fry and the controversial Lancashire fast bowler Mold in England for throwing, and was now travelling with the tourists, called and condemned Australian fast bowler Ernie Jones for similar reasons in England's first innings. One can imagine the irascible Ernie's reaction to this affront. Even the mildest of suggestions was enough to stir 'Jonah' to anger. Once he was asked by Lord Hawke if he had ever been to Adelaide University. 'Yes My Lord', said the bluff labourer, 'with a load of bloody sand'.

England's tale of woe continued in Adelaide in the Third Test where the tourists were again defeated comprehensively by an innings and 13 runs. Medium-paced off-spin bowler Monty Noble followed up his débutant 7-wicket performance in Melbourne by capturing 8 wickets. England's Archie MacLaren scored 124 and Ranji and Tom Hayward each contributed 70s; but these efforts were more than cancelled out by a wonderful 178 from Joe Darling and two 80s from Clem Hill and Frank Iredale.

Once more luck was not with the English side. Fast bowler Tom Richardson left the field on the second day feeling unwell; he was followed to the pavilion by George Hirst who ricked his back and Ranji, who batted courageously in England's second innings in spite of an injured finger. Australia had an unexpected ally in England's second knock. Noble's 5/84 should have gained only qualified official recognition in the record books. The bowler was wind-assisted by a gale which raised a dust storm and willi-willis which blinded the batsmen! There were no wind-blown clouds of dust in Melbourne to defeat the Englishmen. Australia, nonetheless, received more atmospheric assistance. This time it was dense clouds of smoke from the bush fires which encircled the city and obscured the visitors' vision. The air was so thick with smoke that it was said that the reporters in the press box could not see the progress of play in the middle of the ground.

Australia clinched the series by defeating England in this game by 8 wickets. Once more the tourists were afflicted by injury and took the field without the services of all-rounder, George Hirst. To make matters worse, Tom Richardson, England's fast bowler, could not perform in Australia's second innings. It was not surprising after Richardson's marathon effort of 26 overs in Australia's first batting attempt. Clem Hill registered an impressive 188 in Australia's initial total of 323; this still remains a record score for a batsman under the age of twenty-one in Anglo-Australian Test matches.

The meteoric fast-bowling Test career of Tom Richardson embraced only four years, the same number of series, fourteen matches, yet an astounding 88 wickets. It ended on a high note when Richardson played his final game for England in Sydney in the late February and early March of 1898. Free at last from his burdensome cross of rheumatism, he bowled like a man inspired to take 10 wickets in the match—8 of them in Australia's first innings at a personal cost of 94. The fact that Australia won by 6 wickets was due entirely to the initiative of Joe Darling's 160 in Australia's second innings; his innings was based on the sole premise that the only way that Australia could win was by hitting Richardson out of the attack. The English fast bowler had the mortification of seeing innumerable catches dropped off his bowling. Moreover, on one occasion he trapped Darling blatantly lbw with a back-break from around the wicket—only to spoil his chances of gaining the benefit of the decision by running in front of umpire

Tom Richardson

59

Bannerman and obscuring his view of the incident. It was an event which caused Richardson to become visibly angry and this in turn sparked off an unruly demonstration amongst the crowd.

It was an unfortunate but a fitting end to a tour whose general atmosphere was, by common consensus, less than pleasant. Even by the normal oven-like Australian climatic standards the summer of 1897-8 was oppressive and hot. Sleep was a rare commodity for the Englishmen, and not infrequently their games were played in an atmosphere scented by the smell of burning eucalyptus gum trees and hazy with the smoke of the bushfires which ravaged the continent of Australia. Importantly from a future cricketing point of view, the Englishmen made the acquaintance of two hard-hitting left-handed batsmen, Clem Hill and Joe Darling, each of whom averaged over 70 in the rubber. The tourists' batsmen were confused by what Harry Altham called Monty Noble's 'curious flight'; Noble, like George Hirst, was one of the first swervers of the ball. He possessed a suddenly dipping outswinger which was allied to an almost medium-pace ability to bring the ball back off the wicket from outside the off-stump.

Joe Darling, at the tender age of twenty-eight, led the tenth Australian touring side to England. It was a formidable bowling combination, possessing as it did, the express speed of Ernie Jones, partnered in the opening attack by Howell, who could cut the ball back from outside the off-stump like a fast off spinner. These pacemen were supported by the subtle variations of Hugh Trumble and Monty Noble. The tourists' batting included the names of Darling, Iredale, Gregory and Hill—though Hill missed the final two Tests of this first five-match series in England because of the necessity to undergo a minor operation. Lurking significantly at number six in the Australian Test batting line-up was a certain V. T. Trumper; he was invited on the 1899 tour as very much a junior member of the Australian side. His payment was based on performance and was only half of that received by the senior members of the team. He scored a scintillating 135 not out in the Second Test at Lords, and thereafter proved himself to be a player who was not likely to be lightly or cynically discounted either by the treasurer of his own team or the bowlers of the opposition.

The First Test at Nottingham was a match of double-headed importance; it saw the début of Wilfred Rhodes in the England side, and the final bow of Dr W. G. Grace. The match was drawn, with England having very much the worst of the exchange because of the lack of a fast bowler. Only an inspired innings of 93 not out by Ranji in England's second knock allowed the home side to stave off what looked to be certain defeat, after they lost 4 of their last 10 wickets with only 19 runs on the board.

To English partisans it appeared that the Second Test at Lords was lost even before it began. Selection peculiarities led to the omission of W. G. Grace for the first time in a home Test match. He was joined on the sidelines by William Gunn, that most reliable of English professionals, Jack Hearne, and George Hirst. Stranger than the irrational weakening of the England side were the replacements. MacLaren, without any runs to his name or match practice behind him, came into the

Joe Darling

side as skipper; the dropping of Hearne and Hirst meant that the home attack wore the strange and ineffectual appearance embodied in the names of Jessop, Mead, Rhodes, Jackson, Townsend, Ranjitsinhji, and even batsman Tom Hayward. Against such imbalanced bowling it was not surprising that Australia amassed the grand total of 421 in their first innings; but it came as a complete shock when the might of the English batting crumbled before a 10-wicket match performance from Australian fast bowler Ernie Jones. The 21-year-old Victor Trumper, playing in only his second Test, outshone in style, if not in runs, even the established brilliance of Clem Hill, eight months his senior, by equalling the latter's score of 135.

Contemporary factual commentaries leave one to wonder about the psychological approach of batsmen to their allotted tasks in these early days of Tests. When Jackson and Jessop became associated in their seventh wicket partnership of 95, England in their first innings were a precarious 6/66; yet far from being daunted by their side's peril, 'the Croucher' and 'Jacko' added five runs less than 100 in just over an hour. I wonder what might have been Trevor Bailey's dour response to a similar moment of crisis? The Australian win at Lords was only their second on that ground; it set a pattern for future years. Since that time they have only been beaten once in eighty years of Tests at Cricket Headquarters.

The Leeds game was utterly spoilt by rain which made an unseasonal appearance at Headingly at the end of June. Perhaps it was just as well for England that the rains came, since, with both fast bowlers Lockwood and Kortwright unavailable and Richardson not selected because of the dampness of the pitch on the first day, the home side were compelled to rely upon the fast left-handed capabilities of 'Sailor' Young, the Essex bowler, the resurrected pace of Jack Hearne and Lancashire's veteran spinner, Johnny Briggs. Pure tragedy was to deplete the England attack further when, on the first evening of the match, the lovable Briggs was seized by a violent epileptic fit, whilst watching a variety show at the Empire Theatre. This proved to be the unfortunate Briggs' last Test, he died less than three years later at the age of forty-one of the affliction which had plagued him throughout his life. Nowadays, modern medical science and the ageless perseverance of current cricketers would have probably kept him on the field for his native Lancashire for quite a few years beyond his all too short span.

The rain which, as Australian skipper Billy Murdoch would have said, 'washed out the sparrows' at Leeds, was not in evidence when the Fourth Test began at Old Trafford a fortnight later. England, batting first on a hard wicket and in heat-wave conditions, accumulated 372 and, thanks to a fine fast-bowling performance from the Kent bowler, Bradley, who was brought into the England side to replace Briggs, bundled out Australia for 196. Darling's side batted again since in those days the follow-on was compulsory if the side batting second failed to reach a total within 120 runs of that of their opponents. The English attack wilted in the course of two hot days in the field and since only three days were allocated to Tests, with Noble and Trumper defending staunchly, the game was once again inconclusive.

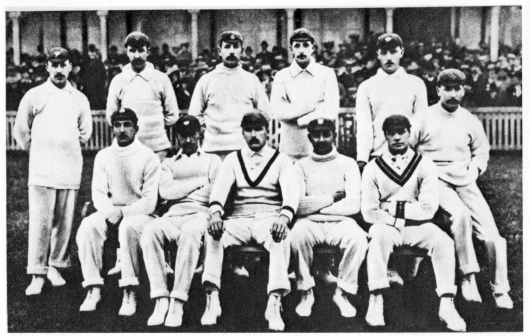

The Great England
Eleven of 1902.
Back row (L to R)
G.H. Hirst, A.A. Lilley,
W.H. Lockwood, L.C.
Braund, W. Rhodes,
J.T. Tyldesley.
Front row (L to R)
C.B. Fry, F.S.
Jackson, A.C.
Maclaren (captain),
K.S. Ranjitsinhji, G.L.
Jessop

The English batting machine was in top gear when MacLaren won the toss in the Fifth Test at The Oval. The home side accumulated a massive 576 with centuries flowing from the bats of Jackson and Hayward; the latter in fact compiled his second hundred in successive Test innings. But even this gargantuan total and the fact that England enforced the follow-on for the second time in successive games, failed to bring victory the home side's way. Inexplicably the selectors had omitted Jack Hearne and 'Sailor' Young and whilst the newly-fit Lockwood returned a first innings analysis of 7/71, the English bowling, even with the spinning additive of Wilfred Rhodes was unequal to the task of bowling Australia out twice in ten and a half hours. Sid Gregory compiled 100, whilst Darling, Worrell and Noble each exceeded the half-century mark to enable their team to retain the Ashes by the narrowest of margins—a disappointing contrast to their 4-1 steamroller victory two years earlier in Australia.

The northern winter of 1901-2 saw the two M.C.C.'s of the cricketing world unable to come to common agreement. The Melbourne Club invited the Marylebone to tour Australia. When their invitation was declined, the Melbourne Club asked Archie MacLaren to organize a privately-managed visit. It was to prove to be the last series conducted under the aegis of a private individual.

MacLaren had the sole responsibility of choosing a side and his innate cricketing judgment was reflected in the flash of inspiration which caused him to choose Sydney Francis Barnes as one of his opening bowlers. Barnes at this stage of his career was an unknown, playing regularly in the Lancashire League, whence he had graduated from his native Staffordshire, and occasionally turning out for MacLaren's county of Lancashire and Warwickshire. The England skipper's acumen was vindicated by Barnes being an immediate success even on the flawless pitches of Australia. Before the great medium-pace bowler twisted his knee during the Third Test he had captured 20 wickets at an average of 16.15. Barnes's career in Test cricket was as brief as it was brilliant, he played in only twenty-seven Tests in twelve years; yet in that time his exceptional match-winning capacity was amply demonstrated by his ability to take each of his remarkable 189 wickets at brief intervals of 42 deliveries. This outstanding achievement increases in stature when one considers that seventeen of his international games were played on bone-hard Australian and South African pitches. It is true that in the days when Test wickets were exposed to the elements, the surfaces in both of those countries could be helpful to the bowler when wet, yet it was a measure of Barnes's greatness that some of his best figures were achieved on perfect batting pitches. With only a cross breeze to help him in the Second Test in Melbourne in 1911-12, Barnes sent back such great Australian batsmen as Kelleway, Bardsley, Hill and Armstrong in the space of 9 overs—at the end of which period of time his figures were 4/3 and Australia were 4/32! Throughout his Test career Barnes's wickets cost him only an economic 16.43 and in the whole history of Anglo-Australian Tests, few major bowlers on either side captured their wickets more cheaply or with greater frequency.

Sydney Barnes

I have often questioned some of his opponents about the origins of Barnes's bowling greatness. His speed never reached express quality, and in the opinion of such judges as the former Australian captain, the late Jack Ryder, who was just beginning his first-class career at the time of Barnes's salad days, never exceeded that of Maurice Tate or Alec Bedser. It is true that Barnes moved the ball both ways in the air and he could spin the ball appreciably from both leg and off; but these had been the characteristics of bowlers before him and they never reached the heights scaled by the Staffordshire man. Harry Altham wrote of Barnes's bowling that 'most deadly of all was the ball which he would deliver from rather wide on the crease, move in with a late swerve the width of the wicket, and then straighten back off the ground to hit the off stump'.

Barnes's greatest bowling attribute lay in his fixity of purpose. There was more of the tensile strength of Black Country steel in his long fingers and soul than the brittleness of Staffordshire pottery. In the opinion of Jack Ryder, Barnes did not know the meaning of defeat. He was pernickety both in the demands he made upon himself and on those who played with him. His exacting standards made Barnes an almost perfect bowling technician. His control was so great that he did not need to employ devious methods. When he was once decried as an imperfect exponent of his art, because he did not possess a wrong 'un, his retort was that he never needed one. The self-confident implication of that remark was that he need not disguise intentions. Even if the batsmen knew full well which way Barnes would swing or spin, his control was so immaculate, there was little they could do to avoid defeat. Graphologists could probably discern Barnes's insistence upon exactitude in the immaculate copperplate handwriting which he still wrote mere months before his death at the age of ninety-four in December 1967. He was known to reproach a fieldsman for wandering only inches from his allotted catching spot thereby missing a chance, and to demonstrate to the culprit where he should stand by means of scoring a cross in the turf with his spikes.

The bowling determination of Barnes knew no bounds. Even advancing age failed to halt him, and when he was sixty-one he captured an incredible 86 wickets at a cost of under 11 runs each in his thirty-eighth season of Staffordshire League competition. England keeper George Duckworth, as a young man on the Lancashire ground staff, played in a game against the great S.F. when he was fifty years old and in spite of the fact that he was batting at the lowest position in the order, was denied permission by his captain to walk around the ground. His leader was convinced, quite rightly as things turned out, that Duckworth would be needed to bat in a very short space of time. The man who was to become renowned for the loudest appeal in Test cricket affirms that this was the only time when he saw the first seven batsmen in the order padded up in the pavilion at the same time.

Barnes's doggedness was reflected in an almost perverse disposition. When the time came to choose J. W. H. T. Douglas's side to tour Australia in 1920, the medium-pace bowler was forty-six years old yet still declared himself available for selection. Writing to an old friend in Australia one leading English cricket administrator said:

> Barnes was the troublesome problem. He always is. He said he would go if we paid for his wife and family and when we said no, he would not answer us. He says he is bowling as well as ever, but as he is seven years older, I doubt it. However, eventually he said no and we are really well rid of him.

That administrator might have changed his tune and welcomed the evergreen assistance of Barnes, had he been able to see into the future and predict that England would lose the 1920-1 series 5-0.

MacLaren's tour to Australia twenty years previous to Douglas's visit was hardly more successful than its successor of two decades later. England lost the rubber 4-1, their sole victory being in the First Test where their skipper sped to a commanding century in only 187 minutes. Barnes in his first appearance at the Test bowling crease captured 5/65, and the Australian discomfiture was completed by Len Braund who, even though confronted with the skill of Gregory, Trumper, Hill, Noble and Darling, captured 5/61 in Australia's second innings with an enigmatic variety of fastish and puzzling leg-spin. England's initial victory by an innings and 124 runs was misleading. The second game in Melbourne very quickly showed that the tourists, without Yorkshire-men Hirst, Rhodes and Jackson and deprived of the brilliance of the oriental Sussex batting combination of Fry and Ranji, were far from an impregnable batting or bowling proposition. On a wet pitch Australia won by 229 runs, but not before Barnes gave an amazing exhibition of bowling endurance by taking 13/163 in the match. In the second Australian knock he bowled 42 overs in succession and at the end of 64 overs had captured 7/121. Unfortunately for MacLaren's XI even the great Barnes was outshone on this occasion by Monty Noble who returned a match analysis of 13/87. Hugh Trumble ended the match by taking the notable hat-trick of Jones, Gunn and Barnes; yet in spite of this performance he had to play second fiddle to a superlative piece of bowling by Noble.

In the second innings at Melbourne, Clem Hill was second highest scorer to Reggie Duff who notched 104; Hill scored a so-near-yet-so-far 99 and began a lucky yet unlucky scoring streak which saw him reach 99, 98 and 97 in successive innings. It must have been a source of major disappointment to his local South Australian supporters that Hill came within a combined total of 5 runs of scoring two separate 100s in the same Adelaide Test. His compact 97 in Australia's second innings on a wicket which was crumbling and turning was accomplished in the face of the substantial overall English lead of 314, yet won the game for Australia by 4 wickets. England for their part, however, must have thought that the decisive factors in their loss were the injuries to both Barnes and Colin Blythe, their two key bowlers. Barnes twisted his knee in Australia's first innings after sending down 7 overs. He did not appear again at the bowling crease on the tour. Blythe, the most beautiful of slow left-arm bowlers, bruised his bowling hand badly and was wicketless after the 23 overs which he sent down in Australia's final innings.

For the remainder of the tour the fast-bowling work-horse was John Gunn, the Nottinghamshire professional. Years later I was to meet Gunn at a Master's Luncheon and he was to provide me with a most salutary lesson which all young cricketers would do well to learn; he was to teach me that no cricketer, irrespective of his experience, ever ceases to learn more about the art of cricket. On the occasion of our meeting, Gunn told me that he was an all-rounder which was quite acceptable to my ears. But when he said that he bowled fast left-arm leg-spinners at about my pace, my reaction became almost incredulous. At this stage of my career I was reputedly bowling at somewhere in the region of 90 mph. When I asked John Gunn how he held the ball to bowl his incredible stock delivery he demonstrated his grip to me by means of scoring a seam with a fruit knife on an orange taken from the fruit bowl and holding it as though it were a ball. Apparently his method was to hold the seam upright with his index and second finger on the one side of the seam, with the other fingers and thumb on the other side of the seam. With a closed action he would then bowl the ball dragging his hand down its left side. The result?—a fast leg-spinner! This seemed hard to believe. Some years later, however, I was talking to my fast-bowling colleague in the England side, Brian Statham, a man whom I knew could bowl a ball which he defined as a fast 'nip-backer'. This was an 80 mph off-spinner which moved back sharply off the seam from outside the off-stump a matter of three to six inches even on hard wickets. When I asked Statham how he held the ball, he showed me the right-handed version of the identical grip to that demonstrated to me by John Gunn! Since that time I have never doubted or questioned other people's bowling methods; I have simply tried them to see if they worked. That way at least lies the empirical path to increased knowledge in a game that is extremely complex.

Australia clinched the Ashes by a 7-wicket victory in the Fourth Test

Hugh Trumble

Monty Noble

at Sydney. Barnes went through a fitness trial before the game but failed the examination; his bowling was sorely missed. Having scored 317 by dint of fine innings from MacLaren and the England captain's Lancastrian stalwart, Tyldesley, England, with Jessop bowling very fast, reduced Australia at one stage to 4 wickets down for 48. The absence of the indefatigable Barnes, however, prevented their pressing home their advantage and a shabby second batting display of 99 lost England the game. The medium-paced left-handed spinner Saunders, playing in his first game for Australia, captured 9/162 and was rewarded for his efforts by being dropped for the next Test!

The fifth and final game took place in Melbourne and resulted in a thrillingly close contest which saw Australia squeeze home by 32 runs. Australia, batting first on a wet wicket were headed on the first innings by 45, probably due to the shock of seeing Jessop open the innings and hit 35 of the first 50 runs in only twenty minutes. The home side, however, reasserted their supremacy when Hill steadied them with a peerless 87; and a joint 9-wicket performance by Noble and Trumble on a pitch which was worsened by rain, steered Australia home by a narrow but deserved margin. If the modern system of sponsorship had applied in the days of 1901-2, the Player of the Series Award would probably have gone jointly to Australia's triumvirate of Hill, Noble and Trumble. In the course of the five games Hill scored 521 runs at an average of 52, whilst Noble and Trumble captured 60 of the 84 wickets which fell to the Australian bowlers during the rubber.

If I were given the choice of one year from the past in which to watch Test cricket, my selection would probably go to the heroic year of 1902. It was a wet English season which saw two magnificently matched sides of formidable talent pitted one against the other. In this golden year of a golden era, England possessed the redoubtable batting ability of MacLaren, Fry, Ranjitsinhji, Jackson, Tyldesley, Jessop, Braund and Rhodes, all of whom scored a century against Australia. The first seven in the Australian batting order had also reached three figures against England. In the ranks of the bowlers there were such fearsome names in the Australian camp as Noble, Armstrong, Jones, and Howell. The English attack has probably never been more glittering in its array of talent, containing as it did the left-handed swerve of Hirst, the break-back of Lockwood, the Keith Miller bowling capabilities of Jackson, the leg-spinners of Braund, and the left-handed guile of Rhodes. So strong was the English bowling that Jessop, who proved himself to be a fast bowler of no mean ability only months previously in Australia, was rarely bowled.

The two new Test venues of Edgbaston and Sheffield were scarcely worthy settings for the contests between the two gladiatorial teams. Indeed no ground in England could have done the rubber justice. It would have probably been more appropriately accommodated in the Coliseum in Rome. The series was the equivalent of the heavyweight boxing championship of the cricket world and boxers such as Dempsey and Carpentier could not have been more evenly matched. A theatrical entrepreneur would have made a fortune out of this English season. It produced a series which saw two heart-stopping matches decided on rain-affected pitches, one going the way of the tourists by a mere 3 runs and the final encounter being won by England by a single wicket.

England enjoyed all the good fortune of Birmingham's First Test. Before the rains came on the first evening, a fine 138 from Tyldesley brought England to the supremacy of 9/351. With the English skipper MacLaren timing his declaration with a finesse which ensured Australia must bat on a sticky wicket on the second day, Darling's side were dismissed for 36: the lowest score ever recorded in Anglo-Australian Tests. The unplayable Wilfred Rhodes repeated the bowling figures of Monty Noble only months before in Melbourne to take 7/17. Significantly, the peerless Victor Trumper scored exactly half of his side's runs. The eighty-five minutes batting ordeal of the Australians, however, was not to be repeated, since the rain which troubled them in their first innings, eventually saved them when they were 2/46 in their second.

The Australians' casualty list for the Second Test at Lords bordered on the appalling. Hugh Trumble who missed the First Test because of injury was still unavailable, as was fast bowler Howell. Joe Darling and Monty Noble had scarcely recovered from influenza and Saunders, their left-handed bowler, was afflicted with tonsillitis. So uneven did the contest promise to be that it was mooted on the eve of the match that the Test should be postponed. The Gods had the ultimate say. The match was utterly ruined by rain which deluged the Lord's ground for the last two days.

The third encounter between the two sides was staged at Sheffield; it was the first and only time that the city, famed for its cutlery and steel, has been the venue for a Test. Now, seventy-seven years after it staged a match between England and Australia, Sheffield is no longer deemed worthy of a Yorkshire county game. The stands of Bramall Lane—a ground originally chosen as a cricket stadium because 'it had the advantage of being free from smoke'—remain unshaken save by the cheers of soccer crowds who frequent the terraces over which Gilbert Jessop hit many of his sixes off Wilfred Rhodes. Jessop, opening England's second innings smote 15 in only half an hour; but it was all in vain, for England lost by 143 runs. An injury to fast bowler Lockwood had brought Sydney Barnes into the Test match arena for the first time in the series; he captured 6/49 in Australia's first innings, but the winds of selection ingratitude were so cold that this was to prove his only Test of the series.

It was a remarkable game. The vision of both sides' batsmen was obscured by palls of black smoke emanating from the surrounding chimney stacks. Someone apparently forgot to tell the unpartisan stokers when the opposition was batting! Another unusual feature of the Test was that Len Braund was chosen to open the England attack. The English skipper, MacLaren, exercised what would be an unusual option in modern times, for Braund was a leg-spinner. The issue of the game was settled by Clem Hill's century and Victor Trumper's 62 in Australia's second innings of 289. Nothing that MacLaren could do by means of his elegant 63 or Jessop's hard-hit 55 in England's second innings could reverse the dismal fate of England on that black day in smoky Sheffield.

The Fourth Test at Old Trafford sealed the fate of England in the series. It was a game marred both by the weather and the pettiness of the selectors, but illuminated by the brilliance of Victor Trumper. Australia were the victors by the slender margin of 3 runs; but it was a hard-won victory. It would probably not have been possible without the collusion of Trumper, the unpatriotic perversity of the English skipper MacLaren and the autocracy of the Yorkshire cricketing magnate, Lord Hawke. Lord Hawke, in his wisdom, refused to permit the Yorkshire all-rounder Schofield Haig to play. MacLaren retaliated by refusing to select the Yorkshire alternative, George Hirst, and opted instead for the fashionable and currently successful talents of Fred Tate, the father of the more illustrious Maurice.

Poor Fred Tate! This Old Trafford game, his only Test, was to go down in the annals of cricket as Tate's game. However, it was not through any outstanding performance on that bowler's part, but rather because of a sequence of misfortunes which caused him to be largely instrumental in England losing the match. When the Australian skipper, Joe Darling, was only 16 in the tourists' second innings, Tate dropped a simple catch off him at square leg; Darling went on to make a decisive 37 in a low total of 86. To add insult to injury Tate, as last man for England, came to the wicket when only 8 runs were required for victory, and just before rain caused the batsmen to retire to the pavilion for a nail-biting three-quarters of an hour. When they returned, Tate immediately hit Saunders for 4, only to be bowled by the very next delivery, swinging wildly at a time when the coolness of Rhodes, who was batting at the other end, could have saved the day. This was the Test which saw Trumper notch 100 out of 168 before lunch on the first day on a sodden wicket. By the time the interval arrived with the Australian score at 173, Trumper was already in the pavilion with 104 runs behind his name—all this after MacLaren had only been seeking to restrain the Australian's rate of scoring, until such time as his bowlers could gain an adequate foothold on the greasy and saturated Old Trafford turf!

Trumper scored the runs for Australia, but no less a hero for the tourists was Hugh Trumble who, with his medium-pace off-spinners, captured 10 wickets and subsequently followed up this feat with a 12-wicket performance at The Oval. In this memorable series the lanky Victorian bowler captured 26 wickets—over a sixth of his eventual bag of 141 victims against England—a final tally which placed him 26 wickets above his nearest bowling competitor in Anglo-Australian Tests.

Trumble according to the Australian cricket historian Johnny Moyes was one of the greatest bowlers in cricket:

Fred Tate

> He bowled at slow-medium from his full height of 6'5'' keeping an impeccable length and spinning the ball slightly either way. He had a great command of flight and often looped the ball on to a shorter length than that expected by the batsman. He was persistent and believed in the adage of bowling to a batsman's strength. Often he would feed the drive until such time as the striker, not being quite to

the pitch of the ball, lofted it into the covers. He possessed such command and control that he conceded a run only once in every three deliveries throughout his career, and he could spin the ball on even the most placid of surfaces.

England won the palpitating final Test at The Oval in 1902; but this was in spite of Trumble, who in the course of the game sent down 64.5 overs to concede only 173 runs in taking 12 wickets. The Oval Test of this epic series is widely and commonly known as 'Jessop's Game'. His pulverizing 104 out of 139 in seventy-five minutes in England's final knock was, in the words of Harry Altham, the English cricket chronicler, 'an innings that will be famous as long as cricket is played'. What is not often mentioned in the recording of this memorable one-wicket English victory is that Jessop, whilst he completely demoralized most of the Australian bowlers, was almost circumspect against the bowling of Trumble. The lofty Hugh probably went to his grave firm in the belief that Australia should have won this vacillating game. The Yorkshireman George Hirst supported by his reliable 'crutch', his fellow 'tyke' Wilfred Rhodes, steered England to the narrowest win of all time in the history of Tests. Yet Hirst, who scored an unbeaten 58, should, to Australian eyes, have been given out lbw to Trumble, bowling his off-spinners around the wicket, before he scored. One wonders what the gentlemanly Trumble said when the umpire rejected his confident appeal!

The English 1903-4 visit to Australia represented a great step forward into the administrative future of cricket. For the first time a party was chosen, not by an individual or private enterprise, but by the club which was to become the organizing genius of English touring cricket for the next half century. The Marylebone Cricket Club selected the England team and nominated the 30-year-old Pelham Warner as its skipper. It was rumoured that the passing over of England's previous skipper, Archie MacLaren, caused bitter animosity between himself and the new M.C.C. leader. In his speech at the Trocadero on the occasion of the M.C.C. banquet to welcome home England's conquering heroes at the end of the tour, however, 'Plum' Warner was at pains to point out that he and MacLaren remained upon the best of terms. Indeed he went on to say: 'We missed him in Australia, and the Australian public missed him, because anyone who has studied the cricket records must admit that Mr MacLaren has been the principal batsman on Australian wickets'.

In the introduction to 'Plum' Warner's book on that tour, *How We Recovered The Ashes,* Bishop Weldon described what must have been an interesting voyage to the antipodes on S.S. *Orantes.* It encompassed an acquaintance with 'the wrong lady who always wanted to sleep in some other cabin than her own; and the other young lady who in a moment of abstraction mysteriously disappeared down an air chute'. The shipboard sports included a cricket match between Pelham Warner's Eleven and an Eleven of the Ladies, with the English cricketers using only their unnatural hands and the ladies not only playing right-handed but making full defensive use of their skirts!

At the end of the tour Warner could look back upon victories in the First, Second and Fourth Tests and an Ashes win by the margin of 3-2. The England side won the First Test in Sydney by 5 wickets due almost entirely to a superb maiden innings by R. E. 'Tip' Foster of 287—a score which remained the highest in England-Australia Tests in Australia until the advent of Bob Cowper. It remains the greatest number of runs notched by any batsman of any nation on his début; no Englishman has scored more runs in a Test in Australia and only Lawrence Rowe of the West Indies has equalled Foster's achievement of aggregating more than 300 runs in his first international. The Sydney Test was not an easy victory for the touring side; it was won in spite of an immortal 185 not out from Victor Trumper in Australia's second innings—an innings which Lilley, the English wicketkeeper, classified as one of the five greatest innings that he had ever witnessed. The game was marred by a violent outburst on the part of the spectators in the members' pavilion. When Hill was adjudged run out for 51 by the Australian umpire Crockett and Australia took another step towards defeat, bottles rained down on the playing arena as pandemonium erupted. This ugly spectacle was to be repeated during the Fourth Test match when, much to the annoyance of the viewers on the famous Hill, umpires Crockett and Argall appeared reluctant to resume the game after rain. When the first ball was bowled after the interruption, 35,000 people chanted in unison: 'Crock, Crock, Crock'. When Rhodes came on to bowl he was counted out. Pelham Warner's imagination, as reported in his book, conjured up visions of an official ringing up the War Ministry to send the message:

> Send Troops, International Match Now On, Crowd On Hill, Armed To The Teeth With Umbrellas, Bottles, Melon Skins and Rude Language Advancing Determinedly On The Wicket. Three Policemen And Groundsman's Dog Doing Good Work. Umpires Crockett and Argall Retreating To The Mountains.

In spite of these discordant incidents Warner still retained sufficient sense of humour and judgment to remark that the Sydney crowd were spicely stimulating and that anyone who took part in a Test match on the S.C.G. may consider himself fit to play before an audience from the Infernal Regions.

The Melbourne match saw Australia trapped on a wet pitch to lose by 185 runs. Only the superhuman ability of Trumper enabled him to score 74 and 35 in sparse totals of 122 and 111 and against an England attack in which Rhodes captured 15/124: a match analysis which remained a record until Verity eclipsed it at Lords in 1934. The home side made up some leeway by winning the Adelaide game by 216 runs on a wicket that Warner described as one of the best he ever saw. Trumper scored his second century of the series against the mystifying leg-spin and googlies of Bosanquet. Fortunately for the nonpareil Australian batsman, the English slow bowler not only puzzled those at the batting crease, but he also baffled the English wicketkeeper, Lilley, who repeatedly moved the wrong way to take the ball and missed numerous stumping opportunities.

70

The culprit remedied his sins of faulty omission in Sydney to make three stumpings in Australia's second innings off what Warner called the 'puzzling, off breaking, leg-break of Bosanquet'. Bosanquet—the very sound of his name had a ring of Gallic trickery about it! So it proved to be in this Test, for the slow bowler captured 6/51 to steer his side home by 157 runs.

Australia slightly redressed the imbalance of defeat by winning the final contest in Melbourne by 218 runs. With the wicket covered before the game, much to the annoyance of Warner, and with rain falling during the course of the match, the Australian first innings total of 247 decided the issue. Trumble playing in his last Test captured 7/28, including a hat-trick. Trumper in Australia's second innings was bowled by Hirst for 0; it was the first duck he had scored in over a year and in 80 completed innings.

Trumble's bowling partner, Monty Noble, continued to play until 1909 and at the conclusion of the 1903-4 series, he received the publicly expressed accolade from 'Plum' Warner of being the finest all-round cricketer in the world on Australian wickets. Johnny Moyes wrote of Noble that, 'as a medium-pace bowler, he had wonderful control, a late swerve which caught the batsman after he had got into his stroke, and an off-break which could be vicious on a pitch that helped'. He also apparently possessed a perplexing degree of flight; Warner confessed that three times in his tour he was bowled by a Noble delivery which appeared to 'flop' in the air.

At Bathurst the English batsmen met the Aboriginal fast bowler, Jack Marsh. Two years previously, Archie MacLaren objected to Marsh's playing against his team on the grounds that his fast bowling —or rather fast throwing—might injure some of his batsmen. In 1904 there was little devil left in Marsh and it was deemed advisable not to question the Aborigine's delivery, although the Englishmen were still of the opinion he threw three balls in every over and the other three would scarcely satisfy English umpires.

Jack Marsh, Aboriginal fast bowler

So ended the first official tour by an M.C.C. side of Australia. Significantly it heralded the dawning of a new era of official Tests between more representative English and Australian teams. On 6 May 1905 precisely twenty-three days before the First Test of that year was played at Trent Bridge, the Australian Board of Control for International Cricket held its inaugural meeting at Wesley College, Melbourne. The newly-born Australian administrative body was too late in the field to select the 1905 touring side to England. Indeed, this party was financed by a loan covering preliminary expenses from the Melbourne Cricket Club and organized and administered by the players themselves, together with their player-manager Frank Laver. Full control of Australian touring sides was not destined to pass into the hands of the Board of Control until after the great confrontation between players and administrators during the 1911-12 series, on the subject of the right of the team to select Laver as their manager.

6. Conflict on Three Fronts

Most players drop from the Test scene on the discordant note of failure; it falls to a privileged few to go out of the game in a blaze of glory. The year 1905 showed, however, that there are exceptions to this general rule. England's home series against the visiting Australians witnessed the glorious exits from Test cricket of Australian batsman Duff and the English captain, the Hon. F. S. Jackson. Duff enjoyed the distinction of scoring a century in his first Test and he finished his career in the same vein at The Oval—by happy coincidence the home ground of the county of his birth. Jackson's performances in 1905 were of such consistent quality and distinction that cricket historians have come to recognize that season as 'Jackson's Year'. In his last full season in the first-class game, the Yorkshire skipper scored two centuries against Australia and averaged over 70 in the rubber. The nearest statistical approach to Jackson's batting performance in both camps were the mean figures of 58 from England's wonderfully versatile athlete, C. B. Fry, and 41 from Australia's vitally aggressive Duff. Nor do these figures encompass the whole of Jackson's achievements for this notable season. In addition, he topped the England bowling averages by taking 13 wickets at an average of 15 and led his side to a 2-0 victory in the series.

Contemporary accounts described Jackson as a paragon of typical English gentility of the Edwardian era. Fry wrote of him as being 'good looking in an Anglo-Saxon guards way'. He was always immaculately dressed on the field and never lost his composure, always maintaining a stiff upper-lip in the most serious of crises. Sir Home Gordon wrote of him: 'It was his unexampled coolness that was so astounding; an unruffled calm arising from what he himself could do. His concentration was abnormal'. The background of F. S. Jackson was that of a gentleman of the English upper class. He was the son of a cabinet minister in Lord Salisbury's Government of 1888. He attended Harrow where Winston Churchill was his schoolboy servant or 'fag': a coincidence which caused Churchill's political opponent of later years, Lloyd George, to remark that he was delighted to meet someone who, in the course of time, had given Churchill a beating.

At Cambridge, Jackson captained the University side for two years in succession, a then unparalleled feat of popularity. During the Boer War he forgot his natural Yorkshire partisanship, to serve in the Royal Lancaster Regiment, attaining the rank of Colonel, a nickname which remained with him for the remainder of his career. Reverting loyally to his own kind at the outbreak of the First World War, he joined the West Yorkshire Regiment, but one year later was elected Unionist MP for a Yorkshire constituency. President of the M.C.C. in 1921, he was appointed the Governor of Bengal in 1927. Characteristically, in India, Jackson survived an assassination attempt with all the icy coolness which characterized his cricket.

His biographer E. H. D. Sewell wrote of Jackson the cricketer: 'All he did on the field, he did so easily that it seemed to be the only thing to do'. C. B. Fry said of him that

F.S. Jackson

> . . . he is versatile to a degree, being able to adapt his play to suit any kind of wicket. On hard, true wickets he can play the free classical style with an execution not inferior to that of Mr Palairet; on a sticky wicket, his scientific back play is equal to that of Arthur Shrewsbury and his driving worthy of Maurice Read. His method of playing back whether the wicket be hard or soft is particularly sound; he judges the length of the ball in time to shape for his stroke without any flurry or uncertainty; stepping back a foot or so towards his wickets and balancing himself nicely on his right leg, he comes down on the ball from well behind its line of flight so as to not only get safely over it but also to force it away hard . . . his driving is beautifully clean and well timed; there is no suspicion of a slog and a mis-hit rarely occurs . . . his stroke to the good length off ball, which he despatches past extra cover, is perhaps the best of all. He is a master of every form of the cut and of all kinds of gliding and forcing strokes to the on and to leg. A great player, he bowls medium to fast-medium with a graceful easy action and plenty of spin. His length is excellent and when the wicket helps him, his off-break is very abrupt.

This was the captain who led England to victory in 1905. The Nottingham Test was won by the home team by 213 runs, due to a century from MacLaren and an 8/107 performance in Australia's second innings from Bosanquet. Three occurrences in this particular game exemplified the spirit in which cricket was played in the early 1900s. There was certainly hostility in the game, for when Australian quick bowler, Tibby Cotter, unleashed a savage barrage of bouncers, it provoked an equally ferocious retaliation from part-time English fast bowler, Jessop. There was also sportsmanship in cricket in those days for, even though the light was generally deemed to be unfit in the last half hour of the match, both sides pressed on to reach a decision. Finally there was courage in this sporting era. The Australian batsman, Victor Trumper, after beginning his second innings in flawless fashion strained his back and was forced to retire. He made a spirited bid to return to the crease to save the game, being supported out of the pavilion by two of his colleagues. He only reached the gate before he collapsed once more and was carried back into the dressing-room.

The Second Test at Lords and the subsequent game at Leeds were both drawn: rain washed out the third day of the Lords encounter and Australia, having been set to score 401 in their final innings at Leeds, hung on to save the game with 3 wickets in hand. Having scored 144 not out before his local Headingley crowd, Jackson followed this with yet another century on the alien turf of Old Trafford in the Fourth Test. Completely at home on the Manchester ground was Lancashire's fast bowler, Walter Brearley, who captured 8 wickets in his first Test and was not the least of the contributing factors to England's victory. Brearley was one of the breed of fast bowlers who were great characters; he was known to have broken a stump in bowling a batsman, raced off to the pavilion, leapt the fence of the members' enclosure and returned to the playing scene with several spares. Handing them to the umpire, he passed the comment, 'Hang on to these, we'll be needing them'. Brearley not only captured 8 wickets at Old Trafford, but supplemented this with a further 6 in the Final Test at The Oval. Yet in a way he was lucky since his selection in the first place was caused by the illogical omission of the Derbyshire fast bowler, Warren, who played in his first game at Leeds, took 5/57 in an innings and was dropped for the subsequent match at Old Trafford.

England's victory in the Fourth Test was only made possible by the impetuosity of the Australian batsmen. Forced to follow on after rain had fallen and England had scored 446, they attempted to hit their way out of trouble and establish a lead which would have been substantial enough to enable them to declare and put England in again on a bowlers' pitch. Not only did they fail to score a large second innings total—they lost by an innings and 80. The Test finished just before lunch on the third day; ironically for Australia, it rained for the remainder of the match. An excellent wicket saw a high-scoring game at The Oval. The game was drawn with Fry, Tyldesley and Australian Duff each scoring centuries. By reputation Fry was predominately an on-side player; the Australian skipper Darling tried to block this scoring avenue only to find that the English batsman was more versatile on the off than rumour would allow.

The biblical parable of the fat and lean kine was paralleled by the fortunes of England in England in 1905 and those of the M.C.C. touring side in Australia in 1907-8. Jackson's fat year of success was immediately followed by the lean winter of A. O. Jones's failure in Australia. From the outset, the 1907-8 tour was nothing short of disastrous. The English captain fell seriously ill soon after his side's arrival in November and did not play until the Fourth Test in the following February. F. L. Fane took over the reins of leadership and immediately found an unexpected and supernumerary recruit to the touring numbers in the person of the Nottinghamshire professional, George Gunn. Gunn was in Australia for health reasons and his trip was being financed through the generosity of a Nottinghamshire supporter. His late addition to the England side was one of those 1,000-1 gambles which occasionally succeed. Gunn proved to be a trump card, scoring two centuries in the series and topping the Test averages with a mean figure of 51.33.

He was a real character and a batsman of perverse brilliance; when the mood seized him he advanced down the wicket to the faster bowlers to despatch them to all quarters of the field. If criticism was levelled at his methods he would retire sulkily into a shell of the most obdurate defence and refuse to hit even the most blatant of half-volleys. In county games he was known to have given his wicket away when the official hour for luncheon did not coincide with his own pangs of hunger. Gunn did not apparently fit into the home selectors' concept of what a Test batsman should be. He played in only one Test in England; yet he possessed enough batting talent to tour Australia in 1907-8 and 1911-12. Then he re-emerged on to the Test scene at the age of fifty to play on the West Indian tour of 1929 together with his old sparring partner of the 1907-8 tour of Australia, Wilfred Rhodes.

The Jones tour was not, in fact, the Australian walk-over that the margin of 4-1 suggests. The home victories were hard-won and in some instances, close. Australia won the first match by only 2 wickets, whilst according to the opinion of Johnny Moyes, the second game in Melbourne should have been the first tied Test in cricket history. When the last two English batsmen, Barnes and Fielder, came together 39 runs were required for victory. When the scores were level, both batsmen were involved in a running embroglio and found themselves in the middle of the wicket; but the fieldsman, Hazlitt, panicked and muffed his return to the keeper, enabling Barnes and Fielder to scramble home for the winning run.

For the first three days of the Third Test, England were the winning side, only to be sent down to defeat by a record eighth wicket partnership of 243 between Hill and Hartigan—an Anglo-Australian record which still stands to this day. The remarkable feature about the partnership was that Hartigan was a Queenslander and at that stage of Australian cricket development, Queensland was not even a first-class Sheffield Shield side. It would be hard to imagine a Minor counties batsman gaining a place in an England Test side in modern times; yet such was the Australian custom in those days. The margin of Australian victory was again slender in the Fifth Test when the home side won by 49 runs, after England had been trapped upon a treacherous rain-affected wicket.

The 1907-8 tour was not one of unmitigated humiliation for England, but rather a period of exciting and youthful batting reconstruction. Included in the English touring party were players of incalculable promise, amongst whom was Kent's Ken Hutchings. Australia's cricket connoisseur, the late Jack Ryder, rated Hutchings as perhaps one of the best and hardest strikers of the cricket ball whom he saw in sixty years experience of the game. Hutchings, however, was not consistent; his reputation was insubstantially grounded on a mere twelve weeks of meteoric brilliance in English county cricket during the 1906 season. Hutchings, however, did score a match-winning 126 in the Second Test in Melbourne; he was the last product of Sherbourne School to reach this pinnacle of fame until Colin Cowdrey repeated his feat forty-seven years later on the same ground. Unfortunately Hutchings, at the time of Cowdrey's success, was not alive to read of his Kentish successor's maiden Test hundred. He was killed in 1916 fighting for his country in the First World War.

On this same tour, Joe 'Hot Stuff' Hardstaff scored a total of 1,384 runs at an average of 51.25. He, too, was only twenty-five and young Joe, who was later to tour Australia like his father, and who was to use the same nameboard on the Melbourne Cricket Ground scoreboard, was as yet unborn. Hardstaff, however, was but a lesser luminary amongst the Young Turks in the England side. Of far greater significance were the names of John Neville Crawford and John Berry Hobbs. Crawford must have been England's nearest approach to the dynamic all-round talents of players such as Jack Gregory and Keith Miller. Tall and bespectacled, he bowled at a distinctly unpleasant, fast pace, hitting the wicket hard and making the ball rear uncomfortably. Whilst he was still at Repton school he played for Surrey, topping that county's averages, and showing himself to be unusually precocious by capturing 100 wickets and making 1,000 runs in the same season. During the 1907-8 tour of Australia, Crawford at the tender age of twenty-one, captured 30 wickets in the series. He liked his host country so much that after a disagreement with Surrey, the tall schoolmaster transferred his allegiance to Adelaide and St Peter's College. He represented South Australia in the Sheffield Shield and when 'Plum' Warner's side visited Australia in 1911-12, he was chosen to play for the Australian XI against the tourists in Brisbane. In the brief space of 110 minutes in that game, Crawford hit an attack which included Barnes, Rhodes, Foster, Hearne and Woolley for as many runs in as many minutes. Crawford could hit like a pile driver. Returning to England after the First World War he played an innings against the Australian Services side which was deemed by contemporary reporters to have 'taken the eyesight away'. In this great knock in 1919 he hit Jack Gregory, then probably at his fastest, straight back over the bowler's head on to the awning of the Surrey Pavilion. Jack Crawford must have been one of the world's natural cricketers. His biographer said of him that 'he wore flannels as if he were born in them'.

Jack Crawford

John Berry Hobbs was, remarkably enough, passed over by the England selectors in the First Test in Sydney in 1907-8. England opted to include their reserve wicketkeeper, Young, in their side to bolster and open their batting. His achievements amounted to a sum total of 16 runs and the dropping of three vital catches behind the wicket! For the remainder of the series and indeed for the next twenty-three years, Hobbs was England's doyen opening batsman.

It is easy to illustrate Hobbs's greatness by statistics; one only has to look at his record of 197 first-class centuries, twelve of them against Australia, and his aggregate of 3,636 runs against the old foe in both England and Australia. A commentary on the skill of Hobbs, however, would have to embrace far more than a mere factual survey. Harry Altham wrote of him: 'He was never very much concerned with a mere amassing of runs but rather with the art of batsmanship and the challenge of a situation. Given that challenge, whether in the form of the great occasion, a difficult wicket, of formidable bowling or as it may be, a combination of all three, and his stature stood revealed beyond question as that of the greatest English batsman since W.G., great in technical resource of course, and in ease of beauty of style, but above all, I feel, in that serenity which was the reflection of the man himself'. When I read such loving appreciation I cannot but feel that Altham himself, as his own biographer Hubert Doggart fully realized, was very close not only to the heart of Hobbs but also to the heart of cricket.

Since the passing of the Hobbs era, Don Bradman has sped like a lingering yet brilliant meteor through the Test heavens. He blinded men with his genius at the batting crease. Surprisingly, however, even the unforgettable experience of watching Bradman at bat has still left many of the older generation of cricket spectators unconvinced that he was better than either Hobbs or Trumper on every kind of wicket.

The fact that England had extraordinary talent at her disposal in 1907-8 begged the question: why did the tourists go down to a 4-1 defeat? The truth of the matter was that Australia, too, possessed her budding cricketing forces in the persons of Ransford, Carter, Whitty and Macartney. Moreover, in Saunders, the Australian skipper Noble possessed the bowler of the series. In his last rubber the tall lean left-handed spinner bowled at a brisk medium-pace around the wicket to capture 31 wickets. By comparison, the English slow bowlers Rhodes and Braund took only 12 wickets between them. They apparently possessed none of the efficacity of Saunders, who it was said could turn the ball sharply, possessed a good yorker, and had an excellent faster ball. His only drawback was that his action was regarded in some quarters as being rather suspect!

Jack Hobbs

Such an accusation could scarcely be levelled at one of Australia's newest recruits for the 1909 tour of England, Bill Whitty. As recently as 1975 the South Australian still frequented the confines of the Adelaide Oval. A man of short stature in his old age with bright twinkling eyes, he was fond of reminiscing about the pre-First World War days of England-Australia Tests. Described as a fast-medium, left-handed bowler endowed with a beautiful action, Bill Whitty left the Test scene after the Triangular Tournament of 1912 in England. In the late 1920s his continuing enthusiasm for the game was reflected by the fact that he was still bowling at a lively medium-pace in the torrid climate and on the unsympathetic pitches of the South Australian provincial city of Mount Gambier. His love of cricket and the name of Whitty will never be forgotten in the city of the Blue Lake.

Hanson Carter kept wicket in all of the five Tests of 1907-8 and thereby established a respect for his ability which was to keep him in the Australian side until 1921. He had his professional undertaker's eye for detail. It was he who, during the 1921 tour of England, and after a blank first day during the Old Trafford Test, prevented the English captain, Tennyson, from declaring at twenty to six on the second day by pointing out that it would be illegal to close in a two-day fixture later than 100 minutes from close of play. Thus it was that 'Sammy' Carter became an accessory before the fact of the only occasion when a player bowled two successive overs in Test cricket. When the Manchester crowd, hostile about the frustrated declaration, caused an interruption

Three Australian cheers for Jack Hobbs in his last Test. The Oval 1930

in play after one Warwick Armstrong over, the wily Australian skipper exploited the pause, prolonged by the intrusion of Tennyson on to the field to explain matters to the crowd, to reintroduce himself into the attack for the next over from the opposite crease!

Also in the 1909 side to England was Vernon Ransford, the batsman who was to prove most consistent in the five Tests by averaging 58.83. His satisfying record included the gratification of a century on his début at Lords. Johnny Moyes described Ransford as even more brilliant than Warren Bardsley, the man who was to make his mark on Test cricket in his first tour of England by scoring the unprecedented double of a century in each innings of The Oval Test. It was in this self-same year that C. G. Macartney, the 'Governor General', made his first visit to England. His average with the bat in Tests was a modest 18.5. Indeed in these early days his forte was as a slow left-hand bowler with a deceptively long run, uncanny control, an acute degree of orthodox leg-spin and a faster ball which he allowed to slip through his outstretched fingers with no perceptible change in action. Later in his life, the 'Governor' was to become one of Australia's batting elite. He was obviously a man who believed in psychological warfare in cricket; he once explained to the future Australian opening bat, Jack Fingleton that he always liked to upset the concentration of the opening bowlers by driving a ball straight back at their heads during the first overs of a match.

The First Test of 1909 at Edgbaston saw England win by 10 wickets. The heroes of the home side's performance were the two left-handed bowlers of contrasting styles: Colin Blythe of Kent and George Hirst of

Yorkshire. The strength of Blythe's violinist's fingers turned in figures of 11/102, whilst the swerve of the medium-pace Yorkshireman rewarded him with a return of 9/86.

Australia gained her revenge at Lords, where the tourists won by 9 wickets. It was a game remarkable not so much by the performances of the participants, as by the prefatory vagaries of the England selectors. England did not choose a genuine fast bowler. Moreover there was no Fry, Blythe, Jessop, Rhodes or Hayward in their select eleven. As a result, Vernon Ransford registered 143 not out; his sole and singular hundred in Test cricket. Seldom has a player scored a unique and maiden Test Century at cricket's headquarters. His winning performance was compounded by the leg-spinning excellence of Warwick Armstrong who took 6/35 in one England innings, turning his leg-spinners down the then pronounced Lords slope. The 38-year-old L. H. King capriciously plucked from the ranks of Leicestershire cricketers, scored 60 in England's first innings, yet, equally whimsically, never appeared again for his country.

The inconsistencies of the English selection policy were underlined when, just before the beginning of the Leeds Test, the home side announced no fewer than six changes in their eleven: a distinct numerical improvement on their previous five alterations. Australia by contrast were unchanged. The fact that Jessop, Brearley, Barnes, Rhodes, Sharp and Fry were all back in the England side made not one jot of difference and England went down to defeat by 126 runs. It was an eloquent commentary on the imbalanced English selection policy of that era that Barnes, playing in his first Test in England for seven years, captured 6/63 in Australia's second innings yet finished up on the losing side. A contributing factor to England's defeat was undoubtedly the fact that Gilbert Jessop strained his back and did not bat in either innings; the low right-handed slinging thunderbolts of Tibby Cotter and the fingers of the diminutive left-handed Macartney, snatched 17 wickets in the game to tumble England to defeat.

At one stage in the Fourth Test at Old Trafford, Australia were 6/66 in their first innings against Blythe and Barnes. Noble's side however struck back vengefully through the ungainly medium-pace of Frank Laver who took 8/31 in England's first innings of 119. Aided by a strong wind from the leg side, Laver swerved the ball abruptly towards the slips to bring it back to the acute embarrassment of the English batsman whenever he imparted off-spin. Determined not to sacrifice the Ashes the Australian skipper, Noble, instructed his side to play no-nonsense cricket in their second innings and the rain-affected match ended in a draw.

The England team for the drawn Oval Test, according to Wisden of the following year, 'touched the confines of lunacy'. On a hard and fast wicket, the home side omitted to choose a fast bowler. Moreover the selectors nominated the 37-year-old, portly D. W. Carr, a leg-spin and googly bowler who was predominantly a club player and was in his first season of county cricket. Cricket is indeed an unpredictable game; Carr not only took 7 wickets in the match, but he actually opened the bowling in the first innings and captured the wickets of Gregory, Armstrong

Frank Laver

and Noble. In a game of unusual incidents, Noble won the toss for the fifth time in the series—the first of the two captains to accomplish the feat for Australia. Bardsley thereupon compiled his then unique double of 136 and 130. He was one of the great discoveries of this visit to England. Moyes described him as being more orthodox than most Australian batsmen, endowed with accurate footwork and an extremely straight bat, a good cutter of the ball and a player who worked the ball deftly on the leg side.

The 1909 tour to England was a momentous one in the development of the Australian Board of Control's influence over their country's cricket. In fact, 1909 was the prelude to the remarkable players' revolt of the years 1911-12. Included in the 1909 side were both Frank Laver and Peter McAlister. Laver was the player-manager nominated by the members of the team themselves, whilst McAlister was the vice-captain and treasurer nominated by the Board of Control to speak for them that year at the Imperial Cricket Conference in London.

Both players began their cricket careers with the East Melbourne Club. Laver was a players' man: a rough and ready but prolific batsman from Castlemaine and pace bowler of great skill and control. McAlister, for his part, was an opening bat who competed in elegance with players of the ilk of Trumper, Noble, Darling and Hill. In 1905 he was omitted from the touring side to England and it was rumoured that Laver was the power behind the throne who had led to his omission. Their former friendship ended, and McAlister made his way to England as only a supernumerary in his fortieth year—in the opinion of many competent cricket judges, ten years too late. When he returned, the Board asked for his accounts. He had none to submit since he laboured under the misapprehension that Laver was keeping the books on behalf of the Board. When the manager was asked for his accounting, Laver refused to produce his balance sheet, stating that he had kept it for the benefit of the players alone. This was the prelude which led to the Australian Board of Control insisting upon their own manager in the person of G. S. Crouch of Queensland for the 1912 side to England. Clem Hill, Warwick Armstrong, Victor Trumper, Vernon Ransford, Tibby Cotter, and Hanson Carter refused to play in the Triangular Tournament unless they were permitted, under rule 9 of the players' constitution, to choose their own manager. The Board of Control refused to back down. None of the rebellious half dozen were selected for the 1912 tour of England. The division between the authorities and the players on the question of selection was exacerbated by the argument which took place between the Australian skipper, Clem Hill, and the Board selector, Peter McAlister, over the choice of the side for the Third Test against the touring England side of 1911-12. Before the game Hill telegraphed McAlister with the request that Macartney and Matthews be included in the team in place of Whitty and Minnett. McAlister replied that he opposed the selection of Macartney and suggested if Hill insisted upon that player's inclusion, then Hill himself should stand down for the match. When the story hit the newspapers, Hill was quite naturally angry.

The disagreement about the selection of the tour manager came into the open when, on 25 January 1912, six of the Australian side wrote to Sydney Smith, the Honorary Secretary of the Australian Board of Control, stating that 'failing compliance with our request (to appoint our own manager under rule 9 of the constitution) we have to inform you with much regret that none of us will be available for selection or to play on the 1912 tour if selected. Signed C. Hill, W. W. Armstrong, V. Trumper, V. Ransford, A. Cotter and H. Carter'. The Board replied that whilst they were 'anxious at all times to send the best team possible, at the same time they were sure they would not permit any number of cricketers to dictate terms or conditions on which a visit was to be made or if a manager was appointed, the terms and nature of the engagement'.

It was quite clear that, after the 1909 embroglio about the tour finances, the Board were determined to have control of future visits to England. The Board's attitude was that they did not see why any future manager of a touring side could not be nominated by the players and accepted by the Board. The nigger in the wood pile was that Frank Laver's unwillingness to produce the books of the 1909 tour had made him unacceptable to the Board as a controller of the 1912 visit to England. The players for their part were equally determined that Laver should go and maintained that, if the Board did not accept him as manager, then rule 9 of the constitution stating that players had the right to appoint their own manager had been broken. In this contention they were correct but, as Johnny Moyes pointed out, if the organization of state and national cricket was to be rationalized within Australia, it was virtually inevitable that control of the game should pass out of the players' hands and into those of the Australian Board of Control and the State Associations. The tragedy of the situation was that the players, by their breach with the Board, lost a golden opportunity to become part of the future administration of Australian cricket as long ago as 1912. The Sheffield Shield captains' sub-committee of the Australian Cricket Board, founded in 1976, could have easily been a more influential part of the Australian cricket administration scene sixty-four years earlier.

Unfortunately, the antagonism between the Board and players descended to the level of physical conflict. When the selection committee met to choose the 1912 side for England on the second floor of Bull's Chambers in Martin Place, Sydney, Clem Hill confronted Peter McAlister over the selection table. McAlister accused Hill of not using his bowlers to the best advantage during the recent series against England, and added that Hill was probably 'the worst captain he had ever seen'. Hill riposted by saying that, had McAlister been captain of the 1909 side, then the team would have probably refused to tour. Hill thereupon threatened to pull McAlister's nose if he continued with his criticism and when the Board of Control man persisted, Hill, according to his own interpretation of the facts, slapped McAlister on the face. McAlister's version, published later in the *Australasian,* alleged that Hill punched him underneath the eye. Thereupon McAlister advanced around the table and for ten minutes there ensued a wrestling match between the two antagonists which ended with Hill standing over

McAlister, who was thrown to the floor. The Melbourne *Argus* newspaper dramatized the unpleasant incident in verse:

Oh listen to me and I'll tell you why.
Peter McKie has a bandaged eye.
And Clement's face is all awry.
Oh listen to me and I'll tell you why.

The upshot of the matter was that Hill resigned as a selector, set down his resignation in writing and, although he was later to represent South Australia on the Board of Control, he was never to forget the bitterness of 1911-12.

In one respect the England side which visited Australia in 1911-12 was identical to that which toured in 1907-8. Its captain, Pelham Warner, like A. O. Jones, his immediate predecessor on tour, fell ill at the outset and played no significant part in the series. Warner's able lieutenant was John William Henry Taylor Douglas—nicknamed by the Australian crowd because of his initials and ultra-defensive outlook, 'Johnny Won't Hit Today' Douglas. He was a person of herculean stature and immense courage; he won the English amateur middle-weight boxing title in 1905 by defeating Snowy Baker and he played soccer for the Corinthian Casuals, winning an amateur international cap. The slowness of his scoring was legendary and it is reputed that on one occasion a member of the Melbourne Cricket Club bet him that in one hour, more trains would pass along the railway track next to the M.C.G. than he would score runs. Rumour has it that the trains won by twenty-three. Douglas recognized his limitations and once said of himself: 'An optimist is a man who, batting with Johnny Douglas, backs up for a run!' He was a medium-pace bowler of great persistence and nip off the wicket. Some idea of his courage can be gained from the circumstances of his death. In 1930 he was drowned when, during a crossing of the Kattegat, his ship was in collision with another during a thick fog and foundered. Douglas saved himself but returned to the bowels of the ship to perish in a forlorn effort to save his father who was travelling with him.

In Australia in 1911-12 Douglas as a late-swinging medium-pacer captured only 15 wickets at 23.66 runs each; as a batsman he could do no better than a mean figure of 14.57. His successful captaincy indeed was founded upon the instrumentality of Barnes, Foster, Hobbs and Rhodes. Barnes captured 34 wickets in the rubber, Foster 32, and Hobbs scored 662 runs whilst Rhodes averaged 57.87 in the Tests.

The bowling combination of Barnes and Foster won the rubber. They were irresistible. Barnes both swung and cut the ball at medium-pace off the unhelpful Australian pitches at will. Foster operating at a lively left-arm medium-fast around the wicket continually rapped the batsmen hip and thigh whilst spreading a net of catching fieldsmen on the leg side which it was difficult to avoid. Some idea of the efficacy and penetration of the Barnes-Foster bowling combination can be gauged from the fact that Hordern, the first of the Australian great leg spin and googly bowlers, captured 32 wickets in the series and yet ended up on the losing side! Hordern had the consolation of being the deciding influence in the First Test in Sydney where he appropriated 12/155; an analysis which, together with a chanceless 130 from Victor Trumper, ensured Australia of a victory by 146 runs.

An unpleasant note crept into the game when the English batsman, Mead, was run out for 25 in the second innings whilst backing up. Surprisingly the name of the bowler was not even deemed worthy of notoriety in the contemporary records. How different it was during India's 1947-8 tour of Australia. The Indian slow left-arm bowler, Vinoo Mankad, ran out Australian batsman Bill Brown whilst he was backing up, and that incident occasioned the coining of the damning phrase of being 'Mankadded' out. Foster and Barnes began in tandem for the first time in the Melbourne Test at the turn of the year. They proved so effective that at one stage in its first innings, Australia was 6/38, and it was only thanks to Hordern's 49 and Ransford's 43 that the home side managed to accumulate an eventual 184. Barnes's pre-lunch analysis on the first day was a parsimonious 4/3 off 9 overs. His final match analysis was 8/140—figures that were matched by F. R. Foster's 7/143.

Frank Foster

What manner of cricketer was Frank Rowbotham Foster? He possessed a very graceful action which was the culmination of a short, prefatory run. He apparently defied the laws of physics by gaining more pace than other bowlers off the wicket. His fast ball was in the lightning category. Normally he bowled to six fieldsmen in leg-side catching positions. The batsmen who played with the angle however, had to be on the *qui vive* for the ball which Foster straightened like a fast leg-spinner to hit the stumps. In the early months of the First World War, Foster's fast bowling career was terminated by a motor cycle accident. He survived to act as advisor to Douglas Jardine about the field settings for pace men, Larwood and Voce, during the infamous 1932-3 bodyline tour of Australia. Whilst Foster himself disapproved of such tactics, in the late summer of 1932 he met Jardine in his London flat to outline the salient features of his leg-theory field placement.

During the 1911-12 tour Foster himself was far from popular with the Australian spectators because of his habit of striking the home batsmen very painfully on the upper thigh. Barnes was even more frequently booed than Foster. It was not unusual for the Staffordshire man to retire to the pavilion for frequent running repairs, and his insistence upon exactitude in his field placement often exasperated the crowd. During the Second Test Barnes was booed for his meticulous time-wasting and at one stage threw down the ball and refused to bowl until the crowd quietened. An unbeaten century from the young Jack Hobbs—the first of his round dozen against Australia—and 114 from the 20-year-old Jack Hearne assured England of an 8-wicket victory.

The margin in England's favour in Adelaide was only 1 wicket less. At one stage Australia, batting first on a reasonable wicket, was 6 wickets down for 88. The strength of the England attack in this series can be assessed from the fact that medium-pacer Bill Hitch coming on as the third change bowler bowled Trumper with his very first delivery. The Australian skipper Clem Hill batting at number seven was stumped for a duck by the English keeper 'Tiger' Smith, standing up to Foster! In later years Smith was to explain that he was preferred as the keeper in this rubber to both Strudwick and Lilley because of his practised county ability in standing up to the Warwickshire bowler. In England's first innings total of 501, Hobbs accumulated 187 and in spite of the fact that Hill scored 98 in Australia's second innings—the third occasion on which he reached the late 90s in Adelaide—the Australian cause was beyond redemption.

The Fourth Test in Melbourne saw England batting second to open with a record first-wicket partnership of 323 between Hobbs and Rhodes; an opening association which remains unsurpassed in Tests and remembered by old M.C.C. members to this present day. With Australia batting unconvincingly on the first day and being caught on a wet wicket on the fourth day, they could muster no more than 191 and 173 to go down to defeat by an innings and 225 runs. This proved to be the Australian fast bowler Tibby Cotter's last Test. Omitted from the final game in Sydney, Cotter refused to go to England in 1912 and was killed in Palestine during the First World War. Of him Johnny Moyes said that 'he could bowl as fast at half-past five as at twelve noon, being a superb physical specimen and a man who felt it a disgrace if it was suggested that he should have a rest even on a boiling Australian day'.

The Fifth Test in Sydney endured for seven days, two of which were lost entirely to rain. England won by 70 runs after having compiled 324

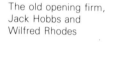

The old opening firm, Jack Hobbs and Wilfred Rhodes

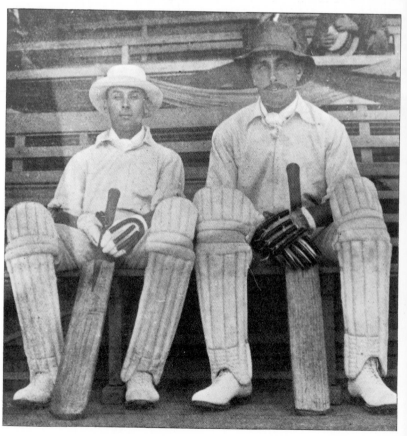

in their first innings, of which Frank Woolley scored an effortless and unbeaten 133. The home side enjoyed scant luck. They were 3/193 when they were trapped on a wet wicket. In spite of that, Australia managed a gallant 292. Trumper, batting for the last time for his country, opened the innings and scored 50. He refused to go to England in 1912 and just over three years later was dead—a victim of that most inappropriately named Bright's disease.

The absence of the six rebels from the Australian side contesting the 1912 Triangular Tournament robbed the competition of much of its glamour. The Australian reserve strength, however, was not so weak as to cause alarm and despondency in the ranks of their supporters. Macartney, Minnett, Hazlitt, Whitty, Bardsley, Kelleway and Matthews were all players of Test experience and maturity. Their 43-year-old skipper, Sid Gregory, already had fifty-five Tests to his name and was described as being 'book perfect in his technique'. Against the M.C.C. in the previous winter he scored 186 for New South Wales. Jimmy Matthews, the leg-spinner from North Melbourne was to establish a unique niche in cricket history for himself during this tour of England in the match against South Africa at Manchester. He became the only bowler to capture a double hat-trick in the same Test on the same day!

The summer of 1912 was so wretchedly wet that the Triangular Tournament was a spectacular flop. The first two Tests between England and Australia at Lords and Old Trafford were completely ruined by rain and a murky gloom, which was slashed only by the gleaming razor sunshine of Hobbs's 107 and McCartney's 99 in the first match. The Third and deciding Test was won by the host country by 244 runs; this victory was in no small way due to Woolley's fine 10-wicket performance with the ball and to Jupiter Pluvius, the God of Rain, who blessed England with opportunely-timed showers to ensnare Australia on a wet wicket on the third day. This misfortune caused a final batting débâcle on the part of the tourists, who were dismissed for 65 in their second innings. There was no shame in that total, for there is no doubt that had England been forced to bat under similar conditions they too would have failed miserably. In fact in their last innings of 175 on this pitch, 5 of their wickets fell in the space of 17 balls and at a personal cost of 1 run to Hazlitt, a medium-paced right-hander with a useful off-break and much swerve. Hazlitt died in 1915 at the early age of twenty-seven and in its obituary on the young schoolmaster from King's School, Parramatta, Wisden stated that in the early part of the tour, Hazlitt 'undoubtedly threw a good deal, but he bowled with a straighter arm later'. Apparently Hazlitt dismissed England too quickly, for Wisden, in describing his 5/1 feat, states that: 'But for this very pronounced success it is certain that Australia would have saved the game, for within half an hour after England had won, the rain descended in torrents and further play would have been impossible'. Faint praise indeed for a man who captured 7/25!

England's second innings owed much of its substance to a magnificent 79 from C. B. Fry. Ironically Fry was bowled three times in the nets before he went out to take strike. When he was twenty, he trod on his own wicket and was given not out—quite rightly in his own opinion, for, as he stated after the match, he had completed his stroke before the wickets were disturbed.

The climatic misery of the 1912 season matched the gloomy air of political foreboding which heralded the cataclysmic First World War: a tragedy which was to transform the noblest human sentiments reflected in the golden age of cricket into the basest, bloodthirsty side of man's nature. Historians tell us in retrospect that Germany had, at enormous expense, been keyed up and prepared, as no nation ever was before, to fight a war at that time. England herself apparently was not loath to take up that challenge; the thirteen years between 1901 to 1914 saw Britain's fighting services' estimates rise by £20,000,000, and the armaments race between Germany and England produced a £19,000,000 inflationary factor in the naval expenditure alone. In October 1912, only two months after the Final Test at The Oval, the Bulgarian War erupted between Turkey and the Slav enclave. The victory of Serbia, Greece, Montenegro, Bulgaria and Rumania in that conflict was a direct threat which the polyglot empire of Austria-Hungary, supported by Germany, could not tolerate and still survive as a nation. Twelve months later Germany had increased her military strength by 120,000 and had seen her arch-enemy, Russia, augment her army by 135,000 men. On 28 June 1914, the Archduke Franz Ferdinand and his wife were assassinated by a Bosnian Serb on the bridge at Sarajevo and Britain was dragged reluctantly into the world conflict.

Sir Edward Gray, Foreign Secretary to England's Prime Minister Asquith, stated that, 'lamps are going out all over Europe, we shall not see them lit in our lifetime'. The glitter, the sweetness and light had gone forever not only from England's Edwardian times but also from cricket's golden age. The game was never to see its like again.

7. The Recovery Cycle

The peace-loving optimists of 1914 deluded themselves into believing that Sir Edward Gray's metaphor about the lights of Europe alluded to a mere dimming process; there could not possibly be a prolonged plunge into stygian gloom. The war would be over in a matter of weeks. Great nations did not engage in a major conflict about the fate of insignificant Balkan states. It required four years of blood-letting on a scale never before envisaged to reveal the enormity of their sanguine self-deception. In four short years 9,700,000 human beings died, 765,399 of them from the tiny island of England. 575,000 men fell in the Battle of Passchendaele, and in the holocausts of Ypres and the Somme, there were 60,000 casualties in one day.

The war which began as a conflict of geographical convenience, motivated by a desire to re-arrange the map of Europe into a more stable and nationalistic format, ended in a welter of high-flown phrases of principle. President Woodrow Wilson declared that the world was being made safe for democracy, whilst Lloyd George, the Prime Minister of England, avowed that his task was to make Britain a country fit for heroes to live in. The world it seemed was changed and there was a new aura of awakened morality abroad.

Cricket like the society around it, was immutably altered. The direct losses in manpower to the game were not as staggering as those suffered by the human race in general. It was, however, symbolic of the ugly impartiality of war that it sought out and destroyed two of England's most graceful cricket artisans. Sergeant Colin Blythe, a slow left-handed bowler of poetic artistry, fell in action in November 1917, the bloody month of Passchendaele. Lieutenant Ken Hutchings of the King's Liverpool Regiment and the hero of the Second Melbourne Test of 1907-8, gained a permanent immortality which far transcended that of his hard-hitting batting genius, when he was killed on 3 September 1916, at the time of the battle of the Somme. At Beersheba in Palestine, Australian fast bowler Tibby Cotter charged to the attack for the last time with Allenby's victorious forces.

The keen edge of war was felt not only amongst the ranks of the recognized champions; its reaping edge cut a swathe through the generation of sprouting ability. Young names such as Booth, Jeeves,

The A.I.F. side 1919.
(L to R) H. Lacy
(manager), C.T.
Docker, J.M, Gregory,
W.L. Trennery, E.J.
Long, C.E. Pellew,
E.A. Bull, J.T. Murray,
H.L. Collins (captain),
W.S. Stirling, W.A.
Oldfield, C.S. Winning,
J.M. Taylor, A.W.
Lampard, C. Willis

Alec Johnson, Jaques, Jennings and G. B. Davies, never reached any mortal or cricketing maturity. To many first-class players, the First World War represented a desert of lost opportunity. Jack Hobbs was thirty-two at the outbreak of hostilities, Charlie Macartney twenty-eight, Frank Woolley twenty-seven, Jack Ryder twenty-five and Herbert Sutcliffe twenty. All of these players wasted four years of their playing sweetness on the gas-laden air of war. At least they were more fortunate than England's former leader, Andrew Ernest Stoddart, who, overwhelmed by the horrific modernity of his times, blew his brains out on 3 April 1915. That year claimed a veritable harvest of old cricketers; for a few short moments, the announcement of the deaths of W. G. Grace and Victor Trumper swept even the casualty lists off the front pages of newspapers.

And after the war? It must have all seemed like a bad dream. The mainstream of cricket flowed on as if there had been no damming up of interest. England and the world had to go on, and where there was England and Australia, there had to be Test matches. In county cricket, the professional cricketer still earned a good living from the game. His wages were three times those of the unskilled labourer and his services were very much in demand. The gates of Test and county matches were swollen by the army of unemployed who could be entertained, and eat and drink like sporting kings, all for a shilling a day.

The war had, however, severely disturbed the balance of cricketing power. England could not point to any youthful ability, whereas Australia, through the unexpected medium of its A.I.F. team, unearthed a mother-lode of golden talent in the persons of fast bowlers Jack Gregory and Ted McDonald, Johnny Taylor, wicketkeeper Bert Oldfield and batsman and fieldsman extraordinaire, Nip Pellew.

The emergence of this bevy of exceptional talent in the Australian side after the First World War was remarkable. Deprivation, food shortages and battlefield casualties sapped the strength of the English game and decimated the ranks of its cricketing youth. Australia not only survived the trauma of the war years, 1914-18, but her players appeared to thrive on the opportunity for overseas experience provided by the Services' games staged in England in the post-war period. It seems that there is a quality of hardihood in the Australian's character which makes him a bouyant survivor of crises. Such an attribute would explain the remarkably parallel revival which will be seen to evolve after the Second World War. After the Great War, many wise heads in English cricketing circles advised that the resumption of England-Australia Tests be deferred. In the opinion of no less an authority than the leading English administrator Lord Harris, the 1920-1 England visit to Australia was too rash, too ill-advised. In deference to the wishes of the Australian camp, the tour was undertaken in spite of the weakness of the England attack. The new ball was virtually the sole responsibility of Hitch and Yorkshire's fast left-hand bowler Abe Waddington; in England, Lancashire's spin bowler, Cecil Parkin, was regarded as a mystery man—the precursor of Australia's Jack Iverson and Johnny Gleeson. Lord Harris thought that Parkin would not pose any problems for batsmen on the harder wickets of Australia. How right he proved to be; and how innocuous the attack of Howell, Douglas, Woolley and Rhodes was on the unyielding Australian wickets. England lost the rubber 5-0, whilst S.F.Barnes, who had offered his bowling services for the tour, sulked at home in England in rejected high dudgeon. Expanding upon his initial theme of the innocuous nature of the English bowling, Lord Harris wrote in terms of pessimistic foreboding to an old friend in Melbourne: 'I doubt Parkin or Howell making much of a show on Australian wickets; indeed I don't see how we are going to get you out, but we've sent you the best we've got so far as we've been able to judge'.

Leadership, too, posed other dilemmas for the England selectors as the celebrated correspondent explained:

The perplexity was an ideal captain. For two weeks we had that in Reggy Spooner, but most unfortunately a little domestic anxiety compelled him, to his bitter disappointment, to resign. It really is a tragedy. You would have liked him so much as well as admired his style. We have done the best we can. Johnny Douglas is indefatigable in the field and has been a lucky captain and, I hope, will hang on to his luck.

I think that you will be quite delighted with Rockley Wilson. He's a fund of information about cricket, of charming manners and a first-rate speaker, if you can give him the opportunity. I don't think it is a great eleven but it is capable of making some big scores. I am very sorry we could not send Pawley to manage but he also has some domestic worries. I only know Mr Toone slightly, but he is a capital man of business.

There was not much perplexity about most of the eleven. They were obvious. There is rather a dearth of Test match players at present. New bowlers of the highest class have not developed and but for a somewhat wet wicket season (1920), scoring would have been very free. I am glad to be able to assure you that cricket has not suffered by the war: it is held in esteem and the affection of the public is undiminished.

Lord Harris

The accuracy of Lord Harris's forebodings exceeded even his anxious expectations. He could not possibly envisage the entry on to the Australian scene of Arthur Mailey, a leg-spinning genius, who brought to polished sophistication the pioneering skills of Hordern. In a five-game series, in which he played in only four, the puckish Lindsay Hassett of slow bowling captured 36 wickets; an achievement which, until 1979, remained the best by a home bowler in Australia in an Anglo-Australian rubber.

Mailey was an expensive proposition for any captain. He conceded more than 4 runs for every Test over which he bowled; but his striking rate of a wicket every 7 overs made him a viable, match-winning luxury. His spinning propensities, even on the best of wickets, demanded the most exacting attention from the most accomplished batsmen. Disconcertingly, he brought to his natural skills the creative imagination of a painter and fine artist. At the crease he was of the impressionist rather than the classical school, preferring the bold, suggestive strokes of the extravagant brush to the fine detail of the pernickety conservative mind. When he suffered at the indiscriminate hands of the Victorian batsmen in 1926, his only comment about the southern state's world record total of 1,107 was that it could have been drastically reduced if the gentleman in the brown derby hat, sitting in the back row of the stands had held at least four catches off his bowling! Mailey's unexpected creativity gave him a novel and personal insight into slow bowling and he was not beyond illustrating his theories to his author friends, Neville Cardus and Denzil Bachelor, at midnight in the middle of London's Piccadilly, clad in the regal magnificence of full evening dress —in which attire he sometimes appeared at the ground next morning. His humour knew no bounds. When he was asked by an affable and considerate dignitary if he was a little stiff from bowling, his answer was: 'A Little Stiff, certainly, sir, but from Sydney, not bowling!'

Mailey's supporting cast in the Australian attack of 1920 included fast-bowling all-rounder, 'Dynamite' Jack Gregory. The versatility of players such as Gregory and his latter-day successor, Keith Miller, made the observer think in cartoon terms of Superman. It was not beyond realistic imagination that they could bowl faster than a speeding bullet and leap over tall buildings in the exuberance of their delivery stride. Gregory once smote a South Africa attack for a century in seventy minutes on one fine Johannesburg day. English bowlers in 1920 suffered to the same three-figure extent in only 137 minutes at Melbourne. More germane to the issue of the series, Gregory was the type of bowler who could turn the tide of a game in the space of a few short overs. From an apology of an approach, in the modern acceptance of the term, and a volcanic action, he generated an eruptive, lift-off speed which threatened the batsmen with decapitation and brought him a harvest of 23 wickets in only 208 overs against Douglas's tourists.

The fortunate captain who held the reins on the formidable Australian attack, was none other than Warwick Armstrong, designated by his adoring Victorian public as 'The Big Ship'—and by the more critical elements of the democratic press as 'The Last of the Cricket Barons'. In 1920 Armstrong was large in every respect. It could easily have been

90

said of Armstrong, as it was of cricket's colossus, W. G. Grace, that in Australia 'he would be worth £3 a week and his tucker merely to walk about the district and crush the vermin with his huge feet that were then destroying the crops'. One of his cricket shirts hangs on display in the Melbourne Cricket Club museum. Its elephantine size still makes one stare and wonder what three-ringed circus of emotion and intelligence used to go on in the breast beneath and the brain above that honest flannel. Employed by the Melbourne Cricket Club, Armstrong was virtually a professional Australian cricketer in an era which was wholly amateur. The early nineteeth century was the time when a feature of the services available to M.C.C. members was the provision of professional ground bowlers. Until his resignation from the position of M.C.C. secretary in 1921, after twenty years in the service of the club, Armstrong's daily two-hour batting stint at the practice nets was a mandatory duty of the 'pro' bowlers.

Jack Gregory

Australia in 1920 also had its leadership problems. The rancour engendered by the players' confrontation with the Board of Control in 1912 lingered on in the minds of the opposing parties. Armstrong, as one of the six rebels, still drew sidelong glances of askance from both the national and state selectors; but his pre-eminent standing in the game was as imposing as his physical stature and brooked no boy-cotting of him as captain. The covert animosity between the Victorian captain and the selectors did, however, emerge into the open on the occasion of his state's game against the tourists. Only a week or two before the Victorian match against Douglas's XI, Armstrong travelled to Sydney for a Shield game. Because of badly bruised legs sustained during the Third Test, he neglected to practise and then omitted himself from the side to play New South Wales in the hundredth game between the two states. The Victorian Cricket Association selectors thereupon demanded a report on the incident and summarily dropped their skipper from the team to meet the M.C.C. before they had heard the evidence! With Hendren scoring a brilliant 271, Victoria subsequently lost the game by 7 wickets amidst howls from the Melbourne outer-ground spectators decrying the merits of the substitute captain, Edgar Mayne, and demanding Armstrong's recall.

The unruly outcome of the sacking of Armstrong was the organiza-tion by a Mr H.D. Westley of a protest meeting at the Atheneum Club and a monster indignation rally outside the Melbourne ground during the Victorian encounter with Douglas's men. The authorities added fuel to an inflammatory situation by requiring patrons who left the M.C.G. to attend the gathering to pay for re-admission. A special meeting of the V.C.A. was convened, and after having heard the medical evidence concerning the Sydney episode, it decided in Armstrong's favour, absolving the capital ship of Australia's cricketing fortunes of all blame. He was nonetheless rebuked with a metaphoric slap over the wrists embodied in the admonition not to behave in similar fashion again. Armstrong survived the captaincy crisis in his own state to lead his country in England in 1921, but rumour had it that his elevation to his select office was only by a single Board of Control vote.

Armstrong vindicated his offical supporters' lukewarm and hesitant

The young Warwick
Armstrong

confidence by crushing England by successive margins of 377, an innings and 91, 119, 8 and 9 wickets. The Sydney Test was a game of ignoble firsts: in the initial match after the war, A. C. Russell in his maiden Test innings was bowled by the first delivery. Jack Ryder, who was later to lead his country, was run out in both innings on his début. Mailey enmeshed the English batsmen in his snares and Armstrong's 158—his first Test century against England since 1908—clinched the game for his team. Heaven knows what the daunting fate of England might have been had not five Australian batsmen run themselves out in the game. In the second encounter the English fieldsmen outdid even their butter-fingered catching propensities of the First Test, thus enabling Gregory to score a century from the lowly, non-opportunist position of number nine. Hearne was sick and missing from the England batting line-up; even a masterly 122 from Jack Hobbs in a total of 251 on a sticky wicket could not compensate for the tourists' numerical deficiencies. If divine justice had maintained its godly impartiality, England should have won the Third Test. For three days they dominated play, with Hobbs maintaining his sparkling centurion form and Russell supporting him admirably with 135. In the final frustrating phases for England, however, Australia's batting depth won the day; Collins, Kelleway, Armstrong and Pellew each contributed hundreds when they were most needed. 'Nip' Pellew's century capped a remarkable athletic career which embraced an outstanding proficiency in football, the quarter-mile race and, finally, cricket.

The season's moment of glory for the veteran players occurred during the Fourth Melbourne Test. The 43-year-old Sammy Carter kept wicket in his usual immaculate fashion for Australia whilst the 38-year-old and rigidly orthodox England opener, Harry Makepeace, scored 117 and displayed a technical correctness which, as coach of Lancashire, he was later to pass on to ensuing generations of young batsmen. It was Warwick Armstrong, however, who at the age of forty-one captured the imagination of the Melbourne public by notching his third century of the rubber and triggering off 'a demonstration of popularity unprecedented in the history of Australian cricket'. The home skipper's hundred was reached in spite of an attack of malaria which he contracted during his war service in New Guinea.

Injuries to England players Hitch, Hearne, Howell, Hobbs and Russell decided the issue of the final game. Hobbs pulled up lame and was cruelly heckled during the third day by the Sydney Hill: a heartless piece of partisanship which later caused Percy Fender and Rockley Wilson to write scathingly of Australian crowd behaviour in those dim and distant days. In his sixteenth Test Macartney scored the first of his five centuries against England. His metamorphosis from left-hand bowler to specialist batsman had followed the Wilfred Rhodes model and was virtually complete. Jack Gregory scored 93 and gave substance to Johnny Moyes's opinion of him that he was

. . . an athletic giant who could bat, bowl and field so magnificently that he was an extraordinary favourite. Everything he did showed clearly that he was a born cricketer, a fitting descendant of the man who led the first Australian team to England.

Douglas's team had not seen the last of the Australian XI after the final ball of the Fifth Test was bowled; the Australian touring side to England for the following season embarked upon the same homeward-bound ship as the returning visitors! The deck sports on board that vessel must have resembled a mini-olympics in the keenness of its rivalry. The Armstrong combination in England in 1921 vies, in the minds of many experts, with the Darling team of 1902 and Bradman's side of 1948 for the accolade of being the strongest party ever to tour that country. Its unbeaten progress through the Test and county programme was marred only by MacLaren's and 'Buns' Thornton's impromptu pot-pourri elevens at Eastbourne and Scarborough in the light-hearted atmosphere of the dying moments of the visit. Only Bradman's unvanquished tourists of 1948 produced a better balance sheet of winning assets than Armstrong's.

The 3-0 success of Australia hinged on the vital roles played in the rubber by fast bowlers Jack Gregory and Ted McDonald and the revolutionary use which their captain made of them. Before the First World War it was not unusual for slow bowlers such as Saunders, Noble, Braund and Blythe to open the attack, adding variety and guile to a foil of speed at the opposing crease. Armstrong, however, according to the contemporary journalistic perception of E. R. Power, 'upset all pre-conceived ideas by opening with his two fastest bowlers on the assumption that if there was any merit in the new shiny ball for one fast bowler, there was more merit in it for two'.

The instruments of torture for the English batsmen could not have been more admirably fashioned. The bucking hostility of the ferocious Gregory was complemented by the insidious feline grace and accuracy of Ted McDonald. The Tasmanian quick bowler toured England only once in 1921, not because of his lack of ability, but because he chose to remain in that country to play county cricket for Lancashire. To my mind's eye McDonald was the beau idéal of a balletomane's cricketer; the effortless elegance of his bowling action, his leading arm upstretched with a delicacy which suggested that he was supporting the most fragile member of the corps de ballet, was reminiscent of Nureyev. His methods were as relentless as those of his Lancashire successor, Brian Statham, and brought him more than 150 wickets on his one tour of England. Yet the fast bowler, and Aussie Rules fullback, who used to draw the spectators into Fitzroy's club games in Melbourne by the thousands, and was hailed by Johnny Moyes as the game's most gifted fast bowler, was both generous and gentle by nature. His death in 1937 was caused by a spontaneous act of concern for other people. He descended from his car on the East Lancashire Road to help a motorist who had broken down. Whilst assisting him, McDonald was struck by another car and killed.

English cricket could have been forgiven its febrile state in the recuperative aftermath of the war; it was impossible, however, to understand and condone the flurry of panic which assailed the England selectors during 1921. They tried no fewer than thirty players in five games. They even issued an invitation to the 41-year-old C. B. Fry to play in the Second Test. Not unnaturally he refused the offer. Who would accept with McDonald and Gregory in the opposition and only ancient reflexes at one's disposal? Bad luck again afflicted the English fortunes. After missing the first two matches because of a strain, the home side's leading batsman, Hobbs, was struck down by appendicitis and took no further part in the rubber. Hearne was fit only for the Leeds Test. Cricketers from north of the river Trent are firm in their belief that when Yorkshire is strong, so is England. The weakness of England in 1921 more than substantiated this theory; after the First Test, the only Yorkshireman by birth to take the field was Sammy Carter, the Australian wicketkeeper!

The summer lightning of Gregory and McDonald struck down the opposition in the Trent Bridge and Lords Tests by 8 and 10 wickets, with the only ineffective insulation against defeat coming from two fine innings of 95 and 93 from the polished Woolley. After seven consecutive losses, Douglas was replaced at the helm for the Leeds Test by the Hon. Lionel Tennyson, grandson of Queen Victoria's poet laureate, later the third baron of the line, and the then current captain of Hampshire. Tennyson was made of the same heroic stuff as his grandfather's Knights of the Round Table. In his baptism of fire as captain of England, he split his hand whilst fielding a hard Macartney drive and trying to thwart the only Australian century of the series. He shrugged off the injury with the same indifference to pain which enabled him to endure his war wounds, and batted twice against the electric speed of Gregory and McDonald using only one hand. His stoic scores of 63 and 36 did not avert defeat but they gave his team new heart.

Lionel Tennyson during his epic one-handed innings at Leeds 1921

Tennyson's county side of Hampshire were made of stern stuff in those days. In its ranks was the 34-year-old wicketkeeper and opening bat, George Brown, a man who, like his skipper, graduated late into international ranks in 1921 and whose answer to the rising delivery was to breast it onto the ground! It is said that the tactic which was efficacious at the outset of his county career in 1908, and which was still being unwisely employed twenty-five years later, caused Brown many heart-searching moments and abrupt collapses in 1933. Brown must have been a remarkable cricketer; not only did he go in first and keep wicket, he was a good enough fast-medium bowler to open his county's attack and take over 600 first-class wickets.

The Old Trafford Test was curtailed by rain on the first day and subsequently drawn—but only after moments of high excitement. A century from Russell enabled Tennyson to think in terms of declaring at ten to six on the second day with the England score standing at an imposing 4/314. The Australian side refused to leave the field, however, and subject their batsmen to an uncomfortable period of survival before close of play. The wily Sammy Carter, with a Yorkshireman's canny knowledge of the rules of the day, pointed out to his skipper, Warwick Armstrong, that it was illegal in a two-day match for the team batting first to close its innings less than 100 minutes before stumps. By the time that Armstrong had left the field to explain the situation to

Tennyson, who was then compelled to venture on to the field to pass on the explanation to the irate Manchester spectators, twenty-five minutes of play had been lost. The Australian captain, taking advantage of the confusion, bowled the next over to complete a totally unlawful two overs in succession! The facet of the match which I find intriguing is that Tennyson's projected declaration actually envisaged the possibility of dismissing a full-strength Australian side twice in the space of the single remaining day of the Test for less than 300! The subsequent game at The Oval was doomed to a drawn fate by the weather.

The 1921 rubber was, beyond a doubt, a contest between two unequally matched sides. Australia's supremacy, however, did not rob the series of all interest. The personalities of the two captains was an intriguing study in itself. It has been stated that if Warwick Armstrong was the Last of the Cricket Barons, Lionel Tennyson was the descendant of the Cricketing Regency Bucks. Equipped with his inseparable companions, his pipe, his lucky shilling and his indomitable courage, Tennyson imbued England with new hope, much as Freddie Brown was to do in Australia thirty years later. Tennyson possessed the same audacity and front foot driving power as Brown, but he was certainly more of a gambler. He disposed of the family property accrued by his grandfather with a throw-of-the-dice abandon. I often wonder what Tennyson's Victorian forefather, dreaming of his utopian world 'bound by chains of gold about the feet of God' would have thought of his descendant. Certainly he would have had to concede that his grandson lacked sententiousness and had an engaging personality. It was said of Lionel Tennyson that whenever he entered a room, everyone broke into a smile.

Warwick Armstrong, 'The Big Ship'

The year 1921 was the last official overseas voyage of Australia's 'Big Ship'. Warwick Armstrong, after a further season with Victoria, was to devote himself to the spiritual matters concerned with his importing agency for John Buchanan's and Peter Dawson's whisky and with the Melbourne Cricket Club. Hailing originally from the country town of Kyneton, Armstrong maintained his rural liaison when he married a wealthy Gundagai grazier's daughter. This New South Wales connection, a subscription of £2,500 from his supporters at the protest meetings of 1921, and his business ventures made Armstrong a wealthy man. When he died in 1947, he was reputed to be worth £90,000. At the time of his retirement from first-class cricket, he weighed twenty-two stone; but his greatness was not merely physical. Armstrong was a person of immense character. During his last tour of England, he attempted to force the hand of the home authorities by asking his manager, Sydney Smith, to demand the re-arrangement of the programme in order to gain a day's rest for his team before a Test. He met his match, however, in the Yorkshire committee who refused to budge an inch from the itinerary which was decided before the Australians left their own shores. When the Final Test was dying to a drawn close, Armstrong angered the crowd and the England officials by bowling batsmen Pellew and Taylor and retiring to the outfield where, in disinterested fashion, he began to read a newspaper. When he was taxed with his irregular captaincy and behaviour, he retorted that he was only perusing the tabloid to see who his side were playing. It was characteristic of the man that he should end his career of fifty Tests, six international centuries and 87 wickets on a note which said quite clearly that when Warwick Armstrong played cricket, he did it—like Frank Sinatra—his way.

The cyclic development of England-Australia Tests in the post-First and Second World War periods was so similar as to suggest that it was more than a coincidence. Their resemblance was so striking that it gives some substance to the theory that there is a clear pattern of cricket renaissance after a major conflict, just as there is a sequence of conservatism, revolution, chaos and totalitarianism in the revolutionary cycle.

The story of Test cricket in both the early twenties and late forties begins with England as the war-battered underdog. In each era the cycle develops as lone victories in a series come her way and finally a win in a rubber by the slender margin of a single game. England's rehabilitation takes exactly nine years in each epoch. Restored to her former strength, she thereupon twice overwhelms her traditional opponent on Australian soil.

In 1920-1 in Australia, the home side annihilated Douglas's team just as they were to crush Hammond's side in 1946-7. Australia maintained its total supremacy in England in 1921 and 1948. This ascendancy was only slightly diminished when England next made comparable visits to Australian shores. England managed to win a Test but lost the series in both 1924-5 and 1950-1. The wheel had almost come full circle when Australia lost the last Test and the rubber in both 1926 and 1953. On each occasion the first four Tests were drawn. When England visited Australia in 1928-9 and 1954-5, they were completely dominant and ran out victors by the respective margins of 4-1 and 3-1. Thereafter the parallel lines of victory and defeat in the post-war periods diverge. England lost the rubber in England in 1930, but won convincingly in 1956: Jardine's combination were victors in Australia in 1932-3 but May's side was demolished by Benaud's XI in 1958-9. The significant factor about the reversal of the comparable trends in 1930 and 1956, however, was that they were engineered by the dominant influence of individual players of outstanding talent: Bradman and Larwood in the earlier era and off-spinner, Laker, in 1956.

Indeed it is a strange feature of the post-war comparisons that the characters of the leading dramatis personae were peculiarly alike. Two senior but outstanding captains in Armstrong and Bradman established Australia's immediate supremacy. Was it, I wonder, as much a reflection on the English social scene of the time as on the strength of the Australian sides, which led to Armstrong's and Bradman's teams being acclaimed as the best ever to leave their shores? The rebirth of England's hopes in 1921 and 1950-1 was rekindled by the same type of Bluff King Hal, inspirational leadership from Lionel Tennyson and Freddie Brown. A duet of great medium-pace bowlers in Maurice Tate and Alec Bedser made the first great inroads into the phalanx of Australian batting might in 1924-5 and 1950-1 and the stability of English batting rested largely on the shoulders of opening batsmen Jack Hobbs and Len Hutton—outstanding players whose careers were bisected by the wars. The catalogue of such similarities lead one to believe that there were more social influences than coincidence in the parallel trends of Anglo-Australian cricket after the two conflicts.

Sussex captain, Arthur Gilligan, was elected to lead England in Australia in 1924-5. Like Freddie Brown's side of 1950-1, his team went down to defeat 4-1, and like their successors of twenty-six years later, they were desperately unlucky. Gilligan himself was chosen as an opening bowler, but a blow over the heart from a fast man in the preceding county season limited his effectiveness. England lost the Third Test by only 11 runs after their attack was reduced to the two regular bowlers, Kilner and Woolley, by injuries to Gilligan, Tate and Freeman. If England had reversed this decision, their subsequent victory in the Melbourne encounter would have made the fifth game in Sydney the decider. In view of the fact that the home side only won the second clash in Melbourne by 81 runs, it can be seen quite clearly that the rubber was far closer than the impersonal analysis of 4-1 indicates.

The touring captaincy was only a small part of the immense contribution made by the Gilligan family to the cause of international cricket. Their close ties with New Zealand and their personal friendship with the Kiwi captain, Tom Lowry, was to lead to Arthur Gilligan taking the first Marylebone Cricket Club party to the Shaky Isles and the inauguration of the England-New Zealand Test competition for the W. J. Jordan trophy in 1929-30. The shipping connections of the family greatly facilitated the importation of English coaches into both New Zealand and South Africa, and their tenure of the England captaincy was perpetuated by the marriage of a Gilligan daughter to Peter May, their country's cricket leader of the late 1950s. Arthur Gilligan was later to become a distinguished President of the M.C.C. As a batsman, however, he did not shine; rumour has it that his daughter, whose cricket judgment was nothing if not realistic, answered the phone on her father's behalf, as he strode from the Sussex pavilion to bat for his county. She advised the caller to hang on if he wanted to speak to Arthur—he would not be long!

In the southern season of 1924-5, England were unfortunate to meet Arthur Mailey's natural successor, Clarrie Grimmett, a leg-spin bowler whom Sir Donald Bradman once described as the best that cricket has ever seen. Grimmett was a strange Australian phenomenon. Born in New Zealand like Spofforth, he migrated to Melbourne and the Prahran club to further his cricket career. The Victorian selectors, however, steadfastly ignored his talents, and it was not until Grimmett transferred to South Australia that he achieved regular state and international recognition at the promising and unusual age, by Australian standards, of thirty-four. In his first Test he outlined his genius by taking 11/82 and thus began a career which should have lasted until the Second World War, but ended contentiously in 1935, at which stage he had a then existing record of 216 victims to his credit.

Grimmett owed much of his success to the driving force of his State captain and Test batsman, Victor York Richardson. On one occasion Grimmett arrived at the South Australian ground for the first day of a game with his bowling hand swathed in bandages. He explained that he

Clarrie Grimmett

had been burning some tall grass in his garden on the previous day and had inadvertently left a metal rake amongst the burning debris. When he later attempted to pick up the rake, he found, to his cost, that it was still red-hot and consequently badly blistered his spinning fingers. Richardson, however, did not brook such excuses and compelled Grimmett to bowl. He captured the lion's share of the wickets and won the game for South Australia, whereupon Richardson advised Grimmett to continue his pyromaniac habits since they seemed to pay dividends.

The England bowling Goliath of the 1924-5 rubber was Maurice Tate, who returned to his native county of Sussex with a record 38 Australian wickets at his belt after his first encounter with the traditional enemy on foreign soil. 'Chubby' was the son of Fred Tate, the unfortunate scapegoat of England's 2-run loss against Murdoch's side at Old Trafford in 1902. He was beloved of his fellow professionals for the enormity of a cheerful heart which was as big as his large feet. Beginning as a slow bowler, he then exploited the natural qualities of his perfect rocking-horse action to develop into a medium-pace bowler with phenomenal nip off the wicket. Whenever I see a photograph of Tate in action, I am astonished at the depth of the placement of his slip fieldsmen, who were almost as far from the stumps as Larwood's catchers in the 1928-9 tour. Tate once confided in me that his bowling technique of holding the seam bolt upright made him unsure of the direction in which the ball would move in the air. If the bowler himself was not certain, he must have created even greater problems for the hesitant batsmen! His swing was so late that many of his contemporaries were of the opinion that Tate's penetrative ability lay in his seaming propensities off even the glassiest of wickets. It was not unusual for county opponents to visit Sussex's seaside ground at Hove and be dismissed by Tate in two successive morning sessions for paltry scores on a wicket enlivened by the sea fret of the incoming tide. In his very first game against Australia in Sydney, Tate captured 11/228 and contemporary reports suggest that, if the English catching had been surer on the second morning, his opening spell of 4/9 could have assumed even more devastating proportions.

The beauty of Maurice Tate's action

Aligned with the opposition to Tate in that First Test was Bill Ponsford, an opening bat of such immense concentration and infallible technique that many regard him as the unlucky precursor of Donald Bradman. He was unfortunate because so many of his staggering scores were soon eclipsed by the performances of the Bowral genius. In the course of the previous Australian season, Ponsford compiled 429 in Victoria's total of 1,059 against Tasmania—a score which he was to exceed by 8 against Queensland five years later. Only Bradman outscored Ponsford's huge totals in Sheffield Shield cricket and to this day some of the bowlers who faced both batsmen still maintain that the breadth of 'Ponny's' bat made him a more discouraging sight at the batting crease. In his first Test, Ponsford, the now retired, self-effacing assistant-secretary of the Melbourne Cricket Club, became one of the few men to score a century in his first international innings.

If Australia possessed promising batting forces in 1924-5, so did

98

Sutcliffe plays O'Reilly hard on to his stumps without dislodging the bails. Sydney 1932

England. It was in this year that Jack Hobbs discovered his perfect opening foil in the person of the immaculate Yorkshire iceberg, Herbert Sutcliffe. The impeccable dress and sleek hair of Sutcliffe was indicative of the iron self-control which until 1930 was to make his name as natural a corollary to that of Hobbs as salt is to pepper. His sang-froid was such that when, in later years, Bill O'Reilly hit his middle stump without dislodging the bail, it is said that Sutcliffe demanded that the game be resumed whilst the fielding side were still clustered around the wicket gawking at the physical impossibility. In his first Test Sutcliffe scored an unflustered double of 59 and 115, adding with Hobbs 157 for England's first wicket.

Six players scored centuries in the First Test, which England lost by 193. They had only themselves to blame since, had they held their catches and batted with more discipline in the lower order, they could have reversed the decision. A new disruptive dimension was added to the records when play on the fourth day was curtailed by high winds. At Melbourne Ponsford scored his second hundred in as many games: a feat which was emulated by Sutcliffe, who became the first English counterpart of Warren Bardsley by notching two three-figure scores in the same match. He and Hobbs were associated in an awesome all-day opening partnership of 283 in England's first innings.

In Adelaide, Tate reduced Australia to 3/22 in his opening spell but was forced to withdraw to the pavilion with an injured foot. He was followed off the field in quick succession by leg-spinner Freeman and captain Gilligan and the English attack was reduced to the spinning remnants of Kilner and Woolley. Rain on the fourth night, after Hobbs had scored his ninth hundred against Australia, afforded the English slow bowlers sufficient assistance to capture the last 7 Australian wickets for 35. In the thrilling climax of the game, England, having been set 375 to win, were still 63 runs short of their target on the fifth evening with 8 wickets down. Further rain overnight sealed her fate and Gilligan's men failed by a meagre 11 runs to gain the first elusive victory for their country after the war.

The tourists did not have to wait long for revenge. They inflicted defeat on Australia for the first time in thirteen years in Melbourne's Fourth Test. England's win by an innings and 29 runs was due largely to a huge first innings total of 548, accumulated by two days of patient batting. Sutcliffe notched his third hundred in the rubber and he and Hobbs opened for the fourth time in seven innings with a century partnership. Astonishingly, Hobbs was stumped for 66 off the fast medium-pace of Ryder by Oldfield who claimed no fewer than four batsmen in the match in this way, an achievement which he was to repeat in the Fifth Test. When showers interrupted play on the third morning Australia's fate was transparently obvious and the home side was forced to follow on, on a drying wicket against the rampant Tate who captured 4/21 in his final match-winning burst.

The last game was played in Sydney where Kippax and Grimmett made their Test bows to the Australian public. For the first time in the rubber both Hobbs and Sutcliffe failed, each collecting ducks, and without their steadying influence, the English batting collapsed twice against Grimmett for 167 and 146. The gnomish leg-spinner throughout his career usually demanded time to work his wily ways; he often complained when he was taken off after bowling 30 overs that he 'was just working out his plan'. Grimmett's systematic approach to life and cricket was exemplified by the fact that he once worked out that if he went through Adelaide's city area at a certain consistent speed in his car, he would not be held up by annoying traffic lights. In his first Test Grimmett did not need temporal latitude for his hip-pocket leg-spinners and wrong 'uns. The match was over in five days as Australia won by 307 runs.

Australia's captain for the 1924-5 series was 'Horseshoe' Collins, a batsman accomplished enough to score a hundred in the First Test and, by profession a bookmaker, lucky enough to win the toss on four out of five occasions. Collins led the next Australian contingent to England in 1929, but this time his good fortune deserted him; he gained the dubious notoriety of being the first Australian captain since the war to lose the Ashes. The ill-luck of the tourists made one wonder whether, like the Ancient Mariner, they had shot an albatross during their sea voyage to England. Gregory, their leading fast bowler, suffered a knee injury and sorely missed his tandem partner of 1921, McDonald. All-rounder Hendry was sick from May until August and Collins was himself laid low by an attack of neuritis in July. Taylor, who led the 1924-5 Test aggregates with 541 runs, also fell ill and played only two innings in the series for 13 runs. The rubber was the end of the international road for Johnny Taylor. The man who began his career as a bank clerk and played regularly in bank matches before the Great War, abandoned Test cricket to concentrate on dentistry—a profession for which he

Bill Ponsford

qualified after his demobilization from the military services.

Ponsford did not enjoy the best of health for three weeks and it was left to the brilliant Macartney to salvage Australia's batting prestige; Macartney averaged 94.6 in the rubber and scored three effervescent centuries in successive innings, including a hundred of incredible, eye-defying brilliance before lunch on the first day at Leeds. His apprentice assistant was a young Methodist schoolmaster from Victoria. Bill Woodfull was the last member of the touring party chosen but he quickly acquired an unbowlable reputation which elevated him to the opening berth by the time that the Third Test arrived, and a technique which subsequently yielded him two three-figure scores in succession.

The home side also had its problems. There was still no automatic solution to the quandary of the choice of captain. In 1926, the stormy-petrel skipper from Nottingham, Arthur Carr, led England in the first four games, but when his form and health declined he yielded his office to Percy Chapman who won the deciding Fifth Test. The crucial victory was a triumph of empiricism blended with a smattering of imagination. The pragmatic England selectors recalled the 48-year-old Wilfred Rhodes, then at the top of the county bowling averages, to lead the spinning attack. On a damp wicket on the fourth day he captured 4/44 from 20 overs and from the time that he went on, according to contemporary reports, 'the match was over'. The imaginative aspect of the England selection for the Fifth and Second Test was the inclusion in the home side of a young Nottinghamshire fast bowler, Harold Larwood. The cricketing miner with a 'carpet slipper' approach to the wicket captured only 9 wickets in his 2 games for 252 runs; but the poetry of his run-up, the geometry of his side-on action and the fact that he could dismiss players of the calibre of Woodfull, Macartney, Andrews and Collins made one thing certain—Australia would hear more of Larwood in 1928-9 and 1932-3.

Rain restricted the First Test at Trent Bridge to precisely 17.2 overs on an improvised wicket, prepared when the original surface was flooded. Play began at 12.15 p.m. on the first day and England reached 0/32 before the flood gates opened and the ground gates closed for the remainder of the game. The home side did receive one sad bonus from the match: fast bowler Gregory injured his knee and was never the same player again. Indeed it was this wrench which was to end Gregory's Test career during the next M.C.C. tour of Australia.

The Second Test at Lords was also inconclusive but was significant because it saw the début of Larwood and the first employment of the bowling tactic of leg theory in Tests. Warwickshire inswing bowler, Fred Root, captured 7 Australian wickets for 42 in the county game preceding the Test by bowling to a packed leg-side field. He did not repeat his success at Lords, where Bardsley, by scoring 193, became the third player to carry his bat through an innings. The perky cockney Patsy Hendren scored his first century against Australia almost within sound of Bow Bells, and Macartney, now in the full flower of his 40-year-old maturity, reeled off the first of three consecutive hundreds for Australia. He was an impudent, experimental and unpredictable batsman who played the ball so late that it became impossible to place a field for him. Johnny Moyes wrote of Macartney that he was 'short and compact, impish, gifted beyond the normal with a touch of genius, a complete stroke maker, brilliant in the extreme, impertinence personified, never admitted the superiority of any bowler and was ready to accept any challenge or to issue one'.

Macartney was to occupy centre stage in the next game at Leeds. Carr won the toss for England and after earnest consultation with the local batsman, Sutcliffe, and the groundsman, he sent Australia into bat. His gambling instincts appeared to have been touched by inspiration when Bardsley, who had batted through the Australia innings at Lords, plumbed the depths of contrasting fortune by not surviving a single delivery at Leeds. He was caught at slip off Tate's first ball and Macartney jauntily survived the fifth ball of the over when Carr at third slip dropped a straightforward opportunity off the same bowler. The batsman's revenge was terrible to behold. Macartney ravaged the England attack to the tune of 100 in 103 minutes and when lunch was taken his score stood at 112. With Woodfull and Arthur Richardson each contributing centuries, Australia totalled 494 and compelled England to follow on; but there was insufficient time for a decision in those times of three-day Tests.

The agitation for longer contests increased when the Manchester Test became the fifth successive drawn game between the two countries. An attack of tonsillitis added to the woes of the England skipper, Carr, who was suffering a wretched series. In three of the games in which he led his country, he had not batted and in his only innings he was dismissed lbw for an unlucky 13. His captaincy at Lords and Leeds had been questioned in high places and now he had to yield his place to Jack Hobbs, the first professional to captain England since the days of Shrewsbury. Poor Arthur Carr! Old Trafford was the last time that he was to lead England against Australia, although he was appointed skipper for two further Tests against South Africa in 1929.

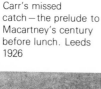

Carr's missed catch – the prelude to Macartney's century before lunch. Leeds 1926

The topsy-turvy fortunes of cricket were admirably illustrated by the Final Test at The Oval. Percy Chapman had been relegated to the lowly role of twelfth man at Old Trafford; now he found himself not only in the side but leading it. Previously only three days had been allowed each game; now there was no time limit on the game. Wilfred Rhodes

had not sent down a ball for England since the Trent Bridge Test of 1921. Now at the age of forty-eight, the extraordinary evergreen was recalled to bowl in the crucial game. He captured 6/79 in 45 impeccable overs and extended his international career even further by going to the West Indies in 1929 where he played in four Tests at the age of fifty-two. Speaking of Rhodes as a bowler, the famous England and Yorkshire batsman, Len Hutton, said in later years that when facing the slow left-hander the batsman sometimes felt that he could cut or drive him; but inevitably one always finished pushing forward defensively.

Chapman's team which regained the Ashes at the Oval, 1926. Standing (L to R) H. Larwood, M.W. Tate, G.T.S. Stevens, G. Geary, H. Sutcliffe, E.H. Hendren. Seated (L to R) H. Strudwick, J.B. Hobbs, A.P.F. Chapman (captain), W. Rhodes, F.E. Woolley

Chapman steered his side to a 289-run victory in the game and the Ashes were back in England after an interval of fourteen years. Chapman's charisma earned him the right to take the next England side to Australia where he reinforced previously won golden opinions of himself by carrying off the series 4-1. The final act of the 1926 rubber produced some extraordinary cricket. In England's first innings Jack Hobbs was bowled by a high Mailey full toss: an event which caused the bowling comedian to remark that perhaps he should have used the tactic earlier and more frequently. In this game Larwood openly demonstrated that he was a bowler of exceptional pace; time and time again he defeated batsmen such as Gregory and Bardsley by sheer speed. On the batting front, Hobbs and Sutcliffe played two incredible innings of 100 and 161 respectively in England's second knock on a sticky wicket! Against the turning deliveries of the left-handed Macartney, Arthur Richardson, Arthur Mailey and Clarrie Grimmett, the two batting maestros added a joint 172 for the first wicket. They scored freely where other players would have been satisfied to survive. The state of the pitch can be assessed from the fact that Australia in their second innings could muster no more than 125 against the guile of Rhodes and the express speed of Larwood.

The year 1926 ended the Australian monopoly of the Ashes since the First World War. It also heralded the marshalling of new potent forces in the Test match field. For Australia, the Bradman era was just around the corner. England's batting was to receive a boost with the advent of Wally Hammond, the batsman with the two hundred habit. More importantly, however, the era of Gregory's supremacy was over and England were about to usurp the fast bowling crown of the world with the discovery of Larwood and his Nottinghamshire companion-in-arms, Bill Voce. Making their last appearance against England in the 1926 rubber were Mailey, Bardsley, Taylor and Collins. It is hard to appreciate that Mailey played in only twenty-one Tests and five series against England and South Africa. It is equally difficult to exaggerate the match-winning powers of the little man with the magic fingers. In six short years Mailey captured 99 wickets—2 wickets more than the much vaunted latter day destroyer of batsmen, Dennis Lillee, in the same number of matches. It was symbolic that Mailey retired; it seemed that he took some of the fun in the game with him. Henceforward cricket was to be the heartless massacre of bowlers by the little batting genius from the New South Wales country town of Bowral, and the equally unfeeling tactical reply of fast bowling directed at the body of the batsmen to an overpopulated leg-side field. Bodyline was six years in the future. The prologue to the drama had still to be enacted in 1928-9 in Australia and 1930 in England.

8. The Coming of Bradman

W. G. Grace's son, Edgar, was quite an athlete. On one occasion he ran second in the local grammar school sports, egged on by his famous parent, who not only yelled his encouragement, but also ran step for step with his offspring over the last 100 yards in the pouring rain. In a paternal keenness for athletics, W.G. had a parallel in Donald George Bradman, whose son was also an accomplished runner; but there were many other points of similarity between the distinguished cricketers. Both men, as batsmen and captains, dominated the world of cricket for long periods of time. The Doctor played his first important game in 1864 and his first Test in 1880; he last trod the first-class field in 1908, latterly saddened by the premature death of his athletic son three years previously. The 'Don' first set foot on the international field at the age of twenty. He was twelve years younger than 'The Old Man' when he made his début in Tests and he was a nonpareil amongst batsmen until, twenty years later, in his own words 'the creaks and groans in his joints made him the best judge of when to retire'.

A regular happening. The 'Don' passes another milestone

Both men were statistical phenomena. Grace registered 126 first-class hundreds and a gross 54,896 runs. In terms of facts and figures, however, even the burly Doctor was outweighed by the diminutive colossus from Down Under: 39 66% of Bradman's innings culminated in a century. The regularity of his hundred habit was almost twice as frequent as that of his nearest rival, fellow Australian, Lindsay Hassett. Bradman remains the only player to have scored 300 runs in a Test match day; in one series he notched 974 runs at an average of 139.14. A single Australian season yielded him 1,690 runs, and when he was bowled by an Eric Hollies wrong 'un in his final innings at The Oval in 1948 for 0, his international average stood at an incredible 99.94 — just a frustrating four runs away from the perfection of batting 100!

Bradman himself stated that comparisons such as that between he and Grace are governed by varying conditions — if not inescapably odious. In his speech on 'A Hundred Years of Test Cricket — Australia versus England' at the Australian Cricket Board Dinner during Melbourne's Centenary Test, Bradman made the point that modern players such as Greg Chappell had to defend stumps which were one inch higher, and twelve per cent wider than those protected by Trumper. Moreover batsmen of the 1977 vintage had to contend with a smaller ball and a more disadvantageous lbw law, even though they did not have to perform on uncovered wickets.

Modestly, Bradman failed to mention that comparisons between himself and the former giants of the game were more than valid. He batted against both the large and small balls. He was playing when the wicket increased in size in 1931. He took guard at the wicket both before and after the lbw law was changed in 1937; and he knew what sticky uncovered wickets were. He had to bat on one in his first Test in 1928. In spite of all of these changing demands, Bradman's triumphal progress remained unchecked. Many deemed him to have failed in 1932-3 during the infamous bodyline series, yet the facts state that at this nadir of his career, he averaged 66.85 per innings and scored 468 runs in eight knocks. Oh for such failure! It was small wonder that the crowds flocked in adulation into the grounds whenever he was batting. Word would travel around the city of his appearance and the turnstiles would begin to click. His fans knew that, like the certainty of death and taxes, Bradman was a short odds 3/1 favourite to score a century at a quick tempo and in an entertaining fashion. His dismissal inevitably produced a depopulation of the outer ground, rivalled only by the glum exodus of Yorkshire crowds in the 1940s and early 1950s when ''Utton was out'.

Bradman first represented Australia in the Brisbane Test of 1928 on the novel venue of the Exhibition Ground. In his previous encounters with Chapman's tourists he had built up an outstanding reputation for himself by scoring 295 runs and only being dismissed twice. The Englishmen, however, at this stage of his development, were still far from convinced that Bradman's technique embodied sufficient text book qualities to make him infallible on all types of wickets. The former England player and Surrey captain, Percy Fender, writing of the Don at the genesis of his Test career, was convinced that he lacked the straight-batted orthodoxy to make him successful on English wickets. One observer of the era commented to the future Prime Minister of Australia, and later to become Sir Robert Menzies, that Bradman was 'frightfully agricultural'. Pragmatist in sport as he was a practical politician, Sir Robert contented himself by remarking: 'Yes, but frightfully fruitful'.

Contrary to early popular belief the Don was not unorthodox in his early days. Former players as expert as Lindsay Hassett, Bradman's successor as captain of his country, are firm in their contention that Bradman's strokes were as correct as those of Trumper. The difference in their eyes between the Boy from Bowral and more mortal players was that his reaction time was like that of boxer Muhammad Ali compared to that of other mundane heavyweights. Bradman did not see the ball earlier than other players; but his response to stimuli was so fast that he was able to position himself and execute cross-batted strokes to balls which would have evinced respectful defence from more conservative players convinced of the limitations of their ability. It is said that a leading Sydney eye specialist once examined Bradman and established that his reaction time was three times faster than that of a normal man. His methods were not agricultural; his judgment and assessment of each delivery was different and uncanny. In justification of this opinion, many of his contemporary players point to the fact that after the Second World War and at a time when Bradman's reactions were slowed by advancing age, he was still statistically successful because he was well served by an orthodox technique which more than compensated for the decline in the acuity of his reflexes.

The supernatural quality of Bradman's batting is exemplified by the tales which are told of his liking for his self-invented pastime of the 'round-up'. A young Victorian appearing for the first time in a pre-war Sheffield Shield game fielded at first slip and was astonished when the Don turned to the keeper, Ben Barnett, and stated his intention of having a 'round-up'. 'What does he mean?' asked the youngster. 'Just wait and see. You will have to chase the first ball', was Barnett's reply. The first delivery was cut delicately past first slip's outstretched hand and the Don thereupon canvassed the whole field in succession; making every player chase a stroke. When one obviously unfit pursuer returned panting from the boundary, Bradman chuckled and said, 'I think we'll give him another'. Whereupon the tortured fieldsman was despatched once again to the very edge of the oval in pursuit of a Bradman drive. There must have been some points of similarity between Victor Trumper and the Don. It was once said of Trumper that he had no style because he was all style. Bradman could not lay claim to an elegance which lay outside the ambit of ruthless efficient savagery, but he did possess the same range of batting versatility as Trumper. I find it hard to sympathize with the alleged opinion of the former England captain, Archie MacLaren, who was once reputed to have seen Bradman amass a large score and then state: 'I wouldn't give tuppence to bat like that'.

It is impossible to identify the inner motivating force behind Bradman's success. The sporting psychologist would probably lean to the opinion that the slender Australian was driven by the motivational factor of independence: the desire to express himself in terms of excellence in a game in which he outstripped his fellows. Bradman's inner fires, however, burned more fiercely than the normal, independently-motivated sportsman. The latter usually discovers a field of proficiency within himself which contrasts with his ineptitude in other spheres. Thereafter he devotes himself with the introverted fanaticism of a long distance runner to his chosen sport. Bradman, however, achieved such heights of concentration in the logical analysis of sport and business that he succeeded in exceptional terms in every task which he faced. He was as accomplished a tennis player as he was a cricketer; at one stage he was torn between the ambitions of playing both games at the highest level. When he abandoned the cricket playing field to devote himself to golf, he reduced his handicap to scratch by assiduous practice. As the leader of a side his success was unspoilt by a series defeat between the years 1936 and 1948. Indeed for twenty years of Test cricket Bradman's presence in the Australian team meant that his country lost only two rubbers and twelve games. As it was in cricket, so it was in business and administration; Bradman's elevation to the knighthood was justified not only by his ability on the cricket field but also by his capability as a stockbroker and Chairman of the Australian Cricket Board of Control.

The single-mindedness of the 'Knight' in pursuit of a goal shut out all other considerations. A touring colleague of Bradman in England recalled to me the time when the Don placed him in an extremely risky fielding position at forward short-leg against a violently aggressive batsman. The expected occurred and the striker, heaving mightily at a slow half-volley on leg-stump, hit the unfortunate close fieldsman on the forehead. As the victim lapsed into unconsciousness he heard the piping voice of Bradman from cover point exhorting some anonymous fieldsman to 'catch it'. Apparently the ball after making solid contact with short-leg's skull, lobbed as a catch towards a neighbouring fieldsman! Concerned to think that a fellow-player should think more of a wicket than his mate's well-being, the suffering short-leg taxed Bradman about his action at a later date. 'Well', said 'Braddles' with frank logic, 'I said it because I realized that we could catch the ball but we had no chance of catching you!'

In some respects, the Bradman syndrome had a deleterious effect on the Australian game and the people around its central personage. His own son could not bear the continuous adulation and comparisons inbuilt into the surname Bradman and changed it. The totality and centrality of the Don's motivating forces was often misunderstood in his playing days; the mellowing years brought greater sympathy but did not completely eradicate the uncompromising memories which were paradoxically allied to unstinting admiration of Bradman as a player and captain. The Australian game suffered with the retirement of Bradman from the active lists. The public, accustomed to the batting fireworks of his era, became listless at the mortal material served up to them as cricket. Crowds diminished as players, seeking to emulate the master without his ability, failed to satisfy them. It was not surprising that the public were momentarily disillusioned; Bradman was a very hard act to follow. Such was his genius that it appears improbable that the game will ever see his like again.

Bradman's achievements in his own time were all the more considerable because of the strength of the opposition with which he had to contend. One of his chief bowling protagonists in the series of 1928-9 was England and Nottinghamshire fast bowler, Harold Larwood, the 24-year-old ex-miner from Nuncargate. Through the ages, the argument has swayed backwards and forwards about who was the best and fastest bowler that cricket has known. Perhaps it was the terrifying Australian, Ernie Jones, who once sent a ball whistling through the beard of W. G. Grace. Opinions vary from Tibby Cotter to his fellow modern-day slinger, Jeff Thomson, and vacillate between England's dark-eyed duet of Tom Richardson and Fred Trueman. One fact remains undisputed throughout the course of all of these arguments: 'Lol' Larwood was amongst the finest exponents of the fast-bowling art.

The scoreboard attendant of many years standing at the Melbourne Cricket Ground is himself a former club cricketer of some distinction, Joe Kinnear. For Joe, Larwood was poetry in flannels seen from his scoreboard eyrie at square leg. He possessed a fluid quality which denied effort and was so accurate that Joe avows that he could 'pitch the ball on a sixpence'. A testimony to Larwood's speed was given to me by George Duckworth, the raucous-voiced England wicketkeeper of the 1928-9 tour and later the baggage-man and the beloved 'Admiral' of M.C.C. touring teams. Lol's pace was such that, standing twenty yards behind the batsman's wicket, George still bruised his hands in taking the Nottinghamshire man's thunderbolts. Finally the keeper had to insert thin slices of steak between his inner gloves and the palm of his hands to give his tender members the black-eye treatment. The ploy worked, but on a hot day on the Sydney and Melbourne Cricket Grounds it was difficult to see George's gloves for the swarm of flies which enveloped them! He told me that the slip fieldsmen were not too keen to come too close to him as the day wore on and the meat lost its freshness.

Making his début against Australia in Brisbane on 30 November 1928, was a certain W. R. Hammond. Hammond had previously appeared for England against South Africa and the West Indies, but without startling success. In his first series against Australia he was to astonish the cricket world by establishing what was to prove a three-year record by scoring 905 runs in five matches at an average of 113.12. For many, Hammond was the acme of elegance on the drive; in his first rubber against the old enemy he notched two double centuries and in the same Adelaide Test, two hundreds. Hammond's main source of runs was the off-side and the principal scenes of his triumphs were the hard wickets of Australia. In later years the Australian bowlers learned how to shackle his scoring by pitching on Hammond's leg-stump, but

The elegance of Wally Hammond's off-drive

even this tactic was a palliative rather than a remedy for Australia's double-century problem.

How good a player was Hammond? An illustration of the batsman's natural talents can be gained from an anecdote recounted about an episode during one of Gloucestershire's county seasons. It was said that, in spite of an easy victory for his side because of a brilliant Hammond innings and an accomplished spell of off-spin bowling on a spiteful wicket from the lanky England slow bowler, Tom Goddard, skipper Hammond was still far from satisfied with his bowler's performance. He transmitted his opinion to Goddard, who thereupon challenged Hammond to face him on the same turning wicket which had seen the end of the match only minutes previously. Not only did Hammond take up Goddard's challenge but he expressed his willingness to bat with the edge ratner than the face of the bat! The two duelists went back out on to the centre of the ground and Hammond proceeded to fulfil his side of the bargain in spite of the turning, lifting ball for a period of three or four overs.

In the First Test of 1928-9 at the Brisbane Showground, England paraded the forces of Hammond, Larwood, Hendren and the slow left-hand bowler, Somerset's 'Farmer' White. Tate, the indefatigable, opened the attack with Larwood and in the gully stood Percy Chapman, the inspirational leader, with ham-like, adhesive hands. By contrast, the Australian combination lacked the youthful freshness of their opponents. Gregory at thirty-three was the youngest of their bowlers; their slow left-hand bowler, Ironmonger, was making his début at an age approaching forty-six. It was in this match that Gregory's suspect knee finally gave way after 4 overs in England's first innings and eight years of joint-jarring international service. He was reputed to have left the field with tears in his eyes, knowing that his Test career was over. With batsman Kelleway stricken with food poisoning and Australia being caught on a wet wicket in their last knock, their luck deserted them. Larwood scored 107 runs in the match and captured 8/62. This contribution and 169 from Patsy Hendren sent Australia to defeat by 657 runs. It was the largest victory margin ever recorded in Tests in terms of runs. Bradman was never to forget it.

Misfortune continued to dog Ryder's side in the second encounter. Larwood broke Ponsford's hand, and he took no further part in the series; but the home selectors compounded ill-luck with bad judgment and omitted Bradman in favour of Richardson—and even dared to take such drastic action for a game played before Bradman's home Sydney crowd. Continuing their policy of encouraging youth, Australia chose the 46-year-old Victorian off-spinner, Blackie, and their spin trio of Grimmett, Ironmonger and Blackie could point to an aggregate age of 129 years! After being out of cricket for a month due to being hit on the nose by controversial West Australian fast bowler, Ron Halcombe, Geary returned to the Test fold to capture 7 wickets and score 74 runs. Woodfull and Hendry revived Australian hopes with second innings centuries, but this was a mere bagatelle against Hammond's massive 251 and England's first innings total of 636. Once more the home side lost by 8 wickets. An unusual feature of this Sydney game was the dis-

An unusual rôle for Bradman — twelfth man in the Second Test 1928-9

missal of Kippax in Australia's first innings. Years afterwards, one of the officiating umpires, George Hele, recounted the story to me. Apparently a Geary delivery passed down the leg-side and rebounded from keeper Duckworth's pads to dislodge the bails. The incident occurred so quickly that most of the England side were under the impression that the ball had touched the batsman's leg-stump. Hele refused the ensuing claim, but Jack Hobbs persisted and referred the matter to the square-leg umpire, Dave Elder. The latter had only seen the end result of the chain reaction and after a long hesitation gave Kippax out, forgetting that only the umpire at the bowler's end could hand down such a decision! Travelling home together in the train that evening, George and Dave hammered out the issue, much to Elder's mortification. He held his head in his hands, whilst, oblivious to Elder's presence, the man in the seat opposite expounded to all and sundry in the carriage what he would do if he could lay his hands on Dave Elder!

George Duckworth

The Third Test in Melbourne was a closer and more distinguished affair with England winning by only three wickets. After Woodfull, Kippax, Bradman and Ryder had each scored centuries and England had replied through another double hundred from Hammond, the tourists found themselves in an invidious position on the sixth day of the game. They required 332 runs for victory and, with rain having fallen overnight, the game was resumed an hour late under a hot sun and on a real Melbourne 'sticky dog'. Melbourne Cricket Club secretary and former Test notable, Hugh Trumble, met Douglas Jardine as he strolled around the ground before play began. He was profuse in his sympathy, stating that the match would be over before tea and England would be lucky if they could accumulate 100 runs. In fact, at tea the two openers, Hobbs and Sutcliffe, were still together with 78 priceless runs on the board! Years afterwards Sutcliffe passed the opinion that England won the match by pure bluff. He and Hobbs repeatedly took hard knocks on the body, with moans of, 'Well bowled', thus conveying the impression that they were in dire trouble against the delivery pitching in line with their bodies and calculated to produce short-leg catches. Blackie, Oxenham and A'Beckett were duped into not bowling at the wicket, and ironically, Ironmonger, the orthodox leg-spinner who could have bowled out the batsmen as quickly as they came in, languished as twelfth man in the pavilion. On the advice of Hobbs, the stoic Jardine was promoted in the order to number three to continue the illusion of difficulty and he and Sutcliffe survived the day on an improving wicket. To the end of his career Sutcliffe deemed his subsequent 135 the best innings he ever played and when he was finally dismissed England were only 14 short of their goal.

In Adelaide, Chapman's side won by an even narrower margin — only 12 pulsating runs. The Test witnessed the auspicious beginning of the tragic career of Archie Jackson, the New South Wales prodigy whom many experts believe would have rivalled Bradman in scoring efficiency and outstripped him in elegance. At the tender age of nineteen years and 152 days, Jackson compiled 164 on his début and thus became the youngest player in Anglo-Australian contests to score a

Archie Jackson

century on his first appearance. He failed by only two runs to register the highest Australian maiden total. Consumption claimed the gentle Archie at the age of twenty-three after only eight Tests. As he lay dying in his hospital bed, he thought of his former opponent, Harold Larwood, during the trying bodyline times of 1932-3. He sent Lol a telegram of sympathy and congratulations which the recipient still treasures to this day.

It was indicative of the batting strength of the tourists that they could include a reserve as able as Maurice Leyland. The pugnacious Yorkshire left-hander immediately responded to the challenge by registering a débutant double of 137 and 53. Phil Mead, of Hampshire renown, played in the First Test of the rubber and, in spite of the fact that he scored 73, did not merit consideration for the next four matches. Hobbs notched his 12th and last hundred against Australia in this Melbourne clash and Hendren reached 95; but their efforts were in vain. In a marathon eight-day endurance Test, the tourists were trapped on a damp wicket in their second innings and collapsed for 257 against the pace of Tim Wall, who captured 9 wickets in the first of his eighteen Tests for Australia. Ryder's unbeaten 57 steered his side home to a 5-wicket victory in what was to prove his final appearance for his country. A selector himself, rumour had it that his colleagues were considering his replacement as he guided his side to this final consolation prize in an otherwise disastrous series. He was dropped at the end of the 1929-30 Australian season. It was said that his co-selectors chose the 1930 touring side whilst he was on the field scoring a century against New South Wales and informed Ryder of his omission when he was out. To the end of his days Ryder never commented on his cavalier dismissal from international circles. He was at the time almost forty years old and must have considered that his race in Tests was almost run. The prisoners in Melbourne's Pentridge gaol thought otherwise and rioted in protest!

In the course of his international career Ryder scored 1,060 runs against England at an average of 44.16. For his native state of Victoria he returned 9,657 runs at a mean figure of 45 and captured 150 wickets with his lofty and lively medium-pace. His record for his local club of Collingwood embraced seventy-one years of service and earned him the nickname of the 'King' of that Melbourne suburb. Strangely enough, Jack Ryder's services to cricket were virtually just beginning when he retired from the active list. He had yet to contribute more than forty years of his life on Australian and Victorian selection committees and as vice-president of the Victorian Cricket Association. He was still to be seen, like his English counterpart, Harry Altham, at club and school nets, encouraging youngsters to drive off the front foot, even when he was in his seventies. A teetotaller to the end of his days, like all of the Australian captains between the wars except two, he loved to refer to himself as 'one of the lemonade brigade'. It was therefore a grand climacteric to a wonderful life that Jack Ryder survived to witness the Centenary Test in Melbourne, celebrating a hundred years of Test cricket which began only twelve years before he was born.

Ryder's successor to the Australian captaincy crown was Bill Wood

112

full: a man who was designated by his contemporaries as 'The Unbowlable'. The Methodist schoolmaster from Ballarat earned his soubriquet. In the last Test match against England in 1929 he was bowled by Hammond for 35; it was the first time in twenty-seven months that his stumps had been hit. It was appropriate that a new 31-year-old leader should take the helm at this stage. Australia was on the verge of a bumper crop of young cricketing talent and needed fresh inspiration. Bradman had already made his mark on Test cricket and it was auspicious that playing for the Southern Districts of New South Wales against Chapman's team was a certain S. J. McCabe, a player who was to bring a new dimension into attacking cricket in the Sydney Test of 1932.

Jack Ryder

Bradman arrived in England in 1930 at the age of twenty-one, hailed as the 'boy wonder' and looking for new cricket fields to conquer. There were Doubting Thomases, who, having seen him play in Australia, were of the opinion that the movement of the ball off the wicket would find him out and that he would not succeed. Bradman asked them to reconsider their verdict by netting 974 runs in the rubber at an average of 139.14. Only in the Old Trafford Test did he fail to score a century. Leeds was the scene of his record score of 334. At Lords the England bowlers suffered to the tune of 254 and The Oval saw him compile a crushing 232. Bradman more than doubled the Test aggregate of any other batsman in either side and made his batting supernumeraries seem almost superfluous. The series went Australia's way by the margin of two Tests to one. It was not surprising, since many of the England contingent who visited Australia two years previously were nearing retirement. Hobbs at forty-seven was playing in his last Ashes contest; Hendren was forty-one, George Geary a greybeard thirty-six for a fast bowler, and Maurice Tate thirty-five. Tate was destined to survive another tour to Australia but did not appear in a Test in 1932-3.

The Trent Bridge Test luckily went England's way by 93 runs. The home side's victory was assured by a man who was not even playing in the match. On the final day of play Australia were 3/198. Bradman was batting at number three for the first time in Tests, together with McCabe, and only 231 runs were needed for victory in four hours. It was an easy task for such brilliance and it was made all the easier by the absence of Larwood from his home field because of an upset stomach. Fielding in his stead was an unknown Nottinghamshire groundstaff player who was not even a regular county player, but an excellent fieldsman; his name was Copley. He was stationed at mid-on when McCabe, who needed a single for his half-century, struck Tate hard in his direction. Falling forward Copley brought off a spectacular catch which Larwood, had he been on the field, could never have imitated. That catch became the young player's sole claim to cricketing fame and it won the match for England in spite of Bradman's 131.

The rubber was squared when Australia won the Lords game by 7 wickets. Duleepsinhji emulated the century achievement of his uncle Ranjitsinhji by notching 173 on his first appearance in a Test. This second highest débutant total was said to have afforded Duleep's relative a great deal of pleasure and was doubtless the topic of many conversations when Duleep became Indian High Commissioner in Canberra. Neither Duleep nor Chapman's 121 could save England from Bradman. His 254 eclipsed Murdoch's previous best of 211 and it was an eloquent commentary on his mastery that he and Australia's other century scorer, Woodfull, added a joint 231 in 154 minutes. It was a case of woe to Duckworth, the England keeper, who missed stumping Bradman off Robins when he was 52.

Tip Foster's record total of 287 was the next hurdle for Bradman to take in his stride in this, his *annus mirabilis*. The 26-year-old Test top score was surpassed by the Australian prodigy in the next game at Leeds. Archie Jackson succumbed to the combination of Tate and the new ball in the first over of the match. To Bradman therefore fell the task of setting the Australian innings on a firm footing. The extent to which he succeeded can be gauged from the fact that he scored 105 runs before lunch, 115 between lunch and tea, and 89 in the last session of play; at stumps he was unbeaten on 309 and Australia had scored at over 70 an hour to be 3/458! Bradman was finally caught behind the wicket off Tate for 334: a record score which was to stand at the top of the honours list until Hutton surpassed it in 1938. The significant feature about the comparison between Hutton's eventual 364 and Brad-

Bradman is caught behind the wicket by Duckworth for his record 334. Leeds Test 1930

man's 334 was that the Englishman's innings occupied over thirteen hours—Bradman's knock ended six and a half hours after he faced his first ball! Even Australia's mammoth score of 566 could not win them the Leeds Test: a downpour on the third day saved England.

A similar soggy fate awaited the inconclusive Old Trafford game, where Bradman, who was apparently ill, had his unique failure in the rubber. Thus the final game at The Oval decided the issue of the series —and Bradman decided The Oval Test by compiling 232 in his single innings. The England keeper, Duckworth had an unfortunate match, missing Bradman, Woodfull and Ponsford, who between them amassed 396 runs. Bradman and Jackson added a combined 243 for the fourth wicket and victory went Australia's way by an innings after the slow-medium left-hander, Hornibrook had captured 7/92 on a rain-affected pitch.

Fast bowler, Harold Larwood, returned the unflattering figures of 1/132; but on one occasion he made a ball rise abruptly to strike Bradman on the chest. As a result of this painful blow, the batsman modified his style against the speedster and backed away to a position outside the leg-stump. The Australian champion's reaction to the lifting ball was noted and from these small beginnings came the tactic which, two years later, was to gain notoriety in the cricketing world as bodyline. Speaking to me years later about the acrimonious 1932-3 M.C.C. tour of Australia, wicketkeeper George Duckworth left no doubt that the strategy of fast leg theory was invented exclusively to combat the prolific scoring of Bradman. When I asked Duckworth why the bodyline weapon was used on the cricket field, he merely replied that I must not think that the touring side of 1932-3 went 14,000 miles 'just to give that little bloke a hand for three days!'

9. Bodyline and the Path to Total War

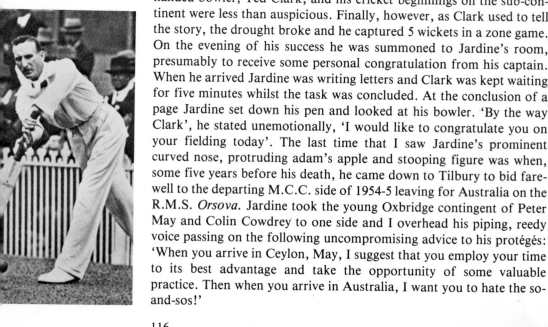

Douglas Jardine

The Australian bodyline season of 1932-3 was a tragic coincidence. It was sheer chance that the blight of Bradman afflicted English cricket and produced a desperate situation which demanded a desperate remedy. There was a large slice of ill-fortune in the fact that England possessed the cricketing brains of F. R. Foster to advise Jardine on the extension of his own former fast skills as a left-handed bowler around the wicket into a leg-side assault on the batsman. It was pure luck that in Jardine, Larwood and Voce, England were endowed with an intransigent captain determined to implement the policy, and two great fast bowlers accurate and swift enough to transform fast leg theory into a weapon of deadly proportions.

There is no doubting that Jardine was a martinet of a captain. During the English winter following the bodyline crisis, Jardine led an M.C.C. party to India. In his side was the Northamptonshire fast left-handed bowler, Ted Clark, and his cricket beginnings on the sub-continent were less than auspicious. Finally, however, as Clark used to tell the story, the drought broke and he captured 5 wickets in a zone game. On the evening of his success he was summoned to Jardine's room, presumably to receive some personal congratulation from his captain. When he arrived Jardine was writing letters and Clark was kept waiting for five minutes whilst the task was concluded. At the conclusion of a page Jardine set down his pen and looked at his bowler. 'By the way Clark', he stated unemotionally, 'I would like to congratulate you on your fielding today'. The last time that I saw Jardine's prominent curved nose, protruding adam's apple and stooping figure was when, some five years before his death, he came down to Tilbury to bid farewell to the departing M.C.C. side of 1954-5 leaving for Australia on the R.M.S. *Orsova*. Jardine took the young Oxbridge contingent of Peter May and Colin Cowdrey to one side and I overhead his piping, reedy voice passing on the following uncompromising advice to his protégés: 'When you arrive in Ceylon, May, I suggest that you employ your time to its best advantage and take the opportunity of some valuable practice. Then when you arrive in Australia, I want you to hate the so-and-sos!'

116

So it was that England in 1932 found themselves in possession of the perfect justification for bodyline in Bradman; they were led by the uncompromising general in Jardine and they could call upon the ideal instruments to implement the policy—Larwood and Voce. The inspiration for the strategy appears to have originated in Jardine's own brain as a result of Bradman's hesitancy against Larwood at The Oval in 1930. He convened an informal meeting at the Piccadilly Hotel in the summer of 1932. It was there that Jardine and his fellow-spirit, the former skipper of England and the captain of the two fast bowlers' county of Nottinghamshire, Arthur Carr, discussed the feasibility of employing fast leg theory against Bradman during the approaching winter. In the light of the previous successes of bowlers such as Barnes and Foster in 1911-12, Root in 1926 and Hirst in 1909 against Australia, Jardine decided to commit himself to the tactic and he began to drop into F. R. Foster's St James's flat to discuss the field placements which the fast left-hander employed so successfully in Australia twenty-one years earlier. The die was apparently cast and Larwood and Voce were to be commanded to bowl short-pitched deliveries at express speed in line with the batsman's body and leg-stump to a packed on-side field.

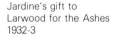
Bill Voce in action

It is important to realize the role played by Larwood and Voce in the unfolding saga of bodyline. They were professional players under the command of an amateur skipper; like the troops in the line when they were ordered, they obeyed under the penalty of losing their cricketing jobs. 'Gubby' Allen was a fast-bowling amateur in Jardine's touring party and disagreed with the policy of his leader; he refused to bowl leg theory and as a person who was not dependent on the game for a livelihood, he could afford the luxury of his decision—and survive. Larwood became a vilified servant in the cricketing dispute which almost alienated a dominion. He did precisely as he was told with unerring accuracy; and for that he was booed and counted out by crowds throughout the length and breadth of Australia. In Adelaide, Larwood told me he was certain that the crowd was going to invade the pitch and attack the England players after Woodfull and Oldfield were injured. So concerned was the fast bowler that he turned to the wicket-keeper Les Ames and said: 'If they come over the fence at us, you take the leg-stump for protection, I'll take the middle'. One person never accused Larwood of anything but obedience: his captain Jardine. Today one of Larwood's most prized possessions is a piece of inscribed silverware—an ashtray bearing the words: 'To Harold for the Ashes 1932-3. From a grateful skipper'.

Larwood was the martyr of bodyline. Jardine survived to play against the West Indies in England and captain a touring side to India. 'Lol', his faithful handservant, walked off the Sydney Cricket Ground with a broken bone in his foot, having accomplished his series-winning task of taking 33 wickets at an average of 19.51. He never played for his country again, even though he continued to play first-class cricket until the outbreak of the Second World War. The seismic tremors of fast leg theory were felt around the world and were not easily forgotten. Larwood returned early as a wounded soldier from his Australian campaign; the press met his ship at Port Said and his own county

Jardine's gift to Larwood for the Ashes 1932-3

captain, Arthur Carr, even travelled to Suez to forestall the reporters and warn Larwood. The fast bowler quickly made it evident through the media that he was unrepentant for his actions. He was equally adamant about his future approach to fast leg theory at a time when new laws against the tactic were being mooted and touring sides were seeking guarantees that it would not be employed against them. His bitterness at his treatment in Australia welled to the surface in a series of newspaper articles and he never took the field against another Australian team. It is perhaps one of the greatest tributes to cricket's powers of friendly healing that Harold Larwood was subsequently persuaded by his former opponent, journalist Jack Fingleton, to emigrate with his family to Australia. It was understandable, however, that Larwood was reticent about leaving his Kingsford home on the occasion of the Centenary Test, to face the Australian public who were the descendants of his vociferous critics in 1932-3.

Harold Larwood today is almost bald, bespectacled, and has lost much of the immense miner's shoulder strength which made him a venomous proposition at the bowling crease. Even when he was at his physical prime in 1932-3, however, his previous record of 22 wickets in two series did not hint at the avalanche of victims which was to follow. Larwood's triumph was almost as unexpected as the bodyline controversy itself.

The irony of the empire-shaking 1932-3 tour was that it began in a blaze of public goodwill. Jardine's manager, Pelham Warner, himself twice a former touring captain, stated in an interview with R. W. E. Wilmot of the *Australasian*:

I believe that cricket has been a great factor in Empire building. It has brought peoples all over the world into closer touch, and has enabled them to understand one another. The very word cricket has become a synonym for all that is true and honest. To say 'that is not cricket' implies something underhand, something not in keeping with the best ideals. There is no game which calls forth so many fine attributes, which makes so many demands on its votaries, and, that being so, all who love it as players, or officials, or spectators must be careful lest anything they do should do it harm. An incautious attitude or gesture in the field, a lack of consideration in the committee room and a failure to see the other side's point of view, a hasty judgment by an onlooker, and a misconstruction of an incident, may cause trouble and misunderstanding which could and should be avoided.

'Plum' Warner as manager of Jardine's touring party

This was a warning which proved to be prophetic in the light of the consequences of Jardine's tour.

Even Jardine's multicoloured Harlequin cap, which became the object of detestation as the series wore on, gained a modicum of praise in the preliminaries. Warner was also a Harlequin and spoke of his headgear as a mascot: 'And even now I wear it, if only having a knock at practice. Jardine wears his too, in all modesty, because it reminds him of the great players who wore it before him. It is not only a headgear but an inspiration. It is part of himself'. The cap became re-

118

cognized as part of the detested leader whom the Australians called 'Sardine' and hissed on sight.

'Plum' Warner's subsequent quote to Wilmot touched the heights of prophetic irony in the light of the developing Australian reaction during the bodyline winter. The England manager went on to say:

> With two men like Douglas Jardine and W. M. Woodfull as the respective leaders, the best traditions of the game will be in safe keeping. Each is a keen sportsman and is imbued with a sense of responsibility. In all the long series of Tests we have had what have been described as 'incidents' and these are inseparable from the game; but never has there been a suspicion of unfair play, or of one side endeavouring to take undue advantage of the other. In all the games that have been played one would think that all the possible happenings would have been disclosed and discovered, but every now and again something occurs which is quite unexpected and is hard to explain. Then must all concerned be patient and view the position fairly. The responsibility is on us all and we must be conscious of it. This game of cricket is too great, too important, to be spoiled by any untoward act, and I am keen to see the present tour an object lesson in fair play all round. Cricket is a happy, friendly game.

Warner's statement in the *Australasian* appeared on 12 November 1932. His admonitions about possible incidents and his plea for patience make one wonder whether he had a vague suspicion about what might happen when Jardine uncovered his secret weapon of fast leg theory in the Tests. If there were niggling doubts about his captain's intentions and their repercussions they were substantiated to the full when, twenty days later, Larwood delivered the first ball in the Sydney Test. Just over two months after this first game, the Australian Board of Control cabled to the Marylebone Cricket Club that, in their opinion, bodyline bowling, the accepted tactic of Jardine and his men, was unsportsmanlike.

From the outset, the atmosphere of the rubber smacked of the unorthodox. Before the first clash in Sydney, Bradman, in defiance of a Board of Control edict, signed a contract to write for a newspaper. He subsequently withdrew from the arrangement but, ironically, was discovered to be unfit on the eve of the match. The game proved to be a triumph for Larwood and England; the fast bowler claimed 10 wickets and his side steamrollered home to victory by the same margin as Larwood's return. The Nawab of Pataudi crawled at a snail's pace to a century on his maiden appearance for his adopted country. He was both supported and outshone by Sutcliffe and Hammond who notched 194 and 112 respectively. Strangely, however, it was not an England batsman who captured the hearts and the imagination of the Sydney Hill on those early December days. Rather it was the quicksilver batting of Stan McCabe, the boy from southern New South Wales, who was to cheer the hearts of all who met him as a player or Sydney sports store proprietor, and who was to die sadly in a cliff fall in 1968. Against the spears of bodyline, McCabe advanced to cut and hook his way to an

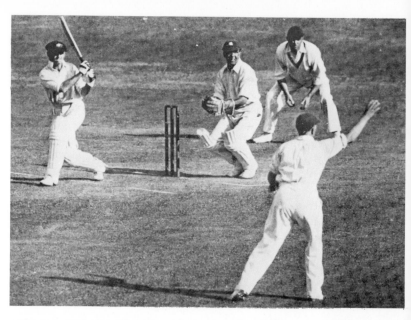

McCabe en route to his brilliant 187 in Sydney

Bradman pulls Bowes on to his stumps first ball. Melbourne 1932-3

unbeaten 187. To this day, this innings is widely regarded as the best played against fast leg theory. Like many of McCabe's knocks, its brilliance dazzled the eye without conveying an impression of anything but absolute surety. In one partnership of 129 with Richardson, McCabe contributed all but 49 runs and his eventual tally represented more than fifty per cent of the Australian first innings total.

Australia gained her sweet revenge in Melbourne by the reputedly unlucky Nelsonic total of 111 runs. Jardine and his selection committee, carried away by illusions of fast bowling grandeur, omitted to select a slow bowler and on a crumbling wicket O'Reilly snared 10 wickets with his medium-paced leg-spinners. Yorkshire fast bowler, the bespectacled Bill Bowes, replaced his fellow 'tyke', left-hand spinner Verity, in the England line-up and claimed the prize wicket of Bradman with the first ball which the Don received. Writing as a journalist in later years, Bowes described how Bradman walked to the wicket amidst a tumultuous reception, took guard and, before the first ball was bowled to him, decided that it would be a bouncer which he would pull. In fact the delivery was of fuller length, though it was still almost a long hop, and Bradman, changing his stroke too late, pulled the ball on to his stumps. The silence was deafening as nought went up on the scoreboard against Bradman's name, and thousands of people left the Melbourne Cricket Ground after one of their briefest visits to a Test match. The Don made amends in his second appearance by recording a remarkable 103 not out in his side's mediocre 191. It was in this innings that Bradman displayed the innovative extremes to which he would go to combat a specific challenge. Against the rearing leg-side deliveries of Larwood and Voce, he adopted the unusual riposte of walking away outside the leg-stump and slashing their fastest deliveries through the wide open spaces in the off-side field. It was perhaps fortunate for the Australian star batsman that the Melbourne wicket for this encounter was at its slowest.

The Third Test began in Adelaide on 13 January 1933 and resulted in a victory for Jardine's XI by 338 runs. The data of the game, however, was as insignificant as the fact that Paynter was introduced into the side for Pataudi, the batsman who had registered a century only two games previously. The true import of the game lay in the ignoble crisis of bodyline which it produced. Nemesis pervaded the normal ecclesastical calm of the Adelaide Oval, for the two balls which injured the Australian captain Woodfull and his keeper Oldfield, and shattered the calm of the cricketing world, were directed at the line of the stumps rather than the batsman's body. Whilst compiling 22 in Australia's reply of 222·to England's 341, Woodfull was struck over the heart by Larwood and upon returning to the dressing-room in a distressed state after his dismissal, he was reputed to have remaked to the visiting and commiserating England Manager, 'Plum' Warner, that, whilst there were two sides on the field, there was only one 'playing cricket'. The comment reached the ears of the press. It was not a surprising leak since there were many press connections in both teams, but it placed the Australian Board of Control in the invidious position of having to back up their captain with action or back down.

Oldfield, by no means a 'rabbit' with the bat, scored 41 before deflecting a short Larwood delivery on to his head whilst attempting to pull. It was this latter incident which so incited the crowd that the bowler himself was certain that they were about to invade the playing area to exact retribution. Oldfield, the darling of the spectators, took no further part in the game; but an equally provoking factor in the near-riot was the action of Jardine subsequent to the injury to Woodfull. Before his heart-stopping thunderbolt, Larwood's field placement had been perfectly orthodox. No sooner had Woodfull partially

Larwood's 'bodyline' field against Bill Woodfull

recovered from his T.K.O., however, and been set upon his feet again, than the England captain with one imperious wave of his hand motioned his men into the threatening, leg-side phalanx of a bodyline field! His action was tantamount to showing a red rag to thirty thousand bulls who were ready to charge.

Woodfull carried his bat through Australia's second innings of 193 for a courageous 73, but his cricketing prowess could not compensate for his previously unguarded remark. The Board of Control's hand was forced and whilst, to their credit, they supported their captain to the hilt, they compounded Woodfull's initial error of judgment with a second diplomatic mistake. Meeting on 18 January they despatched a cable on the subject of bodyline to the governing body of English cricket in London, the Marylebone Cricket Club. Since the telegram contained the unfortunate word 'unsportsmanlike', it provoked a predictable and unsympathetic response.

The body of the Australian Board of Control's cable read:

> Bodyline bowling has assumed such proportions as to menace the best interests of the game, making protection of the body by the batsmen the main consideration. This is causing intensely bitter feeling between the players, as well as injury. It is our opinion it is unsportsmanlike. Unless stopped at once, it is likely to upset the friendly relations existing between Australia and England.

On 23 January, the telegraph wires almost made the Indian Ocean boil as the reply was despatched from London:

> We, Marylebone Cricket Club, deplore your cable. We deprecate your opinion that there has been unsportsmanlike play. We have fullest confidence in captain, team and managers, and are convinced that they would do nothing to infringe either the laws of cricket or the spirit of the game. We have no evidence that our confidence has been misplaced. Much as we regret accidents to Woodfull and Oldfield, we understand that in neither case was the bowler to blame.
>
> If the Australian Board of Control wish to propose a new law or rule, it shall receive our careful consideration in due course. We hope the situation is now not as serious as your cable would seem to indicate, but if it is such as to jeopardize the good relations between English and Australian cricketers and you consider it desirable to cancel the remainder of the programme, we would consent but with great reluctance.

Woodfull is struck by a Larwood bouncer. Adelaide Test 1932-3

Nothing was further from the Australian Board's wishes than the cancellation of a tour which, whilst it was a diplomatic headache, proved to be a financial bonanza. Thus it was that they hurriedly denied their desire to send Jardine's side home with a flea in their collective ear, yet at the same time stuck to their principles on a subject about which they were sure, and their English counterparts totally ignorant. They transmitted the final important telegram in the exchange:

> We do not regard the sportsmanship of your side as being in question. Our position was fully considered at the recent Sydney meeting

and is as indicated in our cable of January 20th. It is the particular class of bowling referred to therein which we consider is not in the best interest of cricket and in this view we understand we are supported by many eminent English cricketers. We join heartily with you in hoping the remaining Tests will be played with the traditional good feelings.

To be fair to all parties in the 1932-3 controversy, these express exchanges must be placed in their proper context and perspective. It is true that the initial Australian cable lacked diplomacy; but it is equally valid to say that the M.C.C. from a distance of 14,000 miles had no correct appreciation of the tactic, the climate of opinion in Australia, and the deadly accurate efficiency with which Larwood and Voce carried into practice the theories of their captain. Only a few months later when English county cricket experienced the trauma of Nottinghamshire bodyline, there was a very swift change in the M.C.C. stance, and bowling aimed at the batsman standing clear of his wicket was outlawed. No stigma for the tactic attached to either Larwood or Voce. They were merely carrying out the instructions of a captain who was intent on reducing the Bradman threat to normal scoring standards. Indeed it is an eloquent commentary on the fairness of Larwood and Voce that in spite of the bodyline ploy, they still contrived to capture 23 of their joint 48 wickets in the series by means of lbw and bowled decisions. Woodfull's role in this drama remained that of a Methodist man of principle; there would be no retaliation and no Australian bodyline policy. Indeed, fast bowler 'Bull' Alexander, introduced into the Australian side for the Final Test, was refused permission to experiment in even the most tentative fashion in the leg-side direction.

In spite of the fact that Larwood was a mere tool in the fashioning of Jardine's master plan, the bodyline series proved to be his condemnation to Test oblivion. The fast bowler broke a small bone in his left foot during the Fifth Test in Sydney. As he limped into the shadows of the pavilion, there were few in the crowd or on the field who realized that this star of the 1932-3 series with 33 wickets to his credit, would never more appear in Tests and never again play against Australia.

Both Larwood and his Nottinghamshire skipper, Carr, later refused to give assurances that fast leg theory would not be used against the touring Australians of 1934. In spite of a confrontation between the Nottinghamshire authorities and the public supporters of Carr and Larwood, the fast bowler was omitted from the county team to play Woodfull's side on the pretext of a leg injury. For another six years Larwood played for his midland county, though he never again reached the pinnacles of pace to which he ascended in 1932-3; he never bowled another ball against an Australian batsman or played for England. After the Second World War, he retired to the obscurity of a small Blackpool sweet shop and so shunned the limelight that he shied at the prospect of advertising his name above his door.

The villain of the 1932-3 melodrama in Australian eyes, Jardine, obviously had a better agent than Larwood, for he obtained other roles on the Test stage. In 1933 he led England against Grant's West Indian tourists and faced with such unflinching stoicism the black bodyline of Constantine and Martindale that he scored 127 at Old Trafford. In the following winter he took an M.C.C. side to India; but as far as Australians were concerned, Jardine remained to the end of his days unrepentant about bodyline, and unyielding, inflexible and unforgiving towards his former opponents. He would not take up the cudgels against Woodfull's 1934 side but preferred instead to report the series for the London *Evening Standard*.

The final two Tests of the 1932-3 rubber saw England maintain the psychological and cricketing dominance which they had fully asserted in Adelaide. In Brisbane, victory came their way by 6 wickets in the first international played on the Woolloongabba Ground. The tourists' win was not as comfortable as the final margin suggested. In reply to Australia's first innings score of 340, England were at one stage 5/198, with their next batsman Eddie Paynter in hospital with tonsillitis. Rebuked by his martinet skipper for not revealing his sickness before the match, Paynter rose like a Lancashire gamecock from his sickbed to score 83 and steer his team to a first innings lead of 16. When Australia collapsed in their second batting attempt for 175, the Yorkshire left-hander, Maurice Leyland guided his side home with an invaluable 86.

At this stage the Australian camp was far from united and it was rumoured several of the home players had been summoned before the Board of Control to answer unspecified charges of an unknown origin of misbehaviour off the field. The defeat of Woodfull's XI in Sydney by 8 wickets came therefore as no surprise. The Australian batsmen performed creditably enough in their first innings, accumulating 435 through the agency of Darling's 85, an innings of 73 from McCabe and a plucky 61 from Victorian left-hander, Leo O'Brien, a state boxing champion, who combatted Larwood's fire with raw physical courage. Hammond's century and a 98 from the rogue bat of Larwood, who strayed into the higher order as nightwatchman, lifted England to 454. When Verity's spin yielded a personal return of 5/33 and tumbled Australia out for another second innings failure of 182, Jardine opened the England innings, scored an unbeaten and disdainful 75, and rang down the curtain on a drama in which he filled the roles of author, director and leading actor.

Larwood's score of 98 was the nearest he ever approached to a Test hundred; many onlookers believed it to be the unluckiest 90 which they ever saw on the international arena. The English fast bowler was eventually caught at mid-on by the worst fieldsman in the Australian side, the 49-year-old Ironmonger, off the relieving Adelaide off-spinner, Lee. For Larwood it was a darkly humorous finale to one of the unfunniest episodes in cricket history.

When the ship bearing the Australian touring side and its Taswegian manager, Harold Bushby, docked in England in 1934, bodyline tactics had not yet been outlawed. Legislation to protect the batsman standing clear of his wicket was not introduced until November of that year. Every county cricketer in England, however, and the man in the street were now more acquainted with the perils of fast leg theory than they had been when Jardine introduced it to Australia. The West Indian fast bowlers had demonstrated its dangers in the previous season's tour of the U.K. and batsmen all over the country had received their fair share of bruises at the whirling hands of enthusiastic fast bowlers. A radically divided consensus of cricket opinion frowned marginally on the concept, and democratic acceptance dubbed it a taboo procedure to be banned by autocratic means. Fast bowler Harold Larwood was a puzzled man. He could not reconcile himself to the realization that bodyline was acceptable in the eyes of the M.C.C. in March 1933, yet totally illegal and unacceptable to the legislators in April 1934. His refusal to accept the M.C.C. volte-face set him on the path to international exile.

O'Reilly's quick leg-spinners won the First Nottingham Test for Australia; his 11-wicket performance eclipsed even the figures of Essex fast bowler, Ken Farnes, whose height, bounce and movement off the wicket yielded him 10/179 in the match. Significantly for Australia's fortunes on the tour, their two nonpareil leg-spinners, Grimmett and O'Reilly moved smoothly and immediately into effective partnership, working in ideal harness; in England's first innings total of 268, Grimmett captured 5/81—figures which were perfectly complemented by O'Reilly's return of 7/54 in the home side's second knock of 141. McCabe completed a fine double 65 and 88 in Australia's scores of 374 and 8/273 declared. But the man who captured the imagination of cricket historians was Arthur Chipperfield, who scored 99 in his first Test. At lunch-time on the second day the diminutive Australian was not out and one short of his century. That lunch must have been a meal of stomach-knotting tension for him, rendered completely indigestible by his falling to the first ball after the interval! Coincidentally, when the next Anglo-Australian game was played at Trent Bridge four years later England batsman, Charlie Barnett, found himself becalmed by Australia's go-slow tactics on 98 not out at lunch on the first day. Unlike the unfortunate Chipperfield, he sped to his century off the first delivery after the adjournment, and was unlucky not to join the select band of players who have reached three figures in the first session of a Test.

Bill O'Reilly

Fortunes were reversed in the Second Test at Lords, where, in a game which by common acceptance has become known as 'Verity's Match', England won convincingly by an innings and 38 runs. The Yorkshire slow bowler, on a pitch teased into a slow turner by heavy rain, returned match figures of 15/104, thus bettering the analysis of the immortal Wilfred Rhodes, who took 15/124 at Melbourne in 1904. The dapper Australian opening bat, Bill Brown, scored an impeccable century on his first Test appearance at Lords, but this was more than outweighed by hundreds from Leyland and Ames; the latter became the first regular wicketkeeper to reach three figures in England-Australia encounters. It was a singular achievement which he was to keep to himself until the coming of his Kentish successor Alan Knott and Australia's Rod Marsh.

Above all, Lords in 1934 meant Hedley Verity, a name which seems peculiarly appropriate for a slow left-hand bowler who was amongst the most serenely true of his kind. I have impersonal yet close ties with

125

Verity; it was as the paid player for my native club of Middleton in the Central Lancashire League that the spin bowler took his first big professional step towards his ultimate selection for Yorkshire and England. When he appeared for a trial at the Headingley nets, coach Wilfred Rhodes was amazed at Verity's comparative speed through the air for a slow bowler and his lack of flight. He called over his fellow coaches with the comment: 'Come and took at our new medium-pace bowler!' Different to the more flighty Rhodes, Verity might have been; but he was not a whit less successful. He still heads the table of remarkable analyses in Wisden with his return of 10/10 in one Nottinghamshire innings at Leeds in 1932. Hedley Verity was the man to have in your corner when the going was tough; he proved this at Lords in 1934, as he did in Sydney's Final Test of 1933. A captain in the Green Howards during the Second World War, Verity was wounded and captured by the enemy in the fighting around Monte Casino in Italy. He died, as unobtrusively yet as nobly as he bowled, of his wounds in a prisoner-of-war camp. As long as subsequent M.C.C. parties travelled to Australia by ship after the war they paused awhile in Naples to make the pilgrimage to Hedley's grave, usually led by his great friend, chief mourner, ex-wicketkeeper and baggage man of later years, George Duckworth. As Rupert Brooke wrote in 1915 of other soldiers' resting places in Flanders, Verity's grave will remain for all cricketers 'some corner of a foreign field that is forever England'—and Yorkshire.

The Third Test of 1934 at Old Trafford eventuated as a high scoring draw with Hendren, now 45, compiling a farewell century for his country. A similar inconclusive fate befell the Leeds clash, though England were lucky to be saved by rain on the last day after an opening phase of swaying fortunes. At close of play on the first day, England had been dismissed for a mediocre 200 yet were still in the game; Australia was in the predicament of being 3/39, Bowes having collected all 3 wickets, remarkably, without expense. The stumbling blocks in the path of the home side proved to be, predictably, Bradman and Ponsford who occupied the batting crease for the whole of the next day to hoist the Australian total to 4/388 and thus place their side in a position to score 584. The Don reached his second triple century against England and when the heavens opened in the last few hours of the match, Wyatt's side were still 155 behind in their second innings, with only 4 wickets in reserve.

The philosophy of the England selectors for The Oval Test was obviously one which laid emphasis on maturity. The 47-year-old Woolley was recalled and spent an age-long and agonizing time in the field as Ponsford and Bradman each contributed liberally to a new record 451 partnership for Australia's second wicket. Australia amassed 701 and, with both Bowes and Ames incapacitated, Grimmett in magnificent form with the ball, and the home fielding inept, England's cause was hopeless. Leyland resisted stoutly for 110 runs in their first innings, but Grimmett's magic fingers conjured up figures of 5/64 and tumbled out his opponents for 145 for Australia to win by 562 runs.

In retrospect, it would be fair to say that the performance of

'Gubby' Allen's M.C.C. team in Australia in 1936-7 exceeded the expectations of all but the most rabid and sanguine of home supporters. Bradman, leading his country for the first time against the traditional enemy, found himself in the invidious position of being two games in arrears after the first two Tests. It was an inauspicious beginning to the Don's subsequently successful career as his country's leader. A remarkable fightback resulted in the first recorded instance of a side winning the final three encounters to completely reverse the trend of the earlier two games and carry off the rubber. The public interest which this series stimulated can be gauged from the fact that an unparalleled crowd of 933,513 paid at the gates to see the five Tests. A total of 350,534 people witnessed the decisive final game in Melbourne—a match attendance figure which still remains unsurpassed after almost half a century.

English hopes could not have been high as their party set sail. There was no bodyline shot in their locker, since the tactic had been outlawed two years previously. On the evidence of the English skipper's opposition to it in 1932-3, Allen would not have used the ploy even if it had been legal. The tourists' batting was depleted by the retirement of Hendren and Sutcliffe and, surprisingly, the leading fast bowlers of the county season, Bowes and Surrey's Alf Gover were passed over in favour of Ken Farnes and Derbyshire's long-armed Bill Copson. It was less surprising that Harold Larwood, who topped the English county averages in 1936, declared himself unavailable for another tour of Australia.

The Brisbane Test saw England coast home by 322 runs after Australia, trapped on a spiteful, wet wicket, collapsed for 58 in their second innings. Left-handed speedster Voce returned match figures of 10/57 whilst his fellow opening bowler and captain, Allen, supported him with an 8-wicket performance. The interesting facet of the game, however, was Australian leg-spinner Frank Ward's match analysis of 8/140. There were factions within the Australian camp which were of the opinion that the South Australian should not have been in the team. He replaced fellow state spinner Clarrie Grimmett in the eleven, presumably on the tenuous argument of age. In 1936, Grimmett was forty-four, but his performances belied his advancing years. During the 1934 tour of England, Grimmett ensnared 109 first-class victims. He exactly equalled the top tally of Bill O'Reilly who was twelve years his junior. Clarrie followed this feat with an even more remarkable achievement: that of taking 44 wickets in the series against Herbie Wade's Springboks in South Africa at a cost of 14.59—a record against that country which younger men have failed to emulate to this present day. In his last meeting with England, the 'Gnome' had taken 5 wickets in an innings. Yet in spite of all of these considerations, Ward, who was destined to play in only four Tests between 1936 and 1938, by comparison with Grimmett's thirty-seven, was chosen as the front-line spinning partner of O'Reilly against Allen's side. There were, and still are, many expert opinions in Australia which say that Grimmett should also have toured England in 1938, even though at that stage he would have been forty-six.

127

The illogical omission of Grimmett from the 1936-7 Test XI leaves the reasons behind the decision open only to frivolous conjecture. Perhaps it stemmed from the humorous incident which occurred in South Africa and is so well recounted by former Australian fast bowler, Ernie McCormick. Apparently during Vic Richardson's side's tour of the Union in 1935-6, slow bowlers O'Reilly and Grimmett came in for some unexpected punishment from a Transvaal batsman, Langton. McCormick, having been removed from the firing line after his new ball spell, watched as Grimmett and O'Reilly bowled and the ball was struck with such force that it soared out of the ground and was lost. Since a ball in a similar condition to the lost one was not available, a shiny new one was produced and McCormick was required to bowl again. When the shine was removed, the slow bowlers, with the whole-hearted co-operation of the batting colossus, once more lost the ball and the fast bowler was recalled to the bowling crease and given yet another new ball. Several times new balls were produced; and each time they were lost! As his captain, Richardson, handed Ernie the last ball, he commiserated with him: 'We've nearly finished the reds and then we can start on the colours'.

The weather again favoured England in the Second Test in Sydney and they won by an innings and 22 runs. Australia sank without trace for 80 in their first knock with bowler Bill O'Reilly reaching the zenith of his batting career by top scoring with 37. Hammond soared to a score of 231 in England's only innings, but Australia's star batsman was suffering badly at the hands of the rain gods. Bradman in four innings had collected two ducks—surely, on the law of his eventual average in Tests, one of the most improbable occurrences in cricket!

'Chuck' Fleetwood-Smith

The tide and the weather of the series turned against the touring side in Melbourne. Australia won by 365 runs, thanks to a rough-hewn first innings bowling performance from tall Melbourne medium-pacer, Morrie Seivers, who captured 5/21 in England's total of 9/76 declared on a damp pitch. Rather than risk his recognized batsmen in treacherous conditions, Bradman displayed his shrewd leadership qualities by opening the second knock with the leg-spinning trio of O'Reilly, Fleetwood-Smith and Ward on an improving surface. It must have been the proud boast of these bowlers in later years that once they batted before Bradman and Fingleton! The next day those two batsmen, on a good wicket, added a joint 346 with Bradman contributing the lion's share of 270. The Australian skipper subsequently contracted a chill, but must have listened to the radio with a great deal of satisfaction from his sick bed as McCabe led the Australians to victory, with the left-handed slow bowler Fleetwood-Smith spinning the ball like a top to take 5/124.

'Chuck' Fleetwood-Smith was a left-arm wrist spinner and the very personification of an erratic genius. In his later years, after having contracted, and spoilt, a good marriage with a soft-drink heiress, the dark good-looking bowler sank to the depths of dereliction and was discovered by his journalistic friends, homeless and alone, sleeping on Melbourne park benches in the icy depths of winter. His bowling, like his life, rose to great heights of inspiration and opportunity, yet plumbed ludicrous levels of failure. When he pitched the ball on a length, his spin was so great that he was unplayable; yet it was not unusual for him to bowl a delivery which bounced twice! Without a shadow of doubt, it was Fleetwood-Smith who, in 1936, won the Fourth Test in Adelaide for Bradman. England outscored Australia in the first innings by 42 and in spite of Bradman's 212, the home side could only set England 392 to win in their final appearance at the batting crease. At the beginning of the last morning's play, Australia's double century hoodoo, Hammond, was still batting with 39 to his name and only 244 required for victory on a blameless wicket. Bradman took Fleetwood-Smith to one side and lectured him like a Dutch uncle about the needs of his side. In the first over of the morning, Fleetwood-Smith applied himself momentarily to produce the perfect 'chinaman' which whipped back from outside the off-stump to bowl Hammond. The match was as good as over; the rest of the bowling task was pure formality. The bowler to whom many captains would have hesitated to give the ball under such circumstances had vindicated his captain's trust.

The gods evened up the climatic fortunes of the two sides when, in the final match in Melbourne, England found themselves, for the second time in the rubber, disadvantaged by a wet wicket just as Australia had been in Brisbane and Sydney. Bradman, McCabe and Badcock each contributed a century to Australia's winning total of 604 before rain on the third evening enabled O'Reilly to reap a harvest of 8/109 and dismiss England twice for 239 and 165. Prominent in the Australian score card was an entry which read: R. G. Gregory c Verity b Farnes 80. Ross Gregory was a 20-year-old batsman of great style and panache. Sadly the Test career of the Wesley College boy who bore the same initials as the statesman product of his school, Sir Robert Menzies, was cut short by his death whilst serving as a sergeant-observer during the Second World War. Today Australian, Victorian and Melbourne cricket remembers him by the St Kilda Cricket Club oval which bears his name.

So ended the 1936 series of topsy-turvy fortunes. At one stage Australia were two matches down with three to play; yet they managed to squeeze through the narrow defile to victory. Bradman showed his resilient genius by collecting two noughts in four innings yet finishing the rubber with an average of 90. Poor Morrie Seivers must have wondered about the vagaries of Test cricket. After capturing 9/161 in three games, he was dropped when fast bowler Ernie McCormick regained fitness, and was never destined to play again for his country.

The fact that England had not been able to translate their initial 2-0 advantage into a series winning margin in 1936-7 clearly suggested that they were a greybeard side and that the time had arrived for an infusion of new talent. The country was fortunate that youthful ability such as that of batsmen Len Hutton, Bill Edrich, Denis Compton and leg-spinner Doug Wright was readily available to confront Bradman's 1938 tourists. Yet England was unlucky, because the redevelopment of their eleven had no sooner begun than it was truncated by the human disaster of the Second World War.

The nineteenth Australian XI to visit England played only four Tests; the third of the scheduled 5-match series game at Manchester was obliterated by rain. In the Nottingham Test, England accumulated a massive 8/658 on a moribund pitch with Hutton and Compton contributing débutant centuries. Charlie Barnett of Gloucester had ample time to think about his hundred over lunch on the first day, being only two short of joining that élite band of players who have reached three figures in the first session of a Test. Those who saw Eddie Paynter's 216 not out in this innings will never forget the nimbleness of the little Lancastrian and his mastery of the battery of Australian spin bowlers which included the formidable O'Reilly, the unpredictable Fleetwood-Smith and Ward. At one stage in their reply of 411 Australia were a precarious 6/194. It was at this crisis point that Maestro Stan McCabe assumed dictatorial powers over the Australian innings and the England bowling. The brilliancy of McCabe's irrepressible stroke play made the most discerning spectator on the ground gasp to see himself 'out-Bradmanned'.

So impressed was the Don that he ordered his players on to the Trent Bridge dressing-room balcony to watch, with the comment that they would never see an innings like McCabe's again. Speaking later of McCabe's brilliance on that occasion, the then Sir Donald Bradman, in a speech at the Australian Cricket Board Dinner during Melbourne's Centenary Test, exclaimed: 'Stan McCabe played the most glorious innings I have ever witnessed. The grace, the beauty and the power of his 232 were unbelievable. Despite five men on the boundary most of the time, he and Fleetwood-Smith put on 77 for the last wicket in twenty-eight minutes, McCabe making 72 of them, and as a writer of the day said, Fleetwood-Smith was just as much a spectator as I was'.

When McCabe batted, even his opponents could scarce forebear to cheer. Former England and Nottinghamshire skipper, Arthur Carr, wrote of 'Napper' McCabe in his book *Cricket With The Lid Off*: 'Here is a grand player to watch, and I feel certain a grand one to have on a side; when all the mysterious manoeuvring was going on to get Bill Voce out of the Notts team (in 1934) after he had bowled these two bumping overs at Woodfull and Brown I was told (and I believe it) that McCabe said: "Well, I don't care if Voce does play tomorrow or how he bowls. I'm going to have my innings". That's the spirit.'

In spite of the respectable size of Australia's first total, Hammond was in a position to afford optimism and enforced the follow-on. He was foiled in his bid for outright victory by Bradman's determined and unbeaten 144 and 133 from the correct blade of opener, Bill Brown. The Nottingham Test was not a game which the bowlers could look back upon with any roseate and fond recollections; the placid nature of the Trent Bridge 'feather-bed' resulted in only 24 wickets falling in four days play for 1,496 runs—an average cost of 62 runs per batsman.

The First Test's high scoring trend continued at Lords; it was a surprising facet of the game since the pitch was officially described as green, and theoretically in favour of the fast bowlers, Farnes and McCormick. McCormick was not enjoying a lucky spell. In the later stages of the tour he was plagued by a leg injury, whilst in his very first

Stan McCabe

county game against Worcestershire he sent down 35 no-balls including 19 in his first three overs in English first-class cricket. This overstepping aspect of McCormick's bowling prompted the waggish Lindsay Hassett to remark to a lady who sat next to Ernie at the dining-room table on the return sea voyage from England, and who continually addressed remarks to the fast bowler without eliciting a response: 'You must forgive him, Madam. Ernie has been deafened by the English umpires shouting "no ball" in his ear all summer!'

The last Test at Cricket Headquarters before the Second World War witnessed a veritable feast of cricket. Wally Hammond, in his most commanding manner, reached 240 before being bowled by McCormick. Equally meritorious on the sloping Lords pitch was Brown's 206 not out in his side's reply of 422 to England's 494. Paynter joined the ill-fated '99 brigade'. When he fell lbw to O'Reilly his average after two innings stood at a remarkable 315. Astoundingly Paynter went on to finish the rubber with an average of 101 and was still only second in the home side's batting figures to Hutton. Denis Compton reached a characteristically versatile 76 not out when England batted again on a spiteful wicket, but Bradman outshone him. When Australia scored 6/204 in 170 minutes in pursuit of 315 for victory, the Australian skipper, batting at number three and coming to the wicket when the score was 8, notched exactly half of his team's total to draw the match. He could probably have won the game single-handed, had the time been available.

Disappointingly for the Yorkshire crowd, neither of their local heroes, Hutton and Leyland, were able to play at Headingley because of injury. No doubt this deficiency led the Leeds spectators to ascribe England's subsequent loss by 5 wickets to a lack of Yorkshire content in their side. The difference between the two teams, in fact, was substantially contained in two names: Bradman and O'Reilly. 'Tiger' O'Reilly captured 10/122 on a pitch which lacked firmness because of preceding rain and turned on the first day.

In the authoritative opinion of Bradman, O'Reilly was the best bowler whom he ever faced. The balding ex-schoolmaster's 144 wickets in only 27 Tests certainly place him in the top drawer of match-winning bowlers; the fact that he captured over 100 wickets in Sydney club cricket in three consecutive seasons and led the New South Wales grade averages twelve times between 1926-49 made him the beau idéal of consistency. His leg-spinners and wrong 'uns, delivered off a run which resembled an aggressive charge, were delivered with a pin-point accuracy which allowed the batsman no respite and at a slow medium-pace which seldom permitted him to carry the battle to the bowler. Tiger's' ferocity towards the batsmen was legendary. He would appeal for lbw against the batsman and when the umpire pointed out that O'Reilly's quivering opponent had edged the ball on to his pad, would growl, 'I know; that's what's wrong with the law!'

On one occasion, when the square-leg umpire had dared to give a decision against him, 'Tiger' snatched the ball and in irritated fashion stormed back to his bowling mark with his head down. As usual he turned without an upward glance and still with head bowed, lumbered in for the next delivery. It was not until he was in the very act of bowling that he realized that the umpire at the batsman's end was still stooping over the stumps, adjusting the bails and exposing an irresistible target. The temptation proved too much for Bill who thought, 'What the hell', and bowled—with his usual, unerring accuracy!

A batsman who played O'Reilly with more relative ease than other players was Lindsay Hassett, a small man who, because of his lack of inches was seldom lured lungingly on to the front foot. In spite of their Victorian-N.S.W. rivalry on the field, Hassett and O'Reilly are the firmest of co-religionist, fellow-fishermen friends off it. They still relate with relish the invitation of the priest who, when the Australian tourists were playing in Ireland, asked Hassett, McCabe and O'Reilly to break as many windows as they could in the nearby Anglican cathedral which he averred was illegally trespassing on Catholic preserves.

Bradman's match-winning contribution to the Leeds game was an inimitable knock of 103 in an Australian moderate first innings score of 242. It was a stay at the wicket which was curtailed merely by the fact that a cricket side only includes eleven players. The Australian skipper rightly concluded that the depletion of the England batting and a wicket to the liking of O'Reilly provided the necessary ingredients for an Australian victory. The tourists' win, however, was not realized without some anxious moments. Australia were in danger on the third day. At one stage they were 4/61 requiring 105 runs with the light bordering on eventide. It was a situation which demanded that linkman Hassett should light Australia's path to victory with a bright innings of 33; it was a will o' the wisp knock, however, since Hassett was missed at slip off the second ball which he received.

With the Manchester game consigned to its watery grave, Australia had only to draw The Oval to win the rubber. The face of fate, however, was set against them and the Final Test not only saw Bradman's XI vanquished by the largest margin in England-Australian cricket but also produced a debilitating crop of injuries, amongst which was one to Australia's leader himself. Bradman injured his ankle in a foothole whilst bowling and did not appear at the batting crease. The magnitude of England's only innings provided an opportunity for all Australian volunteers to bowl. Lindsay Hassett contributed 13 economic overs—a fact which leads one to give credence to Hassett's own opinion, widely canvassed after his retirement from the first-class game, that he was a useful medium-pace bowler. In later years Lindsay was fond of blowing his own humorous bowling trumpet by recalling how he took 3/2—all bowled—in one innings of an international game. The Hassett version of the incident describes vividly the full curve of the ball through the moist atmosphere and the satisfying 'clunk' which it made as it entered the wicketkeeper's gloves. The international occasion was an Australian touring side's game against Scotland!

Kennington Oval in 1938 was the backdrop against which a long drama of English batting records was enacted. Maurice Leyland scored 187 and together with fellow-Yorkshireman, Hutton, established a new best for the second wicket against Australia. Hutton also combined with 'Young' Joe Hardstaff to reach an improved mark of 215 for England's sixth wicket. The main landmark of the match was undoubtedly the performance of Len Hutton. After twelve hours and nineteen minutes at the batting crease, the 22-year-old batsman from Pudsey passed Bradman's 334, scored at Leeds in 1930. When his score was bettered, Bradman was fielding close to the bat; he was the first to reach Hutton and shake his hand in congratulation.

Years later during a television interview at the time of 1977's Centenary Test, Sir Leonard, as he had become, described the mixed feelings of pleasure and sadness which he experienced at The Oval in 1938. Bradman was, after all, the first hero of the young Hutton. His first capital investment in cricket was an autographed Don Bradman bat. As a boy of fourteen he had seen his idol set his world mark; and now he was instrumental in chipping away just a fragment of the Bradman legend. Hutton's eventual tally of 364 was itself a record which endured for twenty years, falling finally to the bat of West Indian Gary Sobers as he played against Pakistan in Kingston in 1957-8. Is it a significant coincidence, I wonder, that each of the Test triple centurions received royal recognition in the form of a knighthood?

Numbers nine and ten in the England batting order at The Oval were the left-handed spinner Hedley Verity and fast bowler Ken Farnes. They shared 6 of the 8 Australian second innings wickets to fall, and theirs was the final satisfaction in their side's decisive victory. It was fitting they enjoyed such a triumphal consolation against the traditional sporting enemy. Pilot Officer Kenneth Farnes was killed by enemy action at the age of thirty on 21 October 1941. Captain Hedley Verity died of his wounds in a prisoner-of-war camp in Italy on 31 July 1943.

The war clouds were gathering even as Farnes took his last wicket in pre-war Anglo-Australian Test cricket—that of Fleetwood-Smith. Six weeks after The Oval Test, English Prime Minister, Sir Neville Chamberlain stepped off his plane at Croydon airport waving aloft the scrap of paper which he had signed with Adolph Hitler in Munich and declaiming that his country had obtained peace with honour. The peace was only temporary and the honour completely illusionary. Germany and Hungary dishonourably dismembered the suffering Czechoslovakia on 31 March 1939—seventeen days after the final pre-war Test between England and South Africa and almost exactly one year after Herr Hitler had stated that he had no territorial designs on that country.

Hitler became Chancellor of Germany on 30 January 1933. It was an unpleasant period both for the world at large, and for cricket: this was just ten days after the bodyline Test in Adelaide and the despatch of the controversial Australian Board of Control cable to the Marylebone Cricket Club. 'Gubby' Allen's touring side lost the deciding Melbourne Test in 1936 just four days before Hitler announced that Germany would re-occupy the Rhineland. In the months preceding the departure of Bradman's 1938 touring side for England, the Führer united Germany with Austria, thus flouting Article 80 of the Versailles Treaty and defying the fifty-three countries of the impotent League of Nations.

A few short weeks after Bradman's men had returned to their Australian homes and whilst Hammond's side was in South Africa Hitler was demanding further 'living space' for his country and championing the cause of the German minorities in the Polish corridor and Danzig. The Polish explosion came on 1 September 1939 and England and her dominions, as guarantors of Poland's independence, found themselves involved in a totalitarian world conflict which was to exceed in horror that of 1914-18. For six years cricket had to take a back seat to more important issues than even bodyline.

10. After the Deluge

The dogs of war, once loosed, were not brought to heel without immense cost. When the cordite fumes dispersed over Europe and the atomic dust finally settled on Hiroshima, the civilized world was left to contemplate the uncivilized ravages of the 1939-45 holocaust. A total of 54,000,000 human beings of every creed, colour and nationality lay dead.

Cricket had aged and was the poorer for the lost years. England's Len Hutton, Bill Edrich and Denis Compton were no longer promising youngsters. They matured harshly in the arid ovens of Indian and Egyptian barrack grounds. Wally Hammond, Australia's Syd Barnes, Lindsay Hassett and the two Dons, Bradman and Tallon, mourned the forfeited opportunities of the five-year hiatus.

Cricket's course after the Second World War ran uncannily parallel to its development in the aftermath of the 1914-18 conflict. Australia's youth escaped the debilitating effects of harsh war-time rationing. As in the early 1920s their physical recovery was quicker than that of the young men of blockaded England, whose batting and bowling stamina was scarcely promoted by a weekly pittance of two ounces of margarine and half a pound of meat. Australian competitive resilience quickly thrust fresh but redoubtable ability into the Test arena. Ray Lindwall, Arthur Morris, Ernie Toshack, Colin McCool, Bruce Dooland and George Tribe were unknown quantities when peace was signed. By the end of 1946 their natural abilities had made them Test identities on both sides of the world. Allied to the formidable talent which, as in 1919, was washed up on the lee-shore of war by the Services Side, these emergent forces gelled into a combination which left Australian cricket almost as strong in 1946 as it was in 1938. Led by an astute if older Bradman, the Australian side of the former year was the precocious infant who became the unbeaten cricketing giant of the 1948 England summer.

It is hard to analyse the reason for Australia's ministry of extraordinary talents in the 1940s. The impact of the Japanese war affected Australians just as much as the conflict on the opposite side of the

Keith Miller

world afflicted the English. Rationing was a reality on the home front and virtually every cricketer was in uniform. However, some cricket was possible on the paddocks of the back-blocks and in the parks of Sydney and Melbourne; the nurseries of the sport did not go completely untended. By contrast, the game in England was in a wasteland. The first-class players who contested the last county games of the fateful September of 1939 were, of necessity, the older, and often still mobilized, soldiers who made up the front line of Hammond's touring party of 1946. They faced a rejuvenated Australia. The vibrant structure of the competitive, amateur Australian game had enabled it to move into top gear as soon as the last shot was fired. There was no shortage of youthful ability which would, in any case, have forced its way into the aging Australian team of 1938, even if the war had not intervened. The fact that the genius of Don Bradman was still on hand to engineer Australia's post-war revival was crucial to the development of his country's dominance in the game over the ensuing years.

When Hammond's post-war tourists disembarked at Fremantle, many experts believed that the world had seen the best of Bradman. Less than fully fit and without the razor-sharp reflexes which made him appear unorthodox at the age of twenty, Bradman was a doubtful starter for the 1946 series. It took only the Brisbane Test to prove Lindsay Hassett's contention that even without his abnormal reaction time, Bradman was still a better, conventional technician than any of his younger contemporaries. True, the Bowral genius no longer despatched the good-length ball with the venom born of his youthful extra-sensory perception; but his total absorption in his batting task and his correctness lived on, bringing him four more centuries against England and three against India in the short span of two years.

The 1946 Australian combination owed much of its strength to the legacy of ability bequeathed to it by Warrant Officer Lindsay Hassett's Services Side. The Keith Miller of the Victory Tests in England was a fast bowler with an immense and ferocious run-up and a voluminous mane of hair. I well remember sitting on the grass at fine-leg at Old Trafford in 1945 and peering through the legs of a fieldsman, as this tall Adonis flung down the ball at an awesome speed, and with an inaccuracy which made it an alarming experience for wicketkeeper Sismey. With the callowness of a 15-year-old, I was of the opinion that both Miller's pace and accuracy would have been greater if he had not paused from time to time in his run-up to toss back his forelock from his eyes.

'Nugget' Miller's talents gained him early recognition in the South Melbourne Club, where, like his team-mate of later years, Lindsay Hassett, he appeared in senior games whilst still wearing short pants. His adult charm on the field was a product of his long apprenticeship and an extension of his personality. He never forgot a name or a face, no matter how boorish its owner. As a batsman of the upright and cavalier ilk, he was a throw-back to the genteel, golden era of Edwardian cricket. Like MacLaren he 'dismissed the ball from his presence' with never a suggestion of malice aforethought to the bowler. In his mature bowling years Miller was comparable to Victor Trumper

136

in the batting sphere; he had, not three different strokes, but three different balls for every situation. Skill appeared to be second nature to him. His approach was now whittled down to a mere half dozen steps of a striding preface to a rhythmic rocking-horse action which lacked the usual convulsive characteristics of a normal speedster. The leading arm was high as the body swayed back into a cocked position of latent power before the silky swing of the bowling arm and the moment of release. Miller, like Maurice Tate, possessed an action as aesthetically appealing as it was effectively utilitarian. There was a natural athleticism about his bowling. It was not unusual for him to drop the ball whilst running up to the crease, scoop it up without pausing in his approach, and bowl a perfect delivery.

There were no bounds to Miller's versatile lack of conventionality. He would follow a fast outswinger, inswinger and a bouncer with a leg-spinner and a wrong 'un—each delivery perfect in concept and execution. Miller could turn the tide of a match and cause inexplicable butterflies even in the stomach of a batsman who had a hundred to his credit on the scoreboard. Once in the Melbourne Test of 1955 against England, though plagued by an injury, he returned a pre-lunch spell of 9 overs, 8 maidens, 3 wickets for 5 runs. On another occasion, however, he threw the ball back to Bradman, his captain, and refused to bowl because of a similar disability! Miller possessed flair, charisma, ability and confidence; but his greatest attribute was that dwindling commodity on the world cricket market—character.

Peter Philpott, the N.S.W. and Australian leg-spinner, made his first appearance on the Sheffield Shield field under the captaincy of Keith Miller. In 'Percy' Philpott's first game, 'Nugget' arrived at the Sydney Cricket Ground, as usual, just a few minutes before he was due to lead his side out to field. On the way to the dressing-room he paused in the press-box to deliver a pithy résumé of what he thought of a certain newspaperman's criticisms of N.S.W.'s performance on the previous day. In consequence, he was both furious and flustered when he led his side on to the oval. Unlike the veterans of the N.S.W. team, Philpott had no specially allocated position in the field, and timidly asked the enraged Miller where he should go. 'Scatter, son,' snarled 'Nugget', 'I'll bowl these so-and-sos out!'—and he did!

Len Hutton, England's skipper and opening batsman, a man of method and a student of his art, hated facing the effervescent Miller. His disguised grip for the outswinger appeared to be that which normal bowlers used for the inswinger; then again, there was no discernible movement of the ball in the air until it had completed three-quarters of its journey down the pitch towards the batsman. The quixotic unpredictability of Miller's bowling was completely alien to Hutton's phlegmatic philosophy of every cobbler to his special last. Miller's triumphs in England were based on the earlier experience which he gained in that country during the war years. As a fighter pilot stationed in the Tyneside area, he occasionally took the opportunity to practise with a local club. One evening he was spotted by a selection committee-man who offered him a game on the following week-end with the second eleven! Grateful, Miller explained that regretfully he would have to

Ray Lindwall, the batsman

decline, because he was playing for the Australian Services at Lords!

The legendary Ray Lindwall was Miller's new ball partner when cricket resumed after the war. In essence he was the very antithesis of all Miller's fast bowling attributes except one: deadliness. He was as orthodox as his partner was unconventional and he was more successful on the Test field in terms of figures. Lindwall was a superb fast-bowling maestro. His approach to the wicket, effortlessly rhythmical and short-stepping until the last few galvanic strides, conveyed the impression that he could bowl all day. It was a tribute to Lindwall's stamina and technique that he survived in Tests until the grand old fast-bowling age of thirty-eight, playing most of his latter-day cricket in the enervating humidity and heat of Queensland. Though Lindwall's bowling arm was low at the moment of delivery, it was perfectly attuned to his swimming outswinger. His gathering stride was superbly athletic and a model for any aspiring fast bowler; but the crowning attributes which raised Lindwall to the pinnacle of the 'Fast Bowlers of My Time' list were his acute cricketing brain and his phenomenal accuracy and control.

'Gubby' Allen, the former England Test bowler and selector, was reputedly unconvinced by the rumours of Lindwall's exceptional control when the fast bowler first arrived in England. He therefore sauntered down to the Lords nets on the occasion of one of the Australians' first airings of their talents for a personal demonstration. At 'Gubby's' behest, Lindwall first bowled an outswinger which pitched on leg-stump and knocked down the off. The second wish was for an inswinger which bounced in line with the off-stump and hit the leg. No sooner said than done—and the selector departed a wiser and no doubt a sadder man, no longer under any illusions about the magnitude of the task which the batsmen he would help to select would have to face in the coming series.

Strangely, little has been said or written about Lindwall's speed. Few commentators place him in the express category of the Wes Halls or Jeff Thomsons of later repute. Yet, as a batsman who was struck on the head by a Lindwall bouncer when the bowler was a ripe thirty-three years of age, I can vouch for the fact that he was very fast. The truth is that the Test scene probably did not see Lindwall at his quickest. When cricket resumed after the Second World War, Lindwall was already twenty-five. On the evidence of Northamptonshire's Australian wicket-keeper-batsman, 'Jock' Livingston, who stood behind the stumps to the fast bowler during the war years when he was only twenty-one, there can be no doubt that Lindwall in the first flush of youth was as mortally fast as any bowler who lived.

Lindwall and Miller hunted in the classical manner of fast bowlers—as a formidable duet of talent. As their cricket business partnership flourished so did the friendship of Ray 'Jackson' Lindwall and Keith 'Nugget' Miller. They were as inseparably hostile on the golf course as they were frighteningly co-operative at the bowling crease. Their bowling figures, however, will live longer than their golfing handicaps in the memory of cricketers.

The Australian Services XI won two of the Victory Tests against England and shared the rubber with a home team which included such illustrious names as Hutton, Washbrook, Hammond, Edrich, Fishlock, Robertson, Wright, Pope and Pollard. The plethora of post-war Australian talent stood revealed when only two of the players who performed so well in 1945 gained selection in their national team of the following year. Whitington, Pettiford, Carmody, Pepper, Christofani, Sismey, Workman and Price each earned themselves wonderful reputations on English fields yet, like the proverbial prophet, failed to gain acceptance in their own land. Workman, Pettiford and Pepper were destined to spend most of their remaining cricketing lives in England. Cecil George Pepper, the batsman who struck a brace of famous sixes over the Lords pavilion and into Scarborough's Trafalgar Square, became the fiery, leg-spinning, all-round doyen of Lancashire League professionals and later a Test match umpire. Jack Pettiford was for years the leading all-rounder for Kent and another veteran of the leagues. 'Picolo Pete', as he was called, collapsed and died of a heart attack in a Sydney taxicab whilst on a visit to Australia. Jim Workman became a coaching institution at Alf Gover's East Hill Indoor Cricket School before his premature death whilst still playing London club cricket.

Lindsay Hassett

Lindsay Hassett and Keith Miller alone survived the transfer of the Services Side to a peace-time footing. Like Puck of Shakespeare's *Midsummer Night's Dream,* the diminutive Hassett threw an unforgettable girdle around the cricketing world. His Test career spanned forty-three games, a war, and culminated in his leading Australia against England, South Africa, and the West Indies between 1949-53. He was the first of a memorable list of players produced by the Victorian public school, Geelong College, and not even his fellow alumni, Ian Redpath, Paul Sheahan and Jack Iverson surpassed Hassett's skill. His judgment, technique and nimbleness were such that he did not fear even the formidable wiles of his life-long friend and Sheffield Shield antagonist, Bill O'Reilly. In his retired days as a commentator, Lindsay would delight in baiting 'The Tiger' with whimsical recollections of the occasions on which he hit him for six or a hundred. Hassett's humour is wickedly dry and delivered with such a twinkle in his eye that it is impossible to take umbrage. He is like a naughty boy, who, tongue in cheek, delights in shocking his elders. During the Australian Services game against the North of England in Blackpool, Lindsay began a speech from the Town Hall steps by looking around the assembled throng and stating quite bluntly: 'Never have I seen so many ugly men!' (Long pause) 'But never so many beautiful women!' The success of the address was assured. The daring of Hassett's wit was matched only by his imaginative captaincy. Few Test leaders could boast, as he could, that in Brisbane in 1950, they had closed an innings against England with 7/32 on the board—and won. Hassett learned his captaincy under the exacting tutelage of Bradman. The Don was a skipper who never left anything to chance. Australian slow bowler George Tribe recounts the story of how, in 1946, Bradman demanded a field setting on paper from each of his bowlers before a Test. With the bowlers' tactics documented, he then analysed the placements, querying the reason for each fieldsman's position, explained in terms of the bowler's intentions and skills. It was a tribute to Hassett's captaincy that he managed to fill Bradman's large boots and lost only one frustrating series in England in 1953.

Bradman's 1946 XI was strong not merely because of its captain's ability and inspiration, but also because of the talents of its constituent parts. The remarkable wicketkeeping omission of the 1938 tour of England had been rectified and Don Tallon, the gloved Bundaburg genius quickly established a matchless reputation for himself as the world's most mobile stumper and a batsman capable of scoring 90 in. the number eight berth. Len Hutton often recalls with wry dismay how Tallon caught him in England's batting débâcle of 52 at The Oval in 1948—off an authentic leg-glance hit in the middle of the bat and deflected literally yards down the on-side.

For Queensland, Tallon worked in humorous conjunction with his brother Bill, a leg-spin bowler. On one occasion when N.S.W. batsman Pepper was in full flight and despatching Bill Tallon with monotonous regularity into the tram depot adjacent to Brisbane's Woolloongabba Ground, his brother Don advised Bill to throw the ball higher and spin it more. Bill replied in his usual stammering fashion: 'I w-w-would, b-b-but I f-f-find the b-b-ball v-v-very h-h-hard to grip. It k-k-keeps c-c-coming b-b-back c-c-covered in t-t-tram t-t-tickets!'

It is doubtful whether Australia have ever possessed a better opening batting combination than that of Arthur Morris and Syd Barnes. Bradman himself categorizes Morris as the best left-handed batsman in his experience. 'Arty's' powers of concentration and defence were inexhaustible and he was an infallible despatcher of the bad ball on the leg-side. The only occasion on which I saw 'Arty' discomfited was when he opened the batting for the Australian tourists in 1953 at Northampton. I was scheduled to send down the first ball but was scarcely visible at the end of my 27-yard run-up when Morris took guard; the slips lurked in distant isolation, twenty yards behind the batsman's wicket and the only fieldsman within communication distance of Arthur was his old friend and former England skipper, Freddie Brown, who was directing Northamptonshire's fortunes from the short-leg position. Feeling as though he had been sent to Coventry, 'Arty' asked if Freddie Brown was joking about the pace of this so-called fast bowler. His only answer was a throaty chuckle from F.R., which became a hearty laugh when the first delivery hit the batsman between thigh and chest before he lifted his bat! Freddie Brown derived a great degree of vicarious pleasure from the fact that after having meted out fast bowling punishment for seven years, Australia were at last on the receiving end—but his delight did not prevent Morris from scoring a faultless 80.

In the course of his 24 Tests and 43 innings against England, Morris acquired the undeserved reputation of being the regular and predictable victim of England's great medium-pace bowler, Alec Bedser. The tag of 'Bedser's Bunny' was really a figment of the imagination of the popular press. It is true that the giant Surrey bowler dismissed Morris on eighteen occasions in Tests, but he sent the left-hander's opening partners back to the pavilion much more frequently. Moreover Morris in those forty-three knocks, scored one double century and seven other

Syd Barnes is carried off the field at Manchester 1948

hundreds, two of them in the same Adelaide game in 1947. His aggregate of 2,080 runs and an average of 50.73 is eloquent testimony to the fact that he was nobody's 'bunny'.

Like that of Hassett, Syd Barnes's Test career survived the war. Writer Ray Robinson in his eloquent vignette on the Australian batsman dubbed him in Dickensian fashion, 'The Artful Dodger'. Certainly there were no flies on Syd, either as a batsman or a man of the world. During the 1948 tour Syd produced a film, which he retailed to audiences upon his return to Australia. A non-playing team-mate was filming the Old Trafford Test for posterity when Syd, fielding in his usual suicidal short-leg position, was felled by a pull shot from the hefty England fast bowler, Dick Pollard. The blow took Barnes in the ribs with the force of a howitzer shell and he was carried bodily off the field by four burly policemen. As he was borne past his fellow film producer who was on location on the terrace of the Manchester pavilion, Syd is reputed to have turned his head towards his collaborator, winked, and asked him if he had got the incident on film. Barnes's later comment about the accident was that the blow 'would have killed an ordinary man!'

Litigation with the Australian Board of Control clouded the twilight of Barnes's career. Barbed asperity, thereafter, seemed to be the keynote of his continuing relations with the game. In the Sydney press Syd wrote trenchantly in a controversial column entitled, 'Like It or Lump It'. His writing was not without appeal, but it was stretching the artistic point a little too far when, on one occasion, he asked the famous littérateur, Sir Neville Cardus to 'put another black (carbon) in his copy' since he felt that he could use it in his column because 'their styles were so similar'. Behind this facade of bravado, Syd Barnes was a generous man. A mate in need never came away from him empty-handed. When he and Bradman added 405 for the record fifth wicket partnership against England in Sydney in 1946-7, Syd was reputed to have given his innings away after he reached 234, the exact equal tally of the Great Man. The cynics said that Barnes sacrificed his wicket to place his name in the record book bracketed memorably with that of 'Braddles'. Barnes said that he lofted a catch deliberately because he did not feel that, in justice or in figures, he could surpass the quality of the superb innings which he had just witnessed from the opposite batting crease.

The post-war players of repute were not all to be found in the ranks of Australian cricketers. Wally Hammond could still inspire the Englishmen under his command as he did in Sheffield with his century in the Victory Test; but Hammond, like Bradman, was far from fully fit and fibrositis was to cause him to withdraw permanently from the Test scene before the fifth game of the 1946 series. He was not equal to the youthful and vigorous Australian challenge of the 1940s. When he captained the first England expeditionary force to visit the antipodes after the war, Hammond appeared to be an elderly, sad survivor of the pre-1939 era. He was not alone in his age group since his team-mate of the bodyline tour of 1932-3, Bill Voce, gained selection in the 1946 touring team; but Hammond created an atmosphere of isolation around himself. He and the M.C.C. manager, Major Rupert Howard travelled around Australia in their Jaguar 'staff' car, leaving the troops to follow by train. It was a policy which did little for the *esprit de corps* of the tourists.

The other ranks under Hammond's command were a body of men redolent with talent. In 1946 Alec Bedser made an 11-wicket début against India at Lords. The performance marked the beginning of a Test career which raised the Surrey bowler to the plane of medium-paced greatness and caused his skills to be compared with those of his nearest distinguished predecessor, Maurice Tate. Statistically there is no disputing Bedser's greatness; he is one of the four bowlers to capture 100 wickets in England-Australia Tests. In two consecutive series against the old enemy in 1950-1 and 1953, 'Big Al' took no fewer than 69 victims in ten games, only two of which were won by his side. His 39 wickets in the latter rubber still stands fourth in the universal roll of honour, second only to Jim Laker's 46 tally in 1956 in Anglo-Australian series.

Bedser is a big man in every way. He stands 6'2'' in his acres of stockinged feet and it seems incongruous that his large muscular frame confined itself to delivering the ball to the batsman at a pace which never aspired to a speed above a lively medium. To look on Bedser is like gazing on one of the Seven Wonders Of The World; every perspective seems to be on a grandiose scale. When Bedser wrapped his mighty right hand about the cricket ball, it disappeared completely from view. His fingers were so long that whereas other medium-pace bowlers were constrained to bowling cutters with most of the spin imparted by the action of the wrist, Bedser made the ball rotate by moving his fingers. He actually spun the ball!

Strangely enough, Bedser discovered his extraordinary gift of bowling the leg-cutter only by accident. On one hot, humid, Sydney day in 1946, the first new ball was proving less than effective against the barn-door tactics of Barnes. Bedser's inswinger was moving so much in the heavy atmosphere that any ball which began its flight just outside the off-stump passed harmlessly down the leg-side or hit the Australian opener on the pads with little hope of a successful lbw decision. Frustrated, Bedser held the ball across the seam and, as a variation, flicked his fingers from right to left as he bowled. The resultant delivery bounced in line with the leg-stump and Barnes, expecting it to pass well clear of the wicket on the on-side did not offer a stroke. Abruptly the ball changed course and clipped the off-bail. Barnes, the victim of a fast leg-spinner, exclaimed: 'Hey, what's going on here?' It was a question which many batsmen were going to ask for the next decade.

Alec Bedser

Bedser's heart was like his frame—giant size. Like his Surrey and England counterpart of half a century earlier, Tom Richardson, he never knew the meaning of the word capitulation. During the Adelaide Test of 1951, in an oven-like atmosphere Bedser bowled without sparing himself and was finally led from the field, exhausted and oblivious of his surroundings. He stood fully clothed for half an hour under a cold shower before returning to reality. 'Big Al' is both a philosopher and a humorist. He would often look at a batsman of dubious technique and say: 'What a terrible player!' This opinion would be repeated time and time again for as long as the opponent remained at the crease; finally, if Alec still could not dismiss him, came the ultimate verdict: 'Damned difficult to get out though!'

Alec and his identical twin, Eric, both represented Surrey in the county championship. Eric was unlucky that his chosen métier—opening bat and a useful off-spinner—was a crowded and talented area of the game when he was in his prime; otherwise he might have graduated into international ranks. The twins were virtually inseparable and indistinguishable, one from the other. Eric usually accompanied Alec on his overseas tours and they always bought items of clothing in pairs and dressed alike. Like two peas in a pod, they attended receptions, attired in identical fashion, right down to the colour of their socks and the handkerchiefs in their breast pockets, and smiled enigmatically as Eric became Alec to one acquaintance but reverted to his normal identity when he was next introduced. The Bedser twins delight in confusing friends, some of whom have never really solved the problem of who is who. It is said that when Alec and Eric are apart, they inform one another of the uniform of the day; even distance cannot destroy the Bedser illusion of inseparability.

A few miles across London from the Bedser's native heath of The

The Middlesex 'twins',
Bill Edrich and Denis
Compton

Oval, at Lords, the Middlesex 'twins', Denis Compton and Bill Edrich, held court in post-war years for their county and country. In their halcyon year of 1947 both batsmen notched more than 3,500 runs and added thirty centuries to the record book. They were commanding figures in Anglo-Australian Tests until 1955. For years Compton's handsome face and luxuriant head of hair peered down from English advertisement hoardings, proclaiming the virtues of Brylcreem hair dressing. The recruitment of Compton for that advertisement was a stroke of inspiration on the part of the Royd's agency; for like his buddy, Keith Miller, Compton embodied the two appealing traits of an attractive personality and sporting genius. Denis was the kindest character who never presumed upon the senior status which years in the international sporting arena brought him. When I first made his acquaintance he was already a veteran of five series against Australia and had won an England soccer cap; yet he was not above performing many small favours for the most junior player in the touring team—if he did not fall victim to his greatest failing—forgetfulness!

As a batsman, Compton was in the genius category. He was unwilling to fetter himself with the shackles of orthodoxy, preferring to improvise according to the challenge of each situation. Like Australia's 'Dasher' Graham and England's William Gunn of the early 1900s, Denis thought little of sauntering down the wicket to the fastest bowlers before they delivered. When they riposted by dropping the ball short he stopped in his tracks half-way down the wicket, leaned back and hooked them unmercifully.

He was endowed with limitless courage and a perverse determination. During the Old Trafford Test of 1948 'Compo's' head was split by a Lindwall no-ball bouncer which he attempted to hook; he retired, but like General MacArthur he returned—to score an undefeated 145 against an attack which numbered in its ranks the combined talents of Lindwall, Miller, Johnston and Toshack! An old soccer injury to his knee occasioned a very lean and inopportune scoring spell during the

144

M.C.C. visit to Australia in 1950-1. In eight Test innings Denis notched a meagre 53 runs in a rubber which his fellow players believed they would have won with their star performing even at half-throttle. Eventually Compton's chipped knee-cap was removed; but even this set-back and a partially stiff leg did not prevent his contributing substantially to England's triumphs in the 1953 and 1954-5 rubbers. Because of his impaired mobility, Denis suffered a sense of frustration in subsequent years against spin bowlers of nagging accuracy.

During a private Cavaliers XI tour of South Africa in 1960 Hugh Tayfield, the Springbok off-spinner, pinned the handicapped 'Compo' to his crease—until one of the last games in Johannesburg when, in an exhibition of daring stroke-play, the English batsman proved that the mind and ability can overcome pain. Denis flayed the off-spinner to all parts of the field, systematically playing his shots in an anti-clockwise sequence and penetrating every gap which was created by the bowler's continual modification of his field placement. It was one of the most brilliant innings which I have seen; and it was all over in the space of 70 runs and one entertaining hour. This was Denis Compton: a gambler in cricket, on horses and even on the frequency with which parking attendants would visit the spot where his car had no right to be. He delighted in cricket's bonhomie, an innocent-looking brand of left-handed wrist-spin which was more subtle than it appeared at first glance, and a *preux chevalier* approach to any bowling challenge.

Bill Edrich was a pugnacious, pocket-battleship batsman at the crease. The Battle of Britain spirit lived on after the war in Squadron-Leader Bill Edrich's cricket. To him no bowler was too fast to hook. On one occasion during a Middlesex-Northamptonshire county game, a Tyson bouncer delivered in the evening gloaming felled the hooking Edrich and broke his jaw. After spending the night in hospital, he appeared at the batting crease next morning at the fall of the following wicket, his head swathed in a bosun's chair bandage. Naturally he tried to hook the next inevitable bumper. Intrepidly Bill walked so frequently to the marriage-altar that his Middlesex team-mate John Warr, when entering the wedding reception on the final occasion informed the enquiring door attendant that he no longer received an invitation—he had a season's pass.

As a bowler Bill generated an amazing degree of slinging pace for his size and could turn his hand to a respectable brand of off-spin. He was a reliable slip fieldsman and the very personification of a good team man—an indomitable and a wholehearted celebrator. The trials and tribulations of a hot day in the field somehow seemed less disastrous when Bill serenaded his team-mates in the dressing-room afterwards, carolling in a husky whisper:

Ginger, Ginger, They all know Captain Ginger.
Jolly old sot. O-T-'ot. Ninety-nine in the shade, wot-wot!
He loves the ladies.
But none of them would he injure.
All the girls are fond of Gin.
Gin-Gin-Gin-Gin-Ginger.

Len Hutton's chinkless defence

England's opening batsman of this post-war generation, Len Hutton, was less of an extrovert than Compton and Edrich. Psychologically he was a conundrum. The profundity of his thoughts were never betrayed on his impassive face—and his mental processes were almost labyrinthine. His captaincy of England between 1953 and 1955 was founded on few words, conservative but astute manoeuvres on the field and a complete knowledge of the opposition's mental make-up. During the 1954-5 series in Australia, Hutton's critics accused him of slowing down play by his continual use of fast bowling which sometimes reduced a full Test day to just over 50 eight-ball overs. His detractors conveniently lost sight of the fact that Hutton won the rubber by establishing a pace-bowling superiority over Australia and not once relinquishing his moral ascendancy. His bowlers sent down few overs in a day—but they took a lot of wickets in those overs.

Beneath his taciturn exterior, Len possesses a wry sense of humour, founded on a great delight in anticlimax. Picture, if you can, the first day of a Test with Hutton leading an English side in the field. The gates of the ground have been closed, the fieldsmen are all in position, the batsman has taken block and looked around the field, and the bowler has measured out his run and is about to start for the first time towards the bowling crease. Suddenly as the buzz of the huge crowd dies into the silence of expectation, Hutton at slip holds up his hand, halts play and walks slowly and solemnly towards Denis Compton at mid-off. 'Ah', say the pundits, 'Hutton is already working out some devious strategy with Compton'. Little do they know that Hutton's words to his senior player are: "Ow are you this morning Denis? Alright? Good, that's alright then'. With the tension increased for the waiting batsman, the England captain then stalks back to his position in the field.

Strange to say, Hutton was a disciplinarian. When he found a member of his side straying from the straight and narrow line of conduct, he communicated his disapproval not by what he said, but by what he did not say. He conveyed an impression of being unable to comprehend the thought processes behind unorthodox behaviour. Once, when he was sipping his créme de menthe frappé, after a good lunch in Sydney's Tattersalls Club, he observed, for a full ten minutes, a drunken Australian steadily and futilely feeding florins into a poker machine. 'Tell me', Len said to his astonished and cricket-loving host, 'Why don't Australians like that learn to do something useful—like playing cricket?'

As a batsman, Hutton was one of the game's greatest exponents of the defensive technique. It seemed to opposing bowlers that the task of dismissing him was hopeless; there were simply no chinks in his armour. He averaged 56.67 in his seventy-nine Tests. Against Australia his mean figure was 56.46 and Sydney, Melbourne, Brisbane and Adelaide crowds will long remember Hutton's skill. He carried his bat for 156 in an England innings of 272 in Adelaide in 1951. It was this same season Down Under which saw Hutton compile a masterly 62 not out on a sodden Brisbane wicket, the unplayable propensities of which caused Hassett to declare his side's second innings closed with 7 wickets down for 32. Statistically, Hutton's achievements, subsequent to his record 364 at The Oval in 1938, lack the Bradmanesque stature of which his pre-war years gave promise. In fact, however, his post-war batting feats bordered on heroic status. They were accomplished in spite of a foreshortened left arm, which was badly broken whilst Hutton was in the army. It was this injury which caused the opener to modify his grip on the bat with the top hand and to hold the handle with the back of his left hand facing diametrically down the pitch towards the bowler. The Yorkshireman's batting task in his later career was also rendered more difficult by crippling attacks of fibrositis.

Len Hutton's post-war grip

The fittest man in England's team of the 1940s and early 1950s was undoubtedly their ebullient wicketkeeper, Godfrey Evans. To see the expertise of Colin Cowdrey clash with Evan's energy on the squash court was a visual experience of sweat, tears of laughter and almost the keeper's blood. Evans was indefatigable in the field on even the hottest Australian day. More importantly he was an inspiration to his side, always alert and perpetually a bundle of energy. Evans was irrepressible. In business he twice suffered financial and partnership reverses; twice he bounced back. Travelling to Australia by ship he was always the life and soul of the party; on shipboard race nights he was the bookie, dressed in loud, check suits; the fancy dress ball usually saw him attired in furbelows and flounces, a bowl of fruit on his head and prancing like the South American bombshell, Carmen Miranda. Off and on the field 'Godders' was unchangeable. When Australian runs were flowing freely, he still dashed up to the wicket to take returns from the outfield with undiminished enthusiasm, red-palmed gloves upraised to provide a target. Before his side took the field he would raise their spirits with cries of: 'Now lads, let's attack with venom!' Out in the middle when things were going badly, he philosophized with frequent exclamations of: 'Never mind boys, they can't stop the clock'.

Evans like Tallon was one of the most mobile stumpers that the game has seen. He covered leagues down the leg-side to bring off impossible catches. His association with Alec Bedser was one of the great spectacles of the game. Bedser's place was on the slippery side of medium; yet he demanded that his keeper should stand up to the wickets and wide of the off-stump, to afford him a point of aim at which to direct his boomeranging inswingers. 'Big Al' occasionally strayed down the leg-side, where not only did Evans take him as cleanly as the proverbial whistle, but not infrequently stumped batsmen losing their balance or caught thin edges. It is reputed that Evans, standing up to Bedser, once caught the left-handed Neil Harvey off a full-bladed leg-glance! Sometimes, as at Leeds in 1948, where he missed both Bradman and Morris, as Australia steamrollered their way to an unlikely and winning total of 3/404, 'Godders' had an off-day; but that Leeds débâcle was probably the only occasion when he was downhearted enough to climb into his car and steal silently away from the ground. Most of his displays were like those in his first two innings behind the stumps against Australia: never a bye in 1,024 runs and a flourishing panache behind the wickets which was an eye-pleasing spectacle in itself for the delighted watchers.

The unusual feature of the years 1946-51 was that, in spite of a

147

plentiful reservoir of talent, England won only one Test in fifteen en
counters with Australia. One of her players of class was Cyril Wash
brook, an opener of world stature, who scored 143 against Bradman'
1948 tourists at Leeds and suffered only from a fatal penchant for the
lofted hook. In scoring 85 not out at Manchester in the same year as hi
century success, Washbrook was missed twice by Lindsay Hassett a
deep fine-leg. Hassett appropriated a policeman's helmet for the nex
opportunity—but Washbrook had learned his lesson, as he proved a
Leeds.

Doug Wright's fast leg-spinning talents also survived the war and
earned him not only a place in the M.C.C. side to Australia in 1946-7
but also unstinting praise from that virtuoso against turn, Lindsay
Hassett. To this day Hassett maintains that Wright was a most difficul
bowling opponent, not merely because of his speed through the air, bu
also because of his steep bounce and acute spin. Wright, however, fel
into the same luckless category as fast bowler of the 1950s, Bria
Statham. Batsmen played and missed at their deliveries with more fre
quency than the law of probability normally allows.

Good fortune, however, was not the determinant factor which
produced the Australian supremacy in the era of the 1940s. Increasing
age, proximity to the trauma of war, dietary deficiences and the
problems of the reconstruction of county cricket, all contributed to
England's lack of success. In the final analysis these factors combined
to produce a situation in which a great Australian team proved itsel
superior to a good England side.

11. The Casualties of War

The M.C.C. tour of Australia and New Zealand in 1946-7 was an extempore affair. The English authorities were reluctant to commit a side, whose strength was a matter of conjecture, to the ordeal of full-scale Tests so soon after the cessation of hostilities. The invitation of the Australian Board of Control, however, was almost insistent and it was supported to the hilt by Labor leader Dr H.V. Evatt, their country's leading diplomat at the United Nations. The fact that the tour would be a great morale booster for the war-weary Commonwealth hardly compensated for the unreadiness of the England contingent. Voce and Pollard, the backbone of the tourists' medium-pace attack, were not even demobilized and had to be given special leave from the Army to make the trip. It was only three weeks before the ex-troopship R.M.S. *Stirling Castle* sailed for Fremantle that the touring party was completed by the inclusion of Edrich, Fishlock and Langridge. Edrich's selection was a fortunate chance since he was one of the successes of an otherwise dismal tour.

England's luck in 1946 was at its lowest ebb. The weather during the tour was most un-Australian and seventeen of the M.C.C. matches were rain-affected. Their early practice was cruelly curtailed. Voce and Pollard waxed fat on Australian food after their meagre English war-time rations and were unable to work off their excess avoirdupoids. Hammond became a martyr to fibrositis during the tour and Hutton was so severely afflicted by tonsillitis that he was compelled to retire ill after scoring a century in the first innings of the Final Test. He flew immediately to England where he underwent a throat operation. The 1946 tour was, in fact, the first occasion when a touring side travelled by plane around Australia. The coincidental event which set the pattern for the subsequent journeys of cricket teams around the continent was a railway strike, which forced the M.C.C. to take a night flight from Adelaide to Melbourne.

The First Test in Brisbane epitomized England's ill-fortune. Not only did Hammond lose a crucial toss and thus condemn his side to batting twice on a wet wicket, but a decisive umpiring decision went against the tourists. England began well when they fielded. Morris fell

149

The disputed Bradman catch. Brisbane 1946

to the third delivery of Bedser's second over, and Barnes was caught at square leg when the score was 46. Bradman scratched together only 7 runs in 40 minutes and when he was 28, he sliced a Voce half-volley to Jack Ikin in the slips, Ikin thought that he had made a perfectly good catch but the umpire ruled not out. It was at this juncture that Hammond was reputed to have exclaimed: 'Well that's a good way to start a series'. Bradman went on to notch 187 and average 97 in the rubber. Had he failed, rumour had it that he would have retired from Tests.

The batsman at the other crease when the crucial incident occurred was Lindsay Hassett, who scored 128 in the same innings. His assessment of the incident was that before lunch on that controversial first day, every England fieldsman thought Bradman was out; after lunch they were less certain and inclined to believe that Bradman had chopped the ball into the ground before it travelled to Ikin.

Australia amassed 645 and England stumbled to 1/21 at the end of the third day. Then it rained—and how it rained! A second thunderstorm followed on the fourth day and flooded the Woolloongabba, according to the eye-witness testimony of Alec Bedser, to a depth which brought the water level to the top of the picket fence surrounding the ground. The stumps floated like disconsolate yellow submarines on the sea that was once a cricket oval.

During the storm hailstones as large as golf balls tumbled from the heavens. The astonished Englishmen goggled at the ferocity of the

150

cyclonic Queensland climate from the shelter of a large wooden hut surrounded by barbed wire—the ancient Gabba pavilion. The inveterate prankster, Syd Barnes, regaled the tourists with tall tales of Brisbane hailstones sometimes a foot in diameter. When they were in the ripe stage of mental credulity, Syd took a large block of ice from the galvanized iron bath which served as a refrigerator to cool the dressing-room drinks and, going to the back of the pavilion, he hurled the icy chunk over the low pavilion roof. The Englishmen were staring out of their dressing-room window as a large hailstone, a foot square, sailed down from the skies and landed with a shuddering thud on the strip of turf before the pavilion. It was weeks before they discovered that there were no square hailstones. After the storm Edrich batted heroically and suffered a fearful battering on the sticky wicket; but England could only accumulate 141 and 172 and went down to defeat by the mammoth margin of an innings and 332 runs. Bradman had gained a modicum of revenge for Australia's humiliation at The Oval in 1938.

The Second Test also went Australia's way by an innings; this time, however, the run bonus was restricted to 33. This Sydney game was the first of England wicketkeeper Godfrey Evan's ninety-one Tests; an international career which was to see him claim an erstwhile record of 219 victims behind the stumps. Evans replaced Paul Gibb, England's hero of the ten-day timeless Test against South Africa in Durban in 1938, and did not concede a bye as Bradman and Barnes each scored 234. For England Edrich scored 119, but the leaden-footed technique of Hammond's batsmen was inadequate to cope with the flight and off-spin of Johnson and the leg-spin of McCool who captured 6/42 and 5/109 respectively.

McCool was an unqualified all-round success in the series. He averaged 54.4 with the bat and captured 18 wickets with his leg-spinners; yet this 1946 rubber was the only occasion on which he played against England. Like spin bowlers, George Tribe and Bruce Dooland, who also made Test appearances in 1946, McCool gravitated towards English county cricket and ended his playing days with Somerset. He was the hero of the drawn Third Test in Melbourne. At one stage Australia were a febrile 6/192 in their first innings; McCool batting at number seven came to the rescue with an unbeaten 104 and bolstered his side's total to 365. It was a tail-ender's match. Batting at numbers eight and nine Tallon and Lindwall scored 92 and 100 in Australia's second innings, and these innings, together with a fine 155 from Arthur Morris, produced 536 runs to guarantee a drawn game. For England, Edrich continued his fine form with a solid 89 and Washbrook scored his first century against Australia in gloomy light and drizzling rain.

The Adelaide encounter was played in extreme heat and humidity with the mercury reaching 104 degrees. Bedser bowled 30 overs in Australia's first innings total of 487 and was led, stupified by heat exhaustion, from the field. On a perfect wicket the batting performances of Morris and Compton alone were enough to make the game inconclusive. They each scored a century in both innings. This is the only time that this feat has been achieved by two players in the same match. With Keith Miller reaching 141 and Hutton producing a fine double of 94 and 76, Adelaide was obviously not a bowler's paradise, though surprisingly, fast bowler Ray Lindwall ended England's first innings by bowling the last three batsmen in the space of four balls.

The final clash in Sydney was won by the home side by a 5-wicket margin. The M.C.C. captain, Hammond, finally yielded to his fibrositis and relinquished his place in the England side. He was the first touring captain to drop himself since Chapman in 1928-9. Hammond's Test career of 85 games embracing the years 1927-46 was over. Yardley was the new king and he began his reign in none-too-auspicious a fashion. Like his predecessor he was unlucky, losing his star batsman and fellow Yorkshireman, Hutton, after the opener scored a brave 122 in spite of acute tonsillitis, a temperature of 103 degrees, and a spate of bouncers from Lindwall and Miller. Wright bowled magnificently for England to capture 7/105 with his fast leg-spin in Australia's first innings; but Australia possessed more than adequate replies to the Kentish man's penetration. Lindwall returned figures of 7/63 in England's first knock and McCool limited their second batting attempt to 186 with a skilful display of leg-spin which yielded him 5/44. Defeat came to the tourists on the fifth day, in spite of the fact that the second day was lost to rain; so much rain fell on the Saturday that the pitch was under water and mushrooms sprang up in the outfield!

Bradman's touring side to England in 1948 has been acclaimed by posterity as the strongest Australian combination ever to visit that country. It won four of the five Tests and was victorious in twenty-three of its matches, without conceding a single triumph to its opponents. Two of its component batting parts, Bradman and Harvey are listed by Wisden as the most prolific Australian scorers in Test history. The side's two opening batsmen, Morris and Barnes averaged over 80 in the five clashes and were so dominant that Bill Brown, Australia's opener of the pre-war era was denied a Test place. Arthur Morris accumulated a huge tally of 696 runs in nine Test innings. The Australian batting juggernaut actually scored 721 in one day's play against Essex! The Essex captain of the time, Tom Pearce, gained one unpalatable crumb of consolation from the match. As he was leaving the ground after his side's game of hunting the leather, an enthusiastic Essex supporter with a sardonic sense of humour congratulated him on being the leader of the first side to dismiss the 1948 Australians in the space of a day. It was reputed that Keith Miller, the tourists' middle-order star, was moved to such pity by the mayhem which was being executed in the middle that, when his turn came to go in with more than 400 on the board, he lifted his bat and allowed himself to be bowled by Trevor Bailey for a duck!

The Australian fast attack of Lindwall, Miller and Johnston was assisted by a selfless innovation in the laws on the part of the English authorities. They were allowed a new ball every 55 overs. As a result, their spinners bowled only just over 200 overs in the series and three quick bowlers, who were expert enough to capture more than 160 wickets each in their Test careers, were permitted to wreak unlicensed havoc on the England batting.

Bradman's last tour was in 1948. As he stated in his farewell speech to the dignitaries of the City of London, the creaks and groans in his bones after a day in the field told him that it was time to quit. When he went to the wicket for the last time in Australia's final innings of the The Oval Test, the England skipper, Norman Yardley, gathered his players around him and led them in three cheers for the Don. The little Australian's run tally for the rubber stood at 508 and his career Test average at 99.94. He was bowled by an Eric Hollies's wrong 'un second ball, some said because his eyes were dimmed by tears. The cynics said that Bradman was too clinically scientific about his cricket to become emotional about it. Whatever the reason for the uncharacteristic finale to Bradman's phenomenal career, his last failure prevented him by a single boundary hit from batting one hundred in international cricket.

England were caught on a damp wicket in the first Test at Nottingham and with the ball rearing nastily were 8/74 in their first innings until a face-saving 63 from slow bowler, Jim Laker, enabled them to reach 165. The home side's chief tormentor was Johnston, a tall, angular left-hander, who captured 5/36 with his late, dipping, fast-medium inswing. Johnston brought the ball down from a great height and his action was so closed at the moment of delivery that he bowled diametrically across his front leg with his leading foot parallel to the popping crease. This action placed a great strain on the bowler's knee and was to cause him injury in his later career. In 1948, however, when he was at the peak of fitness, it afforded him the disconcerting advantage of exceptionally late movement into the right-handed batsman at a pace which was only slightly below that of Miller. As a variant to this delivery Johnston cut the ball appreciably towards the slips. After Bradman and Hassett had each compiled careful centuries and Australia accumulated 509, England batted more competently on their second appearance at the crease to reach 441. Compton scored a brilliant 184 against what the anti-Australian crowd deemed to be more than his rightful share of bouncers; but it was all to no avail and Australia scored the necessary 98 runs for victory for the loss of only 2 wickets. Significantly, however, one of those wickets was that of Bradman who was caught at short-leg by Hutton off Bedser without scoring. He fell in similar fashion in the next Test at Lords thus giving birth to the rumour that Bedser had found a chink in the great man's armour.

The margin of Australia's victory in the Second Test was 409 runs. It was a remarkable commentary on the depth of ability in the Australian team that this crushing win was achieved in spite of the fact that their opening bowler, the all-rounder Miller, appeared solely as a batsman, being unable to bowl a ball because of an injury. The story goes that it was during this Test that Bradman threw the ball to Miller and demanded that he bowl. Miller, who had declared his injury before the game, returned the ball to Bradman in a rare show of defiance which amazed the martinet Australian skipper as much as it did the astonished 20,000 onlookers. Was it coincidence, I wonder, that Miller was omitted from a side, selected in part by Bradman, to go to South Africa in 1949-50?

The absence of Miller from the firing line was more than remedied

Hassett bowled first ball by Yardley. Lords 1948

by the performance of his mate, Jackson Lindwall, who captured 5/70 in England's first innings reply of 215 to Australia's 350. In their second innings, the tourists piled on the agony by garnering 7/460 declared, largely through the agency of a century from Barnes. On the third day of the match Lindsay Hassett, who was batting at number four in the order, sat for six hours in the dressing-room whilst Barnes, Morris and Bradman scored 296 for the first 2 wickets. Television was a sporting novelty in those days, and a set had been installed in the Australian changing-room to enable the visitors to follow the fortunes of their compatriots at the contemporaneous Wimbledon Tennis Championships. Hassett spent hours watching the tennis with his head swivelling from side to side. Suddenly with the dismissal of Barnes, came the laconic summons: 'Taskett you're in'. His head still spinning, Hassett hurried confusedly through Lords' maze of staircases to the centre of the ground. The first ball he received was a gentle medium-paced half-volley from England skipper Norman Yardley. He must have offered a forehand instead of a forward defensive stroke, for he missed it and was bowled. Lindsay swears that when he left the dressing-room the score in the game of tennis at Wimbledon was 15-love; his stay at the wicket was so short that when he returned the score had only advanced to 40-15! Hassett, however, had little reason to be anxious about his second innings failure. Showers added spice to the wicket and Australia's slow-medium left-hand bowler, Ernie Toshack snaffled 5/40 to tumble England out for 186 and win the match.

The Old Trafford Test almost caused Yorkshire to secede from the

United Kingdom. Len Hutton, the hero of the county of the White Rose and the one-time scorer of a record 364 against Australia, was dropped from the opening-bat position which he had held as if by royal prerogative since 1938! How well I remember the indignation and furore which the selection of Gloucestershire's George Emmett caused in Yorkshire. It was commonly held that the old antipathy of southerners towards northerners was solely responsible for Hutton's omission. 'The selectors don't think that anyone can laike at cricket north of the Trent'; such was the angry opinion stormily expressed in the environs of Leeds in July 1948. As it turned out, Emmett scored only 10 runs in 2 innings and was immediately released never to play again for England; but strange to relate, England managed to avoid defeat in Manchester for the only time in the series.

Compton's heroic 145 not out was compiled in spite of a welter of bouncers and a gashed head sustained from a short, Lindwall no-ball. After a remedial tot of brandy and two stitches in his brow, Denis wanted to return to the crease at the fall of the next wicket. Wiser counsels prevailed and he was held in reserve to steer England to 363 and, for the first time in the rubber, into a first innings lead. After being struck in the kidneys by a Pollard 'slog' whilst fielding at short-leg, Australia's opener, Sydney Barnes, attempted to bat but collapsed at the wicket and was replaced by lower order batsman Ian Johnson. An amusing development of the Barnes's injury occurred when he was carried into the dressing-room for the first time. A call for medical help was broadcast over the public address system. This produced a tall, bespectacled local doctor who was a rabid cricket enthusiast, and more than a respectable fast bowler for Royton in the Central Lancashire League. A quick examination sufficed to determine that Barnes was suffering only from bruising and for the rest of the day 'Doc' Longbottom revelled in the atmosphere of the Australian dressing-room, trying Bradman's bat, obtaining autographs and talking with the players whilst lending a sympathetic, but not-too-attentive ear to Barnes's moans. Rain on the fourth day guaranteed a drawn game and not even Yardley's declaration at 3/174 on the fifth morning could force the issue.

Leeds produced one of the most extraordinary Test matches of modern times. Australia won the game against all odds by 7 wickets and in so doing, established a record score for a team batting last and winning the game. Their total of 3/404 came in 344 minutes on a turning last-day pitch; it is perhaps a reflection on the increasingly defensive attitude of the current game that the challenge issued to Bradman on 27 July 1948 would probably have been refused by every Test captain of the last twenty years. Bedi's Indian XI exceeded the achievement of Bradman's combination by totalling a final 4/406 to defeat Lloyd's West Indians in the Third Port of Spain Test in 1976; but the Indian victory bid necessitated a day and a half. It is doubtful whether Bedi would have contemplated the same formidable goal in the short space of a day.

The high-scoring Leeds game yielded no fewer than five centuries, one of them to the 19-year-old Neil Harvey, who thus became the second youngest Australian to score a century on his début in Tests. Harvey was a left-hander of immense talent in an immensely talented family. His brother Merv played against Hammond's tourists in one Test without retaining his opening berth. Neil was an unstoppable rather than an immovable batsman. Against pace bowlers he loved to cut and hook, whilst the spinners who flighted the ball discovered that he was the nimblest of opponents. He always played strokes and thus dangled the attractive carrot of possible dismissal under the noses of his bowling enemies. Once Harvey was in full batting flight, however, he was so destructive of bowlers' analyses and so correctly certain in his technique that no opponent relished bowling against him. The 112 which he scored at Leeds was the first of his twenty-one centuries and 6,149 runs in Tests: statistics which place him second only to Bradman in Australian batting ranks. In my own playing time, Harvey was undoubtedly the most proficient Australian batting artist.

Washbrook with 143, Edrich with 111 and nightwatchman Bedser with 79 boosted England's first innings total at Leeds to 496; but thanks to Harvey's century, 93 from Loxton and 77 from Lindwall, the tourists lagged by only 38. England scored 8/365 when they batted again and prolonged their innings five minutes into the last day in order to accelerate the breaking-up of the wicket with a last application of the heavy roller. Alas for their fond hopes! The wicket turned, but Evans missed both Morris and Bradman off Compton's wrist spin and each of them scored centuries to snatch a deserved Australian victory twelve minutes before close of play. It was a match which completely demoralized England. This fact was abundantly evident when the home side won the toss and elected to bat in the final disastrous encounter at The Oval. The wicket was wet and slow, yet in just over two hours Lindwall captured 6/20 and England were dismissed for 52—their lowest total in post-war Tests. Hutton batted magnificently to be the last man out with his score at 30. When the Yorkshireman was brilliantly caught down the leg-side by Tallon from a stroke which would normally have yielded 4 runs, he was the only man in the home side to have reached double figures. Morris rubbed salt into England's open wound by scoring 196 before he was run out. Australia led by 337 on the first innings and the result was a pure formality. The Test inexperience of such players as Cambridge undergraduate, Dewes, and Glamorgan all-rounder, Watkins, was not equal to the Australian fast attack. England were dismissed a second time for 188 and lost by an innings and 149 runs. Bradman must have regretted, in this his final Test, that his team was so efficient. A second Australian innings would have given him the opportunity of bolstering his final international average to three figures.

Business sponsorship provided the stimulus for the revival of England's Test fortunes of the early 1950s. In the late 1940s the roller-bearing manufacturer, British Timken, sought to boost the cricketing fortunes of the midland county of Northamptonshire by employing many of its players. The chairman of the company, Sir John Pascoe, invited Freddie Brown to join Timken and F.R. took over the captaincy of the county eleven. The former Surrey and England all-rounder, who toured Australia with Jardine's side in 1932-3 was not, at the age of thirty-eight, in the first flush of youth when he made his comeback into first-class cricket. Yet in the 1949 season he captured 111 wickets, only 11 less than Jim Laker, and scored 1,077 runs, just 21 short of Brian Close's aggregate. The following season Brown notched a hard-driven 122 in the Gentlemen versus Players match at Lords and the captaincy of England, which he had usurped from F. G. Mann for the Third and Fourth Tests against New Zealand in 1949, was his for the 1950-1 tour of Australia and New Zealand

Freddie Brown was my first captain in county cricket. As a player under his command I can speak of him with authority. He was a skipper cast in the pre-war mould. He knew his appointed station and the relative situation of the players under him. He was an authoritarian leader, who brooked no disobedience. When he entered the Northants

The aggressive Freddie Brown

selection committee room, he took with him a slip of paper on which were written the names of the players he would be happy to lead in the next game. Since the other members of the committee had no obligation to make a silk purse out of a sow's ear, Freddie deemed the composition of the side to be beyond their ken. Heaven help the twelfth man who forgot that F.R. required a revivifying whisky and water at the afternoon drink interval on a hot day in the field. Woe betide the young player who, as I did, stepped into the bath specially run for him by the twelfth man after each day's play. There was one aspect of F.R.'s cricket, however, which set him above the normal run of amateur captains in those days of the early 1950s. Like the eighteenth and nineteenth century English aristocrat, F.R. was aware, not only of the privileges of his station, but also of its responsibilities. Freddie Brown, even at the age of forty-two never asked a 24-year-old boy like myself to do something which he himself could not do. He would bowl a whole afternoon's spell of twiddling little leg-spinners and googlies on a spot which seldom varied more than a foot in length; then when the second new ball became due, he would assume that it was his prerogative to use it and proceed to send down another dozen overs of medium-pace swingers. As hot hour succeeded hot hour, his rubicund face above the familiar neckerchief became ruddier and ruddier, until one feared that he would be stricken in mid run-up by a heart attack. He soldiered on, however, and thus earned himself a wonderful reputation amongst the Sydney costermongers; they extolled the quality of their cabbages and lettuces in 1951 as having 'hearts as big as Freddie Brown'. If I had been buying the greengroceries, I would have snapped up their merchandise if they lived up to their reputations; they must have been bargains.

The professionals in the Northamptonshire side gave F.R. a grudging respect. Some could not forget the amateur-professional distinction which was only just becoming outmoded; not one player could deny him admiration. So they feared him; not only because he went on to the front foot to drive Lindwall at the age of thirty-nine, not only because he could bowl hour after hour in torrid heat, not only because he was one of the amateur establishment, but largely because of the fact that he drew on sources of inspiration too deep for their comprehension.

A strong body of opinion amongst the senior players who toured Australia under Brown in 1950-1 believed that the series victory, which eventually came England's way in 1953, should have preceded that eventual triumph by two years. Australia won the Brisbane Test by only 70 runs, on the strength of the fortuitous spin of the coin, which condemned the tourists to batting twice on a wet Gabba wicket. The second clash also went to the home team, this time by the tenuous margin of 28 runs. The Englishmen were left to wonder what might have happened if their hero of the 1948 series, Denis Compton, had struck a modicum of form. The fact remains that the batsman, who scored 562 runs in ten Test innings only two years previously, was so plagued by the after-effects of an operation to remove a bone chip from his knee, that he could only total 53 in his next eight knocks! A soupçon of good luck could easily have tipped the scales in England's favour in the first two games of the 1950-1 rubber; with the Third and Fourth Tests going convincingly to Hassett's side, this would have made the final match the tie-breaker—and England won their first post-war victory against Australia in that game at Melbourne by 8 wickets. All this is pure hypothesis on what might have been IF . . .! The fact remains that Brown's touring party was very much under strength in the bowling department. Though the leg-spinner, Eric Hollies, and left-arm slow bowler, Bob Berry, toiled hard they lacked the finger and wrist power to make the ball deviate on the hard Australian pitches and consequently lacked penetration. Hollies, an excellent bowler and prolific wicket-taker in England, had a most unhappy tour—though it would be difficult to determine whether he hated Australian wickets or flying between state matches the more. John Warr, the Middlesex medium-pacer, soon discovered that antipodean conditions were unsympathetic to his swinging skills; when Bailey broke a finger and Wright tore a tendon in the Third Test, Brown was compelled to summon bowling reinforcements from England. The pasty faces of off-spinner Tattersall and speedster Statham appeared in subsequent M.C.C. teams during the tour, but the process of acclimatization was too lengthy and the new chums played no great role in the remainder of the rubber.

Brown was fortunate to be served by the medium-paced artistry of Bedser, who captured 30 wickets in the five Tests. His tally might have been greater if the England fielding had risen even to the moderate heights of competency. Warr, in particular, came in for astringent comment and good-natured advice from former Australian opener, Syd Barnes, who was now on the press sidelines as a result of his legal altercation with the Board of Control. It was alleged that after Warr had missed a few simple outfield catches, Syd took him into the nets to give him a practice session. J.J. always won friends and laughs with his unquenchable wit and unstinting effort wherever he went in Australia—but he only took 1 wicket in his two Tests in that country at a cost of 281 runs.

Australia produced a winning dark horse in the series in the person of the mystery spin bowler, big 'Jake' Iverson. Iverson's methods were unique until John Gleeson imitated them in the late 1960s. He imparted spin to the ball by flicking the bent second finger of his bowling hand to the right or left of the ball with little or no use of the wrist. It was almost impossible to detect the direction of Iverson's turn since he bowled out of the front of his hand. The fact that he delivered the ball from a lofty elevation with little or no flight, great accuracy and a surprising degree of resultant bounce, made him almost impossible to hit. The main problem which he posed to batsmen, however, was the same as that set by Ramadhin, the West Indian slow bowler, in the early 1950s: his opponents were unsure of the direction of his turn. It was not until Len Hutton detected that Iverson only spun his leg-break minimally and began to play him as an off-spinner, that the effectiveness of the Melbourne bowler was, to some degree, curbed. By this stage Iverson had wrought his havoc and he ended the rubber with 21 wickets to his credit at an average cost of 15.23 runs each.

Iverson's lack of cricket background made him an odd intruder on to the Test field. He was the product of a school with a noble cricket heritage—Geelong College—the Alma Mater of Lindsay Hassett, Paul Sheahan and Ian Redpath. When he was at school, however, he was not interested in cricket. He was a rower. Iverson only turned to cricket after the war, when he was thirty. Whilst serving in New Guinea, he discovered his peculiar knack of being able to impart spin to a table tennis ball with a bent second finger. He did not realize that his extraordinary talent could be turned to great use on the cricket field until a few years after the war. Iverson's cricket origins were lowly and his rise to Test fame, meteoric. He began as a 30-year-old 'junior' with the third eleven of the Melbourne sub-district side of Brighton. He did not remain long in cadet ranks. Within a year he was a member of the first eleven of the Melbourne Cricket Club. In his first full season with the M.C.C. he captured 64 wickets at an average of 12.06 and was a major factor in his side winning the V.C.A. premiership. That same year, 1949-50, Iverson really came of cricketing age, taking 46 wickets in the Sheffield Shield and gaining selection in the Australian 'B' side which visited New Zealand in February. The Iverson rags to riches success story continued in the 'Shaky Isles' where he snatched 75 wickets at a cost of 7.73 on the two-month tour—25 of them coming in first-class matches. Even whilst he was baffling Freddie Brown's batsmen in Australia, he was still causing problems for his fellow countrymen in Shield games. He captured 23 wickets for Victoria in 1950-1 at, let it be noted, the greatly increased cost of 25.34 runs each. Then, like a comet, just as suddenly as he arrived on the scene, Iverson was gone. He did not linger to win a place in the 1953 touring team to England.

Jack Iverson

I suppose that the shallowness of Iverson's cricket education made it certain that he would be a five-day wonder. He invented a unique method of spinning the ball which a conventional bowler with a conventional background in the game would never have created in a month of Sundays; but that was really all that Jake ever had of real value. His batting aspirations were limited to the wielding of a mahogany-hued bat in a manner reminiscent of an aborigine's use of the nula-nula. In the field he stood like the Rock of Gibraltar at mid-off and caused many an involuntary shudder down Ray Lindwall's spine by his habit of stopping the ball, even when it was in its shiny youth of the first over, by stepping on it with an enormous, spiked boot! After his retirement from the first-class game big Jake Iverson continued his association with cricket from the broadcasting box, but even this did not last. He returned to the family real estate business and on 24 October 1973 he took the secret of his highly individualistic bowling to the grave; at the age of fifty-eight he took his own life.

Australia won the Brisbane Test of 1950-1 because Hassett won the toss. The home side's first innings total of 228 was not imposing, but it sufficed. Rain carried off the second day and transformed the uncovered wicket into an unpredictable quagmire. Consequently the third day witnessed two declarations, the fall of 20 wickets and the scoring of a paltry 130 runs. On the fourth morning the wicket was slightly improved, and England's opening batsman, Hutton, who had been held in reserve in the second innings in the number eight position, played one of the great wet-wicket innings of modern times. He made 62 not out in a total of 122 with a magnificent display of back foot driving; the surviving habitués of the Gabba still speak of that Hutton knock in hushed and reverent terms.

Melbourne is normally allotted the third game of a rubber. In 1950 it was allocated the second match which was played in the Christmas rather than over the usual New Year period. In that southern season, Yuletide in Victoria was particularly humid, and consequently the swing bowlers on both sides enjoyed a field day in another low scoring clash. Bedser and Bailey toppled Australia for only 194, but at one stage in their reply England were a lowly 6/61. Then came Freddie Brown, whose match this undoubtedly was; he scored 62 with fearless front-foot driving and together with 49 from Godfrey Evans lifted England into a 3-run lead. The tourists' skipper followed his inspirational batting with a 4-wicket bowling performance in Australia's second innings and England were set only 179 to win. Without the injured Compton and against the devastating pace and movement of Johnston and Lindwall, they failed by 29 runs.

Brown continued his purple batting patch in Sydney by notching 79; but the dice was loaded against his men and England were never in the contest. A lifting delivery broke Bailey's thumb and Wright suffered a leg injury whilst being run out. Consequently, when Australia batted they were confronted by only three overburdened bowlers; to make matters worse, Compton's wrist spinners were hardly a viable risk, since the Middlesex man's injured knee was still badly swollen. The result was that Australia totalled 426 and their lead of 136, allied to a crumbling wicket, was enough to gain them a victory by an innings and 13 runs. The unplayable Iverson captured 6/27.

The woeful catalogue of the English wounded was lengthened when their captain missed the fifth day of the Adelaide Test, after he was injured. A car, in which he was travelling, struck a pylon under a dark bridge on one of the city's terraces. The match was virtually lost before the accident, for Australia were already 384 runs in the lead with 5 second-innings wickets remaining. The highlights of the match were undoubtedly Morris's 206—the third time in succession that the left hander had reached three figures against England in the City of Light—and a classic 156 not out from the bat of Hutton. The Yorkshireman's feat of carrying his bat in an England first innings total of 272 must rank as one of his greatest Test achievements. Jimmy Burke, replacing Loxton in the Australian side at number six, scored an unbeaten 101 in his second innings and first game against England, and Australia's totals of 371 and 8/403 were enough to give Hassett's team victory by 274 runs on the sixth day.

England's win by 8 wickets in the Final Melbourne Test gave the title of 'The Elusive Victory' to a subsequent book by E. W. Swanton, the doyen of Fleet Street cricket writers. The win was a notable landmark in the resurgence of English post-war cricket since it was that country's first defeat of the old enemy in five years and it began a period of eight years' supremacy over Australia. The reasons for England's triumph

Reg Simpson

were to be found in the genius of Bedser's medium-pace, the bowling versatility of Brown, and the batting of the mercurial Reg Simpson; Bedser captured 10 wickets in the match, Brown 6, and Simpson ravaged 156 not out against an Australian attack which was the equal of that at Bradman's disposal in 1948.

Simpson was a batsman cast in the classical Nottinghamshire mould of the Hardstaffs. He was beautifully erect in his stance and classically correct in his technique against fast bowling. Like Joe Hardstaff he was handsome from the top of his luxuriant curly hair down to the execution of his strokes. Simpson sometimes erred on the side of impatience, which, I believe, stemmed from his disdain of slow bowlers. On 27 February 1951 in Melbourne, every aspect of Simpson's batsmanship fell into perfect perspective. Going to the wicket with 40 on the board he batted with complete composure against pace and a great sense of adventure against the spin of Iverson and Johnson. When England's ninth wicket fell Simpson had seen the departure of eight partners and 205 runs added to the total. With Tattersall coming to the crease, Simpson threw caution to the winds and sallying down the wicket like a latter day George Gunn, he contributed 64 of the 74 runs scored before Miller bowled the Lancashire off-spinner.

England's total of 320 gave the tourists a lead of 103 over the home side's moderate first effort of 217. When Bedser and Wright demolished the Australian batting a second time for a meagre 197, victory for England was around the corner and Hutton's immaculate 60 not out ensured that there was no disappointing anticlimax for England to the 1950-1 M.C.C. tour of Australia. Lindsay Hassett bowled a whimsical last over; this time his international average read: 6 balls, 0 maidens, 0 wickets and 4 runs.

Australia would have done well to have feared the Ides of March in 1951. The last ball of the last Test against England on the last day of February rang down the curtain on a notable epoch in their cricket history. The post-war era had seen Bradman's and Hassett's elevens win nineteen official and one unofficial Test without conceding a single defeat. The figures were a just reflection on the sporting ability of cricket's Land of Giants. The combined might of England, South Africa, India and New Zealand was no match for the likes of Lindwall, Miller, Morris, Harvey, Hassett, Bradman, Barnes and Johnston. Time, however, erodes all physical talents and it requires time to replace greatness with promise. In 1951 the Benauds, Burkes, Davidsons, McDonalds, Archers and Holes were on the Test horizon but their moments of triumph were still around the corner. In successive Australian summers Hassett's men lost a Test to Goddard's West Indians and drew a series with Cheetham's miraculous young South African fieldsmen of 1952-3. After being undefeated for six years Australia found themselves on the threshold of the 1953 tour of England, with their hitherto unblemished record blotted by four losses in three years.

12. England's Speedy Recovery

In the evening rays of the September sun the 22-year-old aircraftman and Yorkshire fast bowler, Frederick Sewards Trueman, sat exhausted on the chassis of the sightscreen at the Kingston Cricket Ground. The day of 5 September 1953 had been a hard one for the speedster. On a moribund wicket, Australia had scored 4/592 in six hours against the English Combined Services. Miller thrashed a majestic 262 and 'Words' De Courcy registered 204. Trueman, powerless on the sluggish wicket, conceded 95 runs without taking a wicket. In the space of another short day his side were to go down to defeat by an innings and 261 runs. The press castigated the young England bowler's ineffectiveness in the Kingston game, but the Yorkshireman was far from worried. After all, it was only three weeks previously that he had been a member of the England team which won The Oval Test and with it the 1953 series against Australia. That was the match which really mattered.

Enough has been said and written of the ex-miner from Stainton to constitute the longest filibuster of all time or to fill a library. His bowling record stands alone on its statistical merits: 2,304 wickets in first-class games and 307 in Tests. He was the first bowler to break the triple century wicket barrier in internationals, and the speed of his accomplishment was years faster than his rival the West Indian off-spinner, Lance Gibbs. It would be repetitious and boring to retread the ground covered by so many of the chroniclers of Trueman's deeds and sayings. It is better to record my own experiences of a fast bowler who was one of the best produced by his country and the county of the broad acres.

I first saw Trueman in action in 1949, his débutant year in first-class cricket. The scene was the Hull Cricket Ground and the match Yorkshire versus the Army. At eighteen years of age the Trueman characteristics and mannerisms were already well developed. His approach to the wicket was parabolic in contour, beautifully rhythmic, and superbly gradated in acceleration. As he ran rollingly, Trueman swung his arms akimbo in a gesture of arrogant confidence. In his delivery stride Trueman opened his arms like a giant bat unfolding its wings; he was academically side-on, his front arm classically high and his leading

Freddie Trueman, 'like a giant bat unfolding its wings'

leg well clear of the turf and ready to plunge with spine-shattering force to earth. The gleaming metal toecap of his right boot rasped in his drag over three feet of devastated soil behind the bowling crease. The purity of Trueman's action made him a natural swinger of the ball; his out-swinger was curvaceous in flight, vicious in speed and inexorably pitched on the ideal spot. The fast bowler seemed to be in complete control of his every action. Did the style of the opposition batsman demand an inswinger, off-cutter or leg-cutter? No sooner said, than Trueman did it.

The Yorkshireman possessed great faith in himself and he firmly believed that every ball which he delivered possessed unique attributes. When he was asked if he had ever bowled a straight delivery, Trueman paused with comical and studied deliberation and said: 'Nay, I don't think I have—wait on though—I tell a lie. There was this straight full toss I bowled at Martin Horton. Knocked 'is bloody middle-stump out of the ground'.

Fred was the possessor of a fine and natural cricketing brain. He could discover a batsman's Achilles' heel in a matter of minutes and produce the exact delivery to exploit the weakness. It was he who, when he was captaining Yorkshire, detected the failing of the Australian batsman Doug Walters outside the off-stump. Immediately he posted two gully fieldsmen, bowled the perfect outswinger—and Walters was on the way back to the pavilion. Nor was his native intelligence confined to the cricket field. Fred possessed a sponge-like memory for jokes and could reel off funny stories for a full hour to an entranced audience who had seldom heard the anecdotes before and rarely stopped chuckling. For a while Trueman's capacity to amuse brought him a living as a comedian on the club circuit in the north of England. His wit was trenchant, sometimes savage and always spontaneous. He came in to bat at Northampton on one occasion when I was bowling and had dismissed the previous Yorkshire batsman who had shown himself less than enthusiastic about fast bowling. Fred remarked: 'I should have brought a shovel as well as a bloody bat'. When someone asked him what he wanted the shovel for, Fred replied: 'To shovel up the manure yon man's left!'

Fred was contoured for fast bowling. He had no tapering waist. He was as straight and as solid as a tree trunk from shoulder to hip. He possessed a miner's strength in his body which was still surprisingly supple. His strength was self-evident when he batted. Trueman was a dangerous hitter with first-class hundreds to his name. He delighted in striking the ball long distances. Once he played in the Champion County versus the Rest fixture at The Oval. The wickets were pitched on the gasholder side of the playing arena and were literally 150 yards from the boundary on the Harleyford Road side of the ground. This did not deter F.S. from trying to hit a Surrey slow bowler for six over the longest boundary. Inevitably he was caught by Barrington off a towering hit on the very edge of The Oval. When Trueman came into the dressing-room, all of the players commiserated and said that if Fred had really got hold of it, it would easily have gone for six. 'Aye', said Fred, 'I really only edged that one!'

In his youth, Trueman was genuinely very fast, though he tended towards inaccuracy because of his inclination to throw back his head just before he delivered the ball. The 1952 touring Indians ran into the Trueman tempest with a vengeance at Old Trafford and The Oval. In Manchester, Trueman and Bedser reduced Hazare's men to the plight of 5/17 in their first innings. At Kennington, India's fifth wicket fell with only 6 runs on the board! In his later career, Trueman declined in speed but not in cunning and his mastery of every type of fast delivery. The fact that his action was technically correct enabled him to sustain his pace long after the strength of less orthodox bowlers failed them. When the pitch helped the cutter of the ball, Trueman's control enabled him to exploit the wicket's assistance—as he did against Australia on the whitened and crumbling Leeds surface in 1961. As a short-leg fieldsman, Trueman was out of the top-drawer. He had the razor-sharp reflexes of the natural sportsman and hands which, like his inseparable partner of later years, his pipe, seemed huge and cavernous. The opening batsman who took guard and looked around the field to discover Trueman and Lock at short-leg, knew that he would put the ball in the air on the on-side at his own risk.

To tour overseas with Fred was like being a soldier in the front-line trenches: one eventually suffered nervous exhaustion from the continual bombardment of opinions, witticisms and jokes which held one spellbound on the edge of the chair, waiting for the direct hit from the blockbuster which would send everyone scurrying for cover. F.S. not only split infinitives with his expletives, he did not hesitate to carve up adverbs. 'Inci-bloody-dentally', was not an unusual piece of his rough surgery on the English language. Fred's bluntness occasionally landed him in hot water. His omission from the England touring side to Australia in 1954-5 has never been fully explained to my, and doubtless to his, satisfaction. Rumour had it that the selection committee passed over his name because of Trueman's acquired status of *persona non grata* with the West Indian establishment during the previous winter's tour to the Caribbean. It was not a difficult qualification to earn, as Lock and Graveney discovered to their cost, but it was a rough kind of injustice which delivered the verdict of the exclusion of both Trueman and Lock from the subsequent Australian trip. Even cricket justice, it appears, is blind.

The strangest tour on which I accompanied Fred Trueman was a promotional coach trip to Nice on the French Riviera. By the time that the party, which included Fred's new wife, reached the Hotel Splendide on the Boulevard Victor Hugo, they had been royally entertained by Fred's unending stream of jokes on the coach's microphone and a visit to the Beaune wine cellars. Quickly the Yorkshireman set the maitre d'hotel at ease by calling him 'chuff' and asking that no red wine be brought as it sent him to sleep, and he had no intention of going to sleep on that honeymoon holiday. Fred made the tour a huge success. His infectious influence on the humour of the other passengers was such that one day out of Boulogne on the return journey, a middle-aged, impassive and hitherto silent north-countryman suddenly seized the microphone from Fred and outdid his mentor by recounting the most uproariously rude stories! Fred laughed; but he did not laugh when a customs officer wanted to pierce the cork of his bottle of Beaune to see if it was brandy. This was not surprising since Fred had declared his eight-pint jeroboam as a bottle of wine!

England was fortunate to have the young fast bowling force of the ferocious Freddie Trueman in the early 1950s; but the Yorkshireman was only one of a bumper crop of bowlers who seized the initiative for England in Tests against Australia and held on to it for six years. Across the Pennine Hills from Trueman's native Yorkshire, the rival county of Lancashire contributed their speedster Statham to the English revival. Middlesex lent their support in the person of Alan Moss and across the river Thames, Peter Loader, at The Oval, was serving a medium-fast apprenticeship which was to culminate in his capturing a hat-trick against the West Indies in the Leeds Test of 1957. Bedser and Bailey were still bowling strongly for England in 1953, but with Test bowlers such as Jackson, Gladwin, Flavell, Rhodes and Shackleton operating in the county background, it was no sinecure to hold on to their positions in the face of challenges from every quarter.

The Truemans en route to Nice

In spin too, England was strong and well-equipped for every contingency. Laker, Lock and Appleyard were deadly on any pitch which gave them assistance and economical on batting surfaces. Wardle could bowl either left-handed finger or wrist spin as the conditions dictated. Slow bowlers such as Titmus, Allen, Mortimore and Illingworth, who were later to gain regular Test recognition, were afforded only occasional opportunities to prove themselves.

Lancashire's Brian Statham earned himself a permanent fast bowling niche in the England side for 70 Tests and eleven years when, after playing in a single game against Hassett's 1953 Australians, he was chosen in the subsequent year's Tests against the West Indies and Pakistan. Statham was the very antithesis to Trueman in every respect. In contrast to the fire, ferocity and extroversion of Trueman's bowling, Statham's cricket was as placid as a pond, and though the Lancastrian was a formidable opponent, his methods had their source in an almost introspective demeanour. His team-mates dubbed him 'The Greyhound' and sometimes 'The Whippet', because of his lean, india-rubber frame and his lithe approach to the wicket. Statham, with a Walter Mitty outlook, chose for himself the nickname of 'George'. When he was asked why he selected the name, he said with simple logic: 'Because I like it'.

Both as a bowler and a person, Statham was monumentally calm, even in moments of high crisis and emotion. During the Fourth Test against the West Indies in Port of Spain in 1954, England's slow bowler and non-recognized number eight batsman, Jim Laker, was struck an almost blinding blow over the eye by an unwarranted bouncer from the West Indian fast bowler, King. King did not appear at the batting crease during that Test, but when he finally walked from the pavilion to face the music from the touring side, Statham was bowling. His partner in pace, Trueman, remembering the bloody pursuit of the England players in Trinidad after the almost demented Laker, expressed in blunt terms that now was the time for a vengeful bumper. Statham thought a moment, then said: 'Nay, I think I'll just bowl him out!'

Unlike Trueman, Statham relied very little on movement through the air. One of the rare times when he did swing the ball was in the Guyana Test against the West Indies in 1953-4. The Bourda ground at Georgetown is below sea-level and protected, like much of the city, from the incursions of the sea by dykes. Consequently the atmosphere in the centre of the ground is humid and redolent with swing. Statham found on this occasion that in spite of his not attempting to move the ball, it swung unpredictably in all directions. The Lancastrian actually bowled a wide—an occurrence which his regular England keeper, Godfrey Evans, had never seen before. 'Godders' always maintained that he could tell when Statham was about to have an inaccurate day with the ball. His touchstone was Statham being off line with one delivery in his first over. George was a firm believer in the 'dead-on' theory of bowling. He used to say: 'If you bowl on the off-side, all your fieldsmen should be on that side of the pitch. If you aim at the leg-stump, you need everybody on the leg-side; but if you set your sights on middle stump, you don't need any fieldsmen'. Whilst the jocularity of the philosophy is obvious, there is a strong foundation of common sense in the 'accuracy theory'.

Because Statham did not move the ball through the air, there is no reason to presuppose that he did not make the ball deviate at all. He was in fact that most dangerous of bowlers: a person who could make the ball change direction off the wicket. Statham possessed a deadly ball which he termed his 'nip-backer'. It was tantamount to a fast off-spinner, inexorably pitched in the perfect spot and moved off the seam on a remarkable seventy-five per cent of the occasions on which he attempted it. There were few histrionics about Statham's bowling. He employed the bouncer only sparingly, and when he treated the batsman to this form of refined torture, the ball was generally at an awkward, throttling, adam's apple level rather than a spectacular altitude, feet above the striker's head. His length was almost invariable and a yard out of the batsman's reach. Perhaps Statham was too predictable, his attitude too placid, and his methods too punctilious; maybe it was this approach which gave the impression that his speed was not in the highest bracket. If this is the case, I should like to correct the misconception. Statham's speed was measured by the scientific means of a radio beam and a metal-plated ball in Wellington, New Zealand in 1955. The exact conclusion of the scientists was that he bowled at 87 mph by comparison with my 89 mph. His velocity was far below the 96 mph achieved by the Australian speedster Jeff Thomson in 1975. But one must place Statham's not inconsiderable speed in its true perspective by stating that the day on which he was assessed was bleak and windy, the pitch and approaches were saturated by an overnight downpour, and Statham bowled in two sweaters without bothering to change from his grey street trousers! Surely those mitigating factors must have been worth quite a few more miles per hour.

The origin of the Lancashire bowler's speed was puzzling. The sprinting yet effortless fluidity of his approach certainly afforded him a great degree of pacy, forward momentum; but there was little of the Trueman arching of the back in the delivery stride. Statham's front foot was not lifted high and slid rather than pounded into the turf. The real cause of the 'Greyhound's' skidding velocity was to be found in the abnormal physical attributes of his shoulders and elbows. He was double-jointed in both areas. His favourite party trick was to pull off a sweater by reaching over his left shoulder with his right hand and grasping the rear hem of the pullover. Before he delivered the ball, his right elbow straightened beyond the normal 180 degrees; it would have been a fine point of law if an umpire had argued that his hyper-extension of the joint and its straightening constituted a violation of law 26. In its final swing Statham's bowling arm was like a flail delivering the ball with a whipping action and consequently more speed.

George Statham's bowling was stamped with the red badge of courage. His effort was unremitting. Not infrequently, he jarred his leading foot with such consistent violence on bone-hard wickets that the constant pounding of his big toe against his toe-cap ripped off his nail and caused his foot to bleed. When this occurred he would simply cut

Brian Statham
('George')

away the toe of his left boot. It was not unusual to see Statham bowling
with a bloody sock protruding from a hacked and toe-less left boot.
The gods rarely smiled on him. He made top-class batsman play and
miss repeatedly without ever edging the ball. On such exasperating
occasions, the only emotion to which he gave expression was a philo-
sophical shake of the head and a shrug of the shoulders, as he turned to
plod back to his bowling mark. On tour he was the target for bad luck.
Once the sickness of one of his children compelled him to return in
hurried alarm from the West Indies; in Australia in 1958-9 he and Peter
Loader were involved in a car accident at the Rock near Wagga Wagga
and missed the Final Test. Nor was he luckier in business; when he
retired from cricket, his venture into the double glazing industry ended
in failure. On one happy occasion, Statham captured a hat-trick during
an M.C.C. game against Transvaal in Johannesburg. An official party

after the event recognized his rare achievement, but even this celebration could not pass without a minor upset. As the toast was offered: 'To Brian Statham'—a voice from the rear, hilariously disrupted the evening by uttering in thick Jewish accents: 'Vell, vere the 'ell is my drink, den'.

Statham was not the hero of the 1953 series against Australia. Like Trueman, the Lancastrian appeared in only one game in the rubber. The real Titans of the home side were Bedser, Watson and Bailey. Bedser snaffled a remarkable 39 wickets in the 5 Tests. The left-handed Yorkshire batsman, Willie Watson, together with Bailey, rescued England from the brink of disaster by batting for virtually the whole of the fifth day of the Lords Test and adding 163 for the fifth wicket, at a time when the home side were 4/73. Bailey twice assumed the role of the rescuing hero during the rubber—though Australians would doubtless prefer to think of him in villainous terms, if only for the part he played in the Leeds clash. At Headingley, the Essex all-rounder not only batted four and a half hours for 38 in England's second innings, but by wasting time and bowling very wide of the leg-stump, he effectively foiled the Australian attempt to score 177 in 115 minutes to win the game. For Hassett the 1953 series was a frustrating experience. His side went down to defeat by the slender margin of a single game. It was their first loss in a rubber since the war; yet in two Tests, victory eluded their grasp only in the final stages of the game. It was said that during the celebrations after the Fifth Test, a champagne bottle, flung in frustration, inadvertently stopped the clock on the Australian dressing-room wall at The Oval. The timepiece hung there unmoving for a season or two, a witness to the niggling sense of anticlimax which Hassett's side must have felt.

The First Test at Trent Bridge was abortive, largely due to the murky gloom and scudding rain which plagued Nottingham for the full five days. The fourth and fifth days were almost a total climatic disaster, but there was time for the spectators to be treated to the sight of a dapper Hassett century and a magnificent exhibition of medium-pace bowling from Bedser, who captured 14/99 in the game. Nottingham's immigrant West Indian population had turned up to the Trent Bridge Ground in force and were enraptured by Bedser's bowling. They immediately composed a song in the Surrey man's honour and sang in his praise, 'The Alec Bedser Calypso'. The Australian tourists, like the West Indians, were, throughout the series, to ask the question posed by the words of the refrain: 'Alec Bedser, who taught you to bowl Australia?'

The Australian Prime Minister, the then Mr Robert Menzies, was a keen watcher at this dismal First Test. His seat in a viewing room, set aside for dignitaries, was next to a senior member of the English aristocracy, who punctuated every sentence which he uttered with a superfluous and meaningless—'What!' Sipping his G & T before lunch, the noble lord enmeshed his neighbour in a sociable chat.

'Damned dull day—what!'
'Yes, your Grace.'
'This fella, Bedser's bowling frightfully well—what!'

170

'He certainly is, your Grace.'

'If it weren't for Hassett, you wouldn't make 200—what!'

'Oh I don't know, your Grace.'

'Damned good job Miller hung around—what!'

Finally exasperated: 'Not Watt, your Grace. Menzies is the name'.

The Nottingham clash was Don Tallon's last Test before handing over his gloves to Gil Langley. It was also the début of 'Snarler' Jack Hill, Australia's irascible quickish top-spin bowler from Melbourne's St Kilda Club. In England's first innings Hill supplemented Lindwall's 5/57 with a return of 3/35. 'Snarler' was a bowler of remarkable persistence. In his later years he suffered a heart attack whilst playing in grade cricket and when St Kilda refused to select him again for his own sake he left the club to seek a game in junior ranks in the parks. He played there until he died a happy but comparatively young man of the inevitable second stroke at the age of fifty-one.

The overall result of the Second Test at Lords was identical to that of the first. Strangely enough, the stars of the second draw of the rubber were the same personnel who shone in the initial clash. Hassett notched his second century in as many games and Keith Miller translated his half-century at Nottingham into a three-figure score. Once more Bedser with 8 wickets and Lindwall with 7 were the outstanding bowlers of the match. Hutton who aggregated 103 at Nottingham whilst being dismissed only once, compiled his first hundred of the rubber. In spite of the Yorkshiremen's classical innings of 145 in a home side first innings score of 372, England appeared to have lost the match when they resumed their second knock on the final day with 3/20 on the board and 375 needed for victory. Hutton, the first professional to lead England in a series, saw his side plumb even more dismal depths when Compton was dismissed with the score standing at 73. Then came the last-ditch stand of Bailey and Watson which spanned 250 minutes and saved the game.

Watson's contribution to the salvation of his side was 109; Bailey's four and a half hours of perversity realized 71. Trevor Bailey revelled in the type of crisis which faced him at Lords. He loved to drop anchor at the wicket and float becalmed and runless for hours. Once in Brisbane in 1958, 'The Boil', as the Australian crowd called their favourite irritant, occupied the crease during the First Test for more than seven and a half hours for a grand result of 68 runs! Bailey's cricket was tantamount to psychological warfare. He delighted in playing forward to Keith Miller's bouncers and hitting the ball high on the splice of the bat in front of his eyes; then he would slide the bat to one side and smile down the wicket at the infuriated bowler. The strange facet about Bailey's batting was that he could play strokes when the mood seized him. Four years before he tortured the Woolloongabba spectators with his steady blocking, he won a prize of £100 for being the first batsman to hit a six in the Brisbane Test. I doubt whether Bailey will be remembered for that individual stroke; his name will rather be bracketed with the infamous stone-waller Scotton and associated with his celebrated 'post-war prod'.

'The Boil's' cricket was not based entirely on the aggravation and

Trevor Bailey's favourite stroke

frustration of his opponents; it was more of an intellectual exercise for the Cambridge graduate. When he bowled his medium-paced deliveries, his approach was measured out to the nearest inch; a fraction too much or too little caused him to flick the bowling crease with his rear heel and, under the old no-ball rule, concede an unnecessary run. Bailey's body position during his delivery stride was perfectly studied; he used to scrape a deep furrow in the ground a yard behind the bowling wicket with his lagging right boot and this manoeuvre enabled him to draw his body into a geometric side-on position. He used the crease intelligently, realizing that if he released the ball over the middle-stump of the bowler's wicket and aimed at the centre wicket at the opposite end, theoretically he had only to swing the ball two and a quarter inches—or half the width of the bat blade—to pass it. Bailey's movement through the air was not immense, but like every other cricketing skill which he possessed, it was immaculately controlled. He could swing or cut the ball off the wicket in both directions and each delivery which he sent down had a relevance within the context of the discovered weaknesses of the opposing batsman.

The second, third and fourth days of the Old Trafford Test were all rain affected; consequently the game suffered the same fate as its predecessors. There was a time, however, for one serious innings from each side, a century from the bat of Harvey and another 5-wicket performance from the untiring Bedser who sent down 45 overs in Australia's first innings. There were moments of anxiety for England before the follow-on was avoided. Australia's second innings effort of 8/35 was a light-hearted forecast of the fate which was to befall Johnson's side, facing the spin of Laker and Lock four years later, on the same ground.

Leading his country against Australia for the first time on his native ground of Headingley in the Fourth Test, Hutton suffered the worst indignity which could befall a Yorkshiremen before his own people: he lost the toss, was asked to bat and was bowled by Lindwall's second delivery. The chestnut of the day told of a son arriving five minutes late at the match to say to his father, 'I've got some bad news for thee, dad. Mum's run away with the lodger'. To which the father retorted: 'I've got worse for thee, lad, 'Utton's out'.

Australia dominated the Leeds encounter virtually from the first ball bowled. Lindwall's 5/54 sent England back to the pavilion for the first time for 167. After establishing a lead of 99, the batting of Edrich, Compton and Laker set the tourists a moderate task of scoring 177 in five minutes under two hours. With forty-five minutes remaining for play, 66 were required for an Australian victory and there were still 7 wickets in reserve. It was at this stage that 'Operation Fabius Cunctator' was initiated; an unforgettable three-quarters of an hour yielded a Bailey epidemic of slack bootlaces, abnormally long run-ups and deliveries directed feet down the leg-side. England went to The Oval with the rubber still undecided; in their minds such an end had justified the means at Leeds.

The stalemate was broken at Kennington where England won by 8 wickets and thus, as in 1926, carried off the series at the last desperate attempt. This Test established the plans for the nucleus of the England side over the next seven years. Trueman appeared in his first game against the old enemy, and captured 4 crucial wickets in Australia's first innings. P. B. H. May made his bow against Australia and heralded a bright future for himself with a brace of competent 30s. Laker and Lock were now the old established spinning firm and won The Oval Test by capturing 9 wickets in the tourists' second innings. Edrich seemed to have found a niche for himself as an opener. Lindsay Hassett, the Australian skipper, however, was not looking to the future; he was more irritated by the immediate past. The crowds massed under The Oval dressing-room balconies calling for Hutton, the man who had recovered the Ashes for the first time since the war. After almost winning two of the Tests, Hassett's side must have wondered about the justice of the outcome.

The composition of the 1954-5 M.C.C. touring side to Australia was open to censure before the party left Tilbury docks on board the S.S. *Orsova*. Amongst the ranks of England's cricketing notables who were conspicuous by their absence from the passenger list were fast bowler Freddie Trueman and spinners Laker and Lock. The facile explanation of their omission was that the England selection committee were reposing their confidence in youth for the torrid experience of an Australian tour; but that reasoning did not hold water. The replacements for Lock and Laker were Yorkshire's Appleyard and Glamorgan's McConnon, who were as old or older than the players whom they supplanted. As Trueman's substitute, I was one year senior to my predecessor, whilst Loader of Surrey was born a year before Moss, the Middlesex fast bowler, whose touring place he usurped.

The truth about the passing over of Trueman, Lock and Laker for the 1954-5 Australian tour was reputedly to be found in the previous winter's tour of the West Indies. Writing of the Caribbean visit in Wisden, R. J. Hayter said that it was, 'all the more regrettable that the visit of the M.C.C. representatives . . . in the early months of 1954 aroused such controversy and uneasiness . . . only one or two of Hutton's team deserved censure but when even the slightest sign of disagreement became public property, as must be accepted in times when Test matches are given increasing prominence in newspapers, radio and newsreels, self-control should have been regarded as essential'. Apparently a select band of the Caribbean tourists received the brunt of the delayed punishment for the team's ostensible and understandable reaction to the 1954 West Indian political climate.

Bob Appleyard

Hutton's team to Australia was the richer for the inclusion of Bob Appleyard. He was a remarkably versatile bowler who could turn his talents with equal facility either to parabolic medium-pace swingers or to his unique brand of quickish, bouncy off-spinners. He was a bowler who must have resembled England's Sydney Barnes in his accurate command of varied pace, swing and spin. In the county season of 1954 Appleyard was the second highest wicket-taker in the country and he, Tony Lock and Tom Goddard shine on the honour board of bowlers as the only players to have captured 200 wickets in a first-class season since the Second World War. More importantly for the fortunes of Hutton's side in 1954-5, Appleyard's high action and kicking spin were

173

ideally suited to Australian conditions. It was a tragedy for cricket that a lung infection was to rob England of Appleyard's talents and cause his premature retirement soon after his return to his native Yorkshire.

The left-handed spinning skills of Appleyard's fellow countyman, John Wardle were also to prove ideally suited to conditions Down Under during the winter of 1954-5. Wardle's effectiveness, however, was cerebrally induced; brutal experience and only 4 wickets in two Tests in the West Indies proved to his complete satisfaction that finger spin alone would not win matches on bone-hard wickets in tropical countries. Wardle therefore set about the self-appointed task of teaching himself how to bowl wrist-spin during the four weeks he was on board ship en route to Australia. For hours each morning the Yorkshireman was to be seen on the sports deck first throwing and finally bowling chinamen and googlies against a bulkhead from an ever increasing distance. By the time he disembarked at Fremantle, Wardle had perfected the skill to such an extent that the team's reserve wicket-keeper, Keith Andrew, confessed to me that he had more difficulty picking the Yorkshireman's wrong 'un than he did that of more recognized leg-spinners such as George Tribe!

The facts of the 1954-5 series are now history. England won the rubber by the margin of 3-1. The reasons for the first English victory in Australia since the bodyline matches are explicit: the tourists in Statham, Loader, Bailey and myself possessed a better balanced, younger and faster bowling combination than their opponents. Miller, Lindwall, Johnston and Archer were still formidable exponents of their fast art and consistently worried the English batsmen. But the England speed assault troubled the Australian batsmen more, and once they had asserted their psychological superiority over the home side after the Second Test, the England captain Hutton never permitted them any mental respite. The resultant tactical warfare produced a series of unremitting fast attacks, for the most part moderate scores and slow over rates; but it won Hutton the rubber.

Years afterwards, Hutton confided in me that he always felt that he had a chance of winning the 1954-5 rubber after the initial first-class game against Western Australia in Perth. During that match, played on a lightning fast pitch, I hit a local batsman on the pads and bruised him so much through his protective gear that he had to remove it and eventually retire temporarily. Thereafter Hutton was always confident that he possessed in his team a bowler fast enough to decide the destiny of Tests.

There was no mystery about the 28-wicket success which I enjoyed during the rubber; it emanated purely from speed. My action, like that of the javelin thrower, was prematurely open at the hips. This created a tremendous lateral tension across my trunk from the left leg to the right shoulder. Like an extended spring, this muscular stretch imparted great pace to the ball when the rear toe was lifted at the end of the back foot's drag. Shoulder strength built up by felling willow trees during the previous winter imparted additional pace to the ball. My action was not based on perfect technique but on physical power. The pitfall of such an advantage is that the bowler's speed must decline with the onset of weariness, the aging process and physical atrophy. It was characteristic of a strong bowling action that in the course of the 1954-5 series I was able to shorten my original 25-yard approach to the wicket to a mere 15 without any loss of pace. Many observers thought that the curtailed run-up was an innovation; in fact I was merely reverting to the approach which I used at the beginning of my bowling career, but which I had been compelled to abandon because of the stresses which it placed on my body. With my re-adoption of the short run-up, I was increasing my chances of injury and condemning myself to a short but merry bowling career.

The 1954-5 series began disastrously for Hutton; his side were defeated in Brisbane by an innings and 154 runs in the wake of a disastrous series of blunders and unlucky episodes. The M.C.C. game against Queensland in the week before the First Test revealed that the Woolloongabba wicket was green and helpful to the seam bowlers. On the evidence of that State game, the England selectors chose an eleven barren of spin-bowling, and once committed to the pace attack of Statham, Bedser, Tyson and Bailey, Hutton had no option after winning the toss but to bowl and exploit the early life in the pitch. His decision proved to be a gross miscalculation; the Brisbane pitch was as flat as a pancake and placid in the extreme. To compound England's difficulties, Evans contracted influenza and was unable to keep wicket; Bedser was afflicted by shingles, and Compton broke his hand on the boundary fence on the first day whilst attempting to stop a four. Dropped catches assisted both Morris and Harvey to their centuries and the exhausting experience of fielding for two days in tropical humidity sapped the batting resistance of the tourists, who twice succumbed for under 300.

The Second Test in Sydney, however, was a different story. Rain before the game made the wicket green and Morris, acting for the injured Johnson, won the toss for Australia and, like Hutton in Brisbane, sent the opposition in to bat. Once again the gamble misfired and England won by 38 runs. The result, however, could have gone the other way if the tourists' tail-enders had not offered sprightly and profitable resistance in both innings. The contest marked the end of Alec Bedser's distinguished career against Australia; he was omitted from the England side in Sydney because he was still suffering from shingles. It was less than fitting that such a faithful servant of England had to learn of his omission from the team sheet pinned on the dressing-room noticeboard on the morning of the game.

I captured 10/129 in the game after being felled by a Lindwall bouncer which struck me on the back of the head after I lost sight of the ball against the gloomy background of the Noble stand. The unkind blow was perhaps deserved, since I had permitted myself the liberty of a bumper at the Australian fast bowler in the course of his scoring 64 in the Brisbane Test; but it was a vengeance which backfired on the home side. Returning from hospital after a precautionary X-ray, with a lump as big as a billiard ball on the back of my head, I was aroused to vengeance on the avenger; one rub of the bump was enough to revive my pace whenever I felt that it was flagging. Neil Harvey's unbeaten 92 in

Colin Cowdrey's
effortless drive

Australia's second innings was a masterpiece set against a background
of bowling advantage. He and Johnston added a palpitating 39 for
Australia's last wicket, before the left-handed bowler was caught
behind on the leg-side playing his idiosyncratic protective leg-glance off
his rump. Thus the game was lost, but if any batsman had been able to
survive with Harvey, the decision might have been reversed.

England's victory by 128 in Melbourne's Third Test was greater than
the mere statistic suggests. A score of 128 runs on this Melbourne pitch
was probably the equivalent of 300 on a good surface. On the first day
of the game the surface was a cracked mosaic of baked clay. England's
batting task was onerous after winning the toss. They had to contend,
not only with the vagaries of the wicket, but also with the magnificent
Miller who, in spite of the handicap of an injured knee, bowled 9 overs
before lunch to take 3/5! Unfortunately for Australia, Colin Cowdrey
was in the mood to score a century. His 102 was the first of his 23
hundreds in Tests and was compiled in a moderate England innings of
191. The Kentish man was eventually bowled in a most extraordinary

fashion by off-spinner Ian Johnson, who made a ball deviate two feet off a crack in the pitch outside the off-stump to bowl Cowdrey behind his legs as he was padding up!

Australia were 8/188 in their first innings at close of play on Saturday evening. The Sunday temperature was 105 degrees and an uncomfortably hot rest day was spent by both teams. Yet when Statham ran up to bowl the first ball on Monday morning the outfield and wicket were so soft that the fast bowler lost his footing and fell over in his delivery stride. The wicket had been watered! Many excuses, such as excessive condensation underneath the covers and a subterranean spring under the ground, were offered in explanation for the condition of the pitch. Their excuses were simply not good enough—at least not to the extent required to reduce the surface to its eventual soggy state. Fortunately for the Melbourne authorities, England enjoyed the best batting conditions of the match in their second knock; otherwise there must certainly have been a protest from the tourists. When Australia went to the crease for the final innings of the game, the pitch had reverted to its original crazy-paving pattern. On the morning of the last day, 165 runs were required for a home-side victory and there were 8 wickets in reserve. Astonishing to relate, on a wicket of unpredictable bounce, in just under 110 minutes before lunch, Johnson's side lost 8/36 to be all out for 111. Tyson captured 6/16 to go into the pavilion with the flattering innings analysis of 7/27.

The sketch of English fast-bowling supremacy which had been firmly outlined in the Sydney and Melbourne Tests was vividly finished in oils in Adelaide. Not without a few moments of anxiety, and in spite of another inspired spell of bowling from Miller, who had a hand in the first 4 wickets to fall in their second innings for 49, England won by 5 wickets. The game proved conclusively the psychological ascendancy of the tourists' pace attack over the Australian batsmen. Hutton's team led by only 18 runs on the first innings and seemed condemned to batting on a pitch which was already receptive to spin when Australia went to the crease a second time. The first three Australian wickets tumbled to the biting off-spin of Appleyard with only 69 runs on the board. The pundits predicted that the Yorkshire slow bowler would be the demon of the fourth day; in fact he never bowled again after his initial spell of 12 overs had yielded him the impressive figures of 3/13! Australia succumbed for a lowly 111 runs on a paceless wicket to Statham and myself. Needing only 94 to clinch the match and retain the Ashes, Hutton became agitated when Miller raised the spectre of possible defeat. 'The so-and-sos have done us again' was his comment. 'I'll show you who's done who', replied Denis Compton, as he snatched up his bat and strode from the dressing-room at the fall of the third wicket. He and Bailey coaxed the score along to 90 before the all-rounder was lbw to Johnston and made way for Evans, who clumped the winning boundary.

This Adelaide Test must surely have been the only occasion when a home team's wicketkeeper was booed as he came into the members' enclosure on the first morning. Len Maddocks retained his place in the Australian team for the fourth game after he had usurped the post of the injured Gil Langley, the local South Australian hero, behind the stumps prior to the Melbourne clash. When Maddocks entered the pavilion before the match, the Langley supporters gave voice to their disapproval; ironically the Victorian keeper proved to be top scorer in his side's first innings.

Cyclonic rain swept like a curtain from the east to delay the start of the final Sydney encounter for a full three days. The game could virtually have been dismissed as no contest before a ball was bowled; yet an apparent miscalculation by the Australian captain, Ian Johnson, almost gave England the opportunity of carrying off an unexpected victory. Johnson was the last batsman dismissed in Australia's first innings. He was run out when his side were exactly 150 runs in arrears of England's total of 7/371 declared. It seemed that Johnson believed that the follow-on had been averted, whereas, in truth, another run was required. Hutton exercised his privilege of asking Australia to bat again and the home side were still 32 runs from making the tourists go to the crease again with 6 wickets down in their second innings when the final curtain fell on the rubber. The game was a triumph for England's previously unsung heroes. Tom Graveney, opening the innings, was at his elegant best in notching 111. Wardle tantalized every batsman with his mesmeric brand of left-handed wrist spin; the last day saw the Yorkshireman capture 7/115.

Writing of the 1956 series in the Wisden of 1957, Neville Cardus, the literary king of cricket, called it 'Laker's Wonderful Year'. That phrase was one of the few Cardus utterances which could safely be classified as an understatement. Laker dominated the series against Johnson's tourists as no other bowler before or since has done and revised the cricket world's thoughts about the limits of bowling possibilities. The Surrey off-spinner captured 46 wickets at a cost of 9.6 each in five Tests. Only the great Sydney Barnes has ever exceeded Laker's wicket aggregate in a rubber—and Barnes's 49 wickets against South Africa in 1913-14 were captured on matting wickets and at a slightly inflated cost. In the Fourth Test at Old Trafford, the expatriate Yorkshire slow bowler exploited the foibles of the Australian batsmen to capture a monopolistic 19/90. Manchester was not the only scene of Laker's mastery over Australia. In Surrey's match against the tourists at The Oval, he steered his London side to the first victory of a county over the Australians in forty-four years. He captured 12 wickets in the game—astonishingly sweeping the board clean yet again in the tourists' first knock with an analysis of 10/88!

At the time of his *annus mirabilis*, Laker was no youthful prodigy. He was thirty-four years old, had appeared in twenty-four Tests, and had made his international début some nine years earlier. Like good wine he matured slowly. He played in three Tests against the invincible Bradman juggernaut of 1948 in a series which left him with a memory of savage punishment and 9 wickets at a cost of 52.44 runs each. Laker's past sufferings against Australia made 1956 a season of sweet retribution.

The experience of the previous M.C.C. tour of Australia misled many good cricket judges into the expectation that England would exert her bowling supremacy in the pace department. Injury to the home team's speedsters, a disappointing summer and the ubiquity of spinners' wickets, everywhere except at Lords, reduced such hopes to fond illusions. The home selectors were well aware of the pervading character of the Test surfaces; I was actually told that there was no need for me to risk my injured heel in the Old Trafford game since the pitch would favour the spin bowler! To some, such a state of affairs smacked of gamesmanship; the truth was that what was sauce for the goose was sauce for the gander. Australia possessed spinners in the persons of Benaud and Johnson. They were simply inferior to Laker and Lock under English conditions. The 6 wickets of off-spinner Johnson in the Tests cost him 50.5 each by comparison with Laker's 46 at 9.6. Benaud collected eight victims in the rubber at a uniform expense of 41.25 runs; Lock's 15 wickets cost him 22.46 runs each. It was indicative of the ineffectiveness of the tourists' slow attack that in a spinners' season, pace bowlers Miller and Ron Archer were the most penetrative members of the Australian bowling line-up with respective wicket tallies of 21 and 18 to their credit. The batting of both sides, it must be said in explanation of these bowling successes, was less than rock-like. Even the team which won the rubber was compelled to recall veterans such as Washbrook and Compton to the colours and open the innings with Cowdrey.

It is incongruous to look back on Laker in the 1956 series and conjure up the mirage of him as the heartless scourge of Australian batsmen. There appeared to be no animosity in Laker's bowling; at the crease he wore an almost avuncular air. When the batsman played at and missed the ball, the off-spinner would wrinkle his brow in a half-amused, half-quizzical manner and look down the wicket at the striker as if to say: 'Now how did you do that, son?' Then he would hitch up his pants over his well-rounded girth, grab the ball with an overarm snatch as it was returned to him and saunter back to his bowling mark like a farmer behind the plough. Before he bowled, Laker always looked down with concern at his index finger before wrapping it around the seam of the ball. His spinning digit was misshapen like a crescent moon, swollen and stretched by years of constant usage. The Surrey man's approach to the wicket was only of two or three steps duration; he shuffled up to the wicket slowly and with his weight on his heels. His arm was high, however, and the strength of his fingers, prodigious.

Laker was a supreme artist. He controlled the ball both through the air and off the wicket as if it were tied to his bowling hand by a length of elastic. On hard wickets, when turn was denied him, he could still puzzle the batsmen with permutations of drift and looping flight. On spinning surfaces he operated from around the wicket, posted three short-leg fieldsmen and made the batsman play at every kicking, turning delivery. Survival against Laker under such conditions was impossible. Batsmen who faced him on pitches which were slightly receptive to spin could not determine when the ball would turn. The snap of Laker's fingers as he released the ball suggested that he aimed to make every delivery deviate. It was a hoax; sometimes Laker would bowl a non-spinning, curving ball designed to produce a slip catch and click the fingers of his non-bowling hand. With such a master off-spinner and Lock in their side it was small wonder that Surrey won the county championship seven times in succession between the years of 1952 and 1958.

The dozen hours lost to rain during Nottingham's First Test ensured that a draw was the only possible result. It was a low-scoring game of skidding misfortune and mishaps. The England left-handed opener, Richardson, should have been run out at 5 when he slipped on the wet turf. By good fortune he survived to score a fine 81 and then follow his initial success with 73 in the second innings. In reply to the first total of 217 from May's team, Australia could only scrape together 148 against the combined spin of Laker and Lock who reaped a combined harvest of 7 wickets; but even a bold declaration at 3/188 in the home side's second innings could not force the issue and Burke's undefeated 58 enabled Australia to play out time with only 3 wickets down. The match yielded a formidable casualty list amongst the ranks of the fast bowlers. English speedster Moss pulled a stomach muscle and Lindwall strained his thigh. Alan Davidson, the tourists' left-handed paceman, slipped in a bowling footmark and cracked a bone in his ankle. The sound of the fracturing bone echoed around the Trent Bridge Ground as Davidson crumpled into a forlorn heap.

True to their traditional form at Lords, England went down to defeat in the Second Test by 185 runs. The barren hoodoo which had existed since Verity's match at Cricket Headquarters in 1934 remained unbroken. Miller was the magician who produced the victory rabbit from the hat for his side. His 10-wicket performance was virtually a solo fast bowling performance, since his opening partner, Crawford, playing in his only Test, bowled a mere 29 balls before injuring a leg muscle. Benaud, too, made an immense contribution to his side's

Benaud's miraculous gully catch. Lords 1956

triumph. In England's first knock, he caught Cowdrey in the gully off the bowling of Mackay. The speed of the ball off the bat was such that it knocked the fieldsman over backwards after he had clasped the catch above his head in a manner reminiscent of a boxer's victory salute. In his first-class career, Benaud, fielding in the same position, was seriously hurt when a similar stroke struck him in the mouth. If Cowdrey's shot at Lords had been two feet lower, he could easily have suffered the same injury twice. His catch amounted to mere reflex protection—and his sharpened reactions elevated his feat into the greatest catch which I have ever seen in the gully. Benaud later added to his laurels by lambasting an unlucky and unlikely 97, batting at number eight in Australia's second innings. He and Mackay, who persevered for 265 minutes to score 31, raised Australia from the doldrums of 6/112 to 7/229 and eventually to a winning total of 257. England requiring 372 for victory had no answer to Miller's pace and lift on a sloping and still lively wicket. They were dismissed for 186 with Miller's bowling portion being 5/80. As a memento of his achievement, 'Nugget' was presented with a bail by his skipper Ian Johnson. As he left the field, in sporting gesture, he flung his trophy into a crowd of admiring and lucky youngsters who were waiting to acclaim and perhaps touch the great cricketer.

The tide of fortune ebbed dramatically for Australia at Headingley where England's victory by an innings and 42 levelled the series. Despairing of the unfulfilled talent of Graveney and Watson, the 41-year-old selector, Cyril Washbrook, helped to ballot himself into the home batting line-up. He was rewarded for his courage by a match-winning partnership of 187 with May and the individual satisfaction of scoring 98. Australia invited defeat by dropping the veteran twice and thus enabling England to accumulate 325. Thereafter, on a wicket bare of grass, the Australian batsmen accepted as gospel truth the words of the West Indian calypso which says:

Ashes to ashes, dust to dust.
If Lock doesn't get you, Laker must.

Laker captured 11 wickets in the game, Lock 7.

The story of Laker's match at Old Trafford was that of heaven and earth; the Fourth Test was the tale of the beneficence of the gods and the wicket. It was said that when Lindwall bowled the first ball of the England innings it raised a puff of dust! The fast bowler was so disheartened by his obviously limited future in the game that he did not bother to remove his sweater. The Australian fast attack, hamstrung by the paceless surface, were powerless to prevent the home side accumulating 459 through the agency of centuries from Richardson and Sheppard. Even their batsmen had little enjoyment in the offing—at least such was the suggestion contained in the clouds of dust which the groundsman raised as he swept the pitch during the intervals. When Australia went to the wicket they inched their way to 48, only to lose Burke to Lock and their remaining batsmen to the irresistible Laker in the space of eighty minutes. Following on 375 runs behind, Johnson's men surrendered as a body to Laker for 205. Laker's second innings analysis read 51.2 overs, 23 maidens, 10 wickets for 53! He conceded just over a run per over in the course of dismissing a complete team. His match return was even more astonishing: 68 overs, 27 maidens, 19 wickets for 90. It was the highest tally of wickets in a first-class game and the only occasion that 10 wickets had been taken in a Test innings. Laker's performance meant that he had captured 51 Australian wickets in five matches and in two of these games he had swept the board clean of batsmen in an innings.

An even more remarkable facet of Laker's achievement at Old Trafford was that whilst he was mowing down nineteen opponents, Tony Lock, arguably the best slow left-handed spinner in the world, had to content himself with a single victim from the opposite bowling crease. As the generous Laker admitted in later years, his Old Trafford triumph was freakish. Just how much the gods were on the off-spinner's side can be gauged from the fact that Neil Harvey, the leading left-handed batsman in the world, was twice dismissed by Laker for a duck. He could not blame his second nought on the wicket; he struck a full toss straight into the hands of Cowdrey at cover! It was small wonder that Harvey tossed his bat high in dismay as he left the wicket for the second unproductive time. England's win by an innings and 170 runs gave the home side the Ashes; it was the first occasion since 1897-8 that they had retained the coveted urn for three successive rubbers.

The interest in The Oval Test revolved around the return of Compton to the Test scene after having undergone an operation for the removal of a damaged knee-cap in the previous November. Like the recall of Washbrook, Compton's re-emergence proved a triumph. After an anxious scoreless quarter of an hour against the friendly yet furious Miller, the familiar Compton of old stood revealed as he claimed 94 of the 156 runs scored whilst he was at the wicket. England reached 247 before rain intervened to present Australia with the fearsome prospect of facing Laker and Lock on a spinning surface. After slumping to 5/47, the tourists rallied as Miller steered his side's score to the respectability of 202 with an inspired knock of 61. England declared their second innings at 3/182 but the weather had the final say; again the first 5 Australian wickets tumbled for 27 against the Surrey spin twins, but time trickled away as Miller and Benaud defended grimly to draw the match. During the interval between the second innings of the teams at The Oval, the President of the M.C.C., Earl Alexander of Tunis, presented Laker with a silver salver on which was inscribed the full scoreboard of the Manchester Test and the legend of Laker's unique triumph. The Laker record of 46 wickets in an Australian series is one that will endure for many years.

13. Benaud's Throw of the Dice

The volte-face in England's fortunes between 1956 and 1958-9 is one of the mysteries of modern sporting times. The intervening years saw Peter May's team draw a rubber against South Africa on the batsmen's wickets of the high veldt and win seven of the ten games played against John Goddard's West Indians and John Reid's Kiwi side. England arrived in Fremantle in October 1958 at the zenith of their cricketing powers. Their fast bowling quartet of Statham, Tyson, Loader and Bailey had been reinforced by the addition of the rehabilitated greatness of Fred Trueman. Laker and Lock, the slow bowlers who were passed over in 1954 and who won the 1956 series, were once more in official favour. Their inclusion in the M.C.C. party made the tourists one of the most formidable bowling combinations ever to leave English shores. Johnny Wardle's nomination alone was the only possible variation in the selector's choice which could have strengthened May's bowling resources. The Yorkshire slow left-hand bowler was originally included in the band of England's élite seventeen cricketers; but a domestic disagreement with his county caused Yorkshire to discontinue his contract and, as a result of a series of national newspaper articles, Wardle's invitation to tour was withdrawn. As he reported the series from the press box, Wardle must have realized that he was not alone in his opinion that his baffling wrist-spin was sorely missed by an England attack which laboured on unsympathetic wickets.

The omission of one player, however, could not fully explain how a side which had so comprehensively defeated Australia in England two years previously were annihilated by the same opposition in four of the next five Tests. It was true that, apart from May and Cowdrey, the tourists' batting was notoriously unreliable on the unfamiliar, bouncy surfaces which they encountered in Sydney, Melbourne, Brisbane and Adelaide. It was equally true that the English tribulations were exacerbated by an unending list of casualties which soon necessitated flying reinforcements to the original party in the persons of off-spinner Mortimore and batsman Dexter. Subba Row broke his thumb before the First Test and did not appear in the series. Trueman throughout the tour was handicapped by a back injury. Evans fractured a finger and played in only three Tests, whilst fast bowlers Statham and Loader were disabled in a car crash before the final Melbourne encounter and invalided home. Importantly, key slow bowler, Jim Laker, was plagued by an arthritic and misshapen spinning finger throughout the rubber and could not play in Adelaide.

Dexter's recruitment to the colours was one of the happier misfortunes of the otherwise disastrous tour. England were compelled to have recourse to a youthful talent, which was to prove one of the exciting ingredients of their side in the 1960s. Dexter's initiation to international cricket was circuitous, to say the least. At the time of his summons to Australia, 'Lord Ted' was indulging in his hobby of light-plane flying and was fog-bound in Paris. It required much shuttling to and fro over the channel and many aborted landings before he was able to take his seat in the larger plane which transported him to Australia.

In the minds of the numerous pressmen who accompanied the 1958-9 side to Australia, the principal contributory factor to England's repeated batting failures Down Under was the prevalence of bowlers with suspect actions on the local cricket scene. Every state incurred the writers' suspicious wrath. In Perth the tourists had to cope with Keith Slater; in Adelaide they encountered Trethewey and Hitchcox; whilst in Melbourne and Sydney they met Meckiff, Rorke and Burke. In Brisbane, the veteran fast-bowling genius, Ray Lindwall, blithely dubbed himself 'The Last of the Straight-Arms'. The danger of this new breed of pace bowlers lay not in their excessive speed but rather in unpredictability. With little or no change in action they could deliver balls which ranged from slow-medium to blistering fast. In addition they were able to obtain pronounced cut from ostensibly the most unresponsive of pitches. The overall effect of these new secret weapons was that even the natural timers of the ball in the England batting line-up, May, Cowdrey and Graveney, were not infrequently bowled whilst their bats were still at the top of their back-swing. In order to present a completely fair picture, it must be added that accusations of not being above bent-arm suspicion were also levelled at England slow bowler, Tony Lock. It was perhaps significant that, as a result of the M.C.C. legislation which emanated from the experiences of 1958-9 in Australia, both Lock and Derbyshire fast bowler, Harold Rhodes, subsequently spent long periods out of first-class cricket modifying their actions to the satisfaction of the authorities.

The uproar in the English newspapers mounted as May's cricket caravan progressed around the Australian seaboard states and the Tests began; yet there was no official protest about bowlers with suspect actions from the England manager, former skipper Freddie Brown. He could see that the continued failure of the side under his guidance would not be reversed by an expression of opinion which the Australian public would deem to be sour grapes. Indeed the causes of the English flop went much deeper than the misfortune of injuries and unorthodox bowling opponents. Though May did not realize it at the outset of the series, the main obstacle to his ambitions of victory was his own side's blasé professionalism and a new spirit which was abroad in Australian cricket and went under the name of Richie Benaud.

The decision of the Australian selectors to appoint Benaud to lead his country against England in 1958-9 surprised the local *cognoscenti*. Many felt that, on seniority and performance grounds alone, the honour should have devolved upon the shoulders of Neil Harvey—expecially when the chosen one was expected to reverse a losing record of five years. At this stage of his career, Benaud was considered lucky in some quarters to have retained his place in the Australian side between the years of 1951 and 1955. Coming into Hassett's strong eleven at the age of twenty-one, Benaud captured only 23 wickets in thirteen Tests. Between his 1955 tour of the West Indies under Johnson's captaincy and his visit to South Africa with Ian Craig's side in 1957, he developed into a competent all-rounder and when he took over from his youthful predecessor, Benaud at the age of twenty-eight could point to a record of thirty-two Tests, 103 wickets, 2 hundreds against South Africa and a century against the West Indies, as well as 97 against England at Lords in 1956. Without a doubt, however, the new Australian captain owed his promotion to his youth and his successful tour of South Africa. In the series against Van Ryneveld's team he captured 30 wickets and averaged 54 with the bat. Benaud's new responsibilities added cubits to his playing stature and in a further thirty-one Tests he went on to increase his tally of Test victims by 145 and to recover and hold the Ashes until his retirement in 1963 after sixty-three Tests.

In spite of Benaud's eventual claim to fame as his country's greatest wicket-taker, it was virtually impossible to justify the selector's initial preference for him over Harvey on the grounds of playing ability. 'Nina' Harvey, after all, is Australia's most prolific run-scorer, second only to Bradman in a list in which Benaud himself figures in the twenty-third position, almost 4,000 runs in arrears. Yet Benaud's appointment to the Australian captaincy bordered on the inspirational. He added new dimensions to captaincy. He was a master tactician, ranking with such astute generals as Bradman, Armstrong and Hassett. At Old Trafford, in 1961, he tipped the balance of a lost Test by abandoning the stereotyped approach and bowling his leg-spinners and wrong 'uns around the wicket to rout the full strength of the England batting at a time when they were advancing towards victory with the rapidity of a panzer division.

Benaud's greatest attribute as captain, however, was his appreciation of the psychological make-up of the players under his command. The faint-hearted fought like heroes for him; injury-prone bowlers performed longer and better for him than they would for any other leader. When the brilliant catch was made and two or three Australians were gathered together in the name of congratulations, Benaud was there in the middle of the back-slapping throng. In the field he led by the example of unflagging excellence, catching the improbable chance and attempting the impossible one. Benaud rescued lost causes time and time again, lifting his men from mediocrity to an unlikely victory. He gave captaincy a new charisma, communicating, like the good journalist which he is, with his fellow-pressmen at close of play on each day of a Test match. He set an example of mateship within his teams yet

Richie Benaud

remained sufficiently detached to make clinical and unemotional judgments. Australian skippers since Benaud's day have taken him as their beau idéal. Some, like Ian Chappell, have almost emulated Benaud's achievements; none, however, have remotely approached the respected image of captain, mate, player, communicator and gentleman with which he quit the Test arena.

In one respect Benaud was fortunate when he assumed command of the Australian side; his team was a balanced blend of proven experience and gifted youth. His opening batsmen, McDonald and Burke, possessed a joint record of forty-five Tests. Harvey, the senior Australian 'pro', was a veteran of fifty-two international games, whilst all-rounder 'Slasher' Mackay had loped on eleven slack-kneed occasions, like a cricketing Groucho Marx, around a Test field. Pace bowler, Davidson, whilst he had already made seventeen Test appearances, had only recently claimed his rightful and henceforth automatic inheritance of the new ball. At twenty-one, Norm O'Neill, the inexplicable omission from the previous winter's tour of South Africa, was already burdened with the stroke-making reputation of 'another Bradman'. His 1958-9 series average of 56 was not in the class of Bradman, but it held the promise of much greater and exciting deeds with the bat. Indicative of the future strength of Australian batting was the fact that Peter Burge and Bobby Simpson only qualified for a single innings each in the rubber.

Brisbane's First Test established a precedent in the acrimony which was to permeate the atmosphere of the series. The touring side were discomfited in the very first innings of the rubber, both by the green wicket and Meckiff's bowling, and could only manage a paltry 134. After scoring 28 in his side's second innings total, Cowdrey was adjudged caught at short-leg off the fast left-arm bowler and departed to the pavilion, obviously far from convinced that the chance carried to the fieldsman, Kline. Long before that juncture, however, the game had become a grudge match with no quarter asked for or given on either side. Australia only led England on the first innings by 52 runs and when May's side batted a second time, their scoring rate was so painfully slow that 'Barnacle' Bailey occupied the crease for seven and a half hours in scoring 68! Wisden rates this tortoise innings as only the fourteenth slowest in the annals of the game—a fact which the stoic Woolloongabba patrons of that year must have found hard to believe. Requiring 147 to win in their second innings, Australia achieved their goal largely through the nervous brilliance of O'Neill who scored 71 of the 89 runs added by the stodgy Burke and himself for the unfinished third wicket stand. Inappropriately Burke made the winning hit and it was said that O'Neill's nervous tension at the end of the match was such that he vomited when he returned to the dressing-room.

Australia's initial 8-wicket margin of victory was repeated in Melbourne's second game. On an overcast day in the southern capital, May won the toss and unwisely opted to bat. Any self-respecting Victorian cricketer could have informed the England captain that the conditions were tailor-made for swing bowlers. So it proved to be. In the third over of the match, Davidson dismissed 'Pakistan Pete'

Richardson, Willie Watson and 'Long Tom' Graveney—the last being lbw to an inswinger to which he padded up without offering a stroke! England recovered, thanks to stubborn 40s from Bailey and Cowdrey and a peerless century from the bat of Peter May, to reach 259. It was indicative of Meckiff's unexpected extremes of pace that the England skipper was bowled by the left-handed speedster as he was picking up his bat after he had scored 113. Just as May's hundred held the England innings together, the solitary splendour of Harvey's 167 prevented Australia's first knock from falling into ruins. Statham was magnificent. Bowling with an injured big toe which poked bloodily from his decapitated left boot, the Lancashire speedster captured 7/57 to restrict the home side's lead to a mere 49. Within four and a half hours the fast bowler was bowling again. England were dismissed a second time for 87 with Meckiff snatching 6/38. After his herculean bowling effort in the first innings, Statham was filled with righteous anger as Australia scored the necessary 42 runs for victory for the loss of the wickets of McDonald and Grout.

Trueman was fit for the Sydney Test and returned to the England side. He chose his match badly, for the wicket's pace bordered on the turgid. It was remarkable that Benaud's team managed to dismiss England in their first innings for only 219. It was true that Benaud captured 5/83 with his leg-spinners but undoubtedly the greatest contributory factor to England's downfall was the brilliance of the home team's fielding. Harvey, who graduated from the covers to the slips in his years of less mobile experience, gathered in a miraculous catch off Laker when he knocked up a full-blooded slash in the gully and careered after it to complete the dismissal in elongated fashion twenty yards from the bat! When the wicket began to turn, Australia

Harvey's memorable catch, Sydney 1958. The fieldsman knocked up the ball and caught it yards to his right

were in trouble against Laker and Lock and were soon 3/87; but slipshod fielding allowed O'Neill, Favell, Mackay and Davidson to boost their side's lead to 138. It required all the resourcefulness and obduracy of the old firm of Cowdrey and May to bring England back from the brink of disaster at 3/64 and add 182 for the fourth wicket in England's second innings. Defiantly May declared 149 runs ahead, after Cowdrey had completed the slowest century in England-Australia games in 362 minutes. It was a futile gesture for, although the wicket was now turning quite acutely and McDonald and Burke soon fell prey to Laker's spin, Benaud, with the Ashes within his grasp, was in no mood for mock heroics. Australia were content with a draw and the urn remained in the southern hemisphere.

England's cup of misfortune brimmed to overflowing in the Fourth Test in Adelaide. Laker's swollen spinning finger precluded him from selection and an epidemic of influenza amongst the tourists made injections the order of the day in the dressing-room on the first morning. May won the toss and, having been burdened with the Hobson's Choice of four pace bowlers in his attack, made the token gesture of attempting to square the series by sending Australia in to bat on a flawless wicket and in broiling heat. Statham's first delivery to McDonald pitched just outside the off-stump and broke back to pass inches over the top of the middle. Assisted by umpiring blemishes, the opener, together with his fellow batsman Burke, went on to add 171 before the first wicket fell!

Before the score reached the half-century, I was convinced that Burke was caught behind the wicket off one of my rearing deliveries which brushed his glove. Much to the amazement of stumper Evans and the close-to-the-wicket fieldsmen, umpire Mel McInnes gave the batsman the benefit of the tenuous doubt. My own reaction to the incident was predictable and after a succession of Tyson bouncers, Burke, exasperated by the short-pitched assault, came down the wicket and left me in no doubt what he would do with his bat if I bowled him another bumper. I responded like a bull to a red rag and as the next delivery soared over the head of the ducking Burke, McDonald, the master of conciliatory psychology, turned to me and said: 'Well bowled, Frank'. Needless to say, he was spared too many bouncers!

McInnes experienced an unfortunate match. He gave Mackay not out to a catch behind the wicket in spite of the fact that the batsman walked. The culmination of the umpire's misfortunes came when McDonald, who had pulled a thigh muscle en route to his eventual 170 and was employing Burke as a runner, was blatantly run out by a return from cover to the bowler's end. Burke was still yards from safety and McDonald had not moved from his batting crease as the bails were removed. The umpire, concentrating his attention on the unmoving McDonald, smiled relievedly to himself as he gave the batsman run out by the length of the pitch. Inadvertently, however, he had moved to the wrong side of the wicket to make his judgment and at the time the wicket was put down he had his back towards the runner. Since he was in no position to pass judgment on Burke's situation, McInnes was compelled to reverse his decision. The mild-mannered England captain,

Peter May, lost his temper for the only time in my experience. 'Make up your so-and-so mind', is a temperate rebuke in terms of modern players' parlance, but there was no doubting the fact that P. B. H. was furious. Sportingly, McDonald sacrificed his innings as Australia amassed 476. The heat had wrought its work on the tourists' batsmen and against the guile of Benaud, the controlled swing of Lindwall and the ferocity of Rorke the tourists collapsed twice to lose the game by 10 wickets.

The position of the pavilion at square leg gave the England players a box seat from which to observe the phenomenal drag of the giant N.S.W. pace bowler, Gordon Rorke. In the days before the front foot no-ball rule was introduced, the speedster grounded his rear foot a yard behind the bowling crease and skated along on his back toe, not only through the rear line but also beyond the popping crease. He placed his front foot a yard beyond the batsman's block hole! Cowdrey scored 84 in England's first innings before Rorke knocked his stumps awry; but in spite of his success, when he returned to England he was accused of being too defensive against the paceman by an old, gaudy-tied M.C.C. colonel. 'Why didn't you drive him?' enquired the aged member, adding, 'You should have charged Rorke'. 'I didn't dare', replied the placid 'Kipper', 'I was afraid he might step on my toe'.

England were without the services of the incapacitated quintet of Evans, Statham, Loader, Milton and Watson as Benaud's side inflicted the final humiliation on them in Melbourne by 9 wickets. Once more the wicket was green and the atmosphere humid as the Australian skipper, profiting from his good fortune with the coin, daringly sent England in to bat. Twice in the game the scoreboard showed England losing their first wicket without a run on the board; twice 'Barnacle' Bailey, much to the delight of the partisan crowd, failed to score—the first time to the initial ball of the game; twice the 38-year-old Lindwall, bowling for the last time at fast-medium against the old enemy, picked up the wicket of his most inveterate opponent. After having been dismissed for 205, England struck back to capture the first 6 Australian wickets for 209; but a seventh wicket partnership of 115 between Grout and Benaud bolstered the home side's advantage of 146 and, with Cowdrey disputatiously run out when May's side batted again, England could only muster 214 at their second attempt. The only vicarious satisfaction which I, personally, derived from England's 9-wicket defeat was that I claimed the wicket of Jimmy Burke in the second innings—lbw to one of his beloved bouncers which failed to rise.

Ian Meckiff

The shouts of dissension and dispute which arose about controversial actions after the 1958-9 tour of Australia echoed around the cricketing world for five years. Ian Meckiff topped the Australian bowling averages in the rubber with 17 wickets at an average cost of 17.17. It is strange to relate, however, that whilst the fast bowler was selected to tour India and Pakistan in 1959 and appeared in Tests against the West Indies in 1960 and South Africa in 1963, he failed to win a place in the Australian side to England in 1961. Meckiff's politic omission was all the more unjust, since not only did the speedster modify his action but he also became the most successful exponent of medium-fast inswing in

Sheffield Shield cricket. Meckiff was the victim of a dichotomy of philosophies about suspect actions in the cricketing world. Australia was content to leave the judgment about the legality of a bowling action to the individual umpire. It was a piecemeal approach which led to a divergence of arbitrary opinions and left the bowler unsure about his best course of action.

England's law-makers imposed a moratorium on the problem at international level, but reviewed the broad spectrum of their own first-class game as a whole. Bowlers who were not above suspicion were reported to Lords and subjected to the scrutiny of slow-motion cameras. Like a French law-breaker they were presumed to be guilty until they proved their innocence and no one was above suspicion. The difference between the individualistic and the co-operative approaches to the problem was exemplified by the South African fast bowler, Griffin, being no-balled in an unofficial limited-over game after the Lords Test in 1960. In the preceding days, bowling under the protection of the moratorium, he faced the same judges who apparently suppressed their own personal opinions and allowed him enough latitude to take a hat-trick.

Meckiff would have benefitted from an Australia-wide and indeed, an English, judgment on his bowling. He would have been able to determine whether further modification was necessary. In the later stages of his Shield career I personally was convinced that he had purged his action. I could not envisage his bowling such pronounced inswingers if he straightened his arm in his delivery swing. In the final unsatisfactory analysis, Meckiff's condemnation in the South African Test in Brisbane in 1963 was based on the opinion of only one man. He was entitled to a trial by full jury.

The evenly contested rubber of 1961 in England was characterized by wickets of dubious quality, a factor which, after the Australian batting débâcle on the Old Trafford dust-bowl in 1956, must have increased the tourists' scepticism about the fairness of Tests played on alien English surfaces. The Lords game—subsequently dramatized by the press as 'The Battle of the Ridge'—took place on a pitch which caused the ball to either whistle around the batsmen's ears or shoot along the ground. A later scientific survey with the help of a theodolite discovered a pronounced depression in the wicket at the pavilion end and led to the re-laying of the world's premier playing area.

The Leeds match was played on a chemically white surface of only temporary durability. Fast bowler, Fred Trueman, quickly assessed the character of his native heath and, reducing his pace to fast-medium, captured 11/88 in the match with accurate off-cutters. Both teams were handicapped during the series by the absence of their leaders. May was not sufficiently recovered from the back abscess which struck him down in the West Indies to play in the First Test. The Australian skipper, Benaud strained the ligaments in his bowling shoulder during the Edgbaston clash and handed over the captaincy at Lords to Harvey. Indeed, Benaud's injury was so serious that it virtually ended his bowling career, but not before he brought off the one coup which enabled Australia to retain the Ashes. In this, he was aided and abetted by Peter May's one tactical mistake of the series.

The scene was Old Trafford and the time, the concluding phases of Australia's second innings. The tourists were 6/296, 119 runs in the lead with only their tail-end batsmen to come to the wicket, which was turning so much that off-spinner Allen had taken 3 wickets in 15 balls. Sensing that desperate situations demanded radical remedies, the left-handed all-rounder Davidson launched an all-out attack on the slow bowler, hitting him for three sixes over the straight boundary. May immediately took the new ball and on a slow pitch, fast bowlers Davidson and McKenzie added an untroubled 98 for the seventh wicket, thereby asking England to score 256 to win the match at the rate of 67 per hour. A home victory was still possible when, with 9 wickets in hand and Dexter in full flight with 150 runs on the board, Benaud opted to bowl his leg-spinners around the wicket in order to gain turn out of the bowlers' footmarks. Dexter chased a wide delivery to be caught behind and Benaud followed up this success by bowling an incredulous May around his legs as he attempted a Comptonesque sweep. Inspired, Benaud brushed the remaining England batting aside to capture 6/70 as 9 wickets tumbled for a meagre 51 runs. Australia won by 54 runs and Benaud became the first Australian wrist-spinner to decide a series in England since the halcyon days of Bill O'Reilly and Clarrie Grimmett. Once again Benaud proved that he possessed the inspirational Midas touch amongst captains.

Bill Lawry

The First Test in Birmingham ended in stalemate, but not without a few anxious moments in the England camp. In showery conditions the home side could only manage 195 in their first batting attempt—a puny total which stimulated the riposte of a Harvey century and a massive Australian score of 9/516. When the first ball of the final day was bowled England were in grave danger of defeat at 1/106. Dexter saved his team and, though he was missed off Davidson, treated every bowler with scorn to register 180 imperious runs. The left-handed Subba Row contributed 112, thus beginning his brief five-match career against Australia with a century. He was destined to emulate this feat in his last Test at The Oval.

Dexter's batting technique was a study in simplicity. At the crease he addressed the bowler as he would a golf ball. He was beautifully erect and classically side-on. The swing of his bat, like that of his golf club, was as straight as a dye and seldom anything but aggressively full. As a straight-hitter he was without parallel despatching the ball with a flat, skimming power which suggested that he was trying to drive a green, 300 yards away, in one stroke. Like Keith Miller before him, Dexter was a paragon amongst batsmen; he was lean, tall, muscular in physique and disdainfully powerful and correct in his methods. Psychologically, however, the future England captain was more complex. It seemed to me that his nickname of 'Lord Ted' was particularly apposite. His character reminded me of an eighteenth century English nobleman. In the field he conveyed the impression of being a dilettante; he practised his golf swing at cover point if a boring phase of the game failed to capture his interest. When a match demanded a responsible approach, however, Dexter assumed the mantle of leadership as though

191

Ted Dexter ('Lord Ted')

it was his inborn duty to set the example for the peasants of the game. He was a unique mixture of disinterest and vitality.

The traditional setting for the Second Test was Lords. In keeping with the history and traditions of twenty-seven years, Australia won by 5 wickets. The issue of the game was virtually decided before a ball was bowled since, on a pitch of indeterminate bounce, England saw fit to choose two spinners, whereas Australia placed their trust in a match-winning combination of three seam bowlers. The tourists' batting trump-card was undoubtedly their 24-year-old left-handed opener, Bill Lawry, who compiled a brilliant and courageous 130. Lawry was a last minute selection for the touring team and was chosen on the strength of his intense concentration, demonstrated during a marathon innings of 266 against New South Wales in the preceding Sheffield Shield season. Lawry was the batting discovery of the tour, heading both the first-class and Test averages and aggregates, as well as notching two centuries more than his nearest rival on tour. In ten years of Tests he was destined to carve out for himself a niche in cricketing immortality by becoming the third highest scorer for Australia—a formidable achievement when one considers that the only batsmen to outscore him were Bradman and Harvey.

Towards the end of his career, 'The Phantom', as Lawry was known to his team-mates, was to earn himself a reputation amongst the English press as the epitome of unexciting batting dourness. At one stage, a certain English journalist was moved to call him 'a corpse with pads on'. Nothing could have been further from the truth. Lawry was a batting realist who fashioned an innings according to his available material. He was always the possessor of a water-tight front foot defence; but his attacking game progressed in phases, as he reduced batting to the science of percentage yields. In his youth he was a ferocious and uninhibited hooker; when opposing bowlers awoke to his penchant for the lofted on-side stroke he tempered his impetuosity and cultivated his driving. No Victorian captain commanded more respect from the players under his command. He computerized leadership, demanding a high level of performance from his side and seldom affording the opposition an opportunity for artistic licence. In spite of his pragmatism on the field, he was not devoid of a wry sense of humour off it; on one occasion 'Phanto' rooted a fast bowler in his side to the spot in surprise by the simple expedient of nailing his size twelve cricket boots to the pavilion floor! When he was eventually jettisoned by the Australian selectors, both as a player and captain during the England tour of Australia in 1970-1, I was of the opinion that he received rough justice. Though his conservative leadership was open to criticism, Lawry was still by far the best opening bat in Australia. His century at Lords in 1961 and two 5-wicket performances from Davidson and McKenzie meant that Australia required only 69 runs to win the match. Against the venomous pace of Trueman and Statham on a totally unpredictable wicket, Australia lost 4/19. After being dropped before lunch on the last day, Burge threw caution to the wind and his bat at anything short. He scored an adventurous 37 not out and

Benaud's side scraped home by a margin which was not as large as it appeared on paper.

England and Freddie Trueman squared the series' account at Headingley where the home side scored an easy victory by 8 wickets. A surprise inclusion in May's XI was the 40-year-old Derbyshire pace bowler, Les Jackson. For years the tall raw-boned speedster had earned and deserved the reputation of being one of the best fast men in the country. To bat against him was an uncomfortable and rib-tickling experience. If one looked at the wicket after a game in which Jackson bowled, one could normally cover the spots on which he had pitched with a mat three feet long by two feet wide. The greatest condemnation which the purists of the theoretical camp levelled at the former miner was that his shoulder-wrenching action was that of a slinger. Such hypothetical assessment of ability makes me wonder whether Jeff Thomson would ever have gained a place in an England side. Before the Leeds clash, Jackson had played in only one previous Test against New Zealand twelve years earlier.

Two Trueman spells of bowling decided the game. In Australia's first innings he took the second new ball to capture 5/16 in 6 overs. England established a lead of 62 with Cowdrey notching 93 and Lock establishing a record by scoring ninety-three per cent of his moderate 30 runs in boundaries. When Benaud's team batted a second time, they lost their last 7 wickets for 21 runs and Trueman captured his last 5 wickets without conceding a run. England knocked off the 89 runs required for victory for the loss of only Cowdrey and Subba Row.

The deadlocked rubber was resolved by the Old Trafford drama where Benaud's inspirational example and Davidson's herculean hitting steered Australia home by 54 runs with only twenty minutes of the match remaining. The game was an incredible volte-face in fortunes since Australia never looked likely to avoid defeat, let alone win, until the final hours of the contest. Statham's 5/53 analysis on a green wicket, combined with 63 from Pullar, 95 from May and 78 from Barrington gave the home side a 177-run advantage on the first innings. In spite of a fine opening gambit of 113 from the new association of Lawry and Simpson, the tourists were still only 119 ahead when their sixth second innings wicket fell. Then came Davidson's hurricane innings, Dexter's riposte of 76 in eighty-four minutes and Benaud's imaginative 6/70 bowling performance from around the wicket. It was strange to think that the rubber was decided by one original idea.

Such proved to be the case, for at The Oval, England, with a strange sense of the inappropriate, omitted Trueman who watched from the sidelines as O'Neill and Burge compiled masterly centuries and Australia amassed 494 in their first innings. Thereafter, England, who scored only 256 in their first knock, were hard pressed to salvage a draw.

14. The Years of Stalemate

The English visit to Australia in the drab winter of 1962-3 was best epitomized by a cavernous yawn. I suppose that outwardly exciting personalities such as the Australian skipper, Benaud, and his English counterpart, Dexter, misled the antipodean public into the expectation of a re-enactment of the excitement which they witnessed when the West Indies visited Australia under Frank Worrell in 1960-1. Certainly the rival captains promised heart-stopping wares when they went through their usual public relations exercises before the series began. They promised, only to deceive and disappoint, and the series was drawn 1-1. Little else could have been expected from two unadventurous major batting powers who could point to a joint might which included the names of Simpson, Lawry, O'Neill, Harvey, Burge, Booth, Dexter, Barrington, Cowdrey and Sheppard. One of the strange facets of the rubber was the bowling success of the England off-spinner, Freddie Titmus. He turned very few deliveries in the five games, but his nagging drift towards the slips and the penchant of the Australian batsmen for the sweep brought him a rich and unexpected harvest of 21 wickets. It was a classic case of the inadvisability of hitting across the line of the ball on even the best of wickets.

A major bone of contention during the Tests was the question of whether to walk or not when the batsman was aware of the fact that he was out. English professional players have long subscribed to the viewpoint that it is the done thing to help the umpire in making difficult decisions and walk from the wicket if one is sure that one has edged a catch to the keeper or a fieldsman. Any other course of action is construed by the 'pro' as depriving a fellow-workman of his due and just rewards. The Australian viewpoint maintains that it is the responsibility of the umpire to make decisions and that to pre-empt those judgments is tantamount to a motion of no confidence in him. Anyway, they argue, adverse decisions have a habit of being counterbalanced by fortunately favourable ones. It is debatable whether being given not out against all expectations when one is 2, cancels out the error of being given unjustifiably out when one is 173. It should be said, however, that the English opinion on walking is not without its point of weakness. A batsman with a reputation for turning towards the pavilion without the umpire's prompting, could easily provoke wrong decisions by acting out of character in times of stress. The Australian habit of awaiting the umpire's signal before departing caused Dexter's batsmen to imitate their hosts in 1962-3. One of the touring batsmen later confessed that in Brisbane's First Test, when England were floundering in their second innings against McKenzie, Davidson and the second new ball and had lost 2 wickets without scoring a run, he sullied a previously blameless record by not walking for a catch behind the wicket and being given the benefit of the doubt. The result was that Dexter's side saved the match; needing 378 runs to win in six hours, they were still 100 runs behind with only 4 wickets in reserve when the stumps were drawn.

England took the lead in the series when they won Melbourne's Second Test by 7 wickets. Cowdrey re-established his habit of notching a century in Melbourne—a custom which he failed to observe only once in six consecutive tours; but the hero of Albion was the Reverend David Sheppard, yet another in the long line of resurrected batsmen in the tradition of Washbrook and Compton who returned to the Test arena after an absence of five pastoral years to score a match-winning 113. Sheppard was run out when his side was only 4 runs short of victory, after he and Cowdrey added 104 for the third wicket. It was a partnership which should never have materialized since Cowdrey was missed at slip at 149 and Jarman, substituting for Grout behind the stumps, dropped Sheppard 2 runs later. It was an unfortunate series for Jarman. In the next match in Sydney the crowd had not forgotten his Melbourne slip and barracked him continuously when Australia were in the field. When he came off the oval a friend remarked that he looked tired and round-shouldered. 'I should be', replied 'B.J.', 'the crowd have been on my back all day'.

David Sheppard ('The Rev')

It was just as well that Sheppard reached three figures in the Melbourne game, for he had much ground to make up; he missed two important catches in the Australian innings. When the tour started, 'The Rev', as the future Bishop of Liverpool was known to his England team-mate, Fred Trueman, was regarded as a close-to-the-wicket fielding specialist. A series of sins of catching omission, however, brought the penance of a gradual relegation to more distant and less important areas of fielding responsibilty. Such were 'The Rev's' lapses from catching grace that it was said that Fred was heard to doubt whether the cricketing ecclesiastic kept his hands together anywhere except in church! After stints at mid-off and mid-on, Sheppard finally found himself in the last refuge of the hidden fast bowler, at deep fine-leg. Unfortunately for Sheppard his transfer came at a time when Bill Lawry was in his hooking period and Fred Trueman was in his bounciest mood. Inevitably Trueman loosed a bumper and Lawry hooked high and hard to deep fine-leg where Sheppard was the incumbent, firm in faith but lacking in confidence. He launched himself on the crusade after the ball and after a journey of some twenty yards to his left, dived, flung out a hand and, much to his amazement, found that the ball lodged in his hand only inches from the turf. Elated, Sheppard threw the ball high, caught it and threw it up again; he repeated the process three times and as the ball was coming down the third time, he turned to find that Trueman had run down from his position at the end of his bowling follow-through and was standing at his shoulder. 'Rev', said Trueman, 'that was marvellous. Now would you mind throwing the ball in; it was a no-ball and they've run five'.

Australia exacted her revenge in Sydney where the home side won by 8 wickets. After trailing by only 40 runs on the first innings, Dexter's team collapsed against the swing of the left-handed Davidson to be all out for 104 in their second knock. 'Davo' bowled a few deliveries in that innings which he usually described, with justification, as being amongst 'the best I ever bowled'. The two Sheppards in the opposing sides played contrasting roles in the Third Test. 'The Rev' persisted in his attack of dropsy and missed Harvey twice as the batsman scored 64. The burly West Australian batsman, the left-handed Barry Shepherd, scored a fine 71 not out in Australia's first innings yet was dropped after a further trial in Adelaide; ironically he finished third in the Test averages. This was the broad pattern of the Perth man's career which was to extend to the West Indian tour of 1965 and yet embrace only nine Tests. John Murray, the England keeper was, however, the unluckiest participant in the Third Test. He injured his shoulder whilst catching Lawry, quite brilliantly, off the bowling of Coldwell in Australia's first innings. His subsequent disability, however, enabled him to establish a dubious batting record which still exists. In England's second innings the handicapped Murray occupied the crease for 100 minutes whilst scoring 3 not out. These statistics make him the slowest scoring batsman in Tests—twenty minutes faster but 5 runs less prolific than even the redoubtable Trevor Bailey.

The Fourth Test in Adelaide epitomized the conservative approach of the two sides contending for the prize of the coveted Ashes. On the morning of the final day, Australia led by 287 runs, yet Benaud delayed his declaration until lunch, thereby setting England the Everest-like total of 356 runs to score in two sessions of play. Dexter did not even attempt to scale the impossible peak, though Barrington conjured up majestic visions of what might have been by notching a cavalier 132 not out and bringing up his century in less than three hours with a huge six. 'Nina' Harvey scored 154 in Australia's first innings of 393—but not without a little good fortune. He was dropped twice off consecutive deliveries. There is no prize for guessing who missed him on the second occasion. It was once more England's unfortunate clerical fieldsman, Sheppard.

The two teams entered the ring for the deciding Sydney Test like a couple of heavyweight contenders for the world crown. Unwilling to give any advantage, they circled one another warily, with neither side landing a conclusive knock-out punch throughout the game. As a result, England batted supinely for the whole of the first day for a dreary 5/195. The tourists' first innings of 321 occupied nine and a half hours. Nor did the home side step up the pace when they went to the wicket. Simpson spent two hours in compiling 32 runs and Burge's 103 spanned a tardy five and a half hours. Trailing by 28 on the first innings, Dexter's side stayed at the crease until lunch-time on the fifth day before setting Australia the impossible task of scoring 241 runs to win at an even-time rate on a wicket which was now turning. Off-spinner Allen snatched 3 wickets for 26 runs as Benaud's side slumped to 4/70. Lawry batted for four hours for 45 not out. The shutters on the game and the series were conclusively up and for the first time a five-match series in Australia was drawn.

The England batting star who was the only man on either side to top the 500-run aggregate for the rubber, and who was to remain at the head of the England averages for the next two series against Australia, was Surrey's personification of cricket professionalism, Ken Barrington. Barrington's international career began in 1955 against McGlew's South Africans. English cricket writer, Jim Swanton, recounts how he drove Barrington to his first Test, as he had done for Peter May before him in 1951. May scored 138 on his début against South Africa at Leeds; alas Barrington did not emulate his illustrious predecessor and Swanton's superstitious ploy failed. As usual, however, the judgment of the *Daily Telegraph's* cricket correspondent was impeccable. There was no doubting Barrington's innate batting ability even in his early career. He was an exciting stroke-maker at the crease when he was twenty-four; he was an accomplished hooker, and an hour of Barrington's batting was worth driving miles to see. The year 1955 was a vintage year for batsmen in England, however, and the Surrey man had to combat challenges from players of the stature of Graveney, Peter Richardson, Cowdrey, Watson and Parks. For two matches against the Springboks, Barrington occupied a place in centre stage, but his lack of consistency saw his role go to another player. He failed to be selected for the tour of South Africa and was passed over for the 1956 and 1958-9 series against Australia. Barrington re-emerged from his batting chrysalis like a brilliant butterfly in the rubber against India in 1959. The transformation which his game had undergone during his four years in the pupa stage was a complete metamorphosis. His stance was now two-eyed and open; at times he appeared to play his power-laden off-drive light years distant from the recommended hitting area close to his front pad. Importantly, however, his approach to batting had undergone a radical change. His concentration was unshak-able. Barrington never committed himself to a stroke without being assured of the mathematical certainty that it was possible. His defence was water, air and bowling-tight. He was the Complete Professional Batsman and a player who had reduced his own special art form to a percentage science. He was the precursor of the Boycott school of batting, yet in his own way more adventurous and more experimental. It was small wonder that Barrington was to dominate the English stage until 1968.

The Australian team which arrived in England at the end of April in 1964 was yet another in that long line of sides which have been dubbed as 'the worst ever to leave Australia', before they have even flexed their playing muscles on the field. The inspiration of Benaud's leadership had been relegated to the press box and it was this one deficiency in the Australian team which probably led to its general condemnation. It was

Ken Barrington. The Complete Professional Batsman

Grahame McKenzie's shoulder-wrenching power

a strange judgment since, on paper, the tourists were a well-rounded combination. Their batting was redolent with talent in Lawry, Burge, Booth, O'Neill, the young Redpath and Simpson; the Australian bowling was balanced with McKenzie and Hawke in charge of speed and Simpson's leg-breaks and Veiver's off-spinners looking after the slow department.

Grahame McKenzie was the perfect physical summation of a fast bowler, tall and broad-shouldered. It is said that this Adonis of speed was once stripped to the buff, preparatory to taking a shower during the tea interval of a game against Yorkshire at Bradford's Park Avenue ground. Suddenly the door opened and a middle-aged waitress pushed the tea trolley into the Australian dressing-room to serve the mid-afternoon refreshments. She took in the anatomical splendour of McKenzie with one swift glance and simply carried on setting the table. Richie Benaud, the Australian skipper, commented to the waitress that it was perhaps not opportune to serve tea at that very moment. 'Nay lad, don't worry about that', said the Yorkshire lass, with an airy wave in McKenzie's direction, 'I've seen all that before'. 'Madam', replied Benaud, with all solemnity, 'you have been spoiled'.

McKenzie's potential was first discovered and commented on by Frank Worrell when his touring West Indian team played against Western Australia in 1960. The following year 'Garth' McKenzie won the Lords Test for Australia by taking 5/37 in England's second innings total of 202. In Australia in 1962-3 McKenzie attained his Test majority capturing 20 wickets in the series and he was to surpass this figure in England in 1964 by nine more victims. McKenzie was an unassuming, unassertive individual who did not seek the limelight which found him. He was little given to histrionics and the blowing of his own trumpet, and many people would be greatly surprised to learn that the bowler with 246 Test victims to his credit and the cricketer who features second on the list of Australian wicket-takers in Tests and fifth on the world-wide honours board, is none other than Grahame McKenzie. He was only twenty-nine years old when he was controversially omitted from the Fifth Test against Illingsworth's England team at Melbourne. For ten years and sixty Tests he had given his all for his country only to be dropped when he was just 3 wickets short of breaking Benaud's record of 248 victims in three more Tests. It was true that McKenzie's form against South Africa in the Australian winter of 1969 betrayed a certain lethargy and lack of penetration. In a disastrous four-match series for Australia on the high veldt he had captured only 1 wicket for 333 runs in three Tests and 110 overs. I still feel, however, that a fallow season would have done much to restore the spirit of the still young fast bowler, who probably still had two good Test seasons in him when he was retired permanently. As a fast bowler, McKenzie was an interesting study. His approach was angular and brief; his bounding run made him appear driven along by spring-heeled boots. His delivery stride expressed all the powerful ambitions of a fast bowler, being completely closed and overflowing with shoulder-wrenching power. The ball was delivered across a front leg which afforded McKenzie the benefit of a natural outswinger. If there was one fault in McKenzie's bowling it was that his last stride was perhaps too volcanic. Sometimes in his desire to put everything into a delivery, the West Australian dropped into slinging error, thrusting down with his leading arm too soon, and consequently straying into erratic zones of length and direction outside the off-stump.

The First Test unfolded at Nottingham's Trent Bridge and was doomed to a draw by the fact that rain kept the players off the field for half of the scheduled time. A late injury to Edrich and the unavailability of a substitute compelled Dexter to use his off-spinner Titmus as an ersatz opener. The Middlesex man went in first with Boycott and was the central figure in an act of sportsmanship seldom seen on the Test field. As Titmus was going through for a quick single he collided with the bowler Hawke who cut across his bows to retrieve the ball. Since Hawke was a veteran of Australian Rules Football and thoroughly accustomed to 'shirt-front' physical confrontation, the outcome of the meeting of the two forces was predictable. Hawke collected the ball as Titmus snowballed in a muddy heap down the wet wicket. Wicketkeeper 'Griz' Grout, who had been an impartial spectator of this imbalanced physical clash, was up over the stumps at the batsman's end as Hawke's return skimmed the bails with Titmus still grovelling in the mud yards down the wicket. It would have been within the letter of the law for Grout to have run out Titmus—but not, in Grout's estimation, within the spirit of the law. Giving Titmus a half-amused look, as if asking him what he was doing in the mire, the Australian keeper threw the ball away without removing the bails and Titmus was safe. It sometimes makes me wonder about the justice of life when people such as Wally Grout are taken prematurely from the cricket scene; 'Griz' died of a heart attack on 9 November 1968 at the age of forty-one. No one apparently was willing to throw the ball away and not take off the bails when he was still short of his crease.

The Second Test at Lords was also condemned to a watery grave with the first two days of the match lost to rain and only two innings being completed. The deciding match of the rubber was played at Leeds, where 'one of the weakest sides ever to leave Australia' turned on its critics to win the match and the series by 7 wickets. The game was virtually decided by one indiscreet decision on the part of the England captain, Dexter. Chasing England's moderate first innings total of 268 and struggling on a typical dusty Leeds wicket against the spin of the left-handed Gifford and Titmus, Australia were 7/187 when Dexter opted to take the second new ball. England's speedsters Trueman and Flavell attempted to bounce the inveterate hooker Burge and were punished for their pains to such an extent that Australia's last 3 wickets added 211 and Burge scored a lone and masterly 160. Handicapped by Parfitt's suffering a broken knuckle, England collapsed for 229 in their second batting attempt and Australia knocked off the required 109 runs for victory for the loss of the wickets of Lawry, Simpson and Burge. Redpath scored 58 not out, revealing the latent ability against spin bowling which was to make him one of the best batsmen in the world in later years on turning wickets. Some idea of the criticism to which the Australian tourists were subjected throughout the tour can be gained from the fact that Redpath exclaimed to his captain, Simpson, as he came into the dressing-room after winning the match, 'That's one innings for you skipper'. Such was the team spirit of the Australian side.

What Australia had, they were determined to hold; such was the evidence of the next Test at Old Trafford. Australia's batsmen for more than two days ground their way to a huge 8/656 declared, with Simpson compiling a triple hundred and assisting Lawry to add 201 for the first wicket. The strange fact about Simpson's innings was that his 311, the fourth triple century in England-Australia clashes, was his first Test hundred. England's reply to the enormity of Australia's score was an equally massive 611, to which Barrington contributed 256 and Dexter 174. Tom Veivers, the Australian off-spinner, achieved an Anglo-Australian Test record, which he would have been happy to forego: he sent down a marathon 95.1 overs to return figures of 3/155. The batting successes of the first innings left only time for two overs in Australia's second and the match was abandoned as a draw.

Simpson's innings was an eloquent commentary on his batting methods. Concentration and method were in his every movement. It was strange that he had to wait until his thirtieth Test before he reached his first three-figure score in the international sphere; large scores abounded in his first-class career. During his self-imposed Sheffield Shield period of exile in Western Australia, Simpson scored 236 not out against his native New South Wales. He later redressed the balance by notching 247 not out for New South Wales against the Perth side. In the 1959-60 Sheffield Shield season he averaged an astonishing 300.66 in five matches. His batting technique was compact and economical; there were no wasted flourishes in Simpson's stroke-play. He was a master of placement, particularly in his range of back-foot strokes, and his running between the wickets bordered on the intuitive. He and Bill Lawry built up an understanding between the wickets which made calling for a run almost superfluous—it was just a case of a nod and the batsmen were off. I doubt whether there could have been a better pair of single-sneakers in Test cricket since the halcyon days of Hobbs and Sutcliffe. In one respect, however, Simpson's batting approach was personally unique. He never avoided the bouncer by ducking under and inside its line, but preferred to withdraw towards the leg-side. It was an attitude which was to cause him many anxious moments when faced

Bob Simpson

with the fire-power of Wes Hall and Charlie Griffith in the following year's Australian tour of the Caribbean; but it was still effective enough for him to produce 201 runs out of the bag in the Barbados Test.

Simpson's determined approach to batting had its source in the personality of the man himself. The Australian skipper is a man of principle and conviction. I recall his batting for New South Wales against Len Hutton's 1954-5 touring side and being 98 not out when the England skipper convinced the umpires that play should be suspended—because the murky light was militating against the fielding side! Simpson was so angry with the gamesmanship of the English leader that he swung wildly at Johnny Wardle's next delivery and was stumped. It appeared that the 18-year-old batsman, even at that early stage of his career, had clear concepts about the spirit in which a game of cricket should be played.

I do not delude myself into thinking that it was pure altruism which caused the 41-year-old Simpson to re-emerge from ten years of international retirement to lead the youthful and new-look Australian team against Bishen Bedi's touring Indian side of 1977-8. As a public relations consultant, he was astute enough to realize that the decimation of the Australian playing strength as a result of the Kerry Packer crisis was a heaven-sent opportunity to re-establish himself in the public eye. His volunteering for service over and above the demands of duty, however, cannot be dismissed as mere opportunism. By his own admission, there had been offers to him to join the ranks of the private promoter's employees; he rejected them to lead the rejuvenated Australian side to a 3-2 victory over India. Businessman though he is, he realized that there are sporting values on which it is impossible to put a price. Pride in representing one's country figures high on Bobby Simpson's list of priorities in life; he is equally determined for Australia to do well in international cricket. Why else should he agree to guide Bill Lawry gently into the harness of captaincy by playing underneath him, after resigning his captaincy during the Indian series of 1967-8? Why should he risk his already established reputation by challenging the West Indian pace attack at the age of forty-two and agreeing to lead the touring side to the Caribbean? After his marathon 311 at Old Trafford in 1964, he answered the critics of his tactic of batting for more than two days by saying that, with his side one up in the rubber, it was in Australia's interest to play the game in that way. It was a mentality which was not designed to produce exciting cricket but it was a realistic assessment of the situation.

It was a policy which enabled his team to win the 1964 series. Rain obliterated the last day of the final Oval Test and the subsequent draw brought victory to Simpson's team by the narrow margin of the Leeds game. Trueman captured his 300th wicket in Tests at The Oval. When Hawke was caught by Cowdrey at slip, the milestone was passed and Trueman could heave a sigh of fatigue and relief. Obviously at the age of thirty-three there were few other fields which the bowler would possess the physical endurance to conquer. Small wonder that, when questioned about how he felt about his achievement, and whether he thought that anyone would ever surpass his record, F.S. replied with feeling that he did not know, but that if anyone did outstrip him he felt sure that they would be 'bloody tired'. Trueman went on to play in two more Tests against New Zealand and climax his international career with a total bag of 307 wickets. Records it appears are made only to be broken, and even Freddie's formidable achievement did not remain inviolate. In 1976, when West Indian off-spinner, Lance Gibbs, had Ian Redpath caught at long-on in the Melbourne Test, Trueman's figure was only second best. Realistically speaking, however, there was no comparison between the fast bowler's feat and that of Gibbs. The slow bowler required twelve more Tests, 12,000 more deliveries, and five more years in the international arena to capture 2 more wickets than Trueman in official games.

I have often been asked whom I regard as being the best fast bowler of my time. Trueman comes close to qualifying for the accolade; this much must be obvious from his career statistics alone. The Yorkshire bowler captured 79 more wickets than the great Australian pace bowler, Ray Lindwall, yet played in only six more Tests. Figures, however, as Mark Twain remarked, are so often 'damned statistics'. Bowling averages do not reflect the strength of the opposing batsmen; they take no account of prime years lost to war or physical injury. Ray Lindwall celebrated his eighteenth birthday one month after the outbreak of the Second World War. When peace was declared 'Jackson' Lindwall was in his twenty-fourth year and had been bowling as fast as was humanly possible for at least two years. When he topped the Australian Test averages for the 1953 series in England with a 'bag' of 26 wickets at an average of 18.84, Lindwall was almost a year older than Garth McKenzie when he played his last Test. Moreover, Lindwall was to grace the international arena for a further five years, most of which were spent bowling in the heat of Brisbane, for his adopted state of Queensland.

These are the facts which lead me to believe that Lindwall was probably the best fast bowler whom I have ever seen and played against. He will remain long in my mind's eye as an artisan who combined physical beauty and strength with a supreme ability to detect and probe the batsman's weaknesses. In their later phases of development, Lindwall and Trueman had much in common. Both bowlers were endowed with the native shrewdness and patience of a slow bowler and the physical capacities of a fast bowling Hercules. Their actions were classically side-on, though perhaps Lindwall's arm dropped more with the passing years; their pronounced movements towards the slips frequently found the edge of the most watchful and orthodox bat and their range of variations was matched only by a relentless pursuit of their goals.

There were, of course, differences between the two bowlers in both technique and personality. Trueman's approach to the wicket bespoke his more extrovert character. It was bounding, vigorous and hostile. Lindwall by contrast seemed to glide over the ground, for all the world like a middle-aged gentleman out for his Saturday afternoon jog—until the last few explosive strides. Trueman showed that he was giving his all in almost every delivery, Lindwall sometimes suggested that he was hardly raising a sweat even on the hottest of Australian days. 'Lindy' seldom gave outward vent to his feelings on the field; there were few gestures and no expletives. Fred wore his sentiments and his bowling heart on his sleeve. The spectator almost felt that he was bowling every ball with Trueman and experiencing his triumphs and his disappointments. It was small wonder that the Yorkshireman soon won himself the epithets of 'fiery' and 'ferocious'—the adjectives describe Trueman at the bowling crease exactly. There was a charisma about Fred Trueman on the cricket field which made him a legend of a character during his own career. He and I were often compared in pace, and such was Fred's competitive nature that he would not concede inferiority in any department of fast bowling. The Tyson-Trueman rivalry in speed was therefore one of the highlights of any game between Yorkshire and

Doug Walters plays an unorthodox defensive stroke. South Africa 1969-70

my own county of Northamptonshire. Everyone enjoyed it—except the batsmen!

On 2 July 1968, Trueman demonstrated his cricketing shrewdness by substituting for the injured Brian Close and leading Yorkshire to their first win over the Australian tourists in sixty-six years. One of Trueman's outmanoeuvred oppoⅼents in that clash was the unfortunate Doug Walters. Three years earlier the 19-year-old batting prodigy from Dungog was the *enfant terrible* of Australian cricket. He was the most exciting commodity in the game, scoring 155 on his Test début in Brisbane and following this triumph with 115 in the second clash in Melbourne. His early beginnings promised the scoring consistency of a second Bradman. He possessed the same early perception of the ball to hook or pull; the fact that his front foot was not near the pitch of the ball nor his bat in the perfect perpendicular plane did not inhibit his driving. He had the exciting panache of the young cavalier participating in his first charge—and the same weakness of impetuosity. His keen eye gave his batting magic moments of near genius. By scoring 242 and 103 against the West Indies in Sydney in 1968-9 he became one of the four players to have scored a double and single century in the same Test. At

203

Christchurch in New Zealand in 1977, Walters despatched the Kiwi bowler to all quarters of the field to notch 250 in an Australian total of 552, on a reputedly green wicket! Hundreds came his way against England, the West Indies, India and New Zealand—on hard wickets. Not once has 'Bicky' Walters reached three figures against the old enemy in England. Indeed English conditions so militated against Walter's technique in 1968 that his highest first-class score was 95. In 1972 his figures were better and he reached the century milestone against Warwickshire, Kent and Derbyshire. Yet his form in Tests was so poor that he averaged only 7 and he was dropped for the Test which squared the series at The Oval.

Walters is the very personification of the erratic genius. He is almost totally dependent on his innate natural ability. His temperament seems ill-suited to moments of tension. He would sooner chain-smoke and play cards than watch play before going in to bat. Often before going out to the middle he will 'loosen up' by throwing three darts at the dressing-room dart board. When his natural talents are unequal to the batting task which faces him, Walters lacks the technique to fight his way out of a tight situation. In South Africa in 1969-70 the Springbok pace attack of Pollock and the unorthodox, wrong-footed Proctor caused the Australian batsman to duck and weave in the manner of a cornered boxer. Photographs of Walters at the batting crease during that series portray him in some extraordinary evasive postures. Not infrequently he ducked into the line of the ball whilst leaving his bat vertically extended above his head. Perhaps the worst aspect of Walters' failures was his unwillingness to modify his technique to meet the challenges of different wickets. He stolidly refused to be coached or helped out of his errors—perhaps fearing that he would lose the natural ability to hit the ball which God had given him. In the Brisbane motel room of the Australian Broadcasting Commission's commentator, Alan McGilvray, on the very evening of Walters' first Test century, I congratulated him but pointed out that his bat was more than slightly out of perpendicular when playing off the back foot and that could cause him a great deal of trouble in situations where the ball moved off the pitch. 'Bicky's' reply was characteristic and adamant: 'That's the way I play, and I guess I always will'. Such is the path which must eventually lead down from the heights of greatness, since every eminent batsman must learn to come to terms with his own limitations and the conditions under which he plays.

The England side which Walters faced for the first time in Brisbane on 10 December 1965, was at a crossroads in its development. Its star fast bowlers, Statham and Trueman took their final Test curtain call in the previous English summer. Dexter was no longer at the helm and the tourists were led by the tall, bespectacled Warwickshire captain, Mike Smith. 'M.J.K.' was probably as well known in Sydney for his 'reverse scissors' manoeuvre on the international rugby field with his fellow Oxford University centre, Brace, as he was his batting prowess. He was, however, one of the best players of spin bowling in county cricket and a powerful punisher of the ball on the leg-side. His less-than-eagle eye often made him suspect against the quicker bowlers, especially when they pitched in the block hole early in his innings, but once established at the crease, he was a formidable opponent whose Test figures did less than justice to his ability. Only three Test centuries came his way in fifty matches; 69 first-class hundreds and almost 40,000 runs more than suggest that he deserved better. His reputation as a captain was peerless and his public relations image in Australia in 1965-6 stamped him as one of the most accessible and respected of skippers ever to lead his country.

Smith's touring problems were many and varied. Injuries to his fast bowlers Larter, Higgs and Brown and batsmen Russell and Cowdrey made life difficult for his selection committee. His fourth quick bowler, Glamorgan's Jeff Jones, continually incurred the umpires' wrath by running on the wicket. His batting, however, was strong and England often took strike, complacent in the knowledge that the name of all-rounder Barry Knight, the scorer of Test centuries against New Zealand and India, was inscribed in the batting order at number nine. Both teams, in fact, possessed immensely powerful striking power. Australia's opener Bill Lawry scored 592 runs in the series. He was helped by the fact that certain Australian wickets proved unreceptive to the bowlers' art. Melbourne's Second Test witnessed the amassing of 1,347 runs for the loss of only 30 wickets; the lowest score on that ground in two games and five completed innings was 358. It was therefore not surprising that the rubber was drawn. The unusual feature about the divided series, however, was the fact that the two conclusive games were each won by an innings. Significantly Australia won the Adelaide game on a green pitch suited to their pace attack, whilst England carried off the honours on a slow, turning Sydney surface, tailor-made for their off-spinners Titmus and Allen.

Australia's future captain, Ian Chappell, met his English adversaries for the first time in the Adelaide encounter. It was indicative of the prowess of the batsmen playing for Australia in this era that Chappell batted at number seven. One place beneath him was his country's future opener Keith Stackpole, whose selection in those days hinged just as much on his ability to bowl darting leg-spinners as his batting. Chappell's gentle nurturing continued during the 1968 tour of England where he batted at number six in most of the Tests. It was a policy which obviously paid dividends, as the successful career of Australia's regular number three in the early 1970s clearly demonstrated.

Australia's batting rock until the summer of 1967-8 was founded firmly on the opening partnership of Simpson and Lawry. Against Smith's XI they established a first-wicket record of 244 in the Adelaide Test, thereby adding to their reputation as the last of that vanishing race of Australian dinosaurs, a regular opening pair. It was an astonishing reflection on the depth of Australian batting talent at this time that 'Wallaby' Bob Cowper, a left-handed batting artist who scored 99 in the Second Test, 60 in the previous game and was to go on to notch 307 in the final clash at the M.C.G., was discarded in favour of Ian Chappell in Adelaide.

Cowper was one of those imperceptible scorers, who seldom gave the impression of tearing an attack limb from limb, yet, when you took stock, was always 40 runs more than when you last looked at the scoreboard. His defence was compact, his on-driving as sweet as a nut and his square-cut the most powerful weapon in his armoury. Above all Cowper placed the ball superbly, tugging the fieldsmen this way and that with artistic touches supplemented by fleet running between the wickets. In four years at the top of the cricket tree he played in only 27 Tests, cutting short his sporting ambitions to follow his chosen business career at the age of twenty-seven. The wastage of Cowper in 1968 was an eloquent commentary on the financial martyrdom to which players of his era had to submit themselves. Had Cowper been born nine years later, in more affluent times, he would have survived in international cricket much longer.

Rain obliterated the second day of the Brisbane Test and, together with an Australian first innings total of 6/443 and an England second innings rearguard action, produced an inevitable draw. In hindsight, it must be said that England's golden opportunity of winning the series went a-begging in the second clash in Melbourne. The traditional Cowdrey century and a hundred from John Edrich afforded Smith's men the advantage of a 200-run lead on the first innings. Australia had only made good their deficit and were 4 runs ahead when England's self-made stopper-keeper Parks missed stumping Burge off Barber's leg-spin when the batsman was literally two yards down the wicket. Four wickets were down at this moment of truth and only the youthful Walters and the home side's bowlers stood between England and victory. Burge went on to compile 120 and together with Walters add 198 for the fifth wicket and thus steer Australia to security and a total of 426.

Barber's 185 in the Sydney Test was one of the most dazzling displays of batting pyrotechnics which I have ever witnessed. He reduced the varied Australian attack of McKenzie, Hawke, Philpott and Sincock to mere impotence, treating them with a disdain which surely must have been in the vein of MacLaren or Trumper. After Smith won the toss, Barber and Boycott lambasted a third best opening stand against Australia of 234, and with Edrich contributing 103, Booth, leading Australia in the absence of the injured Simpson, must have realized that his side were on the threshold of defeat on the second day. The wicket began to turn on the third day as Australia followed on 267 runs behind, in the wake of a 5-wicket performance from fast bowler Brown. They collapsed a second time for 174 before the wondering eyes of Harold Larwood, the former England fast bowler, who had never seen a Sydney wicket spin so widely.

Larwood, in fact, confessed he had not seen the Sydney ground since he last trod it in 1933. It was a strange admission he made in the English dressing-room on that January day in 1966, since he left his Blackpool sweet shop behind him many years previously and, at the prompting of his former opponent, the Australian opening bat and current cricket writer, Jack Fingleton, migrated to the Sydney suburb of Kingsford. For years 'Lol' lived and worked for a soft-drink manufacturer within a few miles of the scene of his former triumphs; yet he was so retiring and unsure of himself in a country which had such bitter memories of bodyline for him, that he was reluctant to take the few steps necessary for him to reach the Sydney Cricket Ground. To understand Larwood's sentiments it is necessary to comprehend the nature of the man. He has virtually become a 'fair dinkum' Aussie; yet in 1977 he still hesitated to accept the Australian Cricket Board's invitation to attend the Centenary Test. The events of those hostile days of 1932-3 and the feelings which they engendered still rankled, and perhaps he was anxious lest time had not dimmed the bitter memories of the public and opposing players. The story had a happy ending. 'Lol' went to the Centenary Test. During one interval of the game he strolled to the centre of the Melbourne Cricket Ground in company with his fellow opening bowler in Jardine's touring side, Bill Voce. Both players were cheered to the echo by an enormous crowd who remembered, not the acrimony of distant days, but the greatness of the players who peopled them.

Australia won the Fourth Test by an innings and 9 runs—not only by virtue of their superior fast-bowling strength on a strangely uncharacteristic humid first day and green Adelaide wicket, but also because of a quirk of fate. McKenzie, after a lethargic and wicketless display in Sydney was initially omitted from the nominated home side. His replacement, Peter Allan of Queensland, contracted tonsillitis and withdrew from the match leaving the way open for McKenzie's reinstatement. Garth seized the opportunity in both of his enormous hands, captured a match-winning 6/48 in England's first innings and ensured his place for the remainder of the series.

The discarded paceman, Peter Allan, must go down in the annals of Test cricket as one of the unluckiest players ever to hover on the periphery of Tests. I first met him when he played for the Fitzroy Club in Melbourne in the early 1960s. Week in and week out, Peter was one of the most consistent and effective medium-fast bowlers in district cricket. He possessed a lively, bounding, kangaroo approach, a high action and a boomeranging outswinger which made him one of the most feared bowlers in club ranks which were replete with the formidable batting talents of such players as Lawry, Redpath, Cowper, Potter, Shaw and Eastwood. Yet because of the competitive ability of Meckiff, Guest and Connolly and because Victoria pursued the Yorkshire policy of selecting only native-born sons, he could not gain a place in the State team. In 1963 he returned to his home state, Queensland, and was such an immediate success at the Gabba that he gained a place in Simpson's touring side to the West Indies in 1965. However, luck was still against him. He was so plagued by sickness and injury that he bowled only 65 overs and played in four games in the Caribbean. Undeterred he came once more into Test contention by taking 39 wickets in the 1965-6 Sheffield Shield season, finishing second in the first-class bowling averages and playing in the First Test against England in Brisbane. Against Victoria in Melbourne in the early days of the New Year, he exacted a terrible revenge for the slight which he had received at the hands of the southern selectors by becoming one of the three bowlers ever to take 10 wickets in a Shield game. He snared all but one of the Victorian batsmen at a cost of 61 runs in the first innings and gained promotion to his Adelaide Test anticlimax three weeks later. He continued to represent Queensland until the 1968-9 season. In that year he topped the first-class averages with 46 wickets at a cost of 16.36 each, finishing above such illustrious names as McKenzie, Connolly, Mayne, Grant, and 'Froggy' Thomson. After his refusal at the Adelaide barrier, however, he was never again chosen in a representative Australian side and he retired, probably a disillusioned, and certainly an unfortunate and able bowler.

The final contest in Melbourne was a wearisome affair, with the bat once more dominating the ball. Again more than a thousand runs were scored on the M.C.G. wicket and only two innings completed. Batsmen monopolized the limelight in the rubber; seven English players returned averages of more than 40 in the Tests, whilst four Australians had mean figures in excess of 60. Barrington enlivened the Melbourne drabness by scoring the fastest hundred of the series and moving to his century with a magnificent 6 over long-on. The immaculate Cowper batted for more than twelve hours of the home side's only innings to become the fourth man in post-war Tests to score a triple hundred. Cowper's immense concentration took him to within 4 runs of Simpson's score in Manchester two years previously and brought him the distinction of a Test innings in Australia, higher even than any achieved by Bradman.

The Australian tour of England in 1968 was almost theatrical in the manner in which fortune stage-managed the finale. England squared the series with only six minutes of 150 hours play remaining. As Underwood claimed the wicket of Inverarity to win The Oval game for England, nine fieldsmen crouched within three yards of the Western Australian's bat. Thousands of English supporters crowed with delight from their perches on the hard Oval benches. They had every right to be pleased, not only with their champions, but also with themselves. If it had not been for the assistance given to the Surrey ground staff by hundreds of spectators who helped to drain the ground after a thunderstorm flooded it at lunch-time on the last day, the match would never have restarted and would have ended in a draw giving Australia the rubber by a one-match margin.

The year 1968 in England was a season of Jupiter Pluvius; no fewer than four of the five Tests were rain-affected and the youngest Australian side to visit that country had their enthusiasm dampened by losing more than 100 hours play to the weather. It was surprising that they retained enough spirit to earn themselves the reputation of a brilliant fielding combination. At Old Trafford Cowdrey's men could not recapture the shades of 1956, and were beaten by 159 on a pitch taking spin and more suited to their attack. England's selectors did little to boost the confidence of their men. They invited fourteen players to attend pre-match practice and did not announce the eleven in whom they reposed their trust until the morning of the game. Lawry set Australia on the victory trail. At a point in Australia's first innings of 357 when England's 21-year-old off-spinner, Pat Pocock, playing for the first time against the old foe, looked like troubling every batsman, the Australian skipper threw caution to the wind and hit successfully against the spin and percentages to completely unsettle the inexperienced Surrey man. Pocock captured 6/79 in Australia's second knock but did not play again in the series. Indeed Manchester witnessed Pocock's only appearance against Australia in an international career spanning seventeen games and nine years.

He was not the only player to suffer in this year of strange English selection. D'Oliveira put up almost lone resistance in England's second innings of 253 to score 87 not out. He was robbed of his richly deserved century only by some irresponsible tail-end batting; yet he was not chosen again until the Fifth Test. There was even a barb in the tail of his selection for The Oval clash. He only came in at the last moment for the injured Prideaux, and was subsequently omitted from the touring party to go to South Africa in spite of his scoring 158 in England's first innings and making the vital break-through with the ball in Australia's second. 'Dolly's' non-selection after the First Test and his non-inclusion in the Springbok tour smacked of connivance with the apartheid policy of the South African authorities to whom it was deemed that the Cape-coloured D'Oliveira would not be acceptable. The furore which the offensive morality of the issue caused split the M.C.C., and so resounded around the cricketing world that not even the player's late selection in place of the injured Cartwright could assuage it. The South African rejection of a side which included D'Oliveira, on the grounds that England had yielded to political pressure, must surely be the classical case of a black prophet not being accepted in his own land.

At Lords a hailstorm on the first day created a landscape more reminiscent of the Arctic Circle in mid-winter than an English cricket ground in June. The conditions were not unproductive, however, since

England's humorist-batsman, Colin Milburn, seems to be expecting a shooter

England and her eighteen-stone batsman, Colin Milburn, played heroic cricket. The home side were 1/53 when the weather halted proceedings at lunch. Such was the intensity of the storm that Lords resembled the frontispiece of a Christmas card. A white blanket of hail cloaked the outfield, whilst a molten glacier flowed down the Lords slope bisecting the pitch with a spate of water worthy of the Yorkshire moors. It was to be expected that when play resumed, the wicket would fall more into the spiteful rather than the benign category. Such proved to be the case. But when the English batting crisis came with the resumption of their innings, so did the man. That man was Colin Milburn. In eighty minutes on a virtually impossible surface, 'Ollie' (after Oliver Hardy) Milburn smote 67 runs with an exciting range of hooks and back-foot drives which would have been acceptable fare on a good wicket, but which bordered on the miraculous on this Lords quagmire.

The rotund Milburn was a batsman of whom it could be truly said that we shall never see his like again. It was the major tragedy of a cricketing generation that a car accident on the winding country lanes of Northamptonshire robbed Milburn of his sight in one eye and England of her greatest natural batting talent. Milburn's father, Jack, was a hitter of great repute and 'a wrecker of roofs of distant towns' for Burnopfield in the Northumberland League. Colin inherited not only Milburn senior's generous physical proportions but also his uncanny eye. For a man of his build he was unexpectedly light on his feet and as a judge of length and a striker of the ball 'Ollie' was without a peer in the world. He was once persuaded that he should attempt to reduce his figure to a more athletic shape and undertook a slimming course on a health farm; but the ascetic philosophy was out of character with a man who had an enormous enjoyment for food, drink, life and cricket. He was more of a cross between Epicurus and Gargantua, revelling hugely in good things on and off the cricket field. Not surprisingly, the correspondingly enormous circle of friendship which Colin built up around him matched the nature of the man himself. Fittingly, the size of his subsequent benefit was equally large.

His size brought him both advantages and disadvantages. An official at the Northamptonshire County Club once told me that he believed that Milburn was physically incapable of batting for more than three hours. Self-realization of this fact probably conditioned his aggressive approach to batting. If Milburn was at the batting crease for three hours, the spectator was assured of exhilarating batting fare. In two and a half hours of his first Test against the 1966 West Indian bowling might of Hall, Griffith, Sobers and Gibbs, he scored 94 before being bowled attempting to reach his century with his third six. A fortnight later at Lords he scored his first international hundred in a three-hour burst of what Wisden described as 'another amazing display of powerful hitting' which yielded 86 runs in boundaries and added 130 in 110 minutes for a record England fifth wicket stand against the West Indies. The most gratified band of Milburn-watchers, however, were those Woolloongabba habitués who in 1968 saw the Northamptonshire giant score 243 on the opening day of Western Australia's match against Queensland. His adopted team's victory by an innings, and their massive quick-fire total of 5/516 declared was due in no small way to Milburn's feat of scoring 181 in the two hours between lunch and tea on the first day! Only rarely do teams equal this individual scoring rate of Milburn. 'Ollie' later told me that he was so exhausted by the Brisbane heat that he tried desperately to give his wicket away after he reached his hundred, but he kept hitting the ball in the middle of the bat! Ross Duncan, the Queensland medium-pace bowler, spectator and victim of this sledge-hammer hitting said after the game that it was the only time in his career that he felt utterly powerless against a batsman. In March 1969, the Pakistan bowlers had occasion to sympathize with Duncan's feelings. Milburn, flown from Perth to replace England's opener, Prideaux, in the Karachi Test, slammed a hundred off the first 163 balls he received and contributed 139 of England's eventual total of 7/502. It was small wonder that the Pakistan supporters created cricket history by causing the abandonment of the game by rioting. They must have realized that, with Milburn in such form, it was their only way of salvaging a drawn series!

Australia managed to retreat with honours even from the Lords Test of 1968, but not without some moments of high drama. After England declared at 7/351, Lawry's men were shot out on the fourth morning for 78 by the menacing and lifting pace-bowling of Warwickshire's David Brown. Required to follow-on, the tourists survived for two and a half hours, but some idea of the grimness of their struggle can be gleaned from the fact that Sheahan, one of the best stroke-makers in the game, batted for nearly an hour without scoring. The rumour, later bruited in the press, was that Australia's first innings batting débâcle was due to the fact that they had helped Australian pressman Bob Gray celebrate his wedding on the previous rest-day. Nothing could be further from the truth; I can personally vouch for the fact that not an Australian was up at midnight on the eve of Australia's collapse.

Rain obliterated the whole of the first day of the Edgbaston game and mercifully curtailed the final six-hour Australian struggle against spin after they had been set a winning target of 321. The match was perhaps more interesting in its consequences than its unfinished events. Both of the rival captains were injured during the clash. Cowdrey, after notching a century in his hundredth Test, was compelled by a leg injury to hand over the leadership at Leeds to Graveney. Lawry's breaking a finger at Birmingham had far more complex repercussions. At Edgbaston, senior team-member McKenzie led the side whilst Lawry was off the field. For a while it seemed that he might be compelled to assume the same responsibility at Headingley if vice-captain Jarman did not recover from the chipped finger bone which had eliminated him from the Third Test. McKenzie would have thus become one of the few modern fast bowlers to captain his country—the first since Ray Lindwall filled the post in 1956-7. Alas for McKenzie's aspirations, Jarman recovered sufficiently to lead Australia for his one and only time.

There was no doubt in my mind after the Leeds Test, however, that Lawry, determined to maintain his one game advantage in the rubber, dictated Australia's general tactics from the pavilion. After three totals of just over 300, England were set a winning target of 326 at a scoring rate of 66 per hour on a last day pitch which was showing an increasing sympathy towards the spinners. Australia's intentions, however, were more directed towards drawing than winning the game. In spite of the promised assistance in the wicket for slow bowlers Gleeson, Chappell, Inverarity and Cowper, the pacemen Connolly, McKenzie and Freeman delivered 62 of the 84 overs in England's last innings. Not surprisingly, England fell short of their winning goal by 96 runs but with 6 wickets in reserve.

Australia's reluctance to set her sights high at Leeds undoubtedly cost her the series. England should never have been in a position to square the rubber in the palpitating finish at The Oval. To be fair to Lawry's tourists, however, it must be stated that on Kennington's final day, it seemed to me that they were playing not eleven but eleven hundred Englishmen—1,089 of whom were self-appointed groundsmen, without whose assistance the game would never have re-started after a lunch-time thunderstorm. Certainly England outbatted Australia by dint of masterly centuries from Edrich and D'Oliveira and her devil-may-care pursuit of quick runs in its second innings. Justice in the rubber was in the process of seeming to be done when, with four hours play remaining, Australia, in pursuit of 352 runs to win in seven hours, had lost 5/85. As I recall, the lunch-time gong had just sounded in the Australia House tent at the Vauxhall end of the ground when the heavens suddenly opened and it began to rain, as the French so pithily put it, 'à grosses gouttes'. Within the space of a quarter of an hour The Oval resembled the Serpentine Lake and any further prospects of play in the game seemed as remote as an lbw decision against an Indian batsman on the front foot in a Test at Kanpur. Then, just as suddenly as it had started, the storm passed and the sun glowered down on the flooded havoc which was formerly The Oval. With the sun, the denizens of the stands re-appeared from their temporary shelters bearing with them hundreds of wooden staves, which had apparently been secreted in some special cache precisely for such an emergency. They sloshed on to the ground, unmindful of the lagoons, and began prodding the ground with their poles, perforating the turf to assist the escape of the water. Within two hours the ex-officio curators achieved the impossible and the pools of water miraculously drained away; a further forty-five minutes after the tea-break, play began on a sodden wicket and an in-field which was a patchwork quilt of sawdust and turf.

For forty minutes the surviving opening bat, Inverarity, led a heroic Australian rearguard action; but when D'Oliveira clipped Jarman's off-bail with a leg-cutter, the decisive breach was made in the tourists' defences and Underwood's medium-paced leg-spinners, supported by a claustrophobic field-placement, stifled further resistance. Inverarity was the last man out, lbw, playing right back on his stumps for the turn which did not materialize, when every other ball had spun and lifted. It was an unexpected end to an unusual Test.

15. The New Professional Breed

The old cricket quiz chestnut that Captain Cook was the first Yorkshire professional captain to lead an English touring party to Australia is undoubtedly based on fact. Hailing as he did from the beautiful village of Marton, nestling in the Cleveland Hills, Cook would have qualified by birth to represent the County of the Broad Acres at Headingley. He was certainly a professionally competent mariner. I sometimes wonder, however, whether Cook, the countryman, had the same iron in his soul as his cricketing successors at the English helm, Hutton and Illingworth. Both were born amidst the dark satanic mills of industrial Bradford. Indeed it is a strange coincidence that the small town of Pudsey should produce two England captains within the space of sixteen years. Their demanding origins found expression in every disciplined stroke they played, every precise ball they bowled and every calculating move they made on the field.

Ironically Illingworth had migrated from Yorkshire to Leicestershire when he was called upon to lead his country against the West Indies in 1969. His adopted county's rise in first-class stature was due in no small way to their captain's inbred qualities of determination, application and Yorkshire cricketing 'nous'. These were the precise attributes which Illingworth brought to bear on the challenge of leading his country on the Test field. His talents as a batsman and an almost too-mechanical off-spinner were not in the supernatural category; but he utilized every ounce of ability at his disposal. Opposition batsmen's weaknesses were pinpointed and exploited; he seldom indulged in the luxury of extravagant strokes. His tactics on the field were based on scientific fact rather than flights of theoretical fancy. An Illingworth field was positioned to the inch. The players under his command knew precisely where they were with Illingworth. He was not a person to waste words or mince matters when controversy arose. His players admired him as a man and a captain. It must be conceded, however, that he was a professional cricketer's captain and he often came into conflict with players who were the amateur relics of the pre-1963 days.

This was the captain appointed to lead England in Australia in 1970-1. The character of the man made it inevitable that the tour would

Ray Illingworth, a professional cricketers' captain

213

John Snow

not lack moments of controversy both on and off the field. He intended to let the Australians know that they had a fight on their hands. He succeeded in his ambitions by winning the rubber 2-0, in an atmosphere which seldom fell below a dramatic level. In Sydney Illingworth led his team off the field, refusing to continue a Test in which his players were assaulted by spectators on the boundary and subjected to regular bombardments of beer cans and blocks of ice from the outer. The President of the Marylebone Cricket Club, Sir Cyril Hawker, and the tour manger, David Clark, put their heads together with Sir Donald Bradman and the Australian Cricket Board to programme a Seventh Test to replace the rain-ruined Melbourne game. Illingworth reacted by protesting vehemently on behalf of his side because they had not been consulted about this change to their original contractual tour arrangements.

The year 1971 saw England riding on the crest of the Test cricket wave. It was true that the formidable Rest of the World, substituting for the defaulting South Africans, annihilated Illingworth's side in the previous year. No one cricketing country was equal to the galaxy of talent embodied in Sober's team of 1970. On egalitarian terms, however, England demolished the West Indies 2-0 in England in the first season of Illingworth's captaincy. Her subsequent victory in Australia made England cock of the cricketing roost. Illingworth had at his disposal Down Under, a Ministry of Outstanding Sporting Talents. The tour was a personal triumph for the stormy petrel of fast bowling, John Snow. In the six Tests played, the Sussex man captured 31 wickets at the low cost, on Australian pitches, of 23.83

There were many Statham qualities about Snow. Like the Lancashire paceman, Snow was muscular, yet not constructed on the normal solid lines of fast bowlers. His lithe approach to the wicket was a bounding version of George's carpet-slipper run-up. His speed emanated from a whirling arm action rather than a pronounced rocking-horse body movement. Snow's accuracy, like Statham's, was phenomenal and, like his Lancashire and England predecessor, he possessed the capacity to move the ball off even the most unsympathetic of Australian wickets. A point of difference was that Snow depended far more on his ability to impart pronounced cut to the ball, whereas Statham relied on an innate talent to move the ball off the seam. Both were tireless workers, endowed with elephantine hearts and a competitive will to win. It was small wonder that with these attributes, Snow eventually became only the fourth fast bowler to pass the 200-wicket mark for England. On a worn wicket in Australia's second innings in Sydney, Snow was virtually unplayable. His leg-cutter bit and spat with such venom off the scuffed patches of the bowlers' follow-through that the batsmen could not play forward to a full length ball without physical risk. Australian bowlers McKenzie and Jenner were both struck on the head by Snow deliveries which pitched just short of a good length and rose like Apollo rockets off the launching pad. Snow's final analysis of 7/40 in that innings bordered on the unattainable, when set against the handicap of an Australian wicket.

One facet of John Snow's character lifted him out of the ruck of

214

professional cricketers. The shock-headed Sussex fast bowler was an individualist and an artist. Cricketers before him had displayed their creative talents off the cricket field. Felix, the cricketing-schoolmaster of the nineteenth century was, like Colin Blythe, England's slow left-hand bowler of the early 1900s, an accomplished violinist. Australia's beloved and whimsical leg-spinner of the post-Great-War period, Arthur Mailey, expressed his innermost thoughts in caricatures or on canvas. Snow inclined more to the aspirations of a littérateur and poet. He lacked the mellifluence of Cardus, the humour of Robertson-Glasgow and the rhythmic accent of Francis Thompson. But he possessed a certain degree of Matthew Arnold's inner seriousness and an acerbity of opinion and expression which caused him to describe the Test press-box as the refuge of those critics who 'sharpen their carbon claws'.

The 1970-1 England tour of Australia represented the apogee of Geoff Boycott's illustrious career as England's opening bat. This was the epoch in his development when caution had not stifled his sense of adventure and his desire to express his natural batting talents. Boycott was a powerhouse on the back-foot drive and his pulling was fearless.

Geoff Boycott, a psychological puzzle

He had not yet entered his analytical, percentage and defensive phase and his Test average for the series was a remarkably prolific 93.8. The balding Yorkshireman's tour aggregate was 1,535 runs—only 18 short of Hammond's record established in 1928-9 for the number of runs scored on tour. That mark must surely have been surpassed, had Boycott not suffered a broken hand whilst batting against McKenzie on a green Sydney wicket in a one-day game against Western Australia. The England opener subsequently missed the final Sydney Test.

If anyone had suggested to me that three years after Boycott's Australian triumph he would withdraw from Test cricket and not be seen on the international scene for a further four home seasons, I would have feared that, as Dryden suggested, his 'great wit was to madness near allied'. In 1971 Boycott seemed to be on the threshold of Test maturity. In the West Indies in 1974 he was still the dominant figure in the England side; his two innings of 99 and 112 in the final Port-of-Spain Test were the only two knocks of over 45 in his team's efforts, and they enabled Denness's side to win the game by 26 runs with an hour to spare and thus square the series. The next English summer saw him dismissed by the slow-medium inswingers of Indian left-hand bowler, Solkar, four times in six successive innings. Press reports thereupon stated that Boycott had retired to his ivory tower of theoretical analysis to consider the inadequacies of his technique. Steadfastly, the Yorkshireman refused to make himself available for Tests or tours, giving credence to the rumours that he would not serve under the captaincy of Mike Denness or Tony Greig, and that he wanted the leadership of the Test side for himself. His Yorkshire team-mates stuck by their county skipper, giving as his reason for refusing international honours his concentration on seeing the young Yorkshire side restored once more to the top of the first-class table.

Boycott was undoubtedly a psychological puzzle for England's chairman of selectors, Alec Bedser. Significantly, when Boycott declared himself once more willing to appear for his country in 1977, the mass Packer defection of players stood revealed in the glory of its commercialism. Tony Greig and Mike Denness, two of Boycott's former rivals for the England captaincy were amongst the leaders of the exodus from the ranks of Establishment cricket. Boycott, although offered terms by the Australian television magnate, refused them, because such a contract would have infringed his commitments to his native Yorkshire. Whatever the supposed shortcomings of Boycott's earlier judgment, there is no doubting the value which he places on such an intangible commodity as loyalty.

Alan Knott was to join the ranks of the World Series defectors in 1977. In 1970-1, however, he was still one of the linchpins of England's victory over Australia. In six Tests the diminutive wicketkeeper accepted twenty-four chances behind the stumps. No stumper has done better in Anglo-Australian games. It is doubtful that there has been a better keeper than Knott. Evans returned a far higher percentage of stumpings in his Test tally of 219 victims. It would be difficult to find a keeper who worked more competently close to the stumps against all types and speeds of bowling than 'Godders'. Marsh, the Australian keeper and Knott's contemporary, possesses tremendous mobility and his compatriot Wally Grout had a pair of adhesive hands and lightning stumping reflexes. Knott appears to possess all of these qualities. His failure rate behind the stumps is so low that the watcher of Knott's

Alan Knott, 'just the batsman for a crisis'

216

every game has to tax his memory to remember when the Kent stumper last missed a chance. He is a colourful character who brightens up the Test day with callisthenics between each delivery. Many people believe that his stretching exercises are designed to prepare Knott for the sudden athletic demands of his skill. In fact their aim is to retain the suppleness of muscles atrophied by a youthful affliction.

Knott is not only a master of the keeeper's art, he is a skilful and determined batsman with four Test centuries to his credit. That figure would have been augmented by one had not a riot caused the abandonment of the Karachi Test and the airborne evacuation of the England players at a time when Knott was in the 90s. His batting is characterized by immense courage. Crisis is the Kent wicketkeeper's second name. His two hundreds against Australia were both compiled when his side's batting was in dire straits. At Nottingham in 1977, he came to the wicket when his team were 5/82 in pursuit of Australia's total of 243. Knott and Boycott thereupon added 215 for the sixth wicket thereby equalling the record association for that wicket between Hutton and Hardstaff at The Oval in 1938. Knott's batting strength lies on the cut; but it is his determination to position himself behind the line of every ball and play it as though his life and his side's hopes of victory depended on it which makes him such a doughty competitor.

The year 1971 marked the nadir of Australia's standing in the cricket world in recent times. When the last ball of the Seventh Test was bowled in Melbourne, the home side had not won a game against England in eleven encounters. It was true that Lawry's combination defeated Pataudi's Eastern and Sober's West Indians by 3-0 margins in the Australian summers of 1968-9 and 1969-70; but their victory on the sub-continent en route to South Africa in the latter year was followed by a merciless 4-0 drubbing at the hands of Ali Bacher's Springboks. Australia's plight demanded a drastic remedy, and after Lawry's defensive retreat from the inconclusive Adelaide Test, the Night of the Long Selectors' Knives witnessed the savage excision of the scapegoat captain from the Australian XI. Lawry was still by far the best opening batsman in Australia. He proved this fact beyond a shadow of doubt by carrying his bat in Australia's second innings in Sydney, only two games previously; but the selectors were thoroughly exasperated by their skipper's alleged lack of initiative and they indulged in a bout of brutal self-denial. Lawry had to go as captain, and Messrs Loxton, Ridings and Harvey cut off their noses to spite their faces by denying their former blue-eyed leader his well-earned right to open the Australian innings.

The immediate result of the choice of Ian Chappell as the skipper to sweep clean the Australian Augean Stables was that the home side lost the last Test in Sydney by 62 runs. One year later Chappell was to prove during the tour of England that, under his tutelage, the young Australians had regained their shattered confidence and reformed themselves into a spirited cricketing combination. The question is whether the resurgence would have occurred without Chappell at the helm. A captain is only as good as the raw cricketing material at his disposal. Lawry was unfortunate that Dennis Lillee, the match-winner of the near future, played in his maiden Test in Adelaide, as Lawry was, unwittingly, making his final bow. Australia's future batting star, Greg Chappell, played in only four games with the 'Phantom' before Lawry was forced into retirement; Greg in fact made his début in Perth's First Test—the game which saw Lawry pass the 5,000-run milestone in international cricket and score his 2,000th run against England. There is no doubt that Ian Chappell possessed the golden Midas touch of captaincy, but to a lesser degree than Benaud. Chappell was endowed with the ability to remain one of the boys, yet retain the hauteur of a skipper who has to stay aloof in order to make impartial decisions. Of course he commanded his men's respect as a good player; but no one could have been more revered in this respect than Chappell's predecessor.

It is hard to determine why Lawry was not a more successful captain. During his regency, Australia was blessed with great talent which should have yielded her more and greater victories. Perhaps Lawry failed to live up to winning expectations because he, unlike Danton, did not have a motto which advocated 'de l'audace'. During the 1970-1 series, he was criticized for not permitting Rod Marsh to expand his 92 not out in the Fifth Test into the first century ever scored by an Australian keeper against England. His detractors on that occasion forgot that it was Marsh's tardiness and the welfare of the team which demanded the closure at a time which, unfortunately, was inopportune for the individual but necessary for the team. A less serious approach to the game on the field would probably have enabled Lawry to be more imaginative in his captaincy.

Keith Stackpole's favourite hook shot

To Bill, however, cricket was seldom anything but serious. An umpire who officiated in one Victoria-N.S.W. game recounted how after 'Phanto' carried his bat through his side's innings, he was finally caught at slip off a thick edge from the bowling of the left-handed wrist-spinner, Johnny Martin. No one in the N.S.W. team appealed. They simply accepted the blatantly obvious, and walked off the field leaving only the two batsmen and two umpires in the centre of the Melbourne Cricket Ground, marooned as the Australian vernacular expresses it so well, 'like shags on a rock'. Bill was unmoved and uninfluenced by the actions of the opposition and as the last New South Welshman strode into the pavilion, his head was bent and he was intent on taking block once more. 'Bill', said the umpire sympathetically, 'I know there was no appeal, but I think that we had better buzz off; we're starting to look a bit conspicuous'.

Lawry led Australia for the first time in a home game against England in Brisbane, where two first innings totals in excess of 400 condemned the match to a draw. It was not a game without its moments of tension. The main contributory factor towards Australia's first innings score of 443 was a double century from their latest experiment in the realms of opening batsmen, Keith Stackpole. When he was eighteen, Stackpole was given the benefit of the doubt in a very close run-out decision. The English players were transparently flabbergasted by the umpire's decision. Their on-the-field expression of anger produced an equally fiery response from Stackpole and the series was

218

off to an exchange of hostile shots between the two opponents. Significantly, in the light of Lawry's banishment five Tests later, the Australian captain contributed a valiant 84 to the home side's low, but face-saving, second innings of 214.

The Second Test in Perth marked the first appearance of that fair city on the international cricket circuit. The support of business houses, and an incredible amount of fund-raising labour in the Western Australian cricket hinterland, enabled the local cricket associaton to construct a stand to commemorate and facilitate the staging of the western state's first Test. Two large first innings scores in the region of 400 once again left the issue of the game undecided; at one stage in their first innings, however, it appeared that Australia, after having lost 5/107, were in a modicum of trouble. Then it was that the slim and elegant younger of the two Chappell brothers, Greg, came to the wicket for the first time in Tests. His eventual 108 and Redpath's masterly 171 not only revived the ailing batting patient, but enabled him to stage a complete recovery and establish an unexpected supremacy of 43 runs on the first innings.

Perth's débutant Test was one of the first featured on a nation-wide telecast by the Australian Broadcasting Commission. It was an immense technological achievement, since the television links not only spanned a nation and continent of almost three million square miles, but also brought international cricket to state capitals separated by distance and time factors as disparate as three hours. As Greg Chappell neared his maiden century in Perth, the pavilion clock ticked slowly towards 4.30 p.m. In Chappell's native Adelaide, the noiseless clock in the television studios edged towards 7 p.m.—the time for the weather forecast. The announcer therefore interrupted the cricket telecast to let the people of Adelaide know that tomorrow's weather would 'continue fine'. By the time the programme returned to the Western Australian Cricket Association Ground in Perth, the great moment was past. Chappell was beyond the hundred, and his South Australian supporters were denied their instant of reflected glory.

The projected Third Test in Melbourne achieved a degree of pluvial infamy which had previously been reserved exclusively for my native city of Manchester. Because of three days' unremitting rain not a ball was bowled in Melbourne in the New Year's game of 1971. The Lancashire city on the regularly swollen Irwell witnessed similar soggy catastrophes in 1890 and 1938. The Melbourne game of 1971 raised a peculiar problem for cricket's statisticians. The thorny question was: had the game been started or not? The two captains, Lawry and Illingworth completed the formalities of the toss during a unique interval between cloudbursts. For a while there was even jocular surmise amongst the radio commentators about the game starting with coir matting being placed over the miniature bogs which surrounded the pitch. A blanket of torrential rain descended once more, however, and scotched further optimistic thoughts about the future of the match. The question was whether the game should be included in the records as one which got under way. The cricketers' bible, Wisden, did not condescend to give the game official recognition but consigned it to the same watery oblivion as the two previous complete wash-outs. There appears to be dissension in certain quarters with that opinion; the plaque which is set in the wall of the members' pavilion of the Melbourne Cricket Club commemorates the Centenary Test as the 226th encounter between England and Australia. According to Wisden's records, it was the 225th. However, if games which were scheduled and were then completely ruined by rain do count in the facts and figures of the game, the Melbourne plaque should record the Centenary Test as the 228th encounter between the two countries.

England won the fourth encounter convincingly by 299 runs. Monotonously the England openers began with a century partnership—a feat which they were to repeat five times in the rubber, in spite of injury causing Edrich to replace Luckhurst when the latter broke his hand in Melbourne and Boycott being unable to play in the Final Test. The Sydney batting honours belonged to the Yorkshire opener who completed a commanding double of 77 and 142 not out. When Australia batted a second time, their necessary survival time was nine hours. They were no match for the pace and cut of Snow on a crumbling wicket, and their tenure at the crease lasted for only half of the requisite time. The only redeeming feature of the home side's disappointing second innings of 116 was Lawry's undefeated knock of 60—a feat which brought him membership of that élite Anglo-Australian club of seven batsmen who had previously shown the same tenacity of purpose and carried their bats through an innings.

The second appearance of the two sides in Melbourne saw, in my opinion, the beginning of 'the football crowd contagion' amongst the ranks of Australian cricket spectators. Lawry's ultra-cautious approach to his side's second innings batting task when they were already 101 runs ahead and England's eight sins of catching omission—five of them surprisingly by Cowdrey at slip—saw the match grind inexorably towards a draw. Even the crowd's frustration at the refusal of Edrich and Boycott to attempt 271 runs in four hours could not excuse the anarchy in the Melbourne outer. The whole of England's second knock was played to the cacophonous accompaniment of empty beer cans clanked one against the other or against the concrete and railings of the terraces. It was a blatant attempt to distract the batsmen. The previous conduct of the crowd had little to commend it. When Ian Chappell completed the first century of his five-year career against the old foe, the 'madding crowd' swarmed onto the playing arena and, after the police had restored order, it was discovered that souvenir hunters had removed Chappell's cap, Cowdrey's white washing hat and a stump. The observer did not need a crystal ball to foresee that the era of the naked streaker lurked around the corner of every grandstand in England and Australia.

The next step in the deterioration of behaviour on the cricket ground materialized during Adelaide's Sixth Test. It was in South Australia that evidence was produced that the players themselves were catching the 'rudeness disease'. England's opener, Boycott, run out in a photo finish in his side's first innings total of 470, took issue with the umpire's decision and flung his bat to the ground in an expression of his chagrin.

His exhibitionism produced a chain reaction both on the field and amongst the watchers. Several of the Australian players motioned Boycott to the pavilion and it was quite obvious that angry words were exchanged—expressions of dissent for which Boycott later refused to apologize. The Yorkshireman had the final telling word in the argument: after Illingworth neglected to enforce the follow-on in spite of a first innings lead of 235, the batsman from Fitzwilliam notched an impeccable 119 not out and was instrumental in setting Lawry's side the unlikely task of scoring 469 for victory in almost eight and a half hours. The England captain's motives in not asking Australia to bat twice in succession were ostensibly based on the justification that his key bowlers were tired and needed fresh vigour to dismiss Australia a second time on a flawless wicket. The critics who disparaged Illingworth's conservatism quickly changed their tune as the Pudsey man was proven to be—oh so right! Australia coasted to a second innings tally of 3/328 and saved the match with consummate ease thanks to hundreds from Ian Chappell and Stackpole.

The Second Battle of Sydney, which sometimes masquerades under the title of the Seventh Test was memorable. England won this contest in acrimony by 62 runs; but it was the incidents off the field of play and the effect which they exercised on the men in the middle which monopolized the attention of the cricketing world. Sydney turned on a display of crowd hooliganism unparalleled since the turbulent times of bodyline. The famous Sydney Hill was no longer a picturesque tradition in Australian cricket, but an anachronistic crowd hazard. It was a jumble of unruly and, at times, uncontrollable individuals sitting on enormous 'Eskie' beer coolers and hurling abuse and beer cans at the policemen who tried to keep their exuberance within the acceptable bounds of civilized conduct. The behaviour of the Sydney Hill in 1971 was not far removed from the riotous conduct which is normally associated with the politically disgruntled denizens of Calcutta's Eden Gardens. Perhaps the violence which is often seen on the cricket grounds of India, Pakistan or the West Indies is likely in Sydney. But prevention is better than cure—and accessibility to every corner of the spectator areas is a prerequisite for crowd control. It is for this reason that I suggest that some re-arrangement of the spectator accommodation on the Sydney Hill is an urgent necessity.

Not all the censure for the distasteful events of this notorious Sydney Test lay exclusively at the door of the spectators. Lack of judgment on the part of the players, captains and umpires contributed to the combustibility of the fiery situation. The umpires unwisely and prematurely warned England fast bowler John Snow for intimidatory bowling after he had sent down one short-pitched delivery. It struck Australia's slow bowler, Terry Jenner, because he ducked into it and the ball did not rise as high as expected. Naturally, Snow's skipper, Illingworth, protested at this hasty condemnation of his quick bowler. This was the overt display of disagreement which produced an outburst of dissent from the crowd and a hail of projectiles which ranged from beer cans to blocks of ice directed at the England players in the outfield. The Sussex speedster was naturally a prime target for the crowd's violent spleen. It

Umpire Rowan warns fast bowler Snow for short-pitched bowling. This incident was to eventuate in England's walk-off in Sydney 1970-1

was equally logical that Snow should retreat from the pickets and point out to his captain the physical danger of his situation at deep fine-leg. The question then remains unanswered as to why Illingworth toyed with the idea of replacing his fast bowling boundary rider with Willis but then revoked his earlier decision to expose Snow once more to the wrath of the crowd. It was at this unfortunate stage that a drunken spectator on the Paddington Hill beckoned Snow to the fence, as if he wanted to point out to him in reasonable fashion the foolish error of his ways. When the England player approached the drunk he was rewarded by a fumbling grab at his shirt and an attempt to punch him on the nose. Once again England withdrew to a better tactical disposition in the centre of the Sydney ground, where they dug in and sat down in protest at the uproar in the outer and the showers of missiles which now littered the outfield with a gleaming hail-cover of cans of varying degrees of emptiness and weight. Illingworth's next move was to slowly parade his team off the field to the accompaniment of a growing, throbbing roar from the now ferocious crowd. It was easy to understand Illingworth's point of view, since it was hazardous to field close to the fence with the spectators in such a belligerent mood and the grass littered with thousands of stumbling blocks. But it was incomprehensible that the England skipper did not discuss the situation with the umpires and gain their consent before making his move. His arbitrary decision to evacuate the scene of conflict only led to further acrimony.

Since the umpires had not been given the opportunity to talk the matter over with the England skipper, they could only presume that for reasons best known to themselves, the England team members were refusing to play. Once the outfield had been cleared of all obstacles, it was therefore the unpleasant duty of the umpires, Col Egar and Lou Rowan, to go to the English dressing-room and warn Illingworth that he was running the risk of forfeiting the match. The result was further ill-feeling.

The course of the Test followed an unorthodox path — without the further complications of the crowd's intervention. In his first game as Australian captain, Chappell won the toss and asked Illingworth to bat. It was an unusual tactic which was to become a successful norm for 'Chappelli' during his 30-match tenure of office. In this instance his decision was the correct one since the Sydney wicket was undoubtedly green on the first morning. The strange feature of England's first innings was that Australia's pacemen proved ineffectual and it was left to the leg-spinners, Jenner and O'Keeffe, to tumble the tourists out for a meagre 184. The home side led on the first innings by 80, but England recovered through the agency of stalwart innings from Edrich, Luck-hurst and D'Oliveira to set Chappell's batsmen the awkward job of scoring 223 for victory on a pitch which was now thoroughly untrust-worthy.

Snow bowled the left-handed Eastwood immediately, thus ending the opener's one-Test career; but then disaster struck at the heart of England's victory aspirations. The Sussex fast bowler broke his bowling hand on the pickets at deep fine-leg attempting a catch off a lofted Stackpole hook. It was at this juncture that Illingworth revealed his fighting mettle as a player. Stepping into the vacuum created by Snow's compulsory retirement to the pavilion, the England captain dropped his off-spinners on the proverbial sixpence to exploit to the maximum a wicket which was now assisting the spinner. The home batsmen were reduced to fumbling ineptitude and, though Stackpole struggled to 67 after being given the benefit of a disputed caught behind decision off Lever when he was 13, the issue was never in doubt. Greg Chappell tried to bluff his way out of trouble, but when he was stumped off Illingworth's arm ball whilst advancing down the wicket, the end came quickly and Australia's final muster of runs stopped abruptly at 160.

England's 2-0 series triumph over Australia represented the zenith of Illingworth's term of captaincy. Two years later he stepped down from office after having shared a home rubber with Ian Chappell's side and lost to India and the West Indies. His later disappointments, however, were insignificant by comparison with that sweet moment in Sydney in 1971 when he became the second Yorkshire-born professional captain of England to defeat Australia on their own wickets. He and Hutton were to remain the only post-war England skippers to achieve this feat until the coming of Brearley in the troubled times of 1978-9.

16. The Chappell Renaissance

The two colourful characters in the Australian batting spectrum in 1970-1 were the brothers Chappell. Their background in South Australian sport was the envy of their generation. Their maternal grandfather, Vic Richardson, was a football and cricketing legend in Adelaide. A State champion in the winter Rules game, the lovable Victor was also one of the heroes who met the challenge of Larwood and Voce in 1932, and emerged with an enhanced reputation to lead Australia on their 1935-6 tour of South Africa. In later years 'Victor York' comprised one half of that inimitable duet of Australian Broadcasting Commission commentators, Vic and Arthur Gilligan. The exchange: 'What did you think of that Vic?'—'That was a very good shot Arthur'—will be remembered as long as listeners recall Test match broadcasts. Martin Chappell—Chappell senior—was a South Australian administrator of great repute and financial acumen. The Chappell name will live long in Australian cricket records; but so will the name of Richardson, for the eastern entrance gates at the Adelaide Oval are ornamented with the name of Victor York Richardson.

The brothers Ian and Greg are an interesting contrast in style, yet have an equally intriguing common batting factor. Their greatest mutual attribute is total application. When Ian goes out to bat, he peers heavenwards, blinking deliberately to attune his eyes to the harmony of the light—hence his nickname 'Birdie'. For his part Greg stares stolidly ahead, looking in an eyes front position with his bat tucked under his arm like a swagger stick, as he pulls on his batting gloves with an air of nonchalance which has no semblance of affectation. In attitude Ian is the perky cock-sparrow while Greg is the equally confident sergeant-major of the batting discipline.

Their differing interpretation of the skill of batting demolishes the theory of hereditary gifts. Greg is the more natural player. His skill all round the wicket is complete, though one has to admit that his preference is for the wide on-drive, be it in the air or along the ground. His reduction of the element of chance is confined to the early restriction of his straight-batted strokes to a limited arc between mid-on and extra-cover. Once the puberty stage of an innings is past, the younger

Chappell is an unfettered and unfetterable batsman. His only Achilles' heel appears to be against the ball which rises unexpectedly outside the off-stump and moves towards the slips . . . but then every batsman has a vulnerability against such a delivery.

Greg's natural talents found an early interpretation into statistical success in Test cricket. Ian required many a summer to come to batting maturity. The inference of this remark does not relegate Ian Chappell's later status to an inferior plane in relation to his brother. Indeed, many of the Australian players who took the field with both of the Chappell brothers would prefer to have Ian on their side rather than Greg. Their bias probably stems from an opinion that the elder Chappell is an extroverted and articulate captain who expresses his personality in the way in

Australian captain Greg Chappell hooks England fast bowler Bob Willis for four. 1977 series which he plays. Ian Chappell is pugnacity personified. Against the fastest of bowlers his first movement is across the wicket. The manoeuvre defies the speed of the bowler, though in theory it exposes the striker to the vulnerability of giving a catch on the on-side because the fulcrum of the stroke is moving continually away from the line of the ball towards the off-side. The observer has to respect Ian Chappell on and off the field because, no matter how strongly one might disagree with the principle behind his actions, one has to admire the spirit which moves him. This, I suppose, is the apologia which most sincere people offer as an excuse for their aberrations; only posterity will be able to judge whether initially accepted mistakes are, in fact, truths. Sometimes, however, soothsayers do try their utmost to make truisms most unpalatable.

After his inauspicious début as Australian captain in Sydney against Illingworth's England team, Ian Chappell's apprenticeship at the helm received a further setback when his side lost to Sober's World XI, 2-1, in the Australian summer of 1971-2. His leadership was gaining support amongst his fellow players, however, and he took the Australians to England in 1972.

The memories of the 1972 tour of England by Ian Chappell's side are emotive recollections for the Australian xenophobe. That year's series saw Australia turn the corner and head pell-mell down the victory path after a barren period of twelve Tests in the trackless wilderness against England, and three successive defeats in rubbers against South Africa, England and a World XI. By sharing the honours of the summer, Chappell's young side demonstrated that the international standing of any team in any sport hinges on a strong and resilient reserve of ability. Such a side cannot be a regressive red giant of the sporting universe.

Chappell's touring party represented a bold experiment in selection. Only seven of the seventeen 1968 tourists gained re-selection. The experience of Lawry, McKenzie and Redpath was jettisoned. The omission of opening batsman Redpath constituted a major blunder. It was based on the statistical justification of the Victorian's Australian form which varied between the disappointing and mediocre. The statistical blight in the withered imaginations of the selectors lost sight of the fact that Redpath was probably the best technician amongst the ranks of their batsmen on turning English surfaces. The unique feature of the 1972 team was that for the first time in their country's long Test history there was no New South Welshman in the side.

The series proved to be a voyage of discovery through the seas of young Australian talent, comparable to Colombus's venture into the New World. A genuine fast bowler of major stature was unearthed in the person of Dennis Lillee. The West Australian blossomed in the previous southern winter when he captured 24 wickets in a five-match contest against Sober's World XI. Six months later Lillee took another step towards greatness by taking 31 wickets in a rubber in England, thus surpassing the previous Australian best of Grimmett and McKenzie who each captured 29 wickets in the rubbers of 1930 and 1964. On the slow English wickets, Lillee's performance was admirable. His speed

Dennis Lillee.
Australia's fast bowler
of the 1970s

was such that even the normally stoic Boycott showed some appre hension about the prospect of opening the England innings against him Lillee, at this stage of his career, was probably the swiftest bowling phenomenon seen by English batsmen since the salad days of Lindwall and Miller; but there were more shots in the quick bowler's armour than his frightening pace. He possessed a bustling, business-like acceleration to the bowling crease which sometimes surpassed the advisable speed of a run-up, but which always presented him in an admirably closed position in his delivery stride. As a result Lillee was the possessor of a deadly outswinger, which was nearly the equal of any of Fred Trueman's deliveries and almost aspired to the controlled perfection of Ray Lindwall.

Ebullient and fiery in his attitude towards batsmen, Lillee still retained enough native cunning to harness his natural talents to a shrewd perception of the opposition's weaknesses. His Test career was curtailed by a stressed-fractured injury to one of his vertebrae whilst touring the West Indies in 1973. Such was his dedication to his fast bowling shiralee, however, that, after a fallow medium-paced season as an all-rounder in Perth district cricket and a university-supervised fitness programme which would have daunted Muhammad Ali, he returned to spearhead the victorious Australian attack with Jeff Thomson against Mike Denness's English tourists of 1974-5 and capture 25 wickets.

Lillee loved fast bowling—not too wisely but too well. His breakdown in the West Indies was occasioned by the fact that, whilst afflicted by a nagging back injury, he sent down 23 consecutive overs to help medium-pacer Max Walker win the Sydney Test and the series against Pakistan in 1972-3. There has never been a pace-bowler with more of a vocation for his job. He bowled even when he was injured and he seemed impervious to pain. At times he worked himself up into such a frenzy of exasperation and frustration on deadly slow wickets that he did not draw the line at loosing two or three successive bouncers at tail-end batsmen. Yet he did not scorn the subtleties of variation and frequently flustered the batsman by bowling equally as fast off a five-pace approach as he did off his normal twenty-five yard run-up. I still believe that Lillee's burst of 7.1 overs against the World XI on a Perth greentop in 1971, and his resultant figures of 8/29, was one of the most ferocious spells of pace bowling I have ever witnessed.

Lillee's companion in fast-bowling arms in England in 1972 was the ephemeral medium-pacer and fellow Western Australian, 'Gus' Massie. For a while this bowler of phenomenal swing flourished like the flowers of the field, but then the wind of adverse fortune blew on him and he was gone. He simply lost all of the tremendous moving qualities through the air which made him unique in his cricketing craft. No bowler in the history of Tests made so rewarding a début. Massie virtually won his first game against England with the sole aid of his own strong bowling arm. He captured 16/137: a remarkable feat which places him at the head of the table of Australian bowlers who have taken most wickets in a single match. The scene was Lords at the time of the Second Test. The day was overcast and the cloud cover admirably low for Massie's purpose. The degree of movement which the medium-pacer gained through the dank air of those early June days was reminiscent of the skills of his predecessor, the 1867 aborigine tourist, Charlie Dumas, with the boomerang! Some idea of the part which luck plays in producing extraordinary performances can be gained from the fact that the conveniently humid conditions did not change throughout the course of the game. So uncontrollable was Massie's swing that he was compelled to bowl inswingers to the right-hand batsmen from around the wicket in order to pitch the ball in line with the stumps! As quickly as it appeared on the Test horizon, Massie's comet of fame passed into limbo. After four games against England and two more consolation matches against Pakistan, he left the Test field forever. It was as if the conditions at Lords led him to believe that the ball would behave in a similar curvaceous fashion every time he opened the bowling. Back in Australia Massie aimed his out-swinger wide of the leg-stump—which was precisely the line on which it concluded its journey at the other end of the pitch. His inswinger directed extravagantly wide of the off-stump, produced more wides than one normally expects from a Test bowler. Twelve months later one looked back on the 1972 rubber and failed to understand how a key player who helped Lillee to capture 54 of the 83 English wickets to fall to bowlers in five games had so quickly become a shadowy figure in Test history. The truth was that Massie lost a God-given bowling attribute and was never able to re-learn an untaught skill.

The infamous 'fuserium fungus' plague appeared in 1972. This was the grass disease which ravaged the Headingley wicket, transforming it into a happy-hunting ground for England's medium-paced, left-handed spinner, Derek Underwood, and bringing the Leeds Test to an abrupt and premature halt at five o'clock on the third of the five scheduled days. Australia's keeper, Rod Marsh, enjoyed a bonanza series, capturing a record touring bag of 23 victims behind the stumps in Tests. He will, however, long remember those three nightmare days in Leeds where, standing up to the finger-spinners Mallet and Inverarity, he conceded 19 byes on a wicket of surprises. By contrast the England stumper, Alan Knott, thoroughly inured to the vagaries of English pitches, allowed only five sundries in two Australian knocks.

Australians, often the victims of wickets which suit the home bowlers on the first day of a Test in England, cast a jaundiced eye on the Headingley pitch. They doubtless thought back to the Old Trafford dust bowl of 1956 and the havoc wrought by Jim Laker's off-spinners. They entertained bitter memories of this same Leeds pitch in 1961 when a chemically over-prepared surface yielded an unexpected 11-wicket harvest for Freddie Trueman's cutters. Justifiably they bemoaned their 9-wicket defeat in 1972 with cries of: 'Not again'. The truth was that Chappell's team were unlucky, rather than the victims of premeditated gamesmanship. The Leeds pitch was flooded by a torrential downpour during the weekend before the Test—a cloudburst which brought with it the watery consequences of the fungus. These facts were brought to light by the inquest by England's ombudsman-curator on the thoroughly deadly wicket after the game.

As a result of suspect wickets and the effective fast bowling of the tourists, good batting was at a premium throughout this series of swaying fortunes. Not a single hundred was scored by an English batsman in the rubber. Bruce Francis proved inadequate as a replacement for Lawry as Stackpole's opening partner. Ross Edwards, the Western Australian middle-order batsman, acted as a successful proxy number two in the Third Test at Trent Bridge. He scored an accomplished 170 in Australia's second innings. Then, as if to prove that one swallow does not make a summer, nor one innings an opening bat, Edwards bagged a pair in the next game at Leeds.

Illingworth won the toss at Old Trafford on his fortieth birthday. His present was a home victory by 89 runs. Wicketkeeper Marsh enjoyed a wonderful match, collecting an equal record five catches in England's first innings. His batting bonus was a rumbustious 91 in his side's final fling, which added 104 with tail-ender Gleeson for the ninth wicket and enabled his team-mates to glimpse, if only fleetingly, the possibility of an impossible victory. Marsh's hitting with the tide against the left-handed slows of Gifford was a joy to warm the cockles of every spectator's heart—except those seated just inside the boundary at mid-wicket where the pugnacious left-hander landed four enormous sixes.

Bob Massie

Stackpole produced a good double in Manchester, scoring 53 and 67; it must be admitted, however, that the burly Victorian opener enjoyed more than his fair share of good luck in the first innings, since he was dropped three times. Indeed, as the series progressed, Stackpole became the exasperation of the England bowlers. He seemed to lead a charmed life, daring to loft the ball where fielding angels always feared to tread. He scored 114 at Trent Bridge but was missed twice en route to his century. Another 50 at Leeds was made possible only because 'Stacky' was dropped off fast bowler Arnold. England's win at Old Trafford brought her triumph in an initial home Test against Australia after an interval of forty-two years.

Lords was the setting for Bob Massie's remarkable début. His 16-wicket analysis brought Chappell's men a win by a comprehensive 8 wickets and was by far the best maiden Test performance with the ball. The nearest approach to Massie's achievement was that by England's left-handed Martin who captured 12/102 against Billy Murdoch's Australians at The Oval in 1890. There was a strange parallel between the careers of Massie and Martin. Both enjoyed only a brief stay in the Test limelight. Indeed the 1890 game was the only one in which Martin played. Massie survived his Lords apotheosis by a mere five more games.

Batting more worthy of a tortoise race than a cricket match led to the Nottingham Test being drawn. England lingered six and a half hours over their moderate first innings total of 189. Australia, too, were cautious, not declaring their second innings closed until they were a secure 450 runs in the lead with nine and a half hours batting time remaining.

And so the scene moves to Leeds—and the drama of the blighted wicket. The irony of the game was that England were almost hoist on their own petard. Illingworth was quick to realize the character of the pitch and the Headingley spectators were treated to the unusual first morning spectacle of the two England spinners, Illingworth and Underwood, operating in joint harness. It was not surprising that Australia were shot out for 146. There was a humorous quirk of fate on the second morning, however, when the home side themselves slumped at one stage to the inadequacy of 6/108 against the less than venomous finger spin of the left-handed Inverarity and Mallett. The Australian bowlers' lack of experience on slow, turning wickets permitted England to escape the consequences of their inconsequential batting; a partnership of 104 between those bowlers of varying pace, Snow and Illingworth, hoisted the home side's first innings tally to 263. It was a winning score. After the Australian batsmen had again shown themselves unequal to the challenging vagaries of the Headingley pitch to be dismissed for 136 by Underwood, who captured 10/82 in the game, England knocked off the 21 runs needed for victory for the loss of 1 wicket.

Australia provided a thrilling climax to the summer by winning the final clash at The Oval by 5 wickets and thus sharing the honours in an entertaining rubber in which only one game failed to produce a result. For their supporters who lay at home abed, the victory of Chappell's men was a joy to be savoured personally, by means of a direct satellite telecast of the last days of this grand climacteric of the tour. Lillee's 10 wickets made him the man of the moment; but Australia owed a great debt of gratitude to the two Chappells, who in their team's first knock became the only pair of batting brothers to reach three figures in the same innings of a Test. Their cause was bolstered by the absence of Snow, D'Oliveira and Illingworth from the England attack when the tourists batted a second time needing 242 to win. Snow was injured by a Lillee delivery which struck him a painful blow on the arm whilst he was batting, and Illingworth sprained his ankle in a bowling pot-hole. In spite of the blunting of their attack, England fought the good fight. When Sheahan and Marsh came together with 5 wickets down, there was still tension in the atmosphere, with 71 elusive runs required for victory. The batsmen did not falter in their purpose, however, and, with Sheahan playing with complete rectitude and Marsh hitting daringly to leg, they saw their side home amidst scenes of sprinting, batwaving jubilation.

A disconsolate Illingworth appeared on crutches on The Oval balcony to congratulate his opponents. This Oval Test was to be his last appearance after a record of successful captaincy against Australia. He was dismissed from office after the following season's disaster against Kanhai's West Indian side. He had the great satisfaction, however, of knowing that the Ashes still reposed in their usual niche in the Imperial Cricket Memorial Gallery at Lords.

The forecasting of the outcome of the 1974-5 England-Australia series was as difficult as the solution of an algebraic quadratic equation. Circumstantial evidence pointed to a home victory. Chappell's new breed of fierce competitors annihilated Intikhab Alam's Pakistan tourists of 1972-3, 3-0 and accounted for New Zealand 3-1 in a split series played on a home and away basis; within weeks of the end of that rubber, they were in the Caribbean where they won the only two Tests to reach a decision. By contrast, England's statistical record during the same period was singularly unimpressive. Defeated 2-0 in England by the West Indies in 1973, they barely drew the return bout with a scratchy victory in the last hour of the Trinidad Test in the following winter. The England selectors, disillusioned with their former blue-eyed skipper, Illingworth, changed leaders between the West Indian rubbers, and Kent's Mike Denness, albeit insecurely, was in the captaincy saddle. Apparently disgruntled by the way the leadership stakes were being run, their star batsman, Geoff Boycott retired from the international race.

A betting man, however, had enough reservations about the apparently straightforward form-guide to cause him to hesitate about putting his shirt on Australia in the approaching rubber. Chappell's men were not completely convincing against Pakistan. Twice in three Tests, Intikhab's side were in winning positions, yet squandered golden opportunities to gain their first triumph on Australian soil. In the West Indies, Australia's wins were pyrrhic victories. Injury and loss of form robbed them of their potential match-winners of future seasons. A fractured vertebra relegated fast bowler, Lillee, to the international sidelines for a year; even the doctors could not assure him of an early return to full fitness. Bob Massie toured the West Indies, but could not reproduce the figures which made him the five-day wonder of the cricketing world only a year earlier. Even 'Bomber' Hammond, the South Australian medium-fast bowler who substituted so ably for the incapacitated Lillee in the Caribbean, was struck down by a mystery back ailment and was unable to take his hard-earned place in the First Test in Brisbane against Denness's side.

The man on whom the Australian selectors pinned a seemingly unwarranted amount of their 1974-5 bowling hopes was a comparatively unknown 'quickie' called Jeff Thomson. There was little in Thomson's background to reassure the cricketing *cognoscenti* that he was the right man to fill the gaping void in the home atack. After only five first-class games for his native New South Wales, Thomson was chosen for the 1973 New Year's Test against Pakistan in Melbourne. He emerged from the game wicketless, having conceded 110 runs. Within the space of a few weeks Thomson had not only dropped out of the national side, but also out of his state team. In vain he pleaded that he bowled under the handicap of a broken foot in his only Test. The only people whom he impressed were the Queensland batsmen, against whom he captured 7/85 in what proved to be his last game for the state of his birth in 1974. The northern state selectors offered him a place in their team and Thomson migrated to Brisbane in the same season that Denness's Englishmen set foot in Australia.

As the Sheffield Shield games of that year progressed there was little in Thomson's performances to suggest that his country had discovered a fast bowling saviour. Of all the cricket experts whom I met from day to day, only the former Australian opening bat, Jimmy Burke, was convinced of Thomson's true potential. Occasionally when 'Burky' and I were sharing the television commentary box, he would turn to me and say: 'Watch out for this bloke, Thomson. He's quick—very quick!' I should have recognized an expert opinion when I heard it; particularly since Jim was still playing Sydney grade cricket and had faced Thomson on more than one occasion. Thomson proved his speed beyond a doubt in the 1974-5 rubber by blasting his way through the defences of thirty-three English batsmen in only four and a half Tests. Had Thomson not injured his shoulder whilst playing social tennis in the Barossa Valley on the rest day of the Adelaide Test, he would certainly have broken Arthur Mailey's series record of 36 wickets against England.

The classical clinical question is: how fast is Thomson? During the Australia-West Indies clash in Perth in 1975-6, the fast bowler's muzzle velocity was measured scientifically at 99.6 mph. The Physical Education Department of the University of Western Australia conducted the experiment and later published their findings on the comparative speeds of Thomson, Lillee and the West Indian speedsters, Holding and Roberts. In terms of what the batsman can expect from Thomson, their figures proved that the striker has exactly 0.438 seconds grace in which to repulse the bowler's assault. The only problem for the batsman is that a normal person's eyes do not pick up the flight of the ball until 0.3 seconds after its release. It then takes a further 0.3 seconds for the batsman to make all the necessary judgments about the length and line of the delivery and to execute the simplest of movements. Thus 'Thommo's' opponents are placed in the unenviable position of having to initiate their stroke 0.162 seconds before the bowler releases the ball! Their predicament is accentuated by the fact that, in the preliminary swing of his bowling arm, the Queenslander hides the ball behind his back and gives no hint to the batsman about the speed or type of his next delivery.

The question is frequently asked whether Thomson, at his peak, was the fastest bowler the cricketing world has seen. It is an unanswerable conundrum. There have been many attempts to make objective comparisons of the speeds of the bowlers of the last century. No one has arrived at a satisfactory gradation of their relative velocities. The insurmountable barrier in the way of assessment has always been the lack of a common and valid yardstick. Writer Royman Browne recorded jocularly that his namesake of Brighton once bowled a ball so fast that the batsman and wicketkeeper failed to touch it and it passed clean through a coat held by a long-stop and killed a dog on the boundary! Closer to reality was the self-assessment of Kortwright, the famous Essex bowler of the nineteenth century, who apparently paid little attention to the scientific niceties of the game, apart from bowling fast at the off-stump. When asked if he ever swung the ball in the air, he replied: 'No. I just bowl as fast as I can and dare the batsman to cut me'.

A more accurate and mathematical measurement of speed was carried out on Larwood, the England pace demon of the 1930s. He was recorded at speeds ranging between 90 mph and 120 mph. The liberal 30 mph tolerance between his deliveries was apparently due, not to his great variation in pace, but rather to the inaccuracy of the high-speed photographic methods of his judges.

In 1955 the boffins of an aeronautical college in Wellington, New Zealand measured my own bowling speed and that of my opening partner in the England team, Brian Statham. Their metrology was based on projecting a metal-plated ball along a radio beam issuing from a radar-like contraption mounted on the batsman's crease: as the ball travelled through an electrical field it emitted a whistling noise. The length of the sound was recorded and a mathematical equation, based on the length of pitch and the duration of the whistle, produced evidence that my speed was 89 mph and that of Statham 87 mph. The validity of the measurement system was open to question, however, since the ball had to remain in the beam throughout its flight and was not permitted to bounce.

A few years later, Wes Hall, the giant Barbadian and West Indian fast bowler was similarly assessed at approximately 90 mph. By comparison with earlier scientific measurement techniques, the Western Australian University research of 1975 was far more sophisticated and exact. It was based on the use of a very high-speed movie camera, shooting against a scaled background. So precise were the assessments of the Perth physical education scientists that they were able to measure the pace of West Indian speedster, Andy Roberts, at 93.62 mph and that of his compatriot, Michael Holding, at 92.3 mph. Lillee, who at this stage of his career was beyond his peak of pace, could only manage 86.39 mph. A revealing fact which emerged from the experiment was that Holding, a potential 400-metre Olympian, attained a far greater consistency of speed than either Thomson or Roberts. This finding caused a few students of fast bowling to scratch their heads in wonderment, since Holding used his body-weight far less in the delivery stride than either Roberts or Thomson. Whilst he depended for his pace less on his strength, Holding possessed a beautifully lithe and fluid approach, the speed of which he maintained for over after sprinting over. The young Jamaican brought many fast bowling experts to the revolutionary realization that bowlers depend upon their run-ups for their pace far more than had previously been thought.

The fastest bowlers still emerged from the experiment as those who used to the maximum the full strength of a rock-back body-swing. In this respect Thomson is unique. His is perhaps the most closed bowling stride I have ever seen. His penultimate step is short because, like Bill Bowes and Neil Hawke before him, he performs a chassé movement towards the crease with his rear leg passing behind his front in a sideways, crab-like shuffle. This sudden pace to his left necessarily throws Thomson's body perilously close to the return crease. From this vantage point he glares balefully at the batsman from behind his raised front elbow as he thrusts his front leg, not down the wicket towards the batsman, but almost towards square-leg. His action is so shut that the heel of his rear pedestal foot points in the direction of cover! As a result the lateral swing of his powerful shoulders describes an immense sweeping arc before releasing the ball—an idiosyncrasy which has resulted in Thomson being accused of being a slinger and correspondingly inaccurate. The truth is that with such an action, 'Thommo' cannot escape the physical necessity of dropping his bowling arm to

234

The unique action of
Jeff Thomson

deliver the ball. In his early Test career, his release mechanism was not
perfectly attuned and it was not unusual for him to threaten both leg
and first slip with decapitation because he let go of the ball either too
late or too soon. Because he bowls from a position wide on the crease,
Thomson usually pushes the ball into the batsman: a fact which
prevents his following through across his body and mastering the outswinger. The monotony of his line of attack often lulls the unwary into
thinking that he cannot make the ball leave the bat. Thomson delights
in proving them wrong by occasionally sending down a devastating leg-

cutter—though I doubt whether he knows when he will bowl it.

Injury has taken its toll of 'Thommo's' speed. In his jinx city of Adelaide, he twice seriously injured his bowling shoulder—once whilst playing tennis on the rest day of a Test and a second time in a fielding collision with team-mate Alan Turner. Curbed by these physical inhibitions, Thomson, in his later development, has schooled himself into bottling up the detonation of his shoulder thrust. He lengthened his run-up and, following through further down the wicket, took a leaf out of the book of Michael Holding. Without an erratic body explosion at the bowling crease, his control and accuracy increased dramatically, though it must be admitted that the later-model Thomson lacks a little of the unexpected venom of his prototype.

For the press, 'Thommo', in his early days, was Pullitzer prize-winning copy on two legs. He was an unsophisticated individual who revelled in the animal joy of bowling fast; there are no psychological hang-ups in his sport. Once he was barred from Sydney soccer for life for striking a referee in the heat of the moment. His bowling is correspondingly a physical rather than a cerebral expression of his personality. His early passion was surfing and his continued loved of the sea was obvious in his more affluent days in a succession of purchases of expensive boats. During his first Sheffield Shield season in Queensland, he did not concern himself with the necessity of earning a steady livelihood; he preferred to eke out a wage and keep himself fit by hunting wild pigs in the remote bush country.

Cricket writers quickly exploited 'Thommo's' vital and violent image. He became 'The Terror' who was unconcerned when one of his bouncers ripped into a batsman's body. A few unguarded remarks gave him a newspaper reputation of enjoying the good life and appreciating the sheilas and a glass of beer. In real life the Bankstown fast bowler is not the Australian 'ocker' he is made out to be. He is a retiring individual whose roots in his early life go so deep that, when he suffers an injury, he often travels from Brisbane to Sydney to be treated by a physiotherapist friend.

It was one of the supreme ironies of life that this unmaterialistic man became the first plutocrat of the new commercial breed of cricketers. When thoughts crossed his mind of leaving Queensland and returning to his native Sydney, his business manager, David Lord, ensured his immediate future and anchored him to his adopted state by negotiating a contract with the Brisbane radio station 4IP which yielded Thomson $60,000 per annum. The counter-attraction of World Series Cricket and a failed sports business have completely transformed Thomson's financial situation since those early salad days; but there is no doubt that it was this Thomson coup which stirred nascent thoughts in the minds of Australian Test cricketers and private promoters alike about the commercial advertising possibilities in the game at the top.

When Dennis Lillee bowled the first ball of the 1974-5 series in Brisbane, he must have been apprehensive about what the future held in store for him. His superhuman rehabilitation programme had raised him once more to a superficial degree of fitness. In the earlier state games of the season, he proved that he had recovered from his crippling back injury and achieved moderate statistical success. The $64,000 question was whether Lillee would last the full course of six Tests. Not only did the iron-man of pace bowling survive; he played a major role in Australia's 4-1 victory by capturing 25 wickets. I often wonder whether Lillee bowled at times during that series enveloped in pain; if he did, he betrayed no symptoms of the fact. Indeed, I felt that he was the unlucky bowler of the rubber. Denness's batsmen led a charmed play-and-miss existence against the West Australian.

An integral part of Ian Chappell's attack was the giant but benevolent medium-pacer, Max Walker. Born in Tasmania, Walker migrated to Victoria initially to play as a very useful Australian Rules footballer for the Melbourne Club. Like Apple-Islanders Jack Badcock and Ted McDonald before him, however, Walker was to find his sporting niche in Test cricket. He never forgot his Taswegian origins or his cricket-loving father.

Max delights in telling the improbable story of how he and his father won a village match with a last ball hit of 17! When Walker senior emerged from the pavilion as his side's last hope, he was in a predicament. His task was impossible and had been rendered even more impracticable by the fact that the last batsman had broken one of the club's only two bats by attempting to come down hard on the yorker which bowled him. Undeterred by this turn of events, the elder Walker ripped a red gum paling off the pavilion fence as he walked out to bat, and, armed with this improvised weapon he faced the opposing fast bowler scorning to take guard. The latter took in another notch on his snake-skin belt and hurtled up to the wicket to deliver a full-toss of horrific velocity. The paling descended and made audible contact with the ball which thereupon disappeared, apparently in the direction of a sea of long grass at long-on. With a joint bellow of 'come on' the Walker duet embarked upon their first run. By the time that they reached four, the whole of the opposing team were trampling down the grass in the area of the elusive ball like a herd of exasperated buffaloes. The fieldsmen's knowledge of the laws was rudimentary and there was no thought of calling 'lost ball' as the batsmen turned for their seventh run. The ball still escaped detection as the Walkers crossed for their seventeenth and winning run before collapsing exhausted on the ground. 'I'll bet those blokes would like to know where the ball is', crowed Max's father down the wicket to his son. 'I'll let them into the secret.' He reversed his paling bat and there impaled on a six-inch nail was the ball!

As a bowler Max Walker is a peculiar phenomenon. He delivers the ball off the wrong foot with a whirling of windmill arms and legs which seems a physical impossibility. Small wonder that he has earned himself the nickname of 'Tangles'. Walker possesses three attributes which have brought him more than a hundred wickets in Tests and made him a world-class bowler. His heart is always full of bowling optimism, his stamina is unlimited and his ability to swing the ball into the bat and cut it away off the wicket is unique. In the final game of the 1974-5 series, Walker's capacity to bowl better as the Test wore on, transformed an analysis of 3/128 into a final return of 8/143.

The tangled delivery-stride of Australian medium-pace bowler, Max Walker

'Tangles' epitomizes the contrast which England's chairman of selectors, and himself a great medium-pace bowler, Alec Bedser, often underlines between English and Australian inswing bowlers. Bedser maintains that English swing bowlers hold the seam upright and rely on that agency and the shine on the ball to produce movement through the air. Their Australian counterparts work the ball, as Bedser himself used to do and baseball pitchers do, by drawing the fingers of the bowling hand down the side of the ball and imparting vicious cut or spin. The effect of this spin makes the ball curve into the batsman in the air and often move towards the slips after pitching. Australian medium-pacers have evolved this technique because of the hard, unyielding character of their home wickets which removes the shine and flattens the seam of the new ball in the space of a few overs. Evidence suggests that Bedser's theory is correct; there have been very few English medium-pace methods apart from the similar styles of Bedser, Tate, Barnes and Foster which have proved successful Down Under. Walker substantiated Bedser's claim by making a 23-wicket contribution to Australia's triumph in 1974-5.

Fate did not smile kindly on Denness's tourists. A mystery virus restricted the England captain's opportunities for match practice before the First Test. The game itself produced a series of disasters which tipped the scales in Chappell's favour for the remainder of the tour. Brisbane's Lord Mayor and Queensland's Australian Cricket Board representative, Alderman Clem Jones, assumed the responsibility of preparing the Woolloongabba pitch when a curator crisis struck that ground in November. The product of his cutting and rolling was a corrugated surface of uneven bounce, which, in the space of mere days, produced two broken hands in the England batting ranks. Edrich and Amiss were the sufferers. Edrich was to experience a torrid time at the hands of the fast bowlers during the tour. In Sydney, a non-bouncing Lillee bumper crunched into his rib-cage with all the force of a bolo punch and he was forced to retire, scoreless. He returned to the crease like a true Edrich to complete a courageous and undefeated 33 and almost avert an inescapable defeat.

The psychological consequences of England's bone-crushing and bruising loss by 166 runs in Brisbane were immense. The blinding pace of Thomson and the subtleties of Lillee completely bewildered her batsmen. Just before the Third Test, Denness, his confidence shot to ribbons, gained unique notoriety by dropping himself because of loss of form. His honesty made him the only England captain to be omitted from a touring Test team for reasons other than lack of fitness. His self-effacement seemed, in the light of his 188 in the Final Test, completely unjustified.

England's only answer to Australia's dynamic pace duo of Lillee and Thomson throughout the series appeared to be the defiant 'derring-do' of her future leader, Tony Greig. At times his slashing and edgy methods outside the off-stump brought tears to the eyes of the bowlers, apprehension into the eyes of the slip-fieldsmen and their hearts into the mouths of English supporters; but at least Greig showed that he had spirit—a commodity which was in desperately short supply amongst the

England batting survivors. The T.C.C.B. selectors, in one despairing throw of the dice, attempted to shore up the tourists' confidence by despatching as a reinforcement, the experienced, 41-year-old Colin Cowdrey, a man who had never been known to flinch in the face of fast bowling. After an absence of three and a half years from the Test circuit, Cowdrey arrived in Perth only days before the Second Test and was immediately thrown into the fray. He found himself on an alien planet of cricket savagery.

Thomson had worked himself into a fine frenzy of antagonism before Cowdrey came in at the fall of the first wicket. On his way to the centre of the ground, 'Kipper' passed 'Thommo' and extended the olive branch; 'How do you do', he is reputed to have said in gentlemanly tones, 'I believe we haven't met. My name is Colin Cowdrey'. The fast bowler snarled and soon gave Cowdrey concrete evidence of his hostile opinion on the exchange of such civilities on the Test field. To Cowdrey's credit, he scored 22 and 41. His reflexes were obviously not as sharply attuned as of yore, but his spirit was unquenched.

The sudden resignation of the Woolloongabba curator ten days before the First Test rendered Clem Jones less than aldermanic on the eve of the game. In the dead of the night a typical Brisbane downpour flooded the playing area and the Lord Mayor of Brisbane was summoned from his bed to hold back, like Moses, the waves which threatened to inundate the wicket. The substitute groundsman appeared unmoved by the climatic turn of events and the possibility of a soft wicket. On the morning of the match he was seen washing the mud off the approaches to the pitch with a hosepipe! The jeremiahs who predicted that the wicket would be a horror, were disappointed. It was true that the uneven bounce from the surface and the eye-defying speed of the Australian attack made life difficult for the England batsmen, but both teams managed scores in the region of 300 in their first appearance at the wicket. For the tourists, Greig notched a devil-may-care 110 and thus became the first England player since Maurice Leyland in 1936, and only the second in the history of the Gabba, to reach three figures in a Test. The match saw two more statistical landmarks passed: the 100,000th run in Anglo-Australian clashes was recorded and Alan Knott snared his 200th victim behind the stumps. Bravely though England batted in their first innings, their short-lived triumph over the Australian pace attack was dearly bought. Both Edrich and Amiss could scarcely hold their bats when Denness's side went in again. Their team collapsed for 166 against the now dangerous lift of Thomson to lose the game by the same number of runs as their total.

The England survivors of the First Test took the field in poor heart for the second encounter in Perth. Realizing his psychological advantage, Ian Chappell asked Denness to bat. The Australian captain at this time was at the peak of his good fortune—lucky with the coin and blessed with the excellent performances of his side on the field. I do not think that I have ever seen any team give a better catching performance than Australia in Perth in December 1974. Every false stroke from the edge of an English bat seemed to find its way as if by predestination into the unfumbling hands of an Australian fieldsman. The younger brother of the Australian captain, Greg, wrote the name Chappell once more in the record books by accepting no fewer than seven catches. Five of those opportunities came in one innings: a fact which linked the younger Chappell to the name of his grandfather, Vic Richardson, who performed the same feat in Durban against South Africa in 1935-6.

In the only major Australian innings of 481, Doug Walters's flair for the spectacular was revealed when he reached a century in one session of play by hooking Willis flamboyantly for six off the last ball of the day. Ross Edwards's 115 earned him the distinction of being the first West Australian to score a Test hundred before his home crowd. The tourists batted dispiritedly to lose the game by 9 wickets. It was significant that the old hand Titmus, the off-spinner who had not played in a Test since 1968, displayed the most backbone and top-scored with 61.

An enormous first day crowd of 77,165 saw the beginning of a Melbourne Test which was the great disappointment of the New Year. The game was frustratingly drawn with the home side only 8 runs short of victory and England only 2 wickets away from turning the tables. The draw was the result of the perversity of human nature and demonstrated graphically that there is 'nowt so queer as folk' when there is a clash of personalities on the cricket field. Needing 246 to win in their last innings Chappell's team began the last hour only 55 runs from their objective. Outwardly it should have been an easy task in the mandatory 15 overs; yet when the immaculate Underwood and the accurate Greig began a spell of economic finger-spin to a defensive field, Marsh and Walker, who batted competently throughout the series, were assailed by an attack of the sulks. Their attitude suggested that they expected Denness to attack on a good wicket which gave Australia the dual options of either winning or 'putting up the shutters'—but certainly did not expose the home team to the real danger of losing. Incomprehensibly, the two batsmen, entirely on their own initiative by the admission of their captain after the game, blocked their way through 7 dull overs for 7 boring runs. With the spectators still howling their disappointment at the Australian tactics, the second new ball was taken, and they began the assault again. Courageously, with 2 overs remaining, and Australia only 16 runs from victory, Denness asked Greig and Underwood to bowl their spinners once more. Australia refused to take disproportionate risks against their accuracy and the match was left unfinished.

England's abysmal luck throughout the tour continued in Melbourne. Her key bowler, the Derbyshire medium-paced outswinger, Hendrick, pulled a hamstring muscle and joined the growing casualty list. In England's second knock, Amiss played a delightful vignette of an innings which yielded him 90 runs. That score represented a double disappointment for the England opener; not only did he fall 10 runs short of his century but he left the Melbourne wicket on 31 December 1974 with 1,379 Test runs to his credit in the previous twelve calendar months. He was just 2 runs from breaking Bobby Simpson's record.

Sydney's Fourth Test and the series were decided when England's medium-pacer, 'Horse' or 'G.G.' Arnold was caught at short-leg off the bowling of Mallett. The record 178,027 Sydney spectators who witnessed their side's triumph, joined in the jubilation of Chappell's men. It was a rare moment for them to savour. It was the first time since the 1958-9 season that Australia had regained rather than retained the Ashes. Australia had not defeated England in a rubber for ten years.

Denness's abdication of his captaincy responsibilities undermined the confidence of the tourists before the first ball of the match was bowled. Edrich tried manfully to fill his skipper's shoes, but the ill-fortune which had danced attendance on the visitors since they first set foot on the southern continent, still pursued England's tatterdemalion side. Lillee stove in Edrich's ribs with the first ball which he bowled to him in England's second innings. Like General MacArthur, Edrich returned to defy pain and stagger to an unbeaten 33 before Arnold's dismissal put him out of his misery. It was characteristic of England's misfortune during this tour that they failed by only 5.3 overs to save the match.

The unflinching fortitude of that band of Norfolk brothers called Edrich will remain a legend as long as cricket is played in England. Bill Edrich batted in Tests with the same courage which gained him the D.F.C. flying fighters during the battle of Britain. He took more than his share of batterings from the Miller and Lindwall bouncers of the late 1940s and early 1950s. Even the vertical lift-off of a Brisbane 'sticky' did not prevent Bill from positioning himself right behind the line of the most spiteful delivery. Once, during a Middlesex-Northamptonshire county game at Lords, I broke Bill's jaw with a bouncer which brought the automatic Edrich reflex response of a hook. Bill was transported to hospital on a stretcher to spend the night in the drugged arms of Morpheus. The following day he reappeared at the wicket at the fall of the next wicket and proceeded to try to hook the next ball he received! Brother Geoff also suffered at the hands of Tyson; playing for Lancashire on an Old Trafford flier—a wicket which was bone-hard underneath the surface, but damp on top—he was struck on the hand. In spite of the fact that his knuckle was broken, he scored a valiant half-century and refused to be cowed, even when a bumper soared over his head, bounced once and hit the sight-screen. John Edrich came from the same yeoman stock as his cousins and he displayed all of the family traits in his epic Sydney innings. I knew of his resolution first hand; once at The Oval, whilst bowling for my county against Surrey, I cracked a knuckle of the junior Edrich so badly that the injury required a corrective operation. It goes without saying that he only retired to the pavilion with the greatest reluctance.

Against all the laws of probability Australia carried off the Fifth Test by 163 runs. England held all the aces, yet contrived to lose every trick in the game and the match itself with unseeming haste in the space of just over three days. No play was possible on the first day because unusual cyclonic conditions invaded Adelaide from the north on the eve of the match, whipping up gale-force winds which brought torrential rain in their wake. The first element tore the covers off the Test wicket. The second flooded it.

Denness, inspired by a sense of returning luck, won the toss on the second morning and sent Chappell's men in to bat on a still soft pitch. After only 3 overs the England captain flung his medium-paced spinner, Underwood, into the assault. The yielding surface was tailor made for the wiles of the Kent bowler. He was too fast through the air for the batsmen to move down the wicket to meet the ball on the half volley; his mechanical leg-spinning accuracy never wavered from a good length or the line of middle-and-leg stumps. By lunch Australia had lost 5/84, in spite of an inspired start of 52 runs for the first wicket. Such was the flaccidity of the English outcricket, however, that Walters was permitted to defy the odds and mount an effective counter-attack against the turning, lifting ball. His 55 was punctuated with false strokes; but he survived and the wicket improved steadily. Leg-spinner Jenner exploited the firmer conditions to top-score with 74, whilst 41 from fast bowler Walker gave his team's total an unexpected boost to 304.

England's innings disintegrated against a rampant Thomson; it plumbed the depths of mediocrity to sink at 172, after having been an illusionary and buoyant 4/130. When Chappell closed his second innings at 5/272, Denness's batsmen required 405 to win in eight and a half hours of predictable anguish. Within the space of 3 overs and 10 runs they lost 3 wickets including that of Amiss, who became the first of a trio of English batsmen to collect a pair of spectacles. At close of play on the fourth day England were a despairing 5/94. Next morning only Knott's adventurous first century against Australia, his third in Tests, enabled England to redeem a modicum of their pawned batting reputation. When England's last man came to the batting crease, Knott still required 15 runs to join his fellow Kentish man, Les Ames, in the records as the only recognized wicketkeeper to have scored a hundred in the august atmosphere of England-Australia games. Knott slashed and

John Edrich bats with typical family determination. Sydney 1974-5

cut his way excitingly past the three-figure mark, thus momentarily uplifting English spirits downcast by a defeat which should never have occurred. The despondency produced in the minds of the tourists by a combination of the Lillee and Thomson pace blitzkreig, and the contrasting conditions of the first three Tests, denied England a logical victory, even when conditions favoured them in Adelaide.

Dame Fortune proved in Melbourne's sixth encounter that when she changes allegiance, there are no half measures. With Thomson *hors de combat* because of his shoulder injury, the onus of responsibility for the home side's fast attack lay weightily on the shoulders of Dennis Lillee. After bowling six overs in England's first innings, the Western Australian limped off the field with a damaged heel and took no further part in proceedings. Australia's misfortunes originated on the first day when Ian Chappell's underestimation of a damp spot on the wicket, caused by a curator's carelessness in removing the covers after a rainy night, proved the undoing of his side's first innings batting hopes. Lancashire fast-medium bowler, Peter Lever, showing himself for the first time on the tour to be as dangerous as his lengthy run suggested, exploited the soft patch admirably to capture 6/38 and dismiss Australia for 152. For most of the first three sessions, Lever, who had shrugged off an attack of influenza to bowl, was an anxiety in the back of the batsmen's minds rather than a danger. Occasionally, however, one of his low trajectory, skidding deliveries struck the soft bull's eye and spat chest high at the batsman with the venom of a bowler twice Lever's speed.

Mike Denness, England's highest-scoring captain in Australia

The saga of England's prospering cause continued when she batted. Denness not only scored his first and only century against Australia, but he profitted from three fielding lapses to translate his hundred into the enormity of 188, thus surpassing Stoddart's 173 and becoming the highest-scoring England captain in Tests in Australia. Fletcher's 146 and 70 from Edrich helped the tourists along the road to 529 and a first innings lead of 377. That ascendancy proved to be exactly 4 runs beyond the second innings batting capabilities of Australia. Greg Chappell reached 102 and appeared capable of saving his side's unbeaten record in the rubber; then he was bowled between bat and pad by a back-break from Lever which scarcely seemed possible on a then benign pitch. It was a match of unplayable deliveries. In Australia's second innings, medium-pacer Arnold bowled Walters with a ball which pitched in line with the leg-stump and just clipped the off-bail, with surgical precision, off the top of the stumps. I have seen very few unplayable balls in my time; Arnold afforded me one of those rare visual experiences.

Statistically the game wrote a new name at the head of the roll of honour of Test keepers. When Knott caught Ian Chappell off the bowling of Greig, he claimed his 220th victim in Tests, thereby surpassing the previous best tally of 219, established by yet another Kent man, Godfrey Evans. It really is strange how Canterbury is not only the city of England's Primate, but also a prime nursery for stumpers such as Ames, Evans and Knott.

17. The Year of the World Champions

The normal cyclic interchange of tours between England and Australia every two or three years was pleasantly disrupted in the northern summer of 1975. In that year, under the sponsorship of the Prudential Insurance Company, the World Cup Competition was inaugurated. In concept, the one-day knock-out match was a sociological reflection of the times. Spectators clamoured for results in six hours; they spurned the drab Test draw fought out in the technical vacuum of the cricket purist. Entertainment was the 'open sesame' for the busy turnstile. Moreover, the public, after years of comparison and speculation about the respective merits of international sides, looked forward to the days of final decision in The World Championship at Lords and the provincial Test grounds.

Limited-over cricket has been a mixed blessing to the first-class game. On the asset side of the balance sheet, it has proved to be a King Solomon's Mines for the finances of foundering county cricket clubs. Moreover the new format introduced a new urgency on the field of play. Curtailed approaches sped the bowlers through their overs. The art of running between the wickets improved with the startling suddenness of the Olympic 100-metres times. English fielding lost its sedate, middle-aged, save-your-energy approach as singles began to mean the difference between winning and losing and between $100 and $1,000 in prize money.

The argument against strictured cricket reasons that the format does not permit the full development of the batting and bowling skills. Unless a major collapse in the early order thrusts them to the forefront of responsibility, numbers five, six and seven in the batting line-up rarely have the opportunity or time to build a substantial innings. Too often the spin bowler is regarded by his captain as an expensive and expendable luxury. The amended game encourages defensive field-placements and tactics which are aimed at run conservation rather than gaining wickets. The quest for quick singles sometimes encourages bad habits in batting technique. It was noticeable that, during England's disastrous 1974-5 series in Australia, batsmen in posts of responsibility, such as Denness, set a bad example by backing away as fast bowlers Thomson and Lillee delivered. The mannerism had its origins, not in apprehension, but in the batsman's habit of giving himself enough room to steer the ball away through the gully for a single—à la limited-overs game.

The playwright Tom Stoppard's *bons mots* can be applied to my attitude towards one-day cricket: 'I'm not a man of firm convictions . . . I think!' Augmented crowds, additional sponsors and increased gate receipts prove that the limited-over game has a vital role to play in the finances of the first-class and Test game. It has improved the technical skills of cricket in certain directions; in other areas it exercises a deleterious influence, producing side effects harmful to the evolution of a five-day player and debilitating captaincy with the affliction of effective conservatism. To have the best of both worlds of solvency and Test success and to afford the spectator and player alike the maximum enjoyment and fulfilment, the administrator has to maintain a fine balance between the short and stretched formats with all the skills of a second Metternich come to a latter-day Congress of Vienna.

The inaugural World Cup was contested by the full and the major associate members of the International Cricket Conference. The finals were played between the two leading sides in the two divisions and resulted in a narrow 17-run victory to the West Indies over Australia in the deciding encounter. The contest enhanced Australia's image as a hard competitor but did not flatter her generosity as a dominant partici-pant. The tiny Sri Lankan batsmen suffered a fearful battering at the hands of Thomson and Lillee. Mendis, struck on the head, was forced to retire and spent the night in hospital. At one stage of the game against the island republic, a Thomson yorker clubbed Wettimuny on the toe. As a result of the 'sandshoe cruncher' the batsman toppled to the ground outside his crease and, as he lay writhing in pain, Thomson, following through, picked up the ball and threw at the stumps in an unfeeling attempt to run the batsman out.

Since the crowd-pulling Australians travelled half-way round the world to participate in the global knock-out competition, a supple-mentary mini-Ashes series was a logical financial corollary to the World Cup. Chappell consoled himself for his universal loss with a 1-0 victory over the host country. The rubber was a drawn-out war of attrition, decided by the preliminary skirmish at Edgbaston. In Birmingham, Denness, kept in the English captaincy by the life-support system of his recent success in Melbourne, made the worst decision of his ill-fated tenure of office. With rain in the offing, he won the toss and sent Australia in to bat; inevitably his side's batsmen were bogged down on a wet wicket by a thunderstorm. Australia, with 243 runs on the board before the rains came, won by an innings and 85 runs in the space of three and a half days. Overtly willing to resign the leadership, Denness was not given the opportunity to retain his place as a player. He was dropped and the unenviable job of leading a dispirited England side out of the wilderness of defeat was delegated to Tony Greig—a South African of Scottish descent and a man imbued with inspirational qualities of captaincy. This was the captain who, in the following English winter, was to lead his side to their first win over India on the sub-continent since the 1933 era of Douglas Jardine.

The spirit which made Tony Greig an inspirational captain

Greig is a man whose cricket encapsulates his personality. There is an aura of aggression and defiance about his game. He never concedes defeat. In his first game for his adopted county of Sussex he scored a callow but unrepentant 156 against the unrelenting pace of Lancashire's maestro, Brian Statham. In itself that recommendation is enough to place Greig in the highest class of batsmen. He scarcely knows or acknowledges the existence of a defensive stroke. He prefers to drive the good length ball 'on the up' rather than prod. To him the edge over the slips is a legitimate means of scoring; his philosophy discounts the chanciness of the shot and advocates a good hard slash at the ball short of a length outside the off-stump. As a bowler his forte is persistence. There is no great venom in his swinging medium-pace and no acute turn in his steady off-spinners; but he never concedes second-best to the batsman and has the supreme and unexpected ability to make the ball bounce. His elongated agility in the slips enables him to scoop up the widest of catching improbabilities and set standards of fielding excellence which only the dullest of spirits would not try to emulate. He leads by example and force of personality. No doubt it was his unyielding character which steered him into a position of inflexible revolt at the time of the Packer revolution. These contentious times only underline the fact that, right or wrong, Tony Greig never surrenders, either on the cricket field or in his outspoken opinions.

Greig, the captain, did not make an immediate impact on the international scene. His first three clashes with Ian Chappell saw both leaders retire from the ring unbowed and undefeated. Greig's brief moment of glory as skipper came in India where he won the first three Tests against Bedi's men and carried off the series 3-1. The Centenary Test was lost by a narrow 45 runs and when the Australian touring party next flew into Heathrow airport in 1977, the Sussex and England captain's behind-the-scenes negotiations with the Packer organization had pushed him to the brink of his eventual dismissal. The crowning disappointment of Greig's eight-match career as captain was that his inspirational potential as leader did not once yield a much-yearned-for victory against the traditional cricket opponent.

The surprising distinction of being the Man of the 1975 Series fell to the lot of the unassuming number three Northamptonshire batsman, David Steele. The prematurely grey-haired, 33-year-old Staffordshire-born player was a most unlikely saviour of the England batting order. His previous twelve seasons with his county had not stamped him as a stroke-maker of outstanding ability. For seven of those summers his batting average had not exceeded 30 and he was generally regarded by his fellow professionals as a bread-and-butter number three with the inbred tenacity of a Black Countryman. His handicap seemed to be that his less than 20/20 vision required him to bat in steel-rimmed spectacles; his county, however, never questioned his general usefulness—he is a handy slow left-handed spin bowler and an excellent close-to-the-wicket fieldsman. Steele is made of the same obdurate material as was his fellow Staffordshireman S. F. Barnes. His uncle, Stan Crump, was for many years one of the most successful off-spinning all-rounders in the Lancashire leagues and was responsible for Steele's early cricket education on a backyard concrete pitch. His younger brother, Jack, plays for Leicestershire whilst his cousin Brian Crump was, in my time, a persevering all-rounder with Northamptonshire—a county he was later to captain.

Steele's tastes are more inclined to the work-a-day fish-and-chip existence of county cricket, rather than the glamorous caviar atmosphere of the international set. His defensive technique is rooted firmly on front foot play: a fact which led many judges to believe that he would be suspect against the bouncing fury of Lillee and Thomson. Steele confounded this judgment by averaging 60.83 in the three games of the four Test series in which he played. He hooked Lillee as courageously as many a younger batsman with sharper reflexes and his stalwart performance was enough to win the coveted award of England's Sportsman Of The Year. The fates were in Steele's camp in 1975; it was one of the driest English summers of the century and the frustratingly slow pitches drew the sharpest fangs of the essentially pace-orientated Australian attack. In subjective terms Lillee probably never bowled better than he did in that series to capture 21 wickets at 21.9 each.

As for Steele—he was soon to become aware of the meaning of the Australian saying: 'Cock of the roost one minute, a feather duster the next'. It was a damning commentary on the fickleness of English selection that after the Stoke man's 1975 triumphs he was passed over when the side to tour India in the winter of 1976-7 was chosen. The reason given? It was foreseen that his methods would not be effective on the spinning surfaces of the sub-continent. His record against Lloyd's all-conquering West Indians in 1976 did not live up to his performances of the previous summer; but he did score his maiden Test century at Trent Bridge, finish third in an unimpressive catalogue of batting averages and score a brace of 40s in the final crushing subjugation of England by 231 runs at The Oval. He deserved a better future than that meted out by Alec Bedser and his co-selectors; but Steele hails from an unfashionable midland county.

David Steele, England's Sportsman of 1975

The Australian discovery of the 1975 tour was Rick McCosker, a bank clerk and a gem of a find from the northern New South Wales mining town of Inverell. Originally a number four batsman for his state, the tall, broad-shouldered addition to Australia's list of successful country players proved his adaptability by stepping into the opening-bat breach in the Fourth Test against Denness's tourists in Sydney and scoring 80 on his début. In his first rubber in England, the strong on-side player with a bent-kneed stance averaged 82.8, proving himself the most consistent and second prolific scorer in the touring ranks. He overcame the disappointment at being stranded on an unbeaten 95 by the vandalization of the Headingley wicket and reached his maiden hundred in his next excursion to the Test wicket.

The West Indian pace attack of Roberts and Holding exposed McCosker's glaring weakness outside the off-stump during the 1975-6 series in Australia. His confidence suffered a further severe set-back when a Willis bumper fractured his jaw during the Centenary Test. The script-like monotony of McCosker's dismissals 'caught behind' or 'caught slip' led to his being jettisoned for the Sydney Test against

Lloyd's tourists, much to the chagrin of his fellow-players. He returned to the Test fold to score a century against Pakistan in Melbourne, tour New Zealand, and gain a place in the side to England in 1977. Delayed by his recovery from his Centenary Test jaw injury and an air-traffic controllers' strike, McCosker was a late arrival in England, where the form of Australia's two regular openers was so ephemeral that her reserve keeper Richie Robinson was pressed into service to go in first in the initial encounter at Lords. McCosker notched a long-awaited hundred in Nottingham's Third Test to salvage his berth in the Australian XI; but his lack of reliability only served to underline the transience of every Australian opening pair since the halcyon days of Lawry and Simpson. In the only Australian innings at Edgbaston in 1975, McCosker scored 59, providing a glimpse of the sterling form which was to follow and enabling his team to reach 359. England were twice trapped on a wet wicket by repeated thunderstorms and went down to an ignominious innings defeat against a pace attack in which Lillee, Thomson and Walker each captured 5 wickets in an innings.

Under the determined tutelage of Greig, the home side put on a braver front at Lords where their skipper's innings of 96 enabled them to recover from a precarious 4/49 and achieve a first innings respectability of 315. Australia were 7/81 just after lunch on the second day, but the 187-run contribution of the last 3 wickets hoisted their total to 268. Accountant Ross Edwards, the tourists' middle-order linchpin, showed an unexpected lack of appreciation for figures. In his last appearance at the home of cricket, he had the unsatisfactory satisfaction of being adjudged lbw for 99 to the medium-pace of part-time bowler, Woolmer. Edrich became the fourth-ranking scorer of centuries against Australia when he notched his seventh three-figure score against them. His 175 was the second-best English effort at Lords and rocketed his side's lead to 483. Alas for Greig's hopes of victory; the wicket proved the winner in this game as Chappell's men batted solidly to reach 3/329 before the final minutes of the game expired.

The Third Test at Leeds will always have a unique niche in the annals of cricket. Vandals caused the abandonment of the game on the fifth day by infiltrating the ground past the security guards, crawling underneath the covers, digging up the wicket and pouring sump oil on to a good length. No alternative wicket proved acceptable to both captains. Obviously Greig wanted an equitable exchange for the fifth day surface, which would have afforded assistance to his left-handed spin duet of Edmonds and Underwood. Chappell on the other hand wanted a good pitch which would allow his remaining seven batsmen a better-than-even chance of scoring the 225 runs separating them from their second victory. The skippers agreed to disagree and since there was no time to programme a supplementary fixture, the already short series was abbreviated even further. Edmonds made a dream début in this clash by capturing 5/28 against some indifferent Australian batting which realized only 135 in their first innings on a slow turning wicket. Gilmour, the hero of the Prudential Cup, caused me to wonder on the vagaries of the Australian selectors who had ignored him until Leeds, by taking 6/85 in England's first innings. The match had a feeling of futility about it. The Headingley vandals were crusading Visigoths agitating to draw attention to the wrongful identification, conviction and imprisonment of the alleged bank robber George Davis. A wry quirk of fate resulted in Davis being freed shortly after the demonstrators' oily agriculture at Headingley; but it was all so pointless—two years later Davis, convicted on another charge, had homed in once more to one of Her Majesty's Prisons. It was also quaint that the person who was finally arrested for the Headingley outrage bore, coincidentally, the same surname as the Australian captain.

The series came to a lingering end at The Oval. A moribund wicket and the Australian determination to hold on to their one game advantage in the series doomed the game to inconclusiveness. Ian Chappell, leading Australia for his thirtieth and last time before yielding fraternal pride of place to Greg on grounds of fatigue, reached the pinnacle of his batting performances against England by accumulating 192. At the time of his retirement, Chappell's thirty successive games at the helm constituted an Australian record. It was strange to think that the 42-year-old Bobby Simpson would set a new mark in 1977 after an interregnum of ten years, by reassuming command of an Australian XI decimated by the Packer defections.

McCosker collected 127 and assisted Chappell to post an enormous total of 532 before declaring with 9 wickets down. When England collapsed for 191 on a surface enlivened by light drizzle and generally humid conditions, it seemed that Australia might increase their winning margin in the rubber. Woolmer, however, came to the rescue when the home side followed on and his six-and-a-half-hour century—the slowest on record against Australia—enabled England to reach 538 and thus set Chappell's men the impossible task of scoring 198 to win in eighty-five minutes. Realistically, the tourists contented themselves with their one match supremacy.

The Oval stalemate was the sixty-sixth draw in ninety-eight years of competition between England and Australia and the last meeting between the two sides before the Centenary Test. According to Wisden, 224 matches were played between the two countries in that time. Seventy-one times England proved victorious; on eighty-seven other occasions the boot was on the other foot. England had called upon thirty-two amateur and two professional or registered cricketers to lead her since 1877. Apparently for seventy-six years the Powers That Be at Lords echoed Lord Hawke's sentiments when he said: 'Pray God a professional will never captain Yorkshire'. It was therefore ironic that a Yorkshire 'pro', Len Hutton, should prove to be the first of his successful ilk to lead England in 1953. Australia's thirty skippers against England were all, by definition, if not in fact, unpaid.

The characters who peopled the cricketing years between 1877-1977 ranged from the normal to the eccentric. They included a wicketkeeper with a passion for ice-cream, a dread of constipation, and a penchant for the laxative exercise of pedalling a bicycle rickshaw with the coolie-driver in the passenger seat, whenever he visited a city where these vehicles were available

Australian left-handed bowler, Arthur Coningham, appeared in his first and only Test against England in Melbourne in the 1894-5 series and captured the wicket of Archie MacLaren with his first ball! Coningham's claim to fame and notoriety, however, transcended one ball and one Test. He boasted that in his time he won 170 foot races, covered a measured mile in four minutes twenty-four seconds and the 440 hurdles in fifty-eight seconds. In the field events this antipodean counterpart of England's all-round athlete, Charles Fry, had reputedly leapt 21'10'' in length and 5'10'' in height. A man of courage, he jumped into the Thames whilst on tour in 1893 to rescue a drowning boy; for this act of bravery he was awarded a medal. He was the precursor of Warwick Armstrong's tomfoolery at The Oval in 1921; at Lords, the centre of social sensitivity, Coningham, like 'the Big Ship', gathered some waste paper from the outfield on a cold day and lit it to warm his hands—much to the disapproval of the members!

Even this was not the limit of Coningham's outrageous folly. In 1900 he sued his wife, Alice, (nee Dowling) for divorce, naming the Reverend Denis Francis O'Haran, the Administrator of Sydney's St Mary's Cathedral as the co-respondent. It proved to be a trial drawn from the pages of *Alice in Wonderland*, with Coningham outraging the sensibilities of sectarian Sydney by claiming that the Catholic priest was the father of one of his children. The ex-cricketer toted a gun into the court, assumed control of his own case when his lawyer withdrew and, understandably, lost the case, much to the delight of the court gallery.

Arthur Coningham

Ernie McCormick, the Australian fast bowler of the late 1930s, was not so outlandish a character as Coningham—but he enjoyed his humorous day. Once whilst playing in a Victorian country town social game for his club of Richmond, Ernie struck an opposition batsman a painful blow on the foot with a full toss. Unfortunately the player's big toe was broken and he was compelled to retire, very hurt. Some years later Ernie was attending an Australian Rules football game at the St Kilda Oval, when his unfortunate victim caught sight of him from afar and pursued him as he made his way into the luncheon room. Ernie was about to do justice to an enormous barbecued steak when his erstwhile opponent breasted his table. 'I'm glad I saw you', said Old Broken Toe. 'I'd like you to see what you did to my foot.' At this he peeled off his shoe and sock and deposited a maladorous member alongside Ernie's plate. As Ernie later said, the misshapen big toe was 'just like a brown, peeled onion'. Honour satisfied, the former fast bowler's prey replaced his sock and shoe and took his leave. It was at this stage that McCormick's companion, George Schofield, exclaimed succinctly, 'My God Ernie, it's a good job you didn't hit him in the box!'

There have been cricketers in the course of the past century who have aspired to notoriety other than on the Test field. On 31 August 1888, the shortest match ever played between England and Australia ended with a home victory by an innings and 21 runs just before lunch on the second day. That same evening in the dark and narrow streets of White-chapel in the East End of London, Mary Ann Nicholls became the first victim of the infamous and undetected murderer, Jack the Ripper. In December of the same year the body of M. J. Druitt, a cricketer of repute at Winchester College and Oxford University and a member of the M.C.C., was discovered floating in the Thames at Chiswick. The general supposition was that Montague John Druitt, a schoolmaster and lawyer, committed suicide fearing that he would be overtaken by the same insanity which claimed his mother. A document entitled 'The East End murderer—I knew him', later published by a cousin Lionel in Dandenong, Victoria, linked Druitt, by its timing, with the Ripper murders. It was a strange accusation to lay against a man who played cricket with Lord Harris at Blackheath and who was finally laid to rest in Wimborne Minster Cemetery, Dorset, next to Nicholas Wanostrocht—the famous 'Felix', one of the game's earliest professionals and a violinist and Blackheath scholar of repute. As I said before, it takes all sorts to make a world, even in cricket.

18. Happy Birthday!

Melbourne and the cricketing world awoke on 15 March 1977 to wish Test cricket a happy one hundredth birthday. The celebration of the event began three days earlier at the Melbourne Cricket Ground, when, to commemorate the First Test staged between James Lillywhite's touring English side and David Gregory's colonials on the Richmond Police Paddock in 1877, the Centenary Test began with Tony Greig winning the toss and asking Greg Chappell's Australian batsmen to 'have a hit'.

As March 1977 approached, few people realized the significance of the date. One of that minority, however, was Hans Ebeling, a medium-pace bowler who made one appearance against England at The Oval in 1934. Hans is President of the Melbourne Cricket Club and a person with a great sensibility for the historical traditions of the game and the charisma of the ground on which the First Test was played. He was determined that the anniversary should not pass unnoticed and a few years before the momentous occasion, he began a campaign to ensure that the significance of 12 March 1977 should not be overlooked.

Initially the idea was simply that the birthday of Test cricket should be marked by the issue of commemorative stamps by Australia Post. The Australian Cricket Board, however, considered the matter so important that it delegated the Victorian Cricket Association to establish a co-ordinating committee. This embraced the Melbourne Cricket Club and the State History Advisory Council, which were to organize a commemorative Test. Like a bush fire in the back blocks, the idea of a Centenary Test swept through the imaginations of the cricketing and business worlds.

As 1976 came to a close, excitement grew as invitations were extended and accepted by more than 200 ex-Test 'greats'. The evening social programme of the match was bursting at the seams with dinners and cocktail parties given by the sponsors, the Melbourne Cricket Club, the Victorian Cricket Association and the Australian Cricket Board. Apart from the Test cricket itself, the days of 12-17 March 1977 promised to be times of golden memories and events. The walls of the Melbourne pavilion were adorned with the scoreboard name-plates of players of former days; formal dinners, cocktail parties and lunchtime entertainment for the spectators were organized. Happily, the Centenary Test also coincided with Melbourne's Mardi Gras celebration—Moomba. It was a fortunate choice of name for, in the aboriginal language, Moomba means, 'Let's get together and have fun'.

The Centenary Test, however, was more than a game and an exercise in nostalgia. Its links with the past were very real and very much alive. The principal speaker at the A.C.B.'s Centenary Test dinner, Sir Donald Bradman, in his youth met and was photographed with Charles Bannerman, the scorer of the first Test century in the initial game of 1877. When he scored his first hundred against England in Melbourne in 1937, the perpetually beaming Centenary Test celebrant, Jack Badcock, was introduced to the 78-year-old Tom Garrett, who, as an 18-year-old Sydney University student, played in the First Test. Garrett was described as a 'tall, lean all-rounder—a fierce but unreliable hitter, a first-class cover point and a fastish bowler with a sharp break-back'. This image destroys my faith in graphology; for I have a copy of a letter which the young Garrett wrote from his school, thanking his father for the present of a cricket bat. Its copper-plate perfection gave me the impression that Garrett, far from being unreliable, was the epitome of punctiliousness. Perhaps it was just that a demanding schoolmaster supervised the writing of Garrett's letter to his father.

The former Australian skipper, Jack Ryder, led the Australian contingent of captains on to the Melbourne Cricket Ground when the leaders from both sides of the world were presented to the 60,000 crowd before the beginning of the Centenary Test. The 87-year-old Jack was struck down by a virus during the match and died a few months later, a much revered father figure of Australian cricket—and no doubt a happy man that he lived to witness the hundredth anniversary of Test

Who is who? The Bedser twins, Alec and Eric

Percy Fender

cricket. It made one aware of the modernity of the international game. Ryder was born only twelve years after Lillywhite's team lost the first historic Melbourne match by 45 runs. The England keeper of the 1911-12 series, 'Tiger' Smith saw the light of day three years before Jack, and whilst he probably did not remember anything about A. G. Steel's side which whitewashed Scott's Australians in the year of his birth, 1886, he was still alive in 1977 at the ripe old age of ninety-one. Unfortunately 'Tiger', like another two veterans, was missing. He like the 82-year-old Herbert Sutcliffe and the new Canadian citizen, the 89-year-old England's former 'Mr Elegance', the left-handed Frank Woolley, was too frail to make the Odyssey to Melbourne. The senior citizen of the England party was the 84-year-old, moustachioed, Percy Fender, a veteran of the 1920 rubber and, in spite of that unrewarding experience, still a man of indomitable spirit. Because of his failing eyesight, he insisted on coming to Melbourne, bringing with him his grandson Nicholas, to act as his 'seeing eye' during the game.

When the first ball of the Centenary Test was bowled, the match to pay tribute to a hundred years of personalities and players was under way. What a wonderful diversity of people Test cricket has thrown up on the shore of sporting fame: captains like 'Plum' Warner, Freddie Brown, Ted Dexter, 'Gubby' Allen, Jardine and Cowdrey who, far from being true-blue Englishmen, were born in such far-flung corners of the world as Trinidad, Peru, Italy, Australia and India. Even the early Australian representatives in the Test arena were a motley crew. Bannerman came from Kent. Midwinter was born in the Forest of Dean in Gloucestershire, whilst Bransby Beauchamp Cooper added the spice of variety to his life by first seeing the light of day in India and subsequently playing first-class cricket for Kent, Middlesex and the Gentlemen of England.

The Centenary Test was a summation of the various characteristics of Tests over the previous hundred years. The match was not only exciting; it was also an individual art form which permitted the free expression of the players' personalities. As a bonus, by an extraordinary quirk of fate the Centenary Test was identical in one respect to the first contest played between England and Australia on the Richmond Police Paddock in 1877. Australia won the 1977 clash by the same 45-run margin which brought David Gregory's team victory in 1877! It seemed incredible that the arm of coincidence could be so long and there were justifiable thoughts in many people's minds that the result had been stage-managed. I remember thinking as I described the last few hours of the encounter on television: what happens if Australia win by the identical margin as they did one hundred years ago? Events were to prove later that I should have gone into the fortune-telling business.

At one phase of the Test, wickets were falling with such rapidity that it was almost certain that a decision would be achieved long before tea on the final day—the scheduled hour for an official visit from Her Majesty the Queen. Two innings were concluded by stumps on the second day on a pitch which many observers classified as perfect for batting! Such an assessment of the wicket was too facile. During the first twelve hours of the match, there was sufficient moisture in the

Old friends, former antagonists. Sir Donald Bradman with his opponents of the 1932-3 'bodyline' tour, Harold Larwood and Bill Voce. The Centenary Test reception

wicket to enable the faster bowlers to move the ball minimally off the seam. There was enough life-expectancy in the pitch to justify Greig's decision to ask Greg Chappell to bat after winning the toss. Commentators, such as England's batsman-in-eclipse, Geoff Boycott, believed the England captain's decision to be a defensive move and motivated by an unwillingness to expose his batsmen to the ferocity of Lillee on a first-day Melbourne surface. There was justification in such reasoning, but the fact remained that whatever the causative factors were which prompted Greig to 'insert' Australia, it was an inspired decision. At the close of play on the first day, accurate seam bowling by Lever, Willis and Old, plus the habitually accurate spin of Underwood and inspired fielding from the tourists, had Australia back in the pavilion for 138. It must be added that injudicious batting on the part of the Australians was a major contributory cause to their batting débâcle. The unwise hook stroke led to the downfall of Cosier, Walters and McCosker. The last batsman was doubly unlucky for his cross-batted swing at Willis diverted the ball onto his wicket via his jaw, which later proved to be broken as a result of the painful deflection. Australia's batting anguish was augmented by Davis hitting across Lever's angled left-handed medium-pace to be lbw and Hookes, Marsh and Gilmour all falling victims to their own edgy uncertainty outside the off-stump. O'Keeffe was spectacularly caught by the elongated Brearley at slip; it was one of the outstanding catches in a match of outstanding catches. With the reservoir of batting reserves dropping like an Alice Springs dam in a drought, both Chappell and Walker swung agriculturally across the line of the undeviating Underwood to be bowled. Incredibly, an hour before stumps, Australia were all out and when the umpires called it

255

quits for the day England were 1/29 having lost Woolmer caught at slip by Chappell off the bowling of Lillee.

Opposite:
Australia's keeper-
batsman, Rod Marsh

Climatically the second day of the match could not be faulted; but as the bible commentator, Matthew Henry, said, 'The better the day, the worse the deed'. England captain Tony Greig echoed these sentiments on Sunday evening, knowing that the hard-won advantage gained by his fieldsmen and bowlers in the first three sessions of the match had been frittered away by irresponsible batting in the next two. England lost 9 wickets in just over two hours for only 66 runs in a supine display of collective batting suttee. The unpalatable reality of the day's play was that the tourists delivered themselves as willing immolations into Australian hands. Lillee was the destroyer-in-chief of the England innings. He wrested a magnificent 6/26 from the 95 English run ruin; yet Lillee did not hit the stumps once and he claimed only a single lbw victim. No fewer than eight of Greig's men were caught either in the slip cordon or behind the wicket, many of them off deliveries at which they had no need to play.

It was a great day for Australia; they bowled and caught magnificently and were 147 runs ahead at stumps with 7 wickets in reserve. On the individual plane, the home side's wicketkeeper Rod Marsh deserved special mention. When he caught Lever off the bowling of Lillee shortly after lunch he surpassed Wally Grout's Australian record of 187 victims behind the wickets.

The England batting beggared description. Brearley succumbed, caught at third slip off Lillee's sixth ball of the day. Nightwatchman, Underwood, fell in Walker's first over of the morning, jabbing an edged catch to Chappell at slip. In the medium-pacer's next stint Amiss was caught in the gully; then Lillee chipped in to have Randall caught in straightforward manner by Marsh behind the stumps, and England were 5/40. The rot really set in when the total was 61. Greig was yorked and Fletcher caught at slip 4 runs later off a Walker leg-cutter. Just before lunch, Lillee claimed Old with an outswinger which seemed to draw the batsman's glove to the ball like a magnet and give Marsh another opportunity to prove his catching skill. Only 8 runs came after the interval for the loss of the wickets of Knott and Lever who were lbw and caught behind, both off the bowling of Lillee.

Australia's second innings task was to put flesh on their minimal first innings lead of 43. Their problem was that they were without the services of the injured McCosker, their regular opening-bat. The straight-batted and front-footed technique of leg-spinner O'Keeffe was used to plug the gap in the number one position; he performed a creditable job. He and Davis compiled 33 runs before the proxy opener was trapped at third slip off Old. The Yorkshire bowler enjoyed further success when he unexpectedly bowled Chappell through the normally non-existent gate between bat and pad for 2. When Cosier was once more caught off a mistimed hook by Knott, Australia were in trouble at 3/53. Walters was missed at gully by Willis when the batsman was 16. It was the crucial mistake of the innings. The New South Welshman was still at the crease with Davis when the umpires drew stumps, with the scoreboard registering 3/104. It was the end of a day which Greig would have liked to play again. For England it contained two and a half hours of spendthrift batting and one important moment of fielding aberration.

In *The Merry Wives of Windsor*, one of Shakespeare's characters states that good luck lies in the third time and in odd numbers. England's fortunes in the third day of the Centenary Test quickly gave lie to this sixteenth century superstition. The odd day began and finished disastrously for Greig's men. At stumps Australia had stretched their lead to 430 with 2 more wickets in hand. With their wicketkeeper, Marsh, unbeaten on 95 and on the threshold of becoming the first Australian custodian to score a century in a century of Anglo-Australian Tests, the home side was certain to bat into the fourth day and pose a close-to-500 batting problem for England in their second innings. The golden setting for Chappell's day of satisfaction was adorned by one pristine gem of an innings from the young South Australian left-hander, David Hookes, whose 56 caused Sir Donald Bradman to comment at the A.C.B. dinner that evening that he saw hope for the future in the Woolley-like elegance of the youthful trainee teacher.

'Bicky' Walters and Davis took the total to 132 before the latter became the unlucky thirteenth batsman in the game to be caught behind the wicket or in the slips. Walters progressed to a personal 66 before he became number fourteen. Then followed one of the most aggressive partnerships of the match between the two contrasting left-handers, the experienced Marsh and the débutant Hookes. Marsh, with bludgeon-like brutality, scored, but Hookes, the rapier, stole the limelight. In the space of five deliveries from Greig, the Adelaide batsman progressed from 36 to 56. Bowler and fieldsmen alike were powerless to stem a spate of strokes which segmented the M.C.G. from point to backward square-leg. Hookes finally departed, after an unnecessary altercation with Greig, caught off bat and pad at short-leg. Lever immediately yorked Gilmour, but the second new ball failed to disturb the equanimity of Lillee and Marsh. They added a joint 76 in eighty-seven minutes before the fast bowler was caught in the covers off a mistimed and lofted drive. Much to the amazement of the onlookers, McCosker then emerged from the pavilion with a runner. A sling held his broken jaw in its most comfortable, but no doubt excruciatingly painful position, as he batted, looking for all the world like the comic-paper idea of a schoolboy suffering from toothache. He held firm as Marsh drew ever closer to his hundred and at stumps Australia were 8/387.

When the Centenary Test resumed in bright sunshine after the perfectly timed dull interlude of the rest day, all hopes of England saving the match appeared to have evaporated with the morning dew. The vagaries of cricket, however, are as foreseeable as those of the inconstant moon. On an improving fourth-day wicket, the tourists re-emerged into the game by scoring 2/191 in pursuit of the will-o'-the-wisp goal of 463 runs for victory in 650 minutes. Their hero of the hour was the 'cheekie chappie' of Nottinghamshire cricket, Derek Randall, who was unbeaten on 87 at close of play. Greig would have been a supreme optimist to think that his side could notch the necessary 272 on

258

a fifth-day pitch—but at least all was not lost, though the history of past Tests predicted otherwise.

Australia batted for an hour on the fourth day, taking their tally to 419, and losing McCosker to a mid-wicket catch before Chappell applied the closure. Marsh completed his unique hundred and remained unbeaten on 110. England began badly, losing Woolmer lbw before lunch to a Walker delivery which kept low to hit the dissatisfied batsman on the front pad. Between lunch and tea, Brearley and Randall imbued their side's innings with an air of substance by adding 85 without being separated. The tourists' vice-captain was out immediately after the interval in much the same disgruntled way as Woolmer; but the successful bowler, Lillee could not make any further inroads into the underbelly of the England batting which, as Randall and Amiss proved, was far from soft.

In 1877 Gregory's Colonials won the game in the late afternoon of the fourth and last day. A century and two days later Greg Chappell's Commonwealth combination achieved the same result, on the same ground, at approximately the same time on the corresponding day. The incredible coincidence was that Australia's margin of victory in 1877 and 1977 was identical—45 runs! The superstitious enthusiast was convinced that cricket was the game of the gods; the sceptic probably thought that the climax of the game had been skilfully rigged. Whatever their sentiments and differing opinions about the reality of the result, everyone agreed that it was a fitting conclusion to a Test in which neither side gave a moment's thought to the possibility of a draw. On the final day Randall swept through the non-nervous 90s to register his maiden Test hundred with an assured cut off Lillee. Amiss lent his solid support as 46 runs were added in the first hour, before the second new ball was taken. Every spectator was convinced that the moment of truth had now arrived for the England batsmen. The two batsmen were not of the same opinion and when lunch was taken, they were still at the crease with the scoreboard showing a total of 267.

The end of the 166-run third wicket partnership came immediately after the break from the totally unexpected source of Chappell's medium-pace. A ball kept low and bowled Amiss; England were still 184 runs short of victory but with 7 wickets still in reserve. Suddenly England's spirited counter-attack degenerated into a dignified retreat and then into an undisciplined rout. Fletcher was caught for the second time in the match behind the wicket, on this occasion off the bowling of Lillee. Greig and Randall never lost heart and played shots, demonstrating to all and sundry that they still entertained illusions of triumph. Randall enjoyed the benefit of Marsh's sporting largesse. The Trent Bridge batsman was adjudged caught behind off the bowling of Chappell, but the Australian keeper recalled him and informed umpire Tom Brooks that the ball had not carried into his gloves. The gods rewarded Marsh's generosity; shortly afterwards Randall was caught via bat and pad by Cosier at short-leg off an O'Keeffe wrong 'un.

The glorious realization that he had scored 174, and his understandable weariness, blotted physical considerations from Randall's mind. He walked off the field through the wrong gate and had to push his way

The Australian Team, The Centenary Test. Standing (L to R) I. Davis, G. Gilmour, R. McCosker, G. Cosier, K. O'Keeffe, D. Hookes, R. Bright. Seated (L to R) M. Walker, R. Marsh, G. Chappell, D. Walters, D. Lillee

unabashed past the newly-arrived Royal party to reach the England dressing-room. Twenty-three runs later his skipper Greig joined him, caught by the same fieldsman off the same bowler and a similar delivery. Chappell at slip claimed Old off the first Lillee ball he faced and 5 runs later, with the scoreboard registering 385, Lever played back to O'Keeffe and was unarguably lbw. Whilst Knott was still at the crease and throwing his bat at every ball which came within reach, there was still hope for England. Underwood departed at 410, his stumps scattered by a Lillee yorker. Undeterred, Knott laid about him with gay abandon, but with the score standing on 417, the diminutive keeper attempted to pull the wrong ball and was trapped with his pads in front of his stumps. Once more, Lillee wrote 'finis' to an England innings with an analysis of 5/139; his match return in the Test was an impressive 11/165. He was the hard-working artisan who engineered England's downfall by 45 runs.

In 1877, Tom Kendall, the slow left-hander from South Melbourne was adjudged the best colonial bowler of the first Test and awarded a trophy by the *Australasian* newspaper. Kendall's two-pace approach was a complete contrast to the 20-yard run-up of Lillee, Kendall's 1977 counterpart—and Lillee's material rewards from the Centenary Test were commensurately greater. Not only did Lillee receive a replica of Kendall's 1877 cup from the Melbourne Herald and Weekly Times, but he shared in the $9,000 prize money donated to the winning side by the Benson and Hedges Company. Each man in the Australian team received more than $2,000 cash in the hand for his week's contribution to the Centenary Test. The England side were compensated for their disappointment in losing the game by a similar sponsored donation of $4,500 and the consolation of knowing that their Man of the Hour,

Derek Randall, was elected 'The Benson and Hedges Player of the Match'.

So it was that the laudatory song of the Centenary Test ended. The melody lingers on, however, and will continue to do so as long as Test cricket is played. It is a unique refrain recalling, in varying proportions, a Victorian drawing-room ballad, the jingle of an Edwardian music-hall, the frenzy of the Charleston, the rhythm of the Savoy Orpheans, Rock and Roll, the Twist, and a touch of Beatlemania and Abba. The match played between Chappell's XI and Greig's side summarized all the preceding achievements of Test cricket; it foretold a rosy future for the game. It embodied memories of the past and hopes for the destiny of the sport.

Players, former stars and spectators will long remember the events of those days in March 1977. Eddie Paynter, the plucky England batsman of the 1930s, will recall in Valhalla that the generosity of his former team-mates helped him to make the 14,000 mile trek to Melbourne. He will smile to himself when he pictures the confusion of the M.C.G. barman when he ordered his usual Lancashire beverage of warm, not cold, beer. Ernie McCormick, the Australian pace-bowler of Paynter's epoch, will give thanks that he saw the game and is still very much with us in spite of the pronouncement of the spectator who cornered him in the Melbourne pavilion with the remark, 'Didn't you used to be Ernie McCormick?' The descendants of Jack Ryder and Paul Gibb—men who witnessed the Centenary Test and died shortly afterwards—will still say proudly of the game many years from now, 'My grandfather was there'. The cricket battle was not Agincourt, and the day was not St Crispin's—but anyone, in England or Australia, who lay a-bed during those momentous Ides of March, 'must think themselves accurs'd they were not there'.

The England Team, The Centenary Test. Standing (L to R) D. Amiss, R. Woolmer, J. Lever, R. Willis, C. Old, G. Barlow, D. Randall.
Seated (L to R) K. Fletcher, A. Knott, A. Greig, M. Brearley, D. Underwood

261

Acknowledgements

The Century-Makers is about the personalities who were the raw material of the past hundred years of England-Australia Tests. The book would not have been possible without the help of the many men and women who witnessed the feats of the champions of the past and found time to speak to me about them. To former cricketers, administrators and umpires I say thank you for their thoughtful opinions, wisely concluded and too often and too lightly dismissed by modern thinking. The veterans of the media have been a valuable source of oral history stretching back into the twenties and beyond. I count myself lucky to have been present at the Centenary Test in Melbourne in 1977; that particular gathering of the game's notables was a gold-mine of anecdotes for all such as I who were willing to listen.

I should like to single out for my especial thanks George Hele, the leading umpire of the 'Bodyline' series, who at 87 still remembers the events of 1932-3 as though they were yesterday. My appreciation also goes to the late Jack Ryder who was still as lucid in his opinions in his last years as when he captained Australia in 1928-9. Mr F.R.Power provided me with much delightful material in the publications of his father, Ernest Renton Power, a Melbourne journalist of the early 1900, who wrote graphically about the cricketing personalities of his times. It is gratifying that one of Mr Power's nine non-cricketing sons has been able to make a substantial contribution to the history of a game which his father loved.

Finally I say thank you to the myriad of people whose writings, views and photographs have had such a formative influence on the opinions expressed in this book. My gratitude goes to Garry Sparke, Bob Biddle and Mike Ringham for their work on the manuscript and their technical advice. I hope that the combined efforts of all of these people helps to preserve a few memories of cricketers whose characters might have seemed paler had it not been written.

Index

H21 135 063 1

A CHARGE
IS MADE FOR
REMOVED OR
DAMAGED
LABELS.

9936907   TYSON, F.

THE CENTURY — MAKERS — THE MEN BEHIND THE
ASHES. 1877-1977

Please renew/return this item by the last date shown.

So that your telephone call is charged at local rate,
please call the numbers as set out below:

	From Area codes 01923 or 0208:	From the rest of Herts:
Renewals:	01923 471373	01438 737373
Enquiries:	01923 471333	01438 737333
Minicom:	01923 471599	01438 737599

L32b

07 FEB 2002

2 4 NOV 1990

2 4 NOV 1990   1 1 DEC 2009

- 4 FEB 1991   11/12

4 MAR

L 33

COUNTY BOOKSTORE
NF COLLECTION

HERTFORDSHIRE LIBRARY SERVICE

Please return this book on or before the last
date shown or ask for it to be renewed

L32/rev79